Rethinking Congressional Reform

RETHINKING CONGRESSIONAL REFORM

The Reform Roots of the Special Interest Congress

Burton D. Sheppard

Schenkman Books, Inc., Cambridge, Massachusetts

SCHENKMAN BOOKS, INC.
190 Concord Avenue
Cambridge, MA 02138

Library of Congress Cataloging in Publication Data

Sheppard, Burton D.
  Rethinking congressional reform.

  Bibliography: p.
  Includes index.
  1. Pressure groups—United States. 2. Campaign funds—
United States. 3. Political action committees—United
States. 4. United States. Congress. House—Reform.
5. United States—Politics and government—1945–
I. Title.
JK1118.S49   1985   328.73′07   84-29833
ISBN 0-87073-550-0
ISBN 0-87073-690-6 (pbk.)

Printed in the United States of America.

To Annabelle T. Sheppard
and Jack N. Sheppard, Jr.

Contents

If any of the great corporations of the country were to hire adventurers . . . to procure passage of a general law with a view to promotion of their private interests, the moral sense of every right-minded man would instinctively denounce the employer and the employed as steeped in corruption and the employment as infamous. If the instances were numerous, open and tolerated they would be regarded as a measure of decay of public morals and degeneracy of the time. No prophetic spirit would be needed to foretell the consequences near at hand.

—*Trist v. Child,* a Supreme Court decision in 1874 which ruled that a suit to enforce a contract to obtain a certain legislative result through lobbying was contrary to "sound policy and good morals." 21 Wall. 441, 22 L.Ed. 623 (1874).

1963

. . . the lobbies were on the whole poorly financed, ill-managed, out of contact with Congress, and at best only marginally effective in supporting tendencies and measures which already had behind them considerable Congressional impetus from other sources. . . . When we look at a typical lobby, we find that its opportunities for maneuver are sharply limited, its staff mediocre, and its major problem not the influencing of Congressional votes but the finding of clients and contributors to enable it to survive at all.

—assessment of special interest influence on Congressional tariff legislation; Bauer, Pool and Dexter, *American Business and Public Policy*, 1963, p. 324.

1983

A candidate entering politics now must systematically make the rounds of the interest groups and win their approval, and their money, by declaring himself, usually in very specific terms, in favor of the legislative goals they seek. He is therefore imprisoned before he ever reaches Congress. Once there, he must worry about maintaining the groups' support or about finding other groups to support him or about casting some vote that might cause monetary retaliation. He must measure every action in terms of what the financial consequences to himself might be. The difference between that and corruption is unclear.

—assessment of special interest influence on Congress generally; Elizabeth Drew, *Politics and Money*, 1983, p. 94.

Acknowledgments

This book developed in three phases. The first phase was as a college student—political activist, political science student, Congressional intern, and follower of Congress during the turbulent period of anti-Vietnam and Watergate politics. The second phase was as a more detached and leisurely observer of American politics as a graduate student at Oxford. The third phase was an overlapping stint as a college professor of political science conjoined with law school and then the practice of law in Boston and Washington, D.C.

I mention this not so much by way of explaining my perhaps peculiar mix of perspectives, but to introduce the personal debts to a wide range of friends and colleagues incurred along the way. Many such debts are memorialized in footnotes of interviews and some remain undisclosed by request of the interviewee. The following people deserve special thanks.

During the first phase, Milton C. Cummings, Jr., Robert L. Peabody, Paul S. Sarbanes, and James M. Shannon shared with me their interest in, and insights into, the workings of Capitol Hill. Their observations and valued friendship have continued through the ensuing phases.

In England, I was fortunate to have tutors and friends who helped me to learn more about international and comparative politics, and to develop a shrewder perspective on American politics. I am not sure I have succeeded to the extent these friends deserve, but I have tried. Philip M. Williams of Nuffield College, Oxford was a special delight as friend, critic, and French, British, and American politics addict—not to mention peerless scholar. David Butler, Martin Cannon, Sir Norman Chester, Richard P. Conlon, Roger H. Davidson, E. J. Dionne, Jr., Martha Epstein, David Goldey, Nevil Johnson, Walter G. Oleszek, Janet Morgan, H. G. Nicholas, Robert L. Peabody, David Price, Michael Ryle, Jim Talcott, and David Watt were helpful in numerous ways during this phase of research and writing on both sides of the Atlantic. Sir Edgar Williams, Warden of Rhodes House, was a source of excellent advice, encouragement and guidance on a host of issues both personal and academic. I am especially grateful to the Rhodes Trust for the opportunity to pursue the studies which led to this undertaking.

xii   Acknowledgments

During the last, hardest phase of rethinking and re-working, I imposed on still other friends and colleagues (and again on veterans of the earlier phases). Those who deserve special thanks are Duffey A. Asher, William Bulger, Robert L. Calhoun, Richard P. Conlon, Joseph E. Cantor, Martin Cannon, James F. Carlin, Carol Cameron Darr, Susan Estrich, Natalie Goldring, William W. Harris, Jay Hedlund, Paul G. Kirk, Jr., Edward R. Lev, Mary Lyman, Robert L. Peabody, Cheryl A. Publicover, James E. Ray, Vincent J. Rocque, Michael Sandel, Patricia Saris, Eli Segal, James M. Shannon, Lee Webb, S. Ariel Weiss and Mark L. Wolf. Philip M. Williams merits separate and further expression of gratitude for reading the entire manuscript and making detailed and incisive comments throughout. The late Alona Evans, Robert A. Paarlberg, Linda A. Miller, Marion R. Just, Alan H. Schechter and Edward A. Stettner were colleagues at Wellesley College whose insights into related fields of politics were helpful along the way. Alfred Schenkman, Jeffrey Klueter, Julie Mines and Joe Schenkman prodded me along and provided many helpful comments on the draft. Alexandra Acosta, Trisha Meili, and Julie Gess provided indispensable research assistance. Gerry Gaeta, Mary Anne Caporaletti and Linda Rose have expertly produced the manuscript.

I was about to send the galleys of this book to Philip Williams when I received the jolting news of his death. Philip was incomparable as scholar, political analyst, mentor and friend. He had a voracious appetite for political facts and ideas. Once, after I had arranged a dinner for Philip with an eminent American professor, I was distressed to encounter a somewhat disappointed Philip. "Was the dinner all right," I inquired. "Yes," said Philip, "but I fear that *he got a lot more out of me than I did out of him!*" This was Philip's way of saying that he had not managed to get answers to *his* questions. This book "got a lot" out of Philip; its technique of detailed, institutional analysis owes greatly to him. He urged me on to completion, and he submitted painstaking, line-by-line comments. I, and friends and admirers all over the world, will always miss him.

My sisters, Audrey D. Sheppard, Cynthia A. Sheppard, and Melinda C. Sheppard were indulgent and supportive at the various stages of the book's—and my—sometimes erratic development.

This book is dedicated to my parents, Annabelle T. Sheppard and Jack N. Sheppard, Jr., who deserve much more than a book (or at least one they might be interested in reading), but this is a small token of my love and gratitude.

Another acknowledgment is in order. It is to Frank Sieverts who as a member of a scholarship interviewing committee asked me a series of questions about Congress. I responded with comments which were opinionated, highly critical of Congress and undoubtedly simplistic. He asked the appropriate follow-up question: "Since you are so critical of Congress, how would you reform it?" My response at the time is mercifully lost to history. This book, and particularly Chapter Twelve, is my attempt at a belated, and I hope better, answer.

Finally, in a book which devotes attention to the role of reform in helping to shape Congressional biases, it is appropriate to disclose my own. This is on the theory that biases, since everyone has them, are only dangerous when they are unwitting, unacknowledged or undisclosed. The reader is entitled to know that the author, a lawyer and political scientist by training, is a liberal Democrat by conviction. While pinpointing exactly what this means in the context of 1980s American politics is difficult, in my case it is clouded even further by the influences of British party (and particularly Labour and Social Democratic) politics, along with steadying exposure to Massachusetts and Washington, D.C. *realpolitik*. Such crosscurrents of political thought may explain some of my orientations and frames of reference. Certainly, stating these biases is not intended to exculpate; hence responsibility for all that lies herein, of course, is mine.

B.D.S.
Mattapoisett, Massachusetts
February 2, 1985

Introduction

It is a commonplace of contemporary politics that Congress is dominated by special interests. The diffuse structure of Congress, the panoply of Congressional staff, committees, subcommittees and new specialized caucuses, the armada of Political Action Committees (PACs), wealthy individuals, single issue groups, trade associations and lobbies all contribute to the inchoate decision-making process of American politics. They further contribute to the often incoherent policies which emerge from that process—a melange of policy zigzags characterized by delay and obstruction in some areas and headlong lurches in others.[1]

There are also stirrings among commentators, citizens and political practitioners themselves to the effect that the systemic balance has tipped too far in favor of the special interests.[2] Some have called for far-reaching reforms. These calls, and even some of the reforms, are to be lauded. There is, however, a problem.

The problem is that the Congress *has just experienced* a period of perhaps the most concerted and sweeping self-reform in its history.[3] While current discontent—and specifically the excessive role played by special interests—cannot be entirely attributed to reform, the possible complicity of past reforms in these developments ought not to be ignored. Many lessons can be learned from the last wave of reform; and there is little evidence to suggest that a systematic review has yet been attempted. There is a danger that when a political climate hospitable to new reform emerges, reformers may not be intellectually or politically prepared; i.e., they will not be aware of the pitfalls that await them. A critical review of the Congressional reforms is needed. It should include a thorough examination of the assumptions on which the reforms were based, the success or failure they experienced, and their implications for future efforts.

Elizabeth Drew, other journalists, and public interest groups have provided new insights into the PAC-based politics of the early 1980s.[4] While there is disagreement as to just how pervasive the influence of special interests has become, there is little doubt that in many instances the impact is profound. There is a growing recognition that a complicated structure of Congressional power and politics is evolving, one that in new ways cedes substantial and institutionalized influence to outside interests. Less well understood, however, is the process—including well-intentioned reform—by which that new structure emerged. A central conclusion of the book develops: while some observers maintain that Congress's problems can be "cured" by simply tinkering with the system of campaign finance, my contention is that the problems are deeper; they go to the basic structure and processes of Congress. Any truly effective reform plan must address these problems.

In sum, what has been missing in much of the debate about Washington politics and its policy-making shortcomings is a sense of recent institutional history, an understanding of the shifts in internal power relationships, and an appreciation of the connection between past reform and present dysfunction.[5] The Congressional reform movements of the 1970s attempted to address real problems of power and process, and to a large extent they addressed them. Old power alignments centered in the committee chairmen were broken up and replaced by the new power of subcommittees, subcommittee chairmen, individual members and narrowly based outside groups. But the reforms designed to correct the "old" problems created serious new ones. The dynamics of politics within and between American political institutions have also had significant effects. Two related developments seem especially instrumental. First, a "side effect" of the adoption of public financing of Presidential campaigns (but not of races for Congress) was to release for Congressional campaigns vast sums of special interest money previously earmarked for the Presidential election. Secondly, spurred on by the new technology of politics—replete with consultants, direct mail, and television advertising—and fueled by the newly abundant money available from interest groups (often through their PACs), the period from 1976 to 1984 has witnessed a virtual explosion in the costs of campaigns.

A decade of reform activity has played a substantial role in creating and nurturing the "Special Interest Congress" of the late 1970s and the 1980s, hardly the result the reformers intended. Most reformers sought to reorganize and reorient Congress to enable it to make broad, effective, "universalistic" policy; but the Congress—and the policies that emerge from it—are even more fragmented and "particularistic" than before. And to the extent that Congress has succeeded in focusing on broad policymaking, its consideration of such matters has often been slipshod and shortsighted.[6]

The reforms also had some positive consequences, and any plausible analysis must clearly acknowledge that reform was not the *only* factor contributing to the increased activity and prominence of special interest groups. There were also many broad sociological factors, transcending but affecting Congress, which also contributed. These factors included economic uncertainty spurring greater consciousness of interest group identity, the decline of the legitimacy and efficacy of political institutions generally, the increased political activism of American corporations and the relative decline of organized labor's political influence, the demand for greater "participatory democracy" in American society, the growth of ideological and single-issue mass movements, and the rise of the electronic media as a forum for both communicating and asserting interest group demands—to name but a few.[7] Thomas Edsall provides an excellent exploration of the macro forces which have shaped the recent rise of special interest influence and what he calls the "new politics of inequality."[8] The present book traces the internal institutional developments which formed the structural foundation and complement to these outside forces. These internal and external developments taken together help explain ironic results—i.e., how a liberal Democratic inspired Congressional reform movement helped form the cornerstones of a new special interest-oriented and conservative political resurgence.

Yet, while external contributing factors should not be minimized, it remains clear that the reform process itself was an important factor in creating the Congressional system which itself now cries out for reform. The present system amounts to a collection of scandals waiting to happen; and Congress's inability to address coherently the complicated problems facing America is the biggest scandal of all. The analysis which follows examines the *overall* reform experience—the conflicting reform goals and proposals, often contradictory motives, the aggregate implications of reform efforts, and its intended and unintended results.

The detailed description and the conclusions and speculations herein are not intended only to provide historical background and critical analysis. This examination of the dynamics of Congressional reform is a caution signal to future reformers, and an attempt to clarify the success and failure of recent efforts in order to increase the quality and success of future attempts. In rethinking Congressional reform, the goal here is to identify correctives. Creative thinking is needed to help extricate Congress from its increasingly distorting entanglements with modern American special interests and set Congress on a more positive course.

* * *

TOWARD A NEW DEBATE ABOUT THE ROLE OF CONGRESS

There is a contemporary debate in American politics surrounding the impact of PACs on Congress. Journalists and "good government" groups such as Common Cause and Congress Watch search relentlessly for "smoking pistols"—i.e., evidence of PAC campaign contributions "buying" votes, "distorting" the outcome of the elections and influencing the course of legislation. Many members of Congress themselves (including beneficiaries of PACs) and other participants in politics make for willing witnesses to the allegedly pernicious new role of PACs.

Dissenters from this position are the various defenders of PACs, including the PACs themselves and the interests they represent, some members of Congress and other political practitioners. In addition, several political scientists have refrained from drawing conclusions alleging undue PAC influence in the absence of hard statistical evidence and citing the complexity of the problem. Of course, many of the positions arrived at in this debate are products of earlier assumptions, motives and—perhaps—the special interests of the participants.

A large and growing body of literature suggests an increasingly pervasive influence of PACs and lobbyists on electoral outcomes and the legislative process respectively.[9] Much of the evidence on this subject is necessarily anecdotal and circumstantial; it must be understood that the most effective exercise of influence is to keep issues off the political agenda altogether, or to "frame" issues so that they appear in their most favorable setting and circumstances. Consequently, interest group influence and the linkage between campaign contributions and legislative voting behavior are not often visible to the public. And, of course, identification of specific special interest linkages to legislative business is made more difficult by the fact that many large campaign contributions are made by individuals. These contributions often carry with them implied endorsements of certain policies or the imprimatur of a corporate or financial interest. One advantage of PAC contributions over large individual contributions is that at least the disclosure of PAC contributions provides for public knowledge of the interest involved. For these reasons, and also due to the brilliant resourcefulness of interest groups—e.g., using "soft money" to circumvent but not violate Federal election laws, independent expenditures by PACs and the funneling of money to preferred candidates by individual executives—statistical analysis of roll call votes on the floor or even in committee and subcommittee does not adequately capture the nuances of the Congressional process. In fairness, neither do simplistic analyses which state the amount of PAC contributions to individual members, cite voting records on issues of concern to specific PACs and then make the broad assertions that PAC contributions *ipso facto* must have "bought" the members' votes. Here too the positions of the protagonists in this debate are colored by their assumptions and aesthetic perceptions. But assumptions and aesthetics aside, it is hard to miss or dismiss three profound recent developments: the new fragmentation of Congressional politics, the increasing assertiveness of special interests, and the influence over the electoral and Congressional agenda and debate by outside groups.

The contemporary debate about PACs is an important one—affecting public opinion, the reputations of members of Congress and the legitimacy of Congress itself. The debate is also critical in defining the limits and possibilities of any future reforms. More evidence needs to be assembled and rigorously analyzed. But a likely result of this contemporary debate about PAC influence is that the situation is not quite as bad as portrayed by the doomsayers but not nearly as benign as characterized by defenders of PACs. The argument that PACs are healthy new instruments of democratic participation is unpersuasive. But an understanding of what is wrong goes well beyond the positive and negative attributes of PACs. Undeniably their monetary influence skews the political process in different ways. It is ridiculous to think that PACs contributed over $104 million in the 1984 election cycle and close to $85 million in the 1982 election cycle out of charity or a spirit of public service. However, PAC contributions are rarely overt *quid pro quo* matters. They do not constitute *prima facie* evidence of individual or even systemic corruption. It must be understood that in most cases the workings of the Congressional process are subtle. In some ways that subtlety itself is most pernicious. Special interest influence flourishes in many different forms (some involving PACs, others involving individuals); money and campaign contributions "buy" access and sometimes influence for the "purchasing" PACs and individuals. However, access ought not to be *equated* with influence, and influence is rarely monolithic, unopposed or dispositive. The conflict of special interests plays itself out on the wide stage of macro-politics, public opinion and exogenous political developments and forces. Quantitative data do not provide a complete or accurate picture. Direct cause and effect relationships are often difficult to discern. The system—and the solutions to the perceived problems—are more complicated than one might initially expect.

This book argues that the system *is* seriously flawed and needs to be changed. However, it should be stated at the outset that little interest will be served by miscasting the characters or simplifying the complicated characteristics of the process. It does no more good to the overall system to characterize all PACs as evil and all recipients of PAC contributions as corrupt than it does to pronounce that all is well with this sometimes seamy, oftentimes unfair, and increasingly dysfunctional system. Moreover, the search for the major scandal or smaller "smoking pistols" of our admittedly bad system of campaign finance diverts attention from the broader implications of recent reform.

In short, there is a need for a serious new debate about Congress. But it should be different—i.e. broader—than the present debate. The influence of PACs and special interest money is certainly a problem of major proportions. But it is only part of the problem. The larger problem of the Special Interest Congress is the advanced stage of decentralized power in the structure and procedures of Congress. A crazy-quilt maze of subcommittees, committees, caucuses and entrepreneurial individual members—in the absence of any significant centralizing force of party—provides multiple access for the array of special interest groups. These groups are more narrowly based, plentiful, and intimidating than ever before. The result is the mobilization of certain special interest biases on some issues and the immobilization of Congress on others.

Reform played a major role in the creation of this fragmented, special interest-oriented Congress. The process by which reform took place and its implications must be fully understood as a first step toward rethinking and perhaps reorienting the system in a different direction. Thus there needs to be debate, but the debate must be about the quality and efficacy of our representative government and nothing less.

THE NEW POLITICS—AND CONSEQUENCES—OF "THE SPECIAL INTEREST CONGRESS"

Some observers contend that little or nothing is new in the contemporary politics of special interests.[10] This position—while appealing in some ways and drawing on a deep strain of American cynicism—is difficult to sustain. While politics and government—and particularly American politics—has always been subject to the interplay of factions[11] and the lubricating effects of money applied in the right places, the post-reform Congressional system is qualitatively different. It is different in scale, in texture, and in ways both obvious and subtle. Many of the latter defy quantification or often detection. Aside from the exceptions of public disclosure of campaign contributors and regulation by the Federal Election Commission (FEC), these new developments are substantially negative. The aggregate result of a number of factors, including a decade of wide-ranging reform, is a legislative branch which can be generally characterized as the "Special Interest Congress."

A definition is in order. The term "Special Interest Congress" is used here to describe the rambling and decentralized political structure of Congress and all its outside appendages, the special interest groups.[12] Special interest groups are viewed broadly as including business, labor, ideological and issue groups. Even "public interest" groups, including self-styled environmental, consumer, good government, and other organizations "fit," despite the fact that their ends are presumably unselfish or at least less self-interested than those of the traditional "special interests." Most of these organizations merit inclusion because of their role in the process and their participation in its structural and campaign finance aspects. In many ways, so do the many other layers of government—such as regional organizations, states, counties, and municipalities—which maintain lobbying offices in Washington (although they do not typically figure in the campaign finance dimension of special interest influence). Basic components of this broad definition of the special interest groups that compose part of the larger "Special Interest Congress" are 1) organized representation in Washington for a discernible set of policy goals, and 2) a constituency-base outside Washington which brings "grassroots" pressure to bear through incentives and disincentives for support by members of Congress. Any organization which has a PAC fits; organizations which do not have PACs but which have an active presence and/or representation in Washington often fit as well. (To be sure, there are PACs which have no specific legislative agendas, but it usually is the case that an organization with certain interests decides to establish a PAC in order to further those interests.) Of course, this is not to say that all special interests are created equal—some interests are more worthy than others, some downright pernicious.[13] There is much confusion nowadays as to what are and are not special interests. This book uses a very broad definition from the limited standpoint of impact on the Congressional process.

Not included here are so-called "non-monetary" sources of influence such as the media. These are, of course, very important, covered briefly in later chapters, but meriting full length coverage elsewhere. The focal points of the Special Interest Congress are the myriad Congressional sub-institutions—subcommittees, committees, party groups, caucuses, etc.—which become centers of various universes of political concerns and interests. It is also important to note that the Congress itself is so diffusely organized that, even absent the sprawling structure of outside forces, it would be prone to diffuse and often confused decision-making. The fact that this elaborate extra-Congressional web of interest groups exists, adds to the systematic incoherence.

There is no criticism intended as to what these interest groups do, or even that, under the present system, they do it. Criticism is focused on the *system* as it has evolved. This definitional problem is a complicated one,[14] and raises a basic question about who is taking advantage of whom. Is it the special interests "capturing" or "conquering" members of Congress, or is it the members themselves who win re-election and wield power based at least in part on special interest support? The answer implied by the use of the term "Special Interest Congress" is that the relationship is symbiotic. Both sides thrive on this relationship, and though they may sincerely profess not to like it, the system is functional for both.[15] If there is a "loser" in all this, it is "the people"—or another great nebulous concept, the "public interest."

What is strikingly new and different about this "Special Interest Congress" includes the following:

- the diffuse structure on which the special interest infrastructure is formed;
- the burgeoning numbers of organized interests growing from the widespread realization that governmental decisions have great effect on those interests;
- the activism of corporations and the new competitiveness of industry and commerce, domestic and international;
- the increasingly intense rivalry between labor and management, older industries versus high technology and service industries, "sunbelt" versus "frostbelt," etc. as well as the sophistication of the operatives in Washington on behalf of these interests;
- the exponential growth in the size of the campaign coffers at PACs' disposal along with the continued large contribution of wealthy individuals;
- the huge cost of Congressional campaigns weighted heavily toward media and direct mail expenditures;
- the new access to information about details of government policy and its effects, and the ability to monitor Congressional activity;
- the proliferation and prowess of lobbyists in Washington and their technological ability to mobilize ostensibly "grass-roots" campaigns;
- the *modus operandi* of PACs to solicit and spur their grass-root mem-

bers to action—fostering a "knowledge and sophistication gap" between grass-roots PAC members and Washington lobbyists;
- the ability of PACs to recruit and otherwise "make" challengers and intimidate incumbents;
- the ability of lobbyists and PACs to skew issues—i.e. distort the process—so as to put some issues on the political agenda and keep others off;
- the convergence of PACs and other factors to render Congress decreasingly capable of dealing at all comprehensively with large national issues;
- the enhancement of Congress's function of mobilizing *dissent* from proposed policy initiatives (e.g., presidential proposals) as opposed to the mobilization of *consent* for government policies. As such, Congress—and particularly its individual members—have become key access and focal points for interests seeking to undo policies. While in their roles as constituency representatives, members of Congress see themselves as defenders of legitimate interests, the overall effect of this role is to undermine governmental—and Congressional—legitimacy.

The new politics of special interests has created an elaborate system of institutionalized—and legitimatized—conflicts of interest. The structure of politics has evolved to the point that large campaign contributions by PACs and individuals have become important requisites for access. Failure and/or inability to participate is a barrier to that access. The process itself, and the perceptions of that process, have become inherently corrosive of the ideals underlying American government, are increasingly deleterious in their policy impact and may ultimately destroy the legitimacy of the political system. But it is not just the *nexus* between the external interests and internal structure that is the problem; in addition, the diffuse internal Congressional structure and process[16] with which the special interests interact—and around which they cluster—themselves need to be made more coherent.

The Concerns of the Book

The story of reform's progress, and sometimes the lack of it, spotlights the essential political qualities of the contemporary Congress. It is these institutional characteristics—political values and incentive systems—and the implications of reform proposals for these values and incentives, which bear thoughtful contemplation if the overall Congressional reform experience is to be understood.

This reform experience also forms the backdrop to a consideration of Congress's *proper* role with respect to the abundant and politically adept phalanx of interest groups now regularly conquering Congress and dominating the American political system. The ultimate mission of this book is to warn of the adverse consequences of the system as it has evolved, and to stimulate thoughtful efforts to eliminate the more pernicious aspects of special interest participation in Congressional decision-making. The goal—admittedly difficult—is to work toward a more rational political system in which special interest influence on the process is on the basis of the merit of ideas and the force of democratic votes, rather than the size of political campaign chests or the coziness of Congressional relationships. And this goal includes the change of Congress's structure from its present orientation toward fragmented service of those special interests. While this is a complicated dilemma and a challenge which has long been with us, it is a problem which has been rendered all the more pressing by the results of the reforms—intended and unintended—described herein.

The Plan of the Book

Part I introduces the general themes and basic framework of the argument, the political context of Congressional reform and the general argument relating structural reform roots to an increase in special interest influence. The balance of the book explains how and why reform efforts contributed to a growing dependence of Congress on well-organized special interest groups, and explores some of the ramifications and possible recourses.

Part II presents a detailed case study of the two main areas of reform activity in the House of Representatives during the 1970s: Party caucus reform and Committee reform. The two organizational cornerstones of the House power structure are its parties and committees, and they were thus the natural targets—as well as forums— for the reformers. Moreover, if the reform movement had any impact, that impact would no doubt be felt on the party and committee structure. Hence the Party and Committee reform experience is reconstructed in detail 1) as a means of unearthing the main goals, strategies and *modi operandi* of the reformers and their adversaries and 2) as the primary source of data used to form general conclusions about patterns of reform activity and their results.

The patterns which emerge from this inquiry are investigated further in Parts III and IV and are the foundation for the more comprehensive interpretations, speculations and conclusions that follow. Part III concludes the narrative; it recounts the demise of consolidative reform in the late 1970s and traces the rise of PACs as a result of campaign finance reform. Part IV is primarily analytical, exploring possible explanations and implications of the Party and Committee reform experience, reviewing and evaluating the spate of other Congressional reform issues such as reassertion of Congress against the Presidency, budget reform, "sunshine" reforms and assorted other reforms, and summarizing the argument linking the entire reform experience to the growth of the Special Interest Congress. Included within this discussion is a consideration of the subtle, and sometimes more explicit, biases which mobilize, and sometimes immobilize, Congress. The patterns of special interest influence in the contemporary Congress—and the extent to which they were shaped by reform—are explored. Part IV also concentrates on the implications of reform for Congress's future role in American government, and the possibilities of future reform efforts. Beyond the recent combined, unintended consequences of past reforms, the possibility of unexpected future consequences of the reforms in altered political circumstances is also considered.

The final chapters of the book seek to derive the lessons of the reform experience and to suggest some possible correctives. Chapter Twelve reflects upon the future role of Congress, especially its important functions of formulating effective national policy and mobilizing consent for that policy. In this chapter, the likely evolution of Congress, in the absence of any new reform efforts which succeed in shifting Congress in a different direction, is considered. In sketching out a pessimistic picture of the future of Congress if it stays on its present path, Chapter Twelve lays the basis for a rethinking of reform—and a package of recommendations—and proceeds to present recommendations for reform. After first considering the reform roots of the Special Interest Congress and the lessons of the reform experience, the chapter suggests possible approaches to reform designed to unify Congress and reduce its dependence on special interest groups. Both "piecemeal" and "wholesale" reforms are considered, and a proposed "package" emerges which might provide a basis for a new approach when political circumstances once again become hospitable to Congressional reform.

Notes

1. For a good discussion of the tendency for Congress to move either extremely slowly and obstruct policy or sometimes rush through massive pieces of legislation, see James Q. Wilson, "American Politics, Then and Now," *Commentary*, February, 1979, pp. 41–42 and Anthony King, *The New American Political System* (Washington, D.C.: American Enterprise Institute, 1978), p. 393. For a worthwhile historical perspective on Congress which stresses the limits of Congress and the sometimes unreasonable expectations placed on it, see Ralph K. Huitt, "Congress: Retrospect and Prospect," *Journal of Politics*, Vol. 38, August, 1976, pp. 209–227. A more recent assessment of Congress's capacities and tendencies is Philip Brenner, *The Limits and Possibilities of Congress* (New York: St. Martin's, 1983).
2. For an account with a Washington "insider" perspective, see Elizabeth Drew, "Politics and Money," *The New Yorker*, December 6, 1983, pp. 54–149 and December 13, 1982, pp. 47–111. This later appeared in expanded form as a book, *Politics and Money*, (New York: Macmillan, 1983). Mark Green, "Political PAC-MAN, On the Hill, All the Votes Money Can Buy," *The New Republic*, December 13, 1982, pp. 18–25 also takes this position, citing examples of PAC influence and reviewing possible correctives. For a longer list of the growing body of recent literature on the subject of special interest influence on Congress, see the Select Bibliography at the end of this book. A representative comment from a school of Washington columnists is from David Nyhan of the *Boston Globe:* "To qualify as a military expert in this Congress, all you need to know is the phone number of the political action committee guy at your local defense contractor. You simply vote for his overpriced weapons system, ring him up, and wait for the check. The defense industry PACs are whoring their way wholesale through the Congress. It's a matter of record. Vote for my missile system, congressman, and the check's in the mail." David Nyhan, "Someone Must Answer for Deaths in Beirut," *Boston Globe*, November 3, 1983, p. 19. Among politicians, in addition to many other supporters of campaign finance reform, Senator Barry Goldwater has joined the ranks of the reformers. See his statement "Unlimited Campaign Spending—A Crisis of Liberty," Senate Committee on Rules, September 28, 1983.
3. The only serious rival period of reform was 1910–1911 when Speaker Cannon was "overthrown." This wrought significant change of party control and patterns of behavior. But it was not the comprehensive and sustained decade of self-examination and reform that was the 1970s. See Kenneth Hechler, *Insurgency: Politics and Personality in the Taft Era* (New York: Columbia University Press, 1940), Charles R. Atkinson, *The Committee on Rules and the Overthrow of Speaker Cannon* (New York: Columbia University Press, 1911) and James Holt, *Congressional Insurgents and the*

Party System, 1909–1916 (Cambridge, Mass.: Harvard University Press, 1967).

4. See Elizabeth Drew, *Politics and Money, op. cit.* and Mark Green, "Political PAC-MAN," *The New Republic,* December 13, 1982, *op. cit.* and sources cited in the Select Bibliography on Special Interests and Congress. Drew and other journalists have been answered in a volume of detailed analyses of campaign finance in the early 1980s; see Michael J. Malbin, ed., *Money and Politics in the United States* (Chatham, N.J.: Chatham House, 1984). A number of trenchant points about the nature of PAC influence are made in this book. Basic conclusions are that the roles of PACs are highly diverse and that many of the criticisms of PACs are based on overly simplistic, and in some cases fallacious, assumptions and stereotypes. The insights of the Malbin book are taken into account in the present analysis; however, it should be noted at the outset that the complexity and variety of PAC influence, some of it described in chapters of the Malbin book, ought not to distract us from the larger phenomenon of the connection between reform and the growth of special interest influence. In addition, it should be remembered that perception and particularly perceptions of power are highly significant in politics; the perception of PACs and lobbyists and their effect on the process will have as much to do with the future of reform as the precise tabulations of PAC contributions and analysis thereof.

5. A notable exception with respect to the presidential nominating process is Nelson Polsby, *Consequences of Party Reform* (New York: Oxford University Press, 1983).

6. For an intriguing analysis of how Congress does focus on "the common good" as opposed to partisan mutual adjustment—i.e. interest group accommodation—see Arthur Maass, *Congress and the Common Good* (New York: Basic Books, 1983). The present analysis acknowledges that much of Congress's attention is focused on broad policymaking; however, a major point stressed here is that, first, reform made it less likely that Congress deals effectively with broad policy, and secondly, that the exigencies of special interest influence on both elections and legislative business extends well beyond the sphere of the specific issues of concern to those special interests. In short, a greater orientation toward narrowly-focused concerns both in Congress's internal structure and external client groups has made it all the harder to achieve even a consideration of the "common good." The trend toward decentralization of power is, of course, abroad in the society. Technological developments, especially ones involving computers and communications, have been especially instrumental in these developments. Although these broad influences, including the role of the media in shaping increasingly fractionated politics, are not focused on in this study, I agree that they are important. I am grateful to William W. Harris for our ongoing discussion on this and other points.

7. For a sociological approach to the role of special interests, see Amitai Etzioni, *Capital Corruption* (San Diego: Harcourt Brace Jovanovich, 1984).

8. Thomas Byrne Edsall, *The New Politics of Inequality* (New York: W. W. Norton, 1984).

9. See sources cited in the Select Bibliography on Special Interests and

Congress. An important rejoinder and analysis of the complex workings of money in politics in the early 1980s is Malbin, ed., *Money and Politics in the United States, op. cit.*

10. This view has cropped up in various places. See Michael J. Malbin, "Of Mountains and Molehills: PACs, Campaigns and Public Policy," in Michael J. Malbin, ed., *Parties, Interest Groups and Campaign Finance Laws* (Washington, D.C.: American Enterprise Institute, 1980), pp. 152–184. A strong statement defending PACs and criticizing proposals for PAC limitation is "Statement of Ad Hoc Committee for Free and Open Elections," Senator Eugene McCarthy, Chairman; John T. Dolan, Treasurer; Stewart Mott, Secretary; May 17, 1983. A sustained critique of the position taken by Elizabeth Drew and other critics of PACs is found in Robert J. Samuelson, "The Campaign Reform Failure, Money Has Changed, but Not Corrupted, Our Political System," *The New Republic,* September 5, 1983, pp. 28–36. In addition, a good historical perspective is provided in Kay Lehman Schlozman and John T. Tierney, "More of the Same: Washington Pressure Group Activity in A Decade of Change," Paper delivered at the annual meeting of the American Political Science Association, Denver, Colo., Sept. 2–5, 1982.

11. The literature on factions is voluminous. Important in its development were James Madison, "Federalist 10," in *The Federalist Papers,* 2nd. ed., Roy P. Fairfield (Baltimore, Md.: The Johns Hopkins University Press, 1981), Arthur Bentley, *The Process of Government* (Chicago: University of Chicago Press, 1908), E. Pendleton Herring, *The Politics of Democracy* (New York: W. W. Norton, 1940), and David B. Truman, *The Governmental Process,* 2nd ed. (New York, Alfred A. Knopf, 1971). More recent "classics" are Grant McConnell, *Private Power and American Democracy* (New York: Alfred A. Knopf, 1966) and Theodore Lowi, *The End of Liberalism,* 2nd. ed. (New York: W. W. Norton, 1979).

12. My use of the term political structure here focuses on the informal rather than the formal apparatus of politics. It is a focus similar to the distinction made by Professor Black and former Congressman Bob Eckhardt between "constitutive" and "constitutional" politics. "Constitutive" politics and my sense of political structure are directed to how the process really works. See Charles Black and Bob Eckhardt, *The Tides of Power* (New Haven: Yale University Press, 1976).

13. The reader is spared a discourse on the subject but it is worthwhile to note that sometimes PACs are instrumental in persuading Congress to do the "right" thing, albeit perhaps for the wrong reasons. Of course, depending on the rigorousness of one's standards, such result-oriented analysis may not mitigate the intrinsic perniciousness of the process.

14. For recent analyses, see Jeffrey M. Berry, *Lobbying for the People* (Princeton, N.J.: Princeton University Press, 1977), G. David Garson, *Group Theories of Politics* (Beverly Hills, Calif.: Sage Publications, 1978), and Norman J. Ornstein and Shirley Elder, *Interest Groups, Lobbying and Policymaking* (Washington, D.C.: CQ Press, 1978).

15. The recognition of the individual benefits of the system for members of Congress and interest groups has been a prominent feature of recent literature on Congress. Important examples are David Mayhew, *Congress,*

The Electoral Connection (New Haven: Yale University Press, 1974), Morris Fiorina, *Congress, Keystone of the Washington Establishment* (New Haven: Yale University Press, 1977), Rochelle Jones and Peter Woll, *The Private World of Congress* (New York: The Free Press, 1979) and Allan J. Cigler and Burdett A. Loomis, *Interest Group Politics* (Washington, D.C.: CQ Press, 1983).

16. For many reasons, which will become apparent, most of the reform activity was in the House of Representatives; hence, this book focuses primarily on the House. The Senate experience is covered in summary fashion in Chapter 10. References to matters "Congressional" therefore relate mainly to the House side. In addition, because the Democrats controlled the House for all of the period under study and the Senate for most of it, there is an emphasis on the dynamics of reform politics within the Democratic Party. A major shift in internal power within the Republican Party in the House had occurred during the middle 1960s, best symbolized by Gerald Ford's assumption of the Minority Leadership from Charles Halleck, and the new assertiveness of Ford supporters such as Donald Rumsfeld, Robert Dole, Melvin Laird, Robert Griffin and Charles Goodell. A collection of conservative Republican criticisms of the recent Democratic-controlled Congress is found in Marjorie Holt, ed. *The Case Against the Reckless Congress* (Ottawa, Illinois: Green Hill Publishers, Inc., 1976), which gives a flavor of conservative Republican differences with Democrats on policy in the middle 1970s. Minority Leader John Rhodes' views are presented in John J. Rhodes, *The Futile System* (McLean, Va.: EPM Publications, Inc., 1976) especially Chapters 5–7, pp. 70–122. I also was fortunate to have access to files on reform matters from the office of Rep. Barber Conable (R.-N.Y.) and the Republican Policy Committee, both during the middle 1970s. An excellent study of the ebb and flow of Congressional Power in the American political system is James L. Sundquist, *The Decline and Resurgence of Congress* (Washington, D.C.: The Brookings Institution, 1981).

PART I

Toward a Rethinking of Reform

One

The Context of Congressional Reform: Process, Internal Power and External Influences

1:1 PROCEDURE AND REFORM ISSUES AS ESOTERICA: A THRESHOLD POLITICAL PROBLEM

A political cartoon pinpointed the problem. A bearded, early 1960s-style protest singer, guitar in hand, stands before an audience of fellow political activists. He intones: "Next I want to sing a song about the House Rules Committee and how the legislative functions of Congress are tyrannized over by its procedural calendar, dominated in turn by an all-powerful chairman hamstringing the processes of democracy." The throng of listeners, more used to Civil Rights and Peace protest songs, look on in bewilderment.[1]

Such a song, of course, did not exist; and if it did, it probably would have been even more soporific than the cartoonist's apocryphal resumé of its message. The point is that Congress's internal procedures and structures have seldom aroused much interest, whether from the public, the press or even Members of Congress themselves. The very topic conjures up images of dusty sheafs describing parliamentary precedents or nooks and crannies of the labyrinthine committee system. Rules and structure can be counted upon to provoke instant yawns from the uninitiated. Even political scientists, for their part, have paid surprisingly little attention to Congress's over-arching rules, concentrating instead on Congressional behavior and actions: who got what, and how. This tendency is better understood in the context of the prevailing concerns of the participants; i.e. legislators, lobbyists and constituents care most about the results and spoils of the legislative process. Even protesters sought to influence Congress's actions on Civil Rights and anti-war legislation, paying scant attention to the procedural and structural factors which shaped those decisions, with the one notable exception of the filibuster in the Senate during the Civil Rights movement. To most of Congress's clientele and constituents, then, its formal rules and structure remain tucked away in the background, seemingly lifeless or without significance: an institutional "given." Rules and parliamentary points of order are occasionally invoked or taken note of, but more often they go unnoticed—like a family's set of comfortable old living room furniture. Kept in the same places for many years, the tables, chairs and fixtures are bound to be taken for granted.

Yet to infer from this that Congress's rules and structures are innocuous is a great mistake. Although decision-making is obviously important and, for Congress watchers, especially interesting, it is the rules and structures which provide the framework within which all activity takes place. They constitute the basis for politics, a fact which becomes more apparent when existing rules come under challenge. In arranging internal power, rules and norms present imposing obstacles to internal change. Those who hold power are loath to relinquish it, and even those who are not particularly powerful often remain resistant to structural change. A subtle tenacity of institutions renders attempts to change institutional norms a complicated and perplexing process. It is incorrect to assume that this framework is somehow value-free or neutral; certain interests and outcomes are favored by the existing structure, while others are opposed or precluded. Certain parties have definite vested interests in maintaining existing hierarchies and practices. How does one go about rearranging that familiar old furniture, especially when powerful occupants prefer leaving it exactly where it is?

This study examines a problem of "rearrangement": the political process by which the U.S. Congress, and particularly, the House of Representatives went about reforming its rules and practices, and in so doing, shifting internal power alignments—or mirroring shifts which had already occurred. In taking on this subject, I have chosen a political science approach which stresses historical development, implications for the allocation of political power, and the nuances of the process. This concern with process includes both the implications for the *Congressional* process, and the process of reform itself. The approach is to reconstruct events, when at all possible taking into ac-

count the perspectives of the participants. It is easy enough to catalogue the reforms *ex post facto;* it is more difficult but also more
rewarding to explore the causal links that led to these reforms. Thus
there is a great deal of attention paid here to the process of reform: to
the various "key players," their *modi operandi* and goals, and the
genesis of the proposals.

There are, of course, other ways to approach this subject; one
which has received considerable attention from political scientists is
"organization theory."[2] This approach examines Congress as a complex organization and proposals for reform as efforts at "modernization," "innovation," "integration," or "adaptation."[3] While this mode
of analysis may provide some useful insights, it tends to minimize
both the political character of Congress and the stakes involved in
reform. As two political scientists reminded a Congressional reform
panel, "the House, after all, is not an engine factory." Nor, they
added, should reformers consider alternative schemes "as if Congress
were comparable to General Motors or the U.S. Army."[4] This study,
then, treats Congress as a political institution composed not of "organization men and women" but of politicians—with specific, often
conflicting, interests.

The few studies which have delved into aspects of Congressional
procedure serve to reinforce the justification for an approach which
emphasizes the politics of reform. Lewis Froman, writing in 1967—
just prior to the period with which we are concerned—observed: "Few
rules are neutral, politically, in their effects," and he also supplied a
thoughtful description of the political biases of the "Congressional
process" in the middle 1960s:

> I think it is clear that the decentralization of power within Congress,
> the distribution within the decentralized structure, the many steps
> which bills must pass through and the complexity of the rules and
> procedures which protect, quite closely, minorities add up to a decision-
> making body which generally favors conservative interests and the *status
> quo.* In other words, it takes a lot of hard work to pass liberal legislation.[5]

The Congress—and particularly the House[6]—was then organized
in a way which served the interests of its conservative sector. Another
study from roughly the same period probing Congressional attitudes
toward various procedural reforms, identified both a similar conservative bias and cited its discomfiting effect on the prospects for
reform:

> The pessimism that surrounds these proposals for fundamental alter-
> ations of Congress stems from the simple fact that those who are most

likely to be dissatisfied are also those with the least influence and that those with the most influence have nothing to gain by changing the *status quo.*[7]

These two observations taken together provide a useful introduction to the context of reform, and to an understanding of why the reform movement was composed mainly of liberal Democrats (and even further removed from the mainstream of power—Republicans). It also is not surprising that the major targets—and opponents—were the senior "barons" of the committee system and the Democratic party. Much of what follows is in essence the story of how those with the "least influence" worked to dislodge those who, quite clearly, had "nothing to gain" (and probably much to lose) from fundamental structural and procedural reform.

1:2 INTERNAL POWER AND EXTERNAL INTERESTS: THEORETICAL AND METHODOLOGICAL ORIENTATIONS

To the extent that this study has its methodological underpinnings in the literature of political science, those underpinnings are in the American political science debate over "community power." The insights that the participants in that debate have offered have helped in formulating questions concerning power relationships within Congress. The brief outline of the theoretical political science which follows is intended to clarify the methodological approach of this study. It should also lay the foundation for the examination of the relationships between the reform process and interest group power which appear later.

Political scientists have sought for many years to explore the vagaries of power. In most instances they have focused on political decisions and decision-making.[8] However, a few have begun to probe the relationship between procedural norms and substantive decisions.[9] These writers have recognized that norms, the so-called "rules of the game," profoundly affect what is ruled upon. How a polity decides often determines what it decides, and even what it decides upon. E. E. Schattschneider in a much-quoted phrase commented incisively:

> All politics, all leadership, all organization involves the management of conflict. All conflict allocates space in the political universe.
> All forms of political organization have a bias in favor of the exploitation of some kinds of conflict and the suppression of others because *organization is the mobilization of bias.* Some issues are organized into politics while others are organized out.[10]

This notion has had many ramifications for the study of power. Whereas most students of power direct their attention to observable decisions, Schattschneider and a handful of others suggest that decisions are only the most obvious and tangible aspect of a considerably more complicated process.

While pluralists gained ascendancy in political science during the 1960s, recent work has focused on other theories of the subtle workings of power and interest group politics.

Peter Bachrach and Morton Baratz, influenced by Schattschneider, identified a "second face of power": the structural and procedural factors which approximate Schattschneider's "organization as the mobilization of bias." Bachrach and Baratz proposed a framework for analyzing this more expansive conception of political power, and by way of illustration, conducted a study of poverty programs in Baltimore during the middle 1960s.[11] They concluded that a White-dominated political culture and meager Black participation narrowed the range of issues that were considered, and thus limited the possible range of alternative decisions. In a study drawing similar conclusions about the nature of power, Matthew Crenson analyzed the issue of air pollution in two Midwestern American cities, asking why the issue had arisen in one but not the other. Crenson discovered that local political factors facilitated a decision on air pollution in East Chicago, but stifled it in Gary.[12] In the latter instance, the issue had not been decided upon because it simply ran counter to the local "rules of the game." This constituted a "non-decision."

Admittedly, non-decisionmaking as an area of critical study has not won broad acceptance. The very term has an element of self-abnegation and anomaly about it. It has been assailed by political scientists, primarily the pluralists in counter-attack, who maintain that key decisions provide the best subject for the study of power. These critics have directed their attack to the non-decision theorists' problems of methodology, arguing that non-decisions are unquantifiable. A non-decision is a non-event, they conclude, and since non-events are not verifiable, they are empirically non-existent. The major objection has been that the arena of non-decisions presents "insuperable" impediments to research. In response, Bachrach and Baratz, Crenson and others have presented spirited cases for both the existence and verifiability of non-decisions, at the same time conceding certain difficulties of method. Indeed, it is bound to be more difficult to identify the forces that "invisibly" shape decisions than to chronicle the decisions themselves. But this is not reason to shrink from the task.

In agreement with Schattschneider, Bachrach and Baratz, Crenson, Lukes and Gaventa, this study subscribes to the view that process directly affects substance, and that the relationship of process and substance has profound implications for special interests. Further, an appreciation of the implications of process for power relationships is indispensable to understanding the subtleties of any polity's power dynamics. However, it is important also to recognize that there are significant methodological problems, as illustrated by the fact that the empirical sections of the nondecisionmaking studies remain their least satisfying and well-developed sections. Even Crenson's imaginative use of survey research data of the attitudes of community leaders serves to underscore the difficulties of corroborating so shadowy an entity as the "mobilization of bias." And so the debate over alternative theories of community power continues: articles in political science journals proliferate; and the central substantive points of debate are often lost in a welter of obscurantist methodological objections.

It is important, however, not to lose sight of Schattschneider's original point that political organization is essentially about the management of conflict. Political organization, then, should be a prime focus of study; but there are subjects to be studied which are more concrete than the elusive political cultures of cities. The main flaw of the nondecision theorists' case has not been their concepts but their choices of polity. Virtually all the previously cited studies,[13] whether endorsing pluralism or non-decisionmaking, have devoted attention to one level of American politics, that of urban government. This probably owes more to the historical development of the literature than any inherent applicability of the subject. The sociologist Floyd Hunter studied community politics using a reputationist approach, and produced an elitist "stratification theory" of power, i.e. that one homogeneous social and political elite controlled community decisions.[14] Dahl and others studied the government of New Haven and sought to disprove Hunter's theory; in so doing, they developed the pluralist model. Bachrach and Baratz chose Baltimore, and Crenson used Gary and East Chicago, Indiana as the subjects for their case studies proposing an alternative to pluralist theory. Hence the recent political science study of power has been largely the study of power in American cities. Perhaps this was an obvious focus for political scientists in great urban centers: but there is no substantive reason why the debate should be so limited. Since both pluralists and non-decision theorists maintain that their frameworks are applicable to other polities, it is curious that the questions raised by the community power debate have not been asked of other political "communities," particularly in light of the methodological problems encountered by non-decision theorists when studying cities. The pluralists have been able to cling to their claim that manifest decisions remain the best clue to power relations in part due to the fortuitous circumstance that cities lend themselves so poorly to the non-decision framework. Yet this in no way undermines the validity of the concept. Instead, it may simply be a reason to investigate its applicability to other polities. Indeed, insofar as it is a goal here to shed light on the intricacies of Congressional power, it seems logical to draw on the literature concerned with explaining power and interests.

These ideas are particularly relevant to our present subject focus on Congress and its various clienteles. Despite the national and international orientations and concerns, it is readily apparent that Congress is a cloistered political community—with its rules of the game, norms and procedures—and "mobilization of bias." This community power structure has profound implications for interest group participation and influence. Hence, it makes sense to approach this subject as a large community power study.

"Changing the Rules": Reform as Redistribution of Internal Power and External Relationships

If the "rules of the game" skew political institutions toward certain decisions and hence different interests, then it is arguable that different rules might produce different outcomes. Both pluralists and non-decision theorists have been examining "the game," i.e. the process of decision-making and policy outcomes, as a goal in itself in the former case, and as indicators of the "rules" and biases in the latter. In investigating recent reforms in the U.S. House of Representatives this study takes a different tack. It begins with an identifiable set of "rules" governing Congressional behavior in 1968, and seeks to ascertain what happened when one sector of the political community set out to change them. In probing the historical roots of these norms, and the reasons for their political sustenance it is possible to understand better why they met with opposition. And a detailed reconstruction of the overall process of reform—analyzing all its participants and their motivations—should provide insight into how various interests perceived themselves to be directly or indirectly affected, and therefore acted in the way they did.

Reform Process and Reform Results

Internal Congressional reform can be divided into two components: *how* and *what* reform occurred, or reform process and reform results. The former includes the ebb and flow of reform proposals during the course of their consideration. The latter concerns the effect on power relations. The reform process encompasses the configurations of support for, and opposition to, reform proposals: the web of internal maneuver and intrigue, strategies and counter-strategies. It also includes the connivance of groups outside the institution both for and against reform. The reform results are the new political alignments.

The view here is that the two must be taken together in order to understand reform; either alone may produce fragmentary and misleading conclusions. To examine process alone, to borrow Bagehot's phrase, would be a "prologue without a play." To take into account only the results would be to ignore the political circumstances and motives of the participants. By examining process and results together over an extended span of time and experience, we are able to focus on the alternative directions of reform, and understand the process by which reform activity affects the redistribution of power.

Threshold Questions

This study approaches reform as a study in the allocation and reallocation of community power and seeks to answer a series of questions such as how the issue of reform was raised, who raised it, who supported it, and who opposed it. In this case, however, we are dealing not with a substantive issue like air pollution control or a piece of legislation (as in the Congressional "bill becomes a law" case studies), but are concerned instead with the process by which a political institution deals with the changes in the very process by which it commonly makes its decisions. While the conflict over substantive ends may reflect the distribution of power, this conflict concerns the actual source of power. If changing the rules does change the game, in order to further understand the new "games" we must investigate carefully the process by which the rules were changed. It is from such an examination that the following questions arise:

- What was the context of reform, i.e. the political factors which spurred reformers and which created the conditions in which the *status quo* came to be challenged?
- Who were the reformers and what did they intend to accomplish?
- How did they plan their reform campaign, i.e. what were their strategies and objectives?
- What were the alternative directions of reform, the various ways in which internal power could be shifted, i.e. from which, and to which, alternative power centers?

- Who supported, and opposed, which reforms and why?
- What involvement, if any, was there by external special interests in the Congressional reform process?
- Which reforms were accepted and why?
- Which reforms "succeeded" and which "failed" upon implementation? What were the ramifications of reform for how Congress operates as a political institution?
- If reform was essentially about shifting power, to whom (internally and externally) did power accrue?
- What were the implications of reform for Congress's relationship with outside interest groups?
- What were the implications of reform for Congress's role in the American political process?

The answers to these questions serve the basis for the analysis, interpretations and recommendations which follow.

1:3 INTERNAL POWER DYNAMICS AS AN IMPETUS TO REFORM: OLIGARCHIC CHAIRMEN, FRUSTRATED LIBERALS

The Democratic Study Group (DSG) was born out of frustration. Organized in 1959 by liberal and moderate Democrats, the DSG had arisen from informal meetings beginning in 1957 of supporters of Civil Rights legislation, Federal-aid-to-education, and social programs. They had been ingloriously dubbed by the press and insiders as "McCarthy's Mavericks" (after their early leader Eugene McCarthy of Minnesota); "mavericks" aptly described the status of liberals in the 85th Congress of 1957–1958.[15] President Eisenhower had swamped Adlai Stevenson in 1956, removing any possibility that liberal leadership might be forthcoming from the White House. While the Democrats held majorities in both Houses of Congress, liberals found little solace in this, given the conservative tendencies of most of the committee chairmen, and in light of the effectiveness on the House floor of the "Conservative Coalition" of Southern Democrats and most Republicans.[16]

Liberal spirits during the 85th Congress reached their nadir when the Landrum-Griffin bill, legislation strongly attacked by liberals as anti-labor, sailed through the Congress over the objections of a poorly-organized and outnumbered bloc of liberals. This served as yet another reminder of the ineffectiveness of the liberal minority within the Democratic party and served as an impetus for liberal leaders to organize DSG. Initial projects of the fledgling, 94 member group included research, discussion of common concerns and efforts to coordinate legislative activity. The last item took the form of a rudimentary Whip system designed to mobilize liberal strength. In the short term, DSG hoped to make the best of the unfavorable circumstances, and perhaps to salvage a few liberal measures. Looking further ahead, they sought to prepare for effective action in the event of an upturn in liberal fortunes, whenever it might come.

DSG, then, arose from a recognition by liberals of their own paltry impact on House business in the late 1950s. Composed mainly of junior Democrats from the North and West, it followed a conscious policy of making few waves. It was a minority subset of the majority party; its members held no positions of power on committees or in the Democratic party leadership. Indeed, it was this lack of consequence which had impelled them to join together.

The liberals' frustration did, of course, imply criticism of the conservative skew of power in the House; however, little attention was paid to structural reform at the time. Rather than concern themselves with structural or procedural issues, DSG's leaders focused on specific pieces of legislation: Civil Rights bills which were bottled up in committee, as opposed to conservative economic legislation which received friendly attention from such important House committees as Rules, Appropriations, and Ways and Means. Moreover, the committees were virtually controlled by their chairmen,[17] who were often quite elderly (because of the seniority system) and conservative (due to the secure tenure of seats held in conservative areas, especially the South, and the propensity of Southerners to make the House a career).[18] Oligarchic and conservative chairmen resisted or ignored liberal pressures, giving short shrift to liberal legislators and their legislative proposals. DSG's leaders—Reps. Lee Metcalf,[19] Frank Thompson, Chet Holifield, John Blatnik and others, sought to improve the hitherto lacklustre legislative record of liberals. They were all pragmatists anxious to avoid a confrontation with the Democratic leadership, especially Sam Rayburn, the Speaker of the House. They understood that Rayburn had found it difficult to contend with the independently powerful committee chairmen; they also knew that Rayburn was inclined to support liberal programs when politically practicable. Therefore they maintained cordial relations with the Speaker, and kept him apprised of their activities either directly or through his confidant with ties to the liberals, Richard Bolling of Missouri. By working with the leadership rather than against it, DSG's leaders felt they would enhance the prospects of their legislative goals. From the very beginning DSG's primary concern was the passage of liberal legislation.

Still, the first, best hope for liberal programs lay in the election of an activist Democratic president, a strong presidency on the Franklin D. Roosevelt model. There was by now consensus among liberals at the time that such leadership was a prerequisite for liberal success. Thus liberal and moderate House Democrats, many of whom had been elected in 1958 and re-elected in 1960,[20] greeted John F. Kennedy's election with high hopes. Of course, on the House side especially, there was little cause for optimism. It was clear from the outset of the Kennedy Administration that the conservative forces in the House, who had dominated the liberal Democratic minority during the previous administration, were not about to alter their views or relinquish their positions of authority.

Collectively, the committee chairmen constituted a formidable obstacle to Kennedy's programs. Though Democrats all, the chairmen were the most reluctant of "New Frontiersmen." Moreover, they sat atop a Congressional structure which had become well-suited to delay and obstruction, the two most obvious symbols of which were the House Rules Committee, the powerful "traffic controller of legislation,"[21] and the slightly more abstract seniority system. The Rules Committee had been dominated by a coalition of Southern Democrats and Republicans, a strategically important microcosm of the larger "Conservative Coalition," since 1937 when they had forged an alliance to undercut New Deal legislation.[22] The committee had a pivotal position in the legislative process, deciding whether to grant a "rule" for floor consideration of bills, and if so, under what conditions; this position translated into effective control over the flow of legislation to the full House. Conservative domination of the committee made it the bane of many liberals' most cherished hopes.[23]

Seniority, the criterion for promotion on House committees, was attacked as a "senility system,"[24] and had become, in the eyes of one of its beneficiaries and staunchest defenders, "as popular a target as sin itself."[25] However, the seniority system tended to be more criticized than understood. For instance, even some sitting House members failed to appreciate that seniority was a relatively recent evolutionary "custom" which had developed in reaction to abuses by Speakers who, until the early part of the twentieth century, had been empowered to appoint committee chairmen.[26] Nor did many critics take into account the functional benefits of seniority, fulfilling what Nelson Polsby had described as a "universalistic" selection process, important in the developing "institutionalization" of the House.[27] In fact, there was widespread acceptance within Congress of some form of seniority-based recognition of experience and expertise as qualifications for committee leadership. Thus "abolishing" the seniority system always had a fanciful ring about it to Congressional insiders, even those most anxious to depart from its strict observance.[28] In any case, the issue of seniority itself lacked the symbolic visibility of the House Rules Committee. And the figure of the embattled Chairman, Judge Howard Smith of Virginia, neatly evoked both images: a crusty, seniority-ensconced chairman, and the Rules Committee as the most blatant impediment to liberal bills, and after 1960, to Kennedy's New Frontier.

It was not surprising then that most of the criticism of Congress in the late 1950s and early 1960s, both external and internal, focused on its conservative disposition and inertia. It was also predictable that liberal reformist attention was fixed on the Rules Committee. One line of attack attempted to circumvent the committee entirely, either through the unwieldy process of a discharge petition[29] or later, through the 21 and 31 day rules allowing committee chairmen to bring bills to the floor if the Rules Committee had not acted within the allotted time.[30] Some liberals embarked on a more politically perilous but potentially rewarding course, attempting to alter the composition of the Rules Committee by "packing it" with more liberal members. This second approach, the move to enlarge the Rules Committee from twelve to fifteen in January, 1961, was the first major Congressional test of the Kennedy Administration. The new President allied himself with Speaker Rayburn and enlisted the support of moderate and liberal Democrats (including the vigorous assistance of DSG) along with seven maverick liberal Republicans. President Kennedy was stridently opposed by most Southern Democrats, most prominently Judge Smith, and all but seven Republicans.[31] In a fierce battle, with considerable influence exerted on each side, the Kennedy-Rayburn forces triumphed narrowly: 217 to 212 on January 31, 1961. Quickly thereafter, the Democratic leadership saw to it that three new members favorably disposed to the Kennedy program were appointed.[32]

This victory remained, however, only a small chink in the conservatives' Congressional armor; the short tenure of the Kennedy Administration proved to be a story of frustration and logjam in the face of conservative recalcitrance on Capitol Hill. It was obvious that the chairmen bore much of the responsibility for these failures, and as a result, liberals became increasingly aware that their real targets were the chairmen themselves.[33] The obstructionism which committee chairmen embodied continued to be the prime focus of criticism leveled at Congress, initially by Washington-based liberals but increasingly by the less ideologically committed citizenry as well.[34] This popular image of Congress as an "obstacle course" found acerbic expression in Robert Bendiner's description in 1964:

> A United States Congressman has two principal functions: to make laws and to keep laws from being made. The first of these he and his colleagues perform only with sweat, patience and a remarkable skill in the handling of creaking machinery, but the second they perform daily, with ease and infinite variety.[35]

It was not until the advent of President Johnson and the landslide Democratic intake of 1964 that this stereotype was belied by experience. A forceful and Congressionally-experienced President commanded the support of that most fleeting and unusual commodity, a liberal majority in both Houses of Congress.[36] During this period, the Democratic Study Group worked to consolidate its swollen numbers in order to lend effective support to the Administration's programs, even though their legislative leadership was now less necessary. Meanwhile, the committees, the centers of conservative power and obstruction, simply lay low, acquiesced occasionally but only when necessary, and survived.

The most significant procedural reform passed during the 1964–1966 period of liberal ascendancy further tinkered with House procedures to side-step the Rules Committee, this time by means of the 21 day Rule. This was another attempt to undermine the Rules Committee's capacity to act as a legislative roadblock. Instead of devoting attention to issues of internal procedure, i.e. reforming itself, in the middle 1960s Congress was preoccupied with the heady business of reforming the country. In so doing, they produced a spate of social welfare legislation unparalleled since the early days of the New Deal. Of course, some liberals felt that President Johnson was too willing to compromise—in order to lengthen the list of Great Society accomplishments—and that the quality of legislative output was the worse for it. But this was the view of a small band of cynics. Most mainstream liberal Democratic energies were spent working out the legislative intricacies of Great Society programs.[37]

There were occasional rumbles regarding more ambitious internal reform. In fact, the two Houses went so far as to establish a Joint Committee on the Organization of the Congress in 1965. It was modeled on the Joint Committee of 1945–1946 which had produced the sweeping consolidation of committees and other reforms in the Legislative Reorganization Act of 1946, but there was no comparable momentum behind the 1965–1966 Committee's work. Much of this no doubt owed to Congress's recent legislative productivity. The criticism of Congress as an obstructive institution seemed to have been temporarily overshadowed by events. Another explanation was that the House's potentates had no interest in change; it was enough that they had been forced to make concessions to the liberal Administration on policy matters. They had no wish to allow liberals greater access to power in Congress itself. Luckily for these senior members unsympathetic to reform, the reformers were fractious, and their proposals rambling and unfocused. It was for a combination of these reasons that the Joint Committee considered many proposals, but recommended action on only a few.[38] Moreover, it assiduously avoided most controversial issues embracing power relations such as seniority and anti-secrecy reforms, although both subjects had been discussed at the Committee's extensive hearings. It concentrated instead on the more congenial Congressional concerns such as improved staffing, better information facilities, electronic voting and the like. The one contentious issue that the Joint Committee did attempt to deal with was the separation of the House Education and Labor Committee.[39] This provoked such a storm of resistance and criticism that it seemed to justify the caution they displayed in the rest of their recommendations. In fact, although the Legislative Reorganization bill passed the Senate with ease in 1967, it was primarily the controversial Education and Labor provision which caused the House to delay their own serious consideration of the reorganization bill until 1970. The bill's final provisions were relatively modest, concerned mainly with "housekeeping" reforms; in the end, the bill's passage was facilitated by removal of the Education and Labor provision.

The experience of the Joint Committee of 1965–1966 demonstrated the problems any Congressional reform movement would face. Their hearings, taking up 2,322 pages, constituted[40] a rambling potpourri of diverse grievances, claims and proposed reforms. The hearings also indicated the breadth of the subject. Congressmen rode their personal hobby horses, such as expanded student internship programs, radio and television coverage, a bullet-proof glass barrier between the public gallery and the House floor, limiting the seniority system and the proposal—supported by President Johnson—for a four-year House term concurrent with that of the President. This plan could be expected to command enthusiastic support in the House, and contemptuous opposition in the Senate. Senators understandably were not pleased at the prospect of House members being able to challenge them without sacrificing their seats in the House.[41] This proposed reform, like others, was doomed from the start by one compelling political factor. In this case, it was the implacable opposition of the Senate, but there were many more similarly simple reasons why such reforms were destined to fail. In the middle 1960s reform had been tailored to the politics of the times; the liberals, the segment of the House most likely to form the backbone of a reform movement, for reasons of their exclusion from most of the internal positions of power and their presumptive receptivity to change, were temporarily mollified. The sources of obstruction were superable, and their time seemed better spent working on legislation and supporting Lyndon Johnson on the House floor. What little effort liberals did muster found voice in an inchoate collection of criticisms and random targets without any unifying foundation. Reform lacked a political impetus. But this was to change.

1:4 MOVING TOWARD 1968: CONGRESS AND PRESIDENTIAL POWER

The 1964–1966 liberal dominance proved to be short-lived; liberals had lost their majority in Congress and the ambitious optimism of the Great Society quickly disappeared. The mid-term elections of 1966 reduced the number of Democrats by 47 in the House. Those who did return were increasingly divided over American involvement in Vietnam and racial problems. Meanwhile, House conservatives were able to reassert themselves, and Congress as an institution, to revert to its familiar ways.

With its ranks also depleted after 1966[42] and its much-vaunted set of national Democratic programs under fire, DSG was particularly affected by the deepening rifts in American liberalism. Many of its members dutifully endorsed the Johnson Vietnam policy, while others were privately critical; few, in any case voiced their opposition to Administration policies. On domestic policy, liberals indulged in recrimination over the causes and consequences of urban unrest, which the Great Society had seemed only to nourish rather than to allay. Moreover, liberal Democrats in Congress were becoming increasingly defensive about their decreasingly credible President. It was perhaps symptomatic of Congress's thankless position in the American separation of powers system that dissatisfaction with the Johnson Administration not only failed to manifest itself in an upsurge of public confidence in Congress; instead it provided yet another opportunity for critics of Congress to make their point. Only now the liberals' grievance was not what Congress had done to thwart the Administration, as it had been in the Kennedy years; this time it was what Congress—or at least its anti-war members—had not done: it had not blocked President Johnson's escalation of the War in Vietnam. And it had not passed legislation which cured America's urban malaise. Thus only a few years after the perception of Congress as an "obstacle course" had achieved broad acceptance, Congress was now indicted on two new and contradictory counts: on the one hand, it had not been enough of an "obstacle course" to Johnson on Vietnam;[43] and on the other, its Great Society legislation had fallen far short of its advance billing.

Yet the cleavages beginning to reveal themselves in the middle 1960s transcended both the criticism of Congress and the divisive issues of Vietnam and racial inequality. Beyond these, the politics of the Johnson era raised Constitutional questions about the proper relationship between Congress and the President. It was a particularly thorny problem for liberals. The necessity of a strong president had been unassailable liberal doctrine since the 1930s, and had even attracted the support of intellectual opinion expressed in the writings of liberal academics such as Arthur Schlesinger, Jr., James MacGregor Burns, Stephen K. Bailey, Richard Neustadt and David B. Truman.[44]

During the 1950s and early 1960s presidential power had come to be viewed as the indispensable antidote to Congressional conservatism and obstruction. However, by the middle 1960s there were perceptible signs of a new liberal attitude: the view that Congress was, in fact, a valuable forum to criticize and oppose presidential policies with which liberals disagreed.[45] Indeed, unbridled presidential power, especially when accompanied by Congressional acquiescence as in the Gulf of Tonkin resolution, seemed less and less appealing to Congressional liberals. Of course, for many the problem was not liberalism but Johnson. Liberalism, as G. B. Shaw said of Christianity, had not failed; it had not been tried. Thus Johnson was seen in some quarters as having betrayed liberal principles. As such, his failures were seen as bearing no reflection on the intrinsic desirability of an activist presidency. For liberals of this persuasion, the answer was to elect a "real" liberal president. The presidential campaigns in 1968 of Eugene McCarthy, Robert Kennedy, George McGovern, and for some, Hubert Humphrey, are best understood in this context.[46] But there were others who perceived more systemic sources of the problem, concluding that the presidency itself had grown too powerful and unaccountable, and that it had done so at the expense of Congress.

As early as 1965 the political scientist John Manley expressed this view in a statement submitted to the Joint Committee on the Organization of the Congress. "Congress does have a problem," he wrote, "but it is not internal; it is inextricably linked to the dominant center of American government, the President."[47] Manley then alluded to external "Congressional reformers" such as Burns and Bailey, who look upon Congress as the "sick man of American politics."[48] Manley went on to probe more deeply the assumptions and implications of this brand of reformism: ". . . the bacillus is the irresponsible political parties which fragment power, permit the continuation of parochial-oriented bases of power which thwart Presidential programs, and consequently frustrate 'exuberant leadership.' "[49] Alluding to John Stuart Mill's classic work, *On Representative Government,* which suggests a limited role for legislatures, Manley concluded:

> There is an essential similarity between Mill's critique of legislatures and the position of Congressional reformers, and the similarity is that both would tighten the executive's control over the legislature.[50]

Hitherto, those who had advocated Congressional reform—most notably these political scientists who advocated an American version of "party responsibility"[51]—were primarily concerned with removing the Congressional obstacles to presidential leadership. James MacGregor Burns' "deadlock of democracy" thesis suggested that there was a system of not two but four party politics in which the Congressional parties, both Republican and Democrat, were dominated by members conservative on domestic matters and isolationist on foreign policy, and the two Presidential parties, by liberal "internationalists." This typology was plausible when the book went to press in 1963, particularly in light of the liberality of recent Democratic presidents and nominees Roosevelt, Truman, Stevenson, and Kennedy; likewise, the moderate domestic stances and foreign policy "internationalism" of Republicans Wilkie, Dewey, and President Eisenhower seemed to support the idea that would-be presidents seek to appeal to "liberal" national opinion. As for the "Congressional parties" it had become conventional wisdom that the Democratic party in Congress was in the hands of its oligarchic chairmen, whose conservatism owed much to their rural, backwater origins. And the Congressional Republicans were led by the "Taft wing," which was also strongly conservative. These facts seemed to support the conclusion of David Truman's influential study of "the Congressional party" in 1959 that Congressional voting was "essentially sectional, one wing in each set being composed entirely of men from the South and Border and the other including North and Border. . . ."[52] These geographic cleavages also neatly fit Burns' model; the Southern Democrats were, in fact, deeply conservative and clearly wielded a disproportionate amount of power. Their coalescence with the Republicans was the main source of the "politics of stalemate," especially evident in the Kennedy era. Burns' prescription, and that of like-minded political scientists, was for streamlined, assertive parties, led by activist (who were by definition, liberal) presidents.

From 1964 to 1966 the conditions for Burns' "exuberant leadership" were fulfilled: an activist liberal Democratic President leading a solid liberal majority in Congress. However, this blissful realization of American-style party responsibility soon led not to the promised land but to Vietnam and domestic turbulence. Moreover, it became obvious that chunks of Burns' typology stood in need of revision. For a start, the institutional and demographic bases of four-party politics were undergoing significant change. Reapportionment and the age of "one man, one vote" began to erode conservative dominance in the House. And the rise of the suburbs at the expense of big cities had diminished the disproportionate impact of big cities in determining electoral college votes. The "internationalist" aspect of Burns' original formulation had been seen as the natural concomitant of liberalism, but by the late 1960s, anti-Vietnam suspicion of interventionism began to color the foreign policy attitudes of liberals. The new-style liberal anti-interventionism bore a rather striking similarity to the old-style isolationism of the conservatives, and by the end of the decade it was liberals in Congress who were now seeking to obstruct the President. In domestic policy—as James Sundquist later documented[53]—the roots of many liberal policies of the Democratic Administration were to be found not in the basement of the White House or in the recesses of the Executive departments but instead in the draft legislation of Congressional committees. Thus while it was fair to argue that Congress was organizationally haphazard and prone to conservatism when the committee "barons" had their way, it was not true that this necessarily precluded liberal success on a number of specific issues. The parties in Congress were less monolithic than Burns' "Congressional parties" thesis had hypothesized; they had certainly been dominated by conservatives in recent experience, but there was nothing divinely decreed that liberals would be perpetually outflanked in Congress for all time.

The factors of liberal re-evaluation of the strong presidency and their coming to grips with their position in Congress converged after November 5, 1968. The election of Richard Nixon was the crowning blow to the Burns "liberal president, conservative Congress" postulation. Elected during a time of tumult, and purporting to offer conservatism and quiescence, Nixon was seen in many circles to be tilting toward his party's conservative wing.[54] An old adversary of the liberals, he stood for almost everything they opposed. Indeed, for liberals who had grown used to friendly guidance from the White House to compensate for their own weak footing on Capitol Hill, it was doubly distressing. The "liberal hour" had apparently elapsed; and Congressional liberal Democrats found themselves threatened with a set of circumstances reminiscent of the glum days of the 1950s. They no longer faced the benign Eisenhower but Nixon, who was not only a conservative but also an avowed activist. Here was a man whom liberals had no wish to see as a "strong president." After 1968, with the advent of a presumptively hostile conservative Republican Administration, the prevailing characteristic of the House liberals was once again one of frustration.

1:5 GOALS: THE OBJECTS AND DIRECTIONS OF REFORM

The Muddle Over Means and Ends: Criticism and Reformism

The primary impetus to reform was the disadvantaged position of liberal Democrats, especially after 1968. Its underlying theme was the liberals' quest for a greater share of internal power. But for all outward appearances the focus of reform was on specific issues of the day; any sort of underlying connection between the various proposals—or their implications for power—was not readily discernible. Moreover, as the experience of the 1965–1966 Joint Committee on the Organization of the Congress had revealed, "reform" included a variety of things: everything from constructing a bullet-proof glass barrier in the public gallery to dispensing with the seniority system. The abundance of proposals (only a tiny fraction of them plausible, or even, in the eyes of many, sensible) betrayed a marked lack of consensus on what constituted reform. Reform, of course, is highly normative; before too long in the Congressional reform debate it became apparent that reform to one person was regression to another.

Much of this lack of clarity stemmed from the diffuse nature of the grievances the reforms were intended to redress. Columnists Drew Pearson and Jack Anderson, writing in January of 1969, provided a catalogue of Congressional sins:

> Congress has become over-age, out-of-date, pompous, negative, cor-
> rupt, inefficient and occasionally, irresponsible. Its procedures are un-
> democratic, contrary to the speeches which fall so easily from Congres-
> sional lips. Its rules are rigid and often irrational. The legislative
> machinery is creaky and cumbersome.[55]

Presented with such an awesome list of evils, would-be reformers
could be forgiven if they were at a loss as to which to attack first, or
how, or even precisely what it was they were attacking.

"Over-age" implied objection to the seniority system and thus internal, and intra-party, power relations. "Pompous" and "negative" were
impressions of behavior, more likely requiring a change of members'
deportment, or failing that, of members themselves. "Corrupt" and
"irresponsible" may have been applicable to the performance of individual congressmen on specific issues and were arguably rooted in
systemic factors;[56] however, it was unclear how Congressional reform
might eliminate dishonesty or guarantee "responsibility." Such cri-
tiques seemed to call for reform of human nature, not Congress.
Finally, "undemocratic" procedures and "rigid" or "irrational" rules
returned to issues of power relations. But there were few attempts to
extrapolate from this multifarious selection of criticisms the precise
targets, means, or ends of reform. Critics such as Pearson and Anderson, and others,[57] did not even try. They concentrated instead on
Congress's seamier side: the assorted practices of skulduggery often
associated with the legislative process which provided grist for their
investigative reporters' mill. But these were only manifestations, unfortunate by-products rather than institutional sources of the problem. They left it to someone else to identify the objects and objectives
of reform.

As we shall see, this is what the DSG Executive began to do in
December of 1968, and what they and others did in a rather
haphazard, incremental fashion over the next six years. DSG, and
later, external reform-minded groups, attempted to give continuity
and direction to the reform effort; but they too were not immune to
the inconsistencies and confusions which characterized the critics. For
example, DSG, the shrewd instigators and tacticians of reform, at one
point identified their objectives as "openness, efficiency, and responsiveness."[58] Each, of course, was an admirable enough goal; but together they were arguably incompatible. An efficient legislature may
not necessarily be a responsive one. Also, it is useful to ask "responsive
to whom?" The answer in the case of a Congress seeking co-equality
with the presidency was that an "efficient" Congress might well be one

more easily dominated by the executive. In addition, efficiency itself may hamper Congress's other capacities, for instance its representative and deliberative functions. Rep. Richard Bolling was fond of describing the House as "messy;" but concluded that it must be so because "the democratic process is messy."[59] Efficiency reforms, then, often begged further questions.

Openness, another DSG goal, can be gained directly at the expense of efficiency, which is not to say it is a bad thing. But then, openness in some aspects of Congressional practice might run headlong into the reformers' notion of responsiveness. That is, openness meant greater public access to Congress and greater visibility of Congressional processes. Yet open committee meetings could become too "responsive" to the lobbyists who attend them, and not enough so to the citizens who, by and large, do not. Another example was the party caucus: an open party caucus may well be less responsive to party wants, and more importantly, open caucuses may well defeat the main purpose of private meetings: i.e. to develop policy unencumbered by outside scrutiny—including that of the opposition party.[60] A prime institutional and sub-institutional goal, then, is effectiveness, and not all the proposals which were ostensibly designed to foster "openness, efficiency, and responsiveness" would accomplish this. For the most part, these divergent ends of reform were not faced squarely by the reformers. Nor was another key aspect of the DSG reform campaign. This was the discrepancy of purpose involved in meshing procedural reform with substantive policy goals. Some reformers viewed these as synonymous; indeed, DSG's leaders understood better than most that reform, at its root, concerned power and that since the House was presently dominated by the conservatives, they needed to improve their own power base in order to advance liberal policies. But this was not to say that all reforms would enhance the prospects for liberal policies. Indeed, at times proposed reforms might well clash with each other, requiring liberal reformers to decide whether their liberalism or reformism took precedence. These were only two of the more subtle conundrums of reform which would persist throughout the reform debate, and most likely would remain long after these reforms themselves became the targets of future reformers. But there were a number of other intellectual conflicts, the sum total of which was a deep muddle over the means and ends of reform.

Like the rambling and confused criticisms, the specific reform proposals involved a range of different objects. In addition, they necessitated action by different sub-institutional bodies and often led in opposing directions. This point about different objects and forums was illustrated by one liberal organization's identification of its targets: "What's wrong with Congress?" they asked, and promptly answered: "It could be a combination of secrecy, seniority and powerful committees."[61] This blurred distinctions between secrecy (a factor of institutional and party Caucus rules) seniority (the informal intraparty criterion for selection of committee leaders) and committees (the official structure by which legislative and other functions are apportioned). In some cases, it was possible to use the party caucus to commit the majority party to change House rules; in others, reformers sought to change party practice through House legislation.[62]

The intricacies involved in implementing reform were often confusing, especially to the many congressmen and outsiders who were more interested in other Congressional concerns. In fairness, most examples of the amalgamation of different strands were the result of well-intentioned reformers trying to make a complicated subject simple. Still, simplicity did not always produce clarity, and the cases presented made for some rather large reformist mouthfuls, for instance this press account of a speech spreading the reform message:

> Congressmen are finally realizing they have lost power to the President and that they must eliminate secrecy and ease the grip of the seniority system in order to regain public confidence, Common Cause Chairman John W. Gardner said here Monday.[63]

This added the inter-institutional factor of Congress's power in relation to the President to the previously mentioned internal issues of secrecy and seniority. And it raised the further issue of public confidence, an external factor, and a complicated one at that.[64]

Finally, the issues involved in the case for reform were further obscured by an excess of literary embellishment. While every reform proposal was, at least potentially, a redistribution of power, some reforms were clearly more salient in their implications for power relations than others. Perhaps least salient were those which could be placed under the heading "modernization." Thus reformers who concentrated on Congress's obsolescence often proved to be more imaginative in their choice of analogies than incisive about the priorities of reform. For example, one liberal pamphleteer, obviously influenced by the consumer movement, exclaimed: "If Congress were an automobile, its unhappy owner would probably junk it and then sue the manufacturer," and continued, quoting TRB of *The New Republic,* that Congressional procedure was "so awful that it has a kind of charm, like preferring an outhouse to modern plumbing."[65] These were useful pieces of propaganda, yet they somehow failed to increase the understanding of what precisely needed reforming, or why. Clarification was slow to emerge, but for the purposes here, it is useful to pinpoint at the outset the prime objects and opposing directions of internal House reform.

Objects: Parties and Committees

If "organization" determines the skew of power relations and reform is the process of redistributing that power, then the real objects of reform are not such internal practices as seniority or secrecy, or aesthetic values like efficiency and modernization as such. The former are mere manifestations of more basic institutional entities and the latter are normative—and probably unobtainable—ideals. Rather, reform must focus on internal structures which regulate conflict and allocate power. These were the instruments of power over which reformers sought to increase their control. In the House of Representatives there are two such sub-institutions: parties and committees.

Parties, unmentioned in the Constitution or House rules and feared by the Founders as potentially dangerous harbingers of factionalism, in practice have more often been derided as weak "catch-alls," themselves coalitions lacking fixed goals. The economic, geographic, ethnic and racial diversity of American society militates against programmatic, "responsible" parties; although one significant body of writing certainly hoped for their emergence.[66] During the period under study the Democratic president necessary for fulfillment of this form of "responsible party" was missing. This "party responsibility" was not the political scientists' panacea, but was instead a device which liberal politicians used to counter the President and salvage as much as possible of "national Democratic" programs. What DSG Congressional reformers had in mind after 1968 was the responsibility of their "truncated majority."[67] There were two internal political goals: to assert the liberal wing of the Democratic party against the party's conservatives, and (as a means of accomplishing the former) to assert the party, i.e., the Democratic Caucus, against the committee system.

Thus one major sphere of reform activity involved the internal dynamics of party: i.e. Party reform. The other major focus of reform was the committee system itself. Rather than to use the Democratic Caucus as a weapon against irascible chairmen, Committee reform involved a more direct approach. This took the form of a special House committee set up to devise a plan to restructure committees: a bipartisan, institutional approach to reform. Ultimately, the matter involved both party and full House consideration. These two movements, Party reform and Committee reform, comprise the two main structural themes of the reform story. As a consequence, our attention is overwhelmingly devoted to politics inside the majority Democratic party and later, the House committee structure: the two key centers of activity. As would later become clear, Party reform and Committee reform were two vastly different matters. And it would also become clear that there were opposite directions of reform implicit in these two main areas of reform activity.

Directions: Consolidation and Dispersion

Having identified the objects of reform, we are better able to discern its alternative directions. House reform was about power, and, more specifically about three separate loci of power: inside the Democratic party, between the Democratic Caucus and committees, and within the committee system itself. While each aspect involved different customs, practices and procedures, together they constituted the House's system of power relations, i.e. the existing political alignments reformers sought to alter. This system favored the committee chairmen: at the expense of their subcommittee chairmen and junior committee members below them, and the House Democratic leadership above them. The leadership under Speaker McCormack was consciously unassertive, and indeed had little means of being otherwise. Ever since 1910–1911, the Speaker's power had been severely limited. And as for potential sources of power: the Democratic Caucus lay fallow for all but the first organizational session of each Congress. In this political setting, the fragmented committees and their leaders dominated the House.

The status quo at the beginning of the period of reform was a system in which the House's power was dispersed to a small group of committee chairmen and a tiny clique of other key figures who possessed the means of effective—albeit fragmented—power. Moreover, the structure of power is further revealed by the composition of the discontented groups, namely: liberals who disliked the political biases of the committee chairmen, juniors who objected to the dominant authority of the chairmen, and Republicans who resented their virtual exclusion from many decisions by the Democratic committee "barons." All three groups had the common target of chairmen, but their specific complaints pulled them in different directions. For example, middle-level liberals were restless but ambivalent about seniority (and became less restless and more aware of seniority's benefits the longer they served). Junior liberals were frustrated by the seniority system and ambivalent about party discipline. The challenge to the existing system was bound to focus on the most obvious holders of power, the chairmen. If the reforms were successful they could shift this power in two possible directions.[68] First, reform could consolidate power in the leadership, where it had been prior to 1910, as symbolized by such notable "strong speakers" as Thomas Brackett Reed and Joseph G. Cannon.[69] This would entail strengthening the Democratic Caucus, and then providing the Speaker with enough authority to use the Caucus as a device to assert himself in party and committee affairs. Further, consolidation would involve changes in House rules to provide the leadership with greater control of business on the floor, which, in turn, would inhere greater control by the Speaker over the Rules Committee. Finally, such leadership-oriented reform would include rationalizing the diffuse House committee structure. Each of these shifts of power was a possible result of the various reform proposals that might have emerged from a combination of Party reform and Committee reform. However, aspects of these proposals in combination with others also had the potential to lead in exactly the opposite direction.

This alternative direction of reform was further dispersion of power, away from the committee chairmen outward to subcommittee chairmen and members, and to junior members of committees. This would also include endowing rank and file Democrats in their party caucus with greater means of control over party, and House, business.

These were the alternative directions of reform: consolidation and dispersion. The passage of reforms heading in both directions might blunt the effect of reform; or the reforms could shift power in one direction or the other. These opposing directions of reform remained quietly in the background during most of the consideration of reform, surfacing only occasionally in the form of demands for stronger leadership, or pleas for more democratic committee procedures. Typically these opposing directions, as well as a grasp of the other subtle implications for power relations, did not figure prominently in the reform debate. Instead the reform effort proceeded one step at a time, an approach which did not lend itself to grandiose schemes with clear-cut directions. Reformers were frequently preoccupied with the immediate task of devising these incremental aims and mobilizing support for their implementation. This provided quite enough of a challenge, but it also laid the basis for mixed, and ultimately negative, results.

Notes

1. Cartoon by Edward Koren which originally appeared in the *New Yorker* in 1964. It was reprinted in the *Washington Post,* March 11, 1973, p. B5.
2. For example, see Roger H. Davidson and Walter G. Oleszek, "Adaptation and Integration: Structural Innovation in the House of Representatives," a Paper delivered at the 1975 Annual Meeting of the American Political Science Association, San Francisco, September 1–5, 1975. I am grateful to Davidson and Oleszek for providing me with a copy of their paper and to Lowe for his draft (hereafter cited Lowe MS). David Lowe in the manuscript of his Ph.D. dissertation at the Johns Hopkins University—on the Bolling Select Committee on Committees—makes effective use of organizational theory.
3. These terms crop up repeatedly in Davidson and Oleszek, "Adaptation and Integration . . .", *Ibid.*
4. This was testimony by Joseph Cooper and David W. Brady before the Bolling Select Committee on Committees. "Committee Organization in the House," *Hearings of the Select Committee on Committees,* House Documents 94–187, 94th Congress, 1st Session (hereafter cited "Select Committee"), Vol. 12., p. 545.
5. Lewis A. Froman, Jr., *The Congressional Process,* (Boston: Little, Brown, 1967), p. 214.
6. The Senate had developed differently as a result of the "Johnson rule" of 1953 which guaranteed every Democrat a major committee assignment— and operationally, a subcommittee chairmanship early in a member's career. This spread power amongst the membership. As for composition, the intake of liberal Democrats in 1958 and their good fortune to come up for re-election in 1964 and 1970 enhanced the upper chamber's reputation as the "more liberal" body.
7. Roger H. Davidson, David M. Kovenock and Michael K. O'Leary, *Congress in Crisis* (Belmont, California: Wadsworth Publishing Co., 1966), p. 100.
8. This tradition in history and political science is both grand and venerable. The classic examples in American political science are Robert Dahl, *Who Governs* (New Haven: Yale University Press, 1961) and its pluralist progeny.
9. Trailblazing works are E. E. Schattschneider, *The Semi-Sovereign People* (Hinsdale, Illinois: Dryden, 1960), Peter Bachrach and Morton Maratz, *Power and Poverty* (New York: Oxford University Press, 1966) and Steven Lukes, *Power, A Radical View* (London: MacMillan, 1976). For fascinating case studies illuminating the subtle workings of power, see John Gaventa, *Power and Powerlessness* (Champaign/Urbana: University of Illinois Press, 1980) and Matthew Crenson, *The Un-Politics of Air Pollution* (Baltimore: The Johns Hopkins University Press, 1971).

10. Schattschneider, *Semi-Sovereign People, op.cit.*, p. 71.
11. Bachrach and Baratz, *Power and Poverty, op.cit.* Also see Peter Bachrach, *The Theory of Democratic Elitism* (Boston: Little Brown, 1967).
12. Crenson, *Un-Politics of Air Pollution, op.cit.*
13. With the exception of Gaventa, *Power and Powerlessness, op.cit.*
14. Floyd Hunter, *Community Power Structure* (Garden City, N.Y.: Anchor Books, 1963).
15. For a good description of the origins of DSG and the political situation which inspired it, see Mark F. Ferber, "The Formation of the Democratic Study Group," in Nelson W. Polsby, ed. *Congressional Behavior* (New York: Random House, 1971), pp. 249–269.Also see Davidson, Kovenock and O'Leary, *Congress in Crisis, op.cit.*, particularly on the rumblings of reform in the 88th and 89th Congresses.
16. In 1957 and 1958 Southern Democrats and Republicans combined to hold 311 of the 435 House seats. The best source for information on the Conservative Coalition is the Voting Study section of each *Congressional Quarterly Almanac* (cited throughout this study as *CQ Almanac*). These analyses identify votes on which the Conservative Coalition "appeared"— i.e. any vote on which a majority of voting Southern Democrats and the majority of voting Republicans opposed the stand taken by a majority of voting Northern Democrats. In 1958 the coalition appeared on 18% of the votes and won 64% of the time. See *CQ Almanac*, 1960, p. 117.
17. Chairmen appointed subcommittee chairmen, hired staff, set the committee's agenda and could use the prerogatives of the chair to recognize members. They also could draw on informal sources of power, for instance, lending prestige to legislation supported by the Administration or a powerful lobby in exchange for concessions which molded bills to their own liking. Certainly, the committees differed in their internal dynamics—some chairmen ruled with an iron hand; some did not. Some conservative chairmen were in fact the instruments of a conservative coalition on their committees. But the stereotype of the omnipotent chairman had solid basis in fact, and further, had undeniable political allure.
18. See Barbara Hinckley, *The Seniority System in Congress* (Bloomington, Indiana: Indiana University Press, 1971). Hinckley finds that between 1947 and 1966 Southern Democrats held a markedly disproportionate number of committee chairmanships and ranking memberships. She argues that it is not just "safe seats," however, but also turnover of non-Southern seats. Southerners comprised 63% of "seniors" and 45% of all members. See Chapter 3, table II, p. 44. Also see DSG's study, pp. 43–45.
19. Metcalf in 1960, like Eugene McCarthy in 1958, was elected to the Senate.
20. The Democrats increased their margin over the Republicans from 235– 200 in 1956 to 282–153 in 1958, a gain of 47, their highest total since 1936. In 1960, the Democrats lost 21 seats, reducing their majority to 262–175. Thirty-five Democrats elected in 1958 were re-elected in 1960 (by my count, based on a comparison of CQ reports on the results of the two elections). See *CQ Weekly Report*, October 31, 1958, pp. 1410–1411 and *CQ Almanac*, 1960, pp. 764–765.
21. Milton C. Cummings, Jr. and Robert L. Peabody, "The Decision to Enlarge the Committee on Rules: An Analysis of the 1961 Vote," in

Robert L. Peabody and Nelson W. Polsby, eds., *New Perspectives on the House of Representatives* (Chicago: Rand McNally, 1969) 2nd ed., p. 254.

22. *Ibid.* p. 256.

23. For example, the Area Redevelopment Bill (S5722) of 1960 was opposed in the Rules Committee by a 6–6 vote, with Judge Smith and William Colmer allying with the Republicans against the other 6 Democrats (*CQ Almanac*, 1960, p. 294). Another example was the Civil Rights legislation (H.R.8601) which languished in the Rules Committee until a discharge petition to discharge the bill from Rules had nearly gained the number of signatures necessary to bring the bill to the floor. See *CQ Almanac*, 1960, p. 190.

24. This is the title of Chapter 7 of Drew Pearson and Jack Anderson, *The Case Against Congress* (New York: Simon and Schuster, 1968), p. 267.

25. Emanuel Celler, "The Seniority Rule in Congress," *Western Political Quarterly* XIV (March 1961), p. 160. Also quoted in Hinckley, *Seniority System, op. cit.* p. 3.

26. In 1910–1911 Speaker Cannon, a Republican, was "overthrown," i.e. his power to appoint committee chairmen, chair the Rules Committee, and other sources of his autocratic rule were removed after an insurgency by progressive Republicans and the Democrats. See Kenneth Hechler, *Insurgency, op. cit.*

27. Nelson W. Polsby, "The Institutionalization of the House of Representatives," *American Political Science Review* 62 (March 1968), pp. 144–168.

28. See pp. 69–72.

29. Under House rules if a bill has been referred to a committee for 30 days and has not been reported, a member may file a discharge petition asking the House to discharge the bill from that committee and place it on the Discharge Calendar. This requires 218 signatures, a majority of the House. For further description of the Discharge procedure on the floor, see Lewis A. Froman, Jr., *The Congressional Process, op. cit.*, pp. 90–93. The rule is little used and, when used, rarely successful. Froman identifies only 22 bills between 1937 and 1960 which passed the House through the Discharge route, only 2 of which became law: the Fair Labor Standards Act of 1938 and the Federal Pay Raise Act of 1960. A discharge petition is of perhaps more use in nudging an obstructionist committee into taking action it might not otherwise have taken.

30. See Cummings and Peabody, "To Enlarge Rules" *op. cit.*, p. 265.

31. Cummings and Peabody give a good account in "To Enlarge Rules," *op. cit.* Also see Tom Wicker, *JFK and LBJ, The Influence of Personality Upon Politics* (Baltimore: Penguin Books, 1968), pp. 22–84. There was considerable "inside-outside" maneuvering here, by both conservatives and liberals, an unusual, early example of inside forces seeking to mobilize outside support on an ostensibly internal matter.

32. The three were Democrats Carl Elliott of Alabama, a moderate ally of Rayburn's, B. F. Sisk of California, a founder of DSG and the Republican, William Avery of Kansas.

33. The real beginnings of anti-chairman activity were inside a few committees themselves. The most notable example was the Education and Labor

Committee where liberals had waged a battle to change Committee rules in the 1950s so as to dilute the power of the conservative Chairman Graham Barden of North Carolina. Barden retired in 1960, in Tom Wicker's words, "in despair at the twentieth century" (*JFK and LBJ, op. cit.,* p. 83). He was replaced by Adam Clayton Powell who also became the target of procedural change inside the Committee.

34. A Harris Poll on Congress's favorability rating in 1963 was only 33% as opposed to 65% for the President. Interestingly, when Congress began passing (in the eyes of some, "rubber stamping") LBJ's legislation, their rating soared to 59% in 1964 and 64% in 1965. When legislative activity slowed again in 1966 it dropped to 38% and by 1969, was down to 34%. There seems to be a strong tie between activity and public favor. See Charles O. Jones, "Will Reform Change Congress?" Paper prepared for delivery at a conference on "The Role of Congress" sponsored by Time, Inc., at the City Tavern Club, Washington, D.C., May 19, 1975. p. 9.

35. Robert Bendiner, *Obstacle Course on Capitol Hill* (New York: McGraw-Hill, 1964), p. 15.

36. The Democrats had a margin of 295–140. CQ's Conservative Coalition index revealed that from 1964 to 1965 the percentage of Conservative Coalition victories plummeted from 67% to 25%. See *CQ Almanac,* 1966, p. 1010.

37. See James Sundquist, *Politics and Policy* (Washington, D.C.: The Brookings Institution, 1968). Sundquist notes that, as early as the Kennedy years, DSG had "converted itself from a 'guerilla band,' as its role in the Eisenhower years has been described, to a disciplined ally of the House leadership in mobilizing supporters of the Kennedy program (p. 484.)" This continued into the early years of the Johnson Administration.

38. Not least of which was that the Joint Committee was prevented in its terms of reference from considering changes in the rules of either house of Congress.

39. It also provided for separate committees on Education and Labor in the Senate.

40. Organization of Congress. *Hearings Before the Joint Committee on the Organization of the Congress,* 89th Congress, 1965 and 1966, Washington, D.C.: U.S. Government Printing Office, 16 volumes.

41. Accounting for the resounding applause in the chamber—there being over four times as many members of the House as of the Senate! Because of the staggered six-year Senate terms and two-year House terms, the existing situation requires any House member running for the Senate to give up his or her House seat. A four-year House term would provide House members in certain circumstances a "free shot" at incumbent senators.

42. DSG does not provide an official number of members in order to protect House members who might not wish to be identified with the "liberal" organization. However, my interviews with several sources indicated that DSG had suffered a substantial loss.

43. Of course, it is fair to note here that majority public support for the war continued throughout this period; hence, it was by no means unrepresen-

tative of Congress not to pass anti-war measures. Congress's deference to the President on the war was, however, an increasingly thorny problem for Great Society liberal Democrats.

44. See, for example, Arthur Schlesinger's extensive writing on the presidency, his trilogy on Franklin Roosevelt and the New Deal and then his *A Thousand Days* (Boston: Houghton Mifflin, 1965). MacGregor Burns was also a Roosevelt biographer who then turned to Kennedy; see his *John Kennedy* (New York: Avon, 1960) and *Presidential Government* (Boston: Houghton Mifflin, 1966). Bailey's works include *The Condition of Our National Political Parties* (New York: The Fund for the Republic, 1959) and Neustadt's classic study is *Presidential Power* (New York: John Wiley and Sons, 1960). David B. Truman's views on the need for a strong president to counter the "dispersion" of Congress is found in his chapter on "The Prospects for Change" in David B. Truman, ed., *The Congress and America's Future* (Englewood Cliffs, N.J.: Prentice-Hall, 1965), pp. 176–183.

45. See, for example, J. W. Fulbright, *The Arrogance of Power* (New York: Random House, 1966). Fulbright in his writings and deeds expressed this view.

46. Although it should be noted that while McCarthy was then certainly a liberal and anti-Vietnam leader, he did openly espouse a weaker presidency than that of President Johnson, and less activist than that for which Robert F. Kennedy stood.

47. Statement of John F. Manley in Organization of Congress, *Hearings Before Joint Committee, op. cit.,* part 13, p. 2025.

48. *Ibid.* p. 2026.

49. *Ibid.*

50. *Ibid.*

51. The classic case for American party responsibility is the report of the Committee on Political Parties of the American Political Science Association, "Toward a More Responsible Two Party System," *American Political Science Review,* September 1950 (Supplement). Also see the aforementioned work of MacGregor Burns and Bailey, and for a good historical perspective see Austin Ranney, *The Doctrine of Responsible Party Government* (Urbana: University of Illinois Press, 1954). A more recent endorsement of stronger parties is John S. Saloma III and Frederick H. Sontag, *Parties: The Real Opportunity for Effective Citizen Politics,* (New York: Alfred A. Knopf, 1972). A more practical in-house approach can be found in Rep. Richard Bolling's two books: *House Out of Order* (New York: Dutton, 1965) and *Power in the House* (New York: Dutton, 1968).

52. David Truman, *The Congressional Party* (New York: John Wiley and Sons, 1959), p. 150.

53. See Sundquist, *Politics and Policy, op. cit.*

54. Examples of this were Nixon's "Southern Strategy" (held to be in return for the support of Senator Strom Thurmond of South Carolina) and manifest in his selection of Spiro Agnew as his running-mate and his tough "law and order" stance.

55. Drew Pearson and Jack Anderson, "Senility System," *Washington Post,* January 5, 1969, p. B7.

56. Particularly in "post-Watergate" America there was a willingness to accept the notion that corruption was endemic to a system which required expenditure of vast sums of money to get elected. This emerged from the "Watergate hearings" of the Senate Select Committee on Presidential Campaign Practices, the so-called Ervin Committee. Prior to this, it had been left to political scientists to speculate about the connection: for example, Alexander Heard, *The Costs of Democracy* (Chapel Hill, N.C.: University of North Carolina Press, 1960).

57. For example, see Warren Weaver, Jr., *Both Your Houses: The Truth About Congress,* (New York: Praeger, 1972) for a considerably more compelling indictment of Congress than that of Pearson and Anderson but still little in the way of prescriptions for improvement.

58. "Reform Proposals for the 94th Congress," *DSG Issue Brief,* December 1, 1974.

59. Select Committee, Vol. 2, p. 58. Also see p. 119n.

60. See pp. 145–146.

61. "The Need for Congressional Reform," *FCNL Washington Newsletter,* Friends Committee on National Legislation, November, 1972, No. 342, p. 1.

62. For example, the Reuss and Schwengel Anti-seniority Amendments to the 1970 Legislative Reorganization Bill; see pp. 74–84.

63. Jack Jones, "Congress Sees Loss of Power to President, Gardner Claims," *Los Angeles Times,* January 9, 1973, Section 2, p. 1.

64. See public opinion data in Charles Jones, "Will Reform Change Congress," *op. cit.* Also see p. 15n.

65. "New Hope for Reform of Congress," *ADA World,* November–December, 1972, p. 13.

66. See p. 19n.

67. This was a term used by David Truman in *The Congressional Party, op. cit.* See especially pp. 308–316. A "truncated majority" was "one without partisan ties to the President."

68. For an early and perceptive identification of the alternative directions of reform, see David Truman's essay "The Prospects for Change," in David Truman (ed.) *The Congress and America's Future* (Engelwood Cliffs: Prentice-Hall, 1965), pp. 176–185. A more recent discussion of the divergent directions is contained in essays by Harvey C. Mansfield, Sr., "The Dispersion of Authority in Congress" and John G. Stewart, "Central Policy Organs in Congress," in Harvey C. Mansfield, Sr., *Congress Against the President* (New York: Praeger, 1975), pp. 1–33.

69. Richard Bolling's writings reveal a particular admiration for "strong speakers." His *Power in the House, op. cit.* is dedicated to three such speakers Thomas Reed, Henry Clay and Sam Rayburn. Bolling's preferences became clear, as will be seen, at various stages of his involvement in the reform effort.

PART II
Reform Roots

Two

Party Reform I: The Majority of the Majority and the Roots of Party Reform, 1968–1970

2:1 ORIGINS OF A REFORM STRATEGY: DSG AND PARTY REFORM, 1968–1969

Political Background

With the 1968 election behind them, the Democratic Study Group's Executive held a series of meetings in the Rayburn Building office of its Chairman, Rep. James G. O'Hara of Michigan. These November and December post-election sessions had become standard DSG Executive procedure, serving as a forum to assess the election results, to plot legislative strategy and to survey the likely issues and eventualities of the forthcoming Congress. In November 1968, of course, there was one major difference from the circumstances of previous meetings: the spectre of Richard Nixon and his coterie of then little-known aides—Haldeman, Ehrlichman, Mitchell, Chotiner, Colson, Magruder *et al*—who were at the same time planning the first moves of the new Republican administration.

The DSG Executive included many leading liberal Democrats, among them, veteran legislators who were intent on developing ways to rebuff the anticipated conservative aims of Nixon. O'Hara, an amiable lawyer with close ties to organized labor, had built a reputation since his election in 1958 for skill in parliamentary maneuvering in support of liberal measures. Like a few other important DSG figures, O'Hara was an influential member of the noted liberal bastion, the

House Education and Labor Committee. Other charter DSG Executive members who served on Education and Labor were Frank Thompson of New Jersey, a DSG founder and former chairman who had played a prominent role in the Kennedy-Rayburn battle to enlarge Rules in 1961; Phillip Burton of California, an aggressive liberal elected in 1964 who prided himself on his hard-nosed approach to legislative bargaining; and John Brademas of Indiana, a highly intelligent legislative strategist and the acknowledged Congressional expert on education matters. The man who probably possessed the deepest knowledge of House history and rules, and who almost single-handedly had been trying to ignite reformist fire since the early sixties[1] was Richard Bolling of Missouri, the intellectual and ambitious former Rayburn protégé. Don Fraser of Minnesota was a respected liberal activist with an expertise in foreign affairs. Morris Udall of Arizona had already established his reputation as a devoted environmentalist and had staked out a position as an aspiring leader of reformers in the House. Brock Adams of Washington was an ardent liberal who served on the Interstate and Foreign Commerce Committee. Thomas Rees of California was a young and acerbic liberal anxious to shake up existing power alignments. Finally, DSG's new staff director, Richard Conlon—the only non-member of Congress to attend these meetings—was a former journalist and Senate aide who began to take an intense interest in the possibilities of internal House reform, in addition to plans for expansion of DSG's day-to-day operation.[2]

As the DSG leaders discussed the impending session, their usual preoccupation with "implementation of the DSG national Democratic program"[3] was overshadowed by the question which was of more immediate concern: "How can we prevent the entrenched conservative Democrats from acquiescing in the passage of the Nixon Administration's policies?"[4] The question elicited an answer on which all of the Executive could agree, something that was not often easy in this group of assertive and strong-willed politicians. The answer obviously lay in preventing the continued ascendancy of "the people the Democrats give power to."[5] There was no mistaking whom they had in mind: the predominantly conservative committee chairmen whom DSG leaders viewed as likely Nixon sympathizers and as predominantly unrepresentative of the majority of the Democratic party.

While the DSG Executive members could readily agree that most chairmen, and the seniority system which produced and sustained them, constituted the most significant obstacle to overcome, there was little consensus on exactly what liberals should, or could, do about them. Moreover, it seemed that there were almost as many ideas as there were participants in the meetings—each congressman enthusiastically putting the case for his own pet scheme. The proposals varied in both their immediate targets and their ultimate directions. "They ranged from the ludicrous to the most ho hum,"[6] reflected one member. For example, O'Hara suggested that DSG should exercise its influence to try to place "our guys" (new DSG members) on committees such as Judiciary and the House Un-American Activities Committee, where they could assert liberal views. But others on the Executive viewed this concentration on committee vacancies as "piece-meal tinkering," as both ineffective and unexciting.

Bolling, a strong advocate of using the party caucus to regiment party behavior, proposed a plan to strip the seniority from—and thus depose—Mendel Rivers of South Carolina, the irascible chairman of the Armed Services Committee and champion of generous Defense spending. The precedents supporting such a move were the 1965 DSG-led actions by the Democratic Caucus removing seniority from Southern Democrats John Bell Williams of Mississippi and Albert Watson of South Carolina for their support of Barry Goldwater in the 1964 Presidential election.[7] Another case of Caucus discipline was the 1967 removal of Adam Clayton Powell from the chairmanship of Education and Labor after he had been shown to have misappropriated House funds.[8] However, Bolling's idea for an assault on Rivers struck others as an *ad hominem* attack based on little tangible evidence. While Rivers was anathema to liberals because of his extreme conservative voting record and his autocratic ways as chairman, Executive members generally felt that these constituted flimsy grounds on which to commit limited energies. Furthermore, such a move might very well not work, perhaps even producing a backlash of support for Rivers, especially from the chairmen and senior members wary of allowing such a precedent.

Rees suggested deposing Rep. Michael Kirwan of Ohio as Chairman of the Democratic Congressional Campaign Committee which raises and dispenses funds to Congressional candidates. Kirwan was known to be a conservative Appropriations subcommittee chairman, but his campaign committee was hardly well-known, except to Democratic fund-raisers. Rees apparently hoped to open up Democratic campaign coffers to candidates sympathetic to DSG, thus improving their election prospects. However, none of the other Executive members thought that a challenge to Kirwan would be worthwhile.

Brock Adams expressed his dissatisfaction with the incumbent party leadership, especially Speaker McCormack, the aging South Bostonian who had served 40 years in Congress and had been criticized for uninspired leadership. Adams advocated a "Dump McCormack" movement, to the delight of Morris Udall who said he was considering challenging one of the party leaders (either McCormack for Speaker or Carl Albert for Majority Leader) when the new Congress convened. There was at this stage little discussion of, or agreement on, the implications or advisability of such a candidacy.[9]

These proposals represented, for the most part, personal schemes of the leading liberals, and illustrated the general lack of consensus on a strategy for liberal action. They agreed to try to assert themselves against the committee chairmen, but on little else. This disarray persisted through the first few meetings.

Finally, at another meeting in O'Hara's office, in early December 1968, Don Fraser focused on what he saw as the main problem facing the liberal forces in the Democratic party. He said that DSG must find some method to make the people who held positions of power—i.e. primarily the chairmen[10]—responsible to rank and file Democrats. Fraser's solution was to work toward an automatic secret ballot for all committee chairmanships in the Democratic Caucus at the beginning of each Congress. This would neatly do away with any of the unrealistic or at least imprecise notions of "abolishing" seniority. Instead, Fraser simply wanted an instrument of control, an "up or down" vote on the senior Democratic member of each committee.

For the first time "there was absolute unanimity in the room."[11] Fraser had defined the problem and proposed a solution that struck the DSG Executive members as a constructive and plausible long-range goal—and even though they soon reverted to bickering over the relative merits of three alternative solutions, Fraser's remained the plan with the strongest backing.

Activity

These meetings had brought to light the divergence of DSG perceptions of the House's inadequacies and the abundance of possible remedies, even within a relatively like-minded group. The Executive therefore decided to conduct a poll of the full DSG membership, and O'Hara attempted to telephone every DSG member[12] to canvass opinions about the specific reform proposals under discussion. He discovered DSG members to be "all over the world" in their perceptions and attitudes. "There was an awful lot of ignorance," reflected

O'Hara, "some members didn't realize the actual process by which you got to be chairman."[13] Some believed the seniority system to be enshrined in House rules; or in Federal law or even (according to one member) in the Constitution. Members saw it as sacrosanct, so entrenched that they had never investigated its institutional and historical roots. The classic Rayburn "go along to get along" ethos had apparently permeated even the relatively junior DSG troops who benefited least from seniority, and was perhaps best expressed in the famous comment "the longer you're here, the more you like it."[14] The Executive Committee concluded, in the words of another member, that "most of them didn't really understand the power relationships." When O'Hara would mention the possibility of voting on committee chairmen, "many of them wouldn't know what he was talking about."[15] It became obvious that DSG's leaders would be unable to achieve their goals without "a major education effort."[16]

As O'Hara canvassed opinion he became increasingly aware that the DSG membership was not prepared for any sweeping changes in the role of the party caucus. Groping for a modest first step toward the DSG Executive's goal he asked members what they thought of the idea—which had not been discussed in the Executive—of regular monthly meetings of the Democratic Caucus, instead of just one at the beginning of each session. This proposal seemed sensible to a large number of the DSG members polled.[17] On the surface it was innocuous enough; what could be the harm of getting the Democrats together once a month? O'Hara did not explain what the Democrats would do at these monthly meetings or how to increase the responsibility of the Caucus. But he saw the meetings as a forum to educate members about internal party dynamics, and as a crucial take-off point in the long term revitalization of the Caucus, where the party might eventually work out policies (substantive legislative priorities never being far from the minds of the DSG strategists). Perhaps "a Wilbur Mills on medicare or a Judge Smith holding up a rule"[18] could be nudged along by the Caucus.

The Executive, noting the favorable response, decided to work immediately for monthly Caucus meetings and eventually for an automatic vote on chairmen. Of course, the DSG Executive continued to have differences of opinion and emphasis; but now it had a tangible proposal toward which to work. On the afternoon of New Year's Eve, 1968 a delegation of DSG leaders informed McCormack and Albert that they would like to change the Caucus rules to facilitate monthly meetings. The provision would require a meeting of the Caucus upon

the written request of fifty Democratic members who would also suggest an agenda to the Caucus Chairman. The Speaker and Majority
Leader were initially opposed to the idea. McCormack had grown
used to the old ways (including years on Rayburn's "Board of Education"[19]), and though faced with a minor rebellion from disaffected
liberals, was not seriously threatened. Albert was loyal to McCormack
but accommodating and pragmatic in mediating House power disputes. After half an hour, he began gravitating to the side of the DSG
leaders. The proposal for monthly meetings might lend a reformist
tinge to the leadership's image if they were to sponsor it. McCormack
then decided to support monthly meetings on condition that the leadership would put forward the plan as its own. The reformers quickly
assented, and settled for their desired results, although the press
hinted at the source of this new "leadership" initiative.[20]

When the Democratic Caucus met on January 2, 1969, the Caucus
overwhelmingly re-elected both McCormack and Albert, and adopted
the provision for monthly meetings.[21] DSG—now under a new chairman, Donald Fraser—began to discuss how the Caucus might be used.
Fearing it might die from lack of interest without ever demonstrating
its positive possibilities, the Executive was extremely careful about
what subjects were to be raised in Caucus. Their eventual strategy was
to use Caucus meetings for discussion of a few selected issues of
concern to liberals, and in late 1969 and early 1970, of reform itself.

Meanwhile, Fraser and Conlon continued to expand DSG's staff
and array of services. DSG "special reports" and "fact sheets" on
selected issues were becoming valued information sources for DSG
members, in addition to finding their way into the hands of others
both inside and outside the Congress.[22] They were characteristically
laden with facts and analysis, being careful to present arguments
from opposing sides. These reports enhanced DSG prestige around
the House, but perhaps even more conducive to increased dependence on DSG materials was the fact that their reports provided data
in a concise form amenable to hurried perusal by busy members of
Congress and staff. Moreover, their provision of straight facts and
diverse views—before slanting toward the DSG liberal position—had
rendered the DSG imprimatur a seal of reliability.

With their reputation in this regard well-established, DSG set out to
"educate" its members (and anyone else who was interested) about
what they saw to be the realities of power relations within the House
Democratic party. The first such DSG report was a voting study issued
on March 10, 1969.[23] Prepared by the DSG staff under the scrutiny of

Conlon and Fraser, it compared the voting behavior of DSG members with that of non-DSG Democrats and Republicans and presented data on the voting records of committee and subcommittee chairmen. The study was based on thirty "key votes"[24] in the 90th Congress which "were selected to provide a representative picture of voting patterns based on the following four factors: (1) Liberal-Conservative Orientation. . . , (2) Administration Support. . . , (3) Support of Democratic Party Principles. . . , (4) and Party Unity. . . ." Aggregating the above, the study expressed its findings "in terms of support for and opposition to the national Democratic position or Democratic programs and policies."[25]

The results depicted a striking gap between DSG and non-DSG Democrats, and more specifically, the pronounced conservatism of the chairmen and their impact on roll call votes. The study also revealed striking cleavages in party voting habits: in particular that non-DSG Democrats had more in common with the GOP than with their DSG Democratic colleagues. The latter were found to vote 91 per cent in support of Democratic programs as opposed to 31 per cent for non-DSG Democrats and 24 per cent for Republicans.

The "opposition of non-DSG Democrats was responsible for two-thirds of the 17 Democratic defeats on 30 key votes," usually "because of the voting alliance between non-DSG Democrats and Republicans." The Democratic committee and subcommittee chairmen were responsible for over half of the 17 defeats. And most striking of all, "one of every three Democratic committee or subcommittee chairmen—42 of 114—voted more often *against* than in support of Democratic programs."[26] In fact, 34 of the chairmen (including six full committee chairmen) exceeded the Republicans in their opposition to Democratic programs.

The study was circulated to all DSG members, and Richard Bolling placed it in the *Congressional Record*. It demonstrated that, far from the conservative coalition disappearing, "the number of Democrats voting more in opposition than in support of Democratic programs has been steadily increasing over the past 16 years—from 0 in the 83rd Congress to 53 in the 90th Congresss." Members of DSG's Executive were convinced that this study had a "tremendous impact"[27] on the DSG membership.

Slightly less than a year later, another DSG reform-oriented special report, this time on seniority, was produced as part of a DSG plan to get the Democratic Caucus to set up a study committee on reform.[28] On February 25, 1970, DSG issued the study, entitled "The Seniority

System in the U.S. House of Representatives,"[29] which traced the evolution of the seniority rule, and concluded that it had hardened only since 1946 into "an automatic system where seniority is sovereign and inviolate in the selection of committee chairmen."[30]

DSG devoted approximately equal space to the arguments for and against seniority. The arguments in favor of seniority included the lack of workable alternatives, its provision of experienced and expert leadership, its avoidance of divisive competition within committees, and its fostering of "great independence on the part of the committee chairmen since they are not held to the test of party responsibility. This independence prevents the emergence of a strong and autocratic Speaker." There was more conviction in DSG's presentation of the arguments against the seniority system:

> The seniority system has fragmented and diffused power in the House, thereby crippling effective leadership and making it impossible to present and pursue a coherent legislative program. In 60 years time, the pendulum has swung from one extreme where virtually all power was lodged in one man, the Speaker, to the other extreme where power is scattered among dozens of powerful committee and subcommittee chairmen.[31]

Other tenets of the DSG anti-seniority case included its tendency to result "on occasion, in the selection of mediocre, senile, or otherwise incompetent chairmen and [to] preserve them in office," and its denial of "competent younger men a chance to exercise their leadership talents at a time in life when they are most able to meet the rigors of the job." Finally, "the seniority system produces chairmen who are generally unrepresentative of America at large and are therefore unresponsive to its needs."

The report went on to describe possible alternatives and modifications. These included the methods of choosing committee chairmen already discussed in the DSG Executive—i.e. Caucus votes on each chairman by order of seniority; a contest between the top three Democrats on each committee; nomination of chairmen by the Speaker, to be ratified by the Caucus—as well as committee-centered approaches which would authorize the majority on each committee to elect their chairman, or the bipartisan method of having each full committee elect the chairman. Other proposals bearing on seniority concerned the tenure of office, e.g. setting an age limit, or limiting the number of years an individual could serve as chairman, or requiring rotation amongst the top three majority committee members at the beginning of each Congress.

These alternatives anticipated the debate among DSG's reform architects during much of the early seventies. However, before attempting any more inroads through the Caucus on the power of chairmen, DSG and some new allies took on a campaign for bipartisan house reform.

2:2 AN INSTITUTIONAL APPROACH: BIPARTISAN REFORMERS AND THE LEGISLATIVE REORGANIZATION AMENDMENTS, 1970

Political Background

While DSG liberals were busy setting the agenda on reform, Nixon's Washington of 1969–1970 had confirmed their anticipated frustration on policy. In domestic affairs, the Nixon Administration and the committee chairmen were settling into a working relationship, which—in DSG's eyes—left it to them to lead the opposition to Republican initiatives. They invested their energy in the fight for liberal programs such as the 1969 Joelson Federal Aid-to-Education amendment,[32] and continued to expand their services to DSG members. In international affairs, the Nixon Policy in Indochina was provoking hostile reactions from the burgeoning anti-war movement outside the Congress (for example, the Moratorium demonstrations of the Autumn, 1969) and among anti-war liberals within Congress. DSG itself was split on the Vietnam issue, with some senior members (e.g. Bolling, Holifield) continuing their support for the "hawk" position, while other DSG leaders (Fraser, Burton, Udall) became "dove" activists. Liberals, racked by deep divisions on this question, generally agreed to disagree at least until Nixon's Vietnamization policy had had time to succeed or fail. Indeed much of O'Hara's tenure as chairman had been devoted to trying to smooth Vietnam-based rifts. However, this course became increasingly impracticable after May 1970 when President Nixon's order for an incursion into Cambodia elicited an unprecedented groundswell of public protest—symbolized by the massive march on Washington of May 30, 1970 but also manifested in satchels of Congressional mail, regional protests, and anti-war "teach-ins" across the country. New organizations, given the umbrella-term "peace groups," sprang up almost overnight. Those based in Washington began to conduct intensive lobbying campaigns which forced the war issue into the hallways, and often the offices, of the usually cloistered confines of Capitol Hill.

The two anti-war measures pending that summer were the

McGovern-Hatfield plan to cut off funds for the war in Indochina, and the "Cooper-Church" bill forbidding U.S. involvement in Cambodia.[33] The sudden rise in student activism and the growing awareness among the general population sparked an extended discussion of political means and ends, whether "the system" worked, and the viability of particular political institutions. Perhaps most commonly heard—especially from liberal politicians to "radical" students—was the advice to work within the system.

It was against this background of jeans-clad students and Middle-American anti-war lobbyists trudging through the halls of Congressional office buildings they had never visited before, that DSG and an assortment of new allies saw the opportunity for a breakthrough on important procedural reforms. The Legislative Reorganization Bill which had grown out of the Joint Committee on the Organization of the Congress of 1965–66[34] had been languishing in the House since 1967, when the Senate had passed it (S.355) by an overwhelming 75-9 margin. The most contentious aspect of an otherwise rather modest bill (primarily providing for expansion of staff and information facilities) was a provision to split the House Education and Labor Committee and the Senate Labor and Public Welfare Committee into four new committees. Two would be devoted exclusively to education and two would be primarily concerned with labor issues. This provoked serious cross-cutting opposition, ranging from organized labor's skepticism towards the prospect of isolated labor committees which might become polarized along strict labor versus management lines, to the venomous contempt for the proposal that was expressed by the Chairman of Education and Labor, Adam Clayton Powell.

This dispute over the division of Education and Labor and a few other minor problems in the reorganization plan kept it bottled up in the House Rules Committee where in April 1969 it was referred to a special subcommittee of five under the chairmanship of B. F. Sisk of California, with active participation by Bolling. This subcommittee adopted a pragmatic approach which sought passage of a reorganization bill less ambitious than the original Joint Committee plan, and without the controversial provision to split Education and Labor. Unanimously approved by the full Rules Committee in May 1970, the bill seeemed fairly certain of passage when it was scheduled to come to the House floor during the Summer and Autumn of 1970. But the rule adopted for floor debate allowed wide-ranging amendments from the floor (except regarding committee jurisdiction),[35] making it possible to expand the bill, or to kill it—or by attempting the former to achieve the latter.

DSG leaders, some of their members, and an emerging bloc of reform-minded Republicans, viewed the Reorganization bill as tame or even innocuous. As one key DSG strategist put it, "it wasn't really reform."[36] The DSG leaders hoped to use the amendment process on the floor to tailor the bill more to their liking. Their strategy was based on one over-riding issue: secrecy. They had learned over the years that closed committees and unrecorded voting procedures served the interests of the conservatives. They also suspected that liberals in general had poor attendance records. Conlon and Fraser had both become convinced that DSG's whip system was essentially inadequate. Many liberals were prominent members of the "Tuesday to Thursday Club," spending much time away from Capitol Hill in their districts or speaking around the country.

These suspicions of desultory liberal voting habits led DSG to undertake a private survey by their staff. Hitherto, their previous published study had shown that in the 90th Congress, cohesive voting by DSG members had provided the margin of victory on all the 13 key roll votes (in a sample of 30) in which they had won. The average margin of victory was 13 votes, and DSG cohesion ranged from 90 percent to 100 percent.[37] Of course, the votes studied were recorded roll call votes on the floor of the House. The study had no way of measuring the voting performance of members on unrecorded "teller votes" concerning crucial amendments in the Committee of the Whole: an adaptation of British parliamentary pratice. In 1641 the Commons stopped recording teller votes in the Committee on the Whole in order to protect the rights of members in dispute with Charles I. The practice survived until the reformed House of Commons convened in 1832.

The Committee of the Whole has a quorum of 100 instead of 218 (a majority of the entire membership) so that amendments can be—and usually are—voted upon by a smaller number. It has its own chairman, whom the Speaker appoints. There was no record of how members voted: congressmen acting as tellers counted the numbers—without recording names—as their colleagues filed down the center aisle in two columns—Ayes and Noes—and then reported the totals to the chairman. Few observers in the galleries could recognize many of the members, and even those few found it hard to compile a record of votes on amendments. Some "peace groups" and others sent gallery "spotters" (armed with Congressional pictorial directories) to try to identify prominent members—but the Doorkeeper's rule forbade anyone but the press from taking notes in public gallery.

This device for sheltering members from any accountability for their votes enabled them to escape taking tough public positions on controversial provisions of bills. During the debate on House rules and Legislative Reorganization amendments, the *National Journal* found that on many of the most contentious issues of the early Nixon Administration, every vote in the House was an unrecorded teller vote. (These issues included attempts to cut appropriations for the ABM anti-ballistic missile program, MIRV rocket project, the C-5A cargo plane, the B-1 bomber, F-111 Fighter plane, and other military-related projects. They also included the SST Supersonic Transport plane, anti-pollution programs, and pieces of domestic legislation such as the "no-knock" provisions of the District of Columbia Crime Bill, and desegregation programs. Finally, the key amendments to foreign aid bills involving troops in Vietnam and Cambodia were also disposed of under the non-record procedure.)[38] The refusal of the House to face these issues publicly was, apart from the substantive questions involved, itself objectionable to those who believed in open government.

Moreover, every one of these issues divided the House on fairly straightforward conservative-liberal lines, and on every one the liberals had lost. The DSG objected to the Committee of the Whole procedure because it afforded moderates and liberals a suitable veil enabling them to vote in favor of conservative positions, especially if there was some persuasive constituency or pressure group interest in doing so. The liberal failure on these votes was also a result of their dismal attendance. DSG members attended an average of 85 per cent of the roll call votes, 80 per cent on quorum calls—which are also publicly recorded—but only 38 per cent of non-recorded teller votes, according to the private DSG study.[39] Conlon concluded, and persuaded the DSG Executive, that "record votes bring people to the floor."[40]

DSG therefore decided to sponsor anti-secrecy amendments, and to seek to carry them by forging a bipartisan coalition with "Young Turk" Republicans who had suffered from a similar lack of access to power. Most of those involved were fairly young, relatively junior, assertive GOP congressmen who had begun meeting informally in the 90th Congress, and who were intent on reforming House rules to facilitate a greater legislative impact by the minority party. Known as "Rumsfeld's Raiders" after Rep. Donald Rumsfeld of Illinois who had served in the House until 1969 when he became an advisor to President Nixon, they were led after his departure by Barber Conable, a shrewd Upstate New York member of Ways and Means, John Dellenback of Oregon, and William Steiger, a youthful moderate from Wisconsin.

They organized a policy-oriented Republican group which had entertained hopes of becoming a powerful intra-party force aspiring to wider impact within the Congress in the event of a Republican House majority in the 1968 election. When this did not come to pass, the group, generally seen to consist of moderate Republicans[41] but probably brought together less by ideology than by their common junior positions within their party, focused their collective impatience on unwieldy House procedures. Moreover, all of these Republicans, like their former leader Rumsfeld, were enthusiastic supporters of the Nixon Administration who saw reform as a possibility of opening up the Democrat-controlled Congressional system. In so doing, they might be able to expand the opportunities for Republicans to advance the Nixon policies through the legislative process, especially in committee where minority participation—particularly by lower ranking members—was often limited.

Activity

At the end of May, 1970 the DSG leaders decided over their usual Wednesday breakfast to launch a campaign for anti-secrecy reforms, focusing primarily upon "record teller" votes in the Committee of the Whole. The DSG strategists included Fraser, Conlon, and Brademas, as well as James Corman of California who was then the DSG's Chief Whip, and Sam Gibbons of Florida who at the time chaired a special DSG task force on Congressional reform. In the meantime, DSG staff had sent out discreet feelers to staff on the Republican side about a possible mutual interest in reform. Shortly thereafter, Republicans Dellenback and Steiger were invited to a Wednesday breakfast where representatives of the two camps began plotting a bipartisan campaign. The Republican reformers, as with Republicans generally, had less at stake politically than senior Democrats, and as one respected Republican tactician put it, had "decided that we couldn't make this a political issue because we'd lose the reforms we sought [and they] were more important than scoring some political points."[42] The bipartisan group agreed to mobilize the campaign around the issue of secrecy, the subject most likely to transcend partisan politics and to unite forces on each side of the issue inside and outside the Congress.

The two groups held a series of meetings in a Capitol hideaway which had quietly been loaned to them by Majority Leader Carl Albert, who offered mild encouragement to the reformers without as yet publicly embracing their cause. The bipartisan reformers discussed which amendments, acceptable to each side, had realistic chances of approval by the full House. Their "package" included seven "key" amendments, five of which dealt with secrecy in some form. The top priority was the "record teller." Other amendments endorsed by the bipartisan group included proposals which would:

- open up all committee meetings unless members in recorded votes voted to close them (many meetings—especially mark-up sessions—were then still closed);
- record votes on all roll calls within committees (not then required);
- require a three day layover before a Senate-House Conference report could be considered in the House;
- guarantee ten minutes of debate time on any motion to recommit a bill to committee (existing practice allowed forty minutes, but often was pre-empted by a majority vote cutting off all debate).[43]

There was bipartisan backing for two major provisions not concerned with secrecy. One made the Fiscal Year coincide with the Calendar Year, allowing Congress six more months to consider requests before the Budget became effective. The other, increased Minority staffing, was generally seen as a "pot sweetener" designed to attract Republican support for the other amendments. Instead of the existing situation where Minority staff allotments were left to the whim of individual chairmen, at least one third of funds for committee investigatory staff were to be allocated to the Minority. The bipartisan reform leaders feared that less pragmatic reformers might try to go too far—and thus jeopardize the whole bill. Congressman Rees and others had put forward a lengthy list of proposals, including assaults on seniority (including a "negative pension scheme")[44] which particularly worried the DSG and Republican reformers.

Perhaps the most striking aspect of the bipartisan reform effort was its ambitious "inside-outside"[45] strategy to mobilize pressure on congressmen. Hitherto, procedural reform had been viewed by members—and most of the Washington political community—as essentially an in-House affair. But now both DSG and the Republican reformers had independently decided to enlist outside support through press relations and coordination of pressure group activity. Conlon was particularly active in developing a strategy by which DSG and the Republican reformers would direct the "inside effort" while at the same time there would be "outside" pressures (with bipartisan information and connivance) goading undecided members into support.

Inside-outside alliances had served liberals as well in the past on such crucial House votes as the Rules Committee enlargement in 1961, the Civil Rights Act of 1964, and the Joelson Federal Aid-to-Education amendment in 1969. In these cases, outside support from either the Administration or specialized lobbies had complemented inside whipping and had resulted in liberal successes. But this time the Administration, fearing to offend senior members, was taking a "hands-off" line. Conlon knew of a number of organizations who might join their campaign, particularly the growing liberal and "public interest" groups, the "peace groups," and other "good government" organizations. He also sought to awaken the interest of newspaper editorial writers. But first the bipartisan group was concerned with internal strategy. They set about cultivating member interest and awareness and trying to attract a broad range of support.

The "Inside Strategy"

The bipartisan alliance consisted of 57 Democrats and Republicans.[46] While this formed a solid core, it was obvious to the strategists that they would need further support—or at least benign neutrality—from the House power centers and from members usually unreceptive to reform. Indeed, only strong majority sentiment for the plan would insure passage in the face of the probable procedural wrangles and unreliable attendance which characterized the practice of the Committee of the Whole.

The bipartisan leaders set out to assure that their amendments would be presented in the most favorable circumstances. The key record teller amendment, they decided, should not be sponsored by anyone identified with liberal or reformist causes who might alienate the broad mass of potential supporters. Pragmatic reformers feared that "knee jerk liberals" or "bombthrowers" would attempt to "load" the bill and so imperil all of their amendments, or even the bill itself. Thus bipartisan strategists recruited two more senior and "reliable" members not previously associated with reform efforts to co-sponsor the record teller amendment. The DSG leadership approached Thomas P. "Tip" O'Neill of Massachusetts, a respected House insider who combined close ties to McCormack with a seat on Rules, and wide popularity with members outside his own big-city, House "Establishment" circles. O'Neill, a burly and likeable Irish politician from Cambridge, Massachusetts, had served in the House since 1952, and had earned the approval of anti-war activists when he came out in 1967 against the war. Lyndon Johnson suggested that he was merely responding to the "peaceniks" in the colleges and universities in his district, but O'Neill told the President he had switched his views because he had discussed it at length with his children and returning Vietnam veterans, and had simply decided the war was wrong.[47]

Without question, O'Neill had been affected by the swirl of activism encircling Capitol Hill at the time, yet he maintained his good relations with all sections of the party. When the bill eventually came to the floor, he felt compelled to explain that rumors of his reformism were greatly exaggerated.

> I have been in politics or in public life for more than 35 years. I have never considered myself a reformer. I do not know exactly what a reformer is. To me if one has a private opinion that the rules and regulations of the Congress should be changed, he should act upon the belief.[48]

Reformers on the Republican side enlisted the assistance of Rep. Charles Gubser of California, a senior conservative who served on the generally pro-Pentagon Armed Services Committee. Gubsen was also not oblivious to the citizens filling the hallways of Congress and streets of Washington. In a "Dear Colleague" letter of June 2, 1970, Gubser observed: "As you know, a number of student groups have raised a very legitimate point regarding meaningful and important 'teller votes' which are not a matter of record."[49] Later, during the debate on the amendment, Gubser reflected the tenor of the times:

> It is not just American youth that has lost faith in the Congress. Our press corps, both privately and in print show disdain for this great parliamentary body. The executive branch often considers the Congress as an albatross. The taxpayers are up in arms. The poor, the rich, men of all races, and everyone view the Congress with a minimum of high regard . . .[50]

Gubser also had a specific reason for his advocacy of the record teller which had appeal for conservative members. "Procedural votes" technically were votes on solely procedural questions but often they had direct bearing on the substance of legislation. Gubser argued, "The absence of a recorded vote on specific issues has created a situation where individual groups now place their own interpretation on the strictly procedural vote on the 'previous question.'" Gubser and others saw the record teller as a protection against anticipated accusations by outside groups. He also stated unequivocally: "I firmly believe that taking a stand and being recorded on the important issues of the day is an obligation we owe our constituents and the country, and we should take steps to make our stand a matter of public record . . . Congress, as an institution, is under attack. The charge of secrecy is a valid one and we should move forthwith to correct what is wrong."[51] In O'Neill and Gubser the reformers had managed to recruit sponsors with impeccable reputations as dependable party and House members. Though O'Neill was a member of DSG, he had never taken a particularly active role. And Gubser could not have been a more staunch conservative Republican. Thus DSG and the Republican reformers had buttressed their own fragile positions in the House with two men with unimpeachable Establishment credentials who could make a classic Burkean "reform in order to save" appeal.

In the meantime, DSG was building bridges to the Democratic leadership. McCormack, who had already decided to retire at the end of the Congress, was deferring to his heir-apparent Carl Albert on issues affecting future Congresses. McCormack had no strong objection to the record teller provision. A DSG leader told the *National Journal,*

> Carl . . . [is] always weighing his position against that of the committee chairman. He knows that if he wants to be a successful Speaker that he has to play ball with them.

Minority Leader Gerald Ford was in much the same position; a leading Republican reformer reflected:

> Gerry is genuinely interested in reform. But he can't afford to antagonize the barons. He's got to work with them on White House legislation all the time. Dellenback and Steiger went to see him and he agreed with their proposals right down the line. Yet as leader, he can't say so.[52]

Both Albert and Ford later publicly endorsed the record teller provision.

As the intensive campaign moved towards a climax, with the amendment expected to come to the floor at the end of July, O'Neill and Gubser wrote a long "Dear Colleague" letter which included their rationale for the provisions, along with a copy of the exact language and a list of the 141 (later 182) co-sponsors. The O'Neill-Gubser letter argued:

The amendment is designed to make the least change in present procedures . . . we have purposely avoided specifying any particular method
so as to give party leaders and House officials maximum flexibility to
develop and implement the best possible system.[53]

The inside strategy was to be complemented by an attempt to do
what Congressional reformers had rarely accomplished, awakening
outside interest and mobilizing outside support for reform.

The "Outside Strategy"

DSG's "outside strategy" was designed to "make reform popular,"[54]
in contrast to the existing image of reform as the dubious province of
a claque of disgruntled liberals. The 1965–66 Joint Committee's lack
of success had shown that virtually anything labeled reform was immediately suspect in many sections of the House. Moreover, the tendency of the press and outside groups to ignore internal reform matters allowed congressmen a free hand. Under Conlon's guidance
from the background, the bi-partisan group held a series of meetings
with invited representatives of outside groups. The Democrats called
on groups they had worked with in the past on particular pieces of
legislation; and the Republicans did likewise. There were three such
meetings in which the "insiders" alerted the "outsiders" to the potential importance of these amendments, and they discussed what the
various organizations could do to help the campaign. "Public Interest" groups, which often had been involved in support of liberal bills,
rallied to this procedural cause: organizations such as Americans for
Democratic Action, the National Committee for an Effective Congress, the Anti-Defamation League, as well as the political arms of
interest groups, the AFL-CIO,[55] the National Education Association,
and the National Farmers Union. Other groups of a more conservative cast showed limited interest (a representative of the U.S. Chamber
of Commerce came along to one meeting "just out of curiosity").[56] But
the bulk of support came from established liberal-leaning groups with
some participation from the newly-created "peace groups."[57] Conlon
accounted for outside attraction to this issue, "They understand that
this bill, with our revisions, is really going to revolutionize this
place."[58] These organizations encouraged their own members to contact congressmen, and made known their interest in the success of
H.R.17654, the bipartisan amendments, and the record teller provision.

In addition, DSG mounted a massive press campaign. The reform
effort was depicted as primarily about secrecy, a subject which "would
make editors salivate."[59] Conlon, a former journalist, saw this as a way

of mobilizing the unanimous support of journalists from Washington to the smallest of small town newspapers.

Further, the carefully cultivated bipartisanship of the campaign assured a non-partisan aura—"openness versus secrecy" and "good government"—to the anti-secrecy amendments.

Perhaps the single most productive ingredient in the campaign was a series of letters sent to the press across the country. DSG Chairman Fraser sent out 600 letters to editorial page editors, and a similar letter to political columnists. The University of Missouri's Freedom of Information Center wrote to 770 daily newspapers and 600 radio and television stations. Other groups joined in the information blitz. Twenty-two bipartisan activists[60] signed a letter to editors which began "We are members of Congress, Republican and Democratic, liberal and conservative. We are writing to seek your help . . . We think the public has a right to know what is happening in Congress and how Members vote on major national issues. . . ."[61] After describing their aim to remove "unnecessary secrecy in the legislative process," they warned that acceptance of these reforms "will depend, at least in part, on the amount of public visibility they receive and the extent to which the public and the press—demands them."[62]

Developments

The Legislative Reorganization Act (H.R. 17654, H.Rept. 91-1215) was the subject of eleven days of debate on the House floor, on four separate occasions,[63] under the very procedure that "record teller" reformers were attempting to reform. The House considered some sixty-five amendments, of which thirty-six were accepted. Of the ten amendments sponsored by the bipartisan group, nine were adopted. In opening debate on the bill on July 13, 1970, George Mahon of Texas, the influential Appropriations Committee chairman and exponent of fiscal conservatism ("Appropriating money on the basis of need is not practical") touched on the policy implications of the reforms when he noted:

> I sense there are those who feel that by changing certain techniques it will be possible to have larger and larger appropriations above the budget of any President for various laudable purposes when we do not have the revenue to provide for them.[64]

Although appropriations were clearly not the main focus of reform, the point was essentially accurate. Mahon was warning the members that supporters of the new rules hoped to use them in future to pass liberal legislation. Fiscal conservatives, who counted among themselves many of the Republican reformers, saw this simply as a risk that had to be taken in the interest of greater House accountability.

Despite his objections, Mahon eventually voted for final passage. The Democratic leaders, Majority Leader Albert and Majority Whip Boggs, as well as Republican leader Ford had endorsed the record teller amendments, as had the influential Southern Democrat, Joe Waggonner of Louisiana. The record teller was adopted by voice vote, and the Act passed overwhelmingly by 326-19 on September 17, 1970. Only one sector of the House showed reluctance: the committee chairmen, of whom less than half supported the bill.[65] Three voted "nay"[66] and the rest were absent.

The bipartisan reformers succeeded in carrying provisions for minority staffing, public disclosure of all roll call votes taken in any committee meeting and for opening up committee meetings and hearings unless the committee decided by a record vote at the beginning of a meeting to keep it closed (typically, it was suggested, on grounds of national security).

Passing the "Record Teller"

The most significant breakthrough was the passage of the record teller. O'Neill had proposed it in the full Rules Committee mark-up of the bill, but it was defeated 6-6—a tie being insufficient for passage. With the co-sponsorship of Gubser, and the connivance of the bipartisan reform group, he proceeded to offer it on the floor, arguing in terms of maximizing public accountability while down-playing the reform label. He came to the nub of the matter when he stated:

> If we were recording these votes, if the people at home knew how we actually voted, I believe we probably would have had some different results. Probably we would have passed more pieces of legislation.[67]

O'Neill-Gubser was the target of several amendments regarding specific methods of electronic voting which were interpreted by its sponsors as possibly jeopardizing passage. O'Neill and Gubser resisted these amendments and accepted an amendment offered by Rep. O'Hara which left open the method of electronic voting. All obstacles removed, the O'Neill-Gubser record-teller was adopted by voice vote.

The victory for the bipartisan forces was testimony to the effectiveness of their "inside-outside" strategy. The difference in attitude before and after the mobilization of pressure was reflected in a statement by Bolling during the course of the debate:

> This is a very interesting legislative situation. I believe in all frankness we should say that the Subcommittee and Committee on Rules were overrun by the interest of members in having record votes on amendments. There was extraordinarily little interest in the subject when we had our long hearings and consideration, but there developed in the past few months a tremendous amount of interest.[68]

The bipartisan effort had converted a little-known mechanism to reform technical procedure into a major "consensus issue" that members apparently had come to feel they could oppose only at their peril. The reform effort had recruited respected bipartisan leaders and had assiduously avoided conflict with established powerholders. The bipartisan institutional approach was in marked contrast with the experience on the more contentious, party-based issue of seniority.

The Seniority Issue: "The Wrong Forum and the Wrong Time"[69]

The bipartisan group's success contrasted sharply with the defeat of other reform amendments that did not bear the bipartisan label of endorsement. These included a few proposals which many sympathetic bipartisan reformers did not support because they were afraid of "loading" the bill. Some measures sponsored by individual bipartisan leaders did not have the group's endorsement such as Rep. Steiger's sensible but unpopular proposal to require that the *Congressional Record* be a *verbatim* account of House proceedings (this was rejected). Rep. Andrew Jacobs sponsored an amendment designed to prevent the Rules Committee (and Ways and Means Committee's tax decisions) from avoiding the scrutiny of the rest of the House by sending a bill to the floor under a "closed rule" which forbade or limited House floor amendments. Ways and Means Chairman Wilbur Mills had used this device with extraordinary success on tax legislation, arguing that it was impossible to "write tax legislation on the floor," thus insuring (until his power ebbed in 1973 and 1974)[70] that tax bills emerging from his committee would be unencumbered by amendments from the 410 non-Ways and Means Members. This effectively limited liberal impact on tax legislation, and with it, the possibility of tax reform.[71] The Jacobs amendment to prohibit closed rules was summarily killed when a point of order[72] was sustained against it.

Other rejected amendments broached issues that would come to be important when the first reforms had time to germinate: such proposals as establishing budget priorities, proxy voting (which passed the Committee of the Whole but was over-turned on the House floor) and the inevitable Republican mainstay, Minority staffing (which also was approved, then over-turned).[73]

However, the major target of the more aggressive reformers was the seniority system. The bipartisan bloc had agreed that this bill was simply not the place for an assault on seniority; at least, as a collective entity they had spurned all moves for an anti-seniority amendment. Indeed, this was undoubtedly the kind of issue to which H. Allen Smith had referred when he mentioned "foolish stuff" that could make him, one of the Bill's drafters, "walk away from"[74] it. And there were, no doubt, many others around the House similarly inclined.

Yet some strong-willed reformers disagreed. From its inception DSG had included some who looked askance at their leaders' pragmatic maneuverings. The Minority Republicans, unlikely to achieve majority status, had little at stake in choosing committee and subcommittee chairmen; although their method of selecting ranking members was not unimportant.

Two major amendments to the Legislative Reorganization Bill were designed to attack seniority. One, sponsored by Henry Reuss of Wisconsin and the Banking and Currency Committee, would have altered Rule X of the House by adding that the chairman selected "need not be the Member with the longest consecutive service on the committee."[75] The other—sponsored by Republican Fred Schwengel of Iowa—provided for election of committee chairmen in the individual committees themselves, with full participation of Minority members—a much greater departure from existing practice. These two amendments deserve close scrutiny, first because they show how unenthusiastic the House was at the time for far-reaching reform, second because the individual statements and colloquies traverse the bounds of feeling about seniority in the House; much of the later discussion about seniority took place behind closed doors in party sessions.[76] The debate on these amendments also illuminates the intricacies of the reform process on such a decidedly contentious issue. Finally, a few of the contributions to this debate illustrate the inimitable Congressional mixture of cliché and eloquence—on an issue which one long-time Capitol Hill participant described as "the trunk of the tree around here."[77]

The Reuss amendment was unambitious and limited. But, he argued: "We should not spend weeks on a Congressional reorganization bill and neglect seniority. Let us take, therefore, this modest step . . .

[the] wooden application of the seniority custom is a luxury we can no longer afford."[78] He made clear his personal opinion that the seniority system was in need of drastic revision·

> It is my own view that this body should select the ablest, the best, and the most just men as the chairmen of its committees just as it exercises that power with respect to the Speaker of the House.[79]

It was generally understood that all Reuss's amendment accomplished was to put the House on record as recognizing other possible criteria in selecting chairmen but that more sweeping inroads in the party caucuses might provide the means for practicing this principle. Later when Reuss's amendment was attacked for "not doing anything," Reuss responded that his amendment "does do something. It acts as a signal and a symbol to the Caucus that they must take into account factors other than pure longevity of service."[80]

Schwengel quickly offered a substitute amendment in the form of a substitute which provided the rather startling transfer of responsibility for selecting chairmen to the individual committees. These chairmen would be selected from the top three members of each committee (i.e. the two senior Majority members and the ranking Minority member; under such conditions insurgents on a committee could "bargain" with a chairman by threatening support for the next-in-line or even the ranking Republican).

This amounted to a broadside attack on the entire structure of House and party prerogatives. The two amendments were debated at the same time, so that Members could address themselves to either or both.

The "establishment" view was one of unequivocal opposition to any seniority provision in the bill—as articulated by Sisk, the floor manager:

> I am not afraid to study and take a look at seniority. We have committees among the Democrats who are today looking at it, and I know there is a committee working among my friends on the Republican side on this question of seniority, but certainly so far as this Subcommittee and the Committee on Rules are concerned, this is not the bill and not the time to get involved in this subject.[81]

Sisk contended that a seniority provision "will create a load that this package simply cannot carry."[82] Rep. John Moss of California concurred that this was the "wrong forum and the wrong time."[83] Among the bipartisan leadership, both Conable and Fraser expressed misgivings. And Richard Bolling proceeded with a masterful lecture to the

House: "the problem of seniority when the Democrats are in the majority is the problem of the will of the majority of the Democrats. If they choose to modify seniority, they have the power to do so."

The Schwengel amendment spurred Bolling to his brand of incisive and unsparing oratory that had won him both respect and a measure of unpopularity within the House:

> Now, the Schwengel amendment is something else again. The Schwengel amendment demonstrates a well-intentioned complete misunderstanding of legislative institutions. There is no institution within the House of Representatives that acts. Only the House of Representatives, under the Constitution of the United States, can act. President Wilson has been misquoted. President Wilson has been misquoted to the effect that the only time Congress was at work, in effect, was when it was in committee. Well, a great deal of the preliminary work of the Congress is and must be done in committee, but the committees are creatures of the House in their performance, and to give to the committee the right of the institution as a whole to select chairmen is to state flatly that we are not a unified entity. . . .
>
> It seems to me absolutely clear that both these amendments should be defeated and we should proceed to face the problem of seniority in a reasonable, meaningful, and rational way in our two parties.[84]

If there was any question about the breathtaking potential impact of the Schwengel substitute, a colloquy between Fraser and Republican Alphonso Bell of California removed any doubts:

> Fraser: . . . Supposing the majority of my colleagues on the Democratic side decided they wanted to change the chairman of a committee of the House.
>
> We now have that power, through our Caucus, to do so; that is true, is it not?
>
> Bell: That is right.
>
> Fraser: The power in the majority to make a decision would be stripped away from us and conferred upon a much smaller group.
>
> Bell: It would be conferred upon the members of the committee itself.
>
> Fraser: That's right; so the members of the Caucus would lose control over the chairmanship.
>
> Bell: The members of the Caucus would, but who properly knows more about the workings of the committee, about the eligibility and ability of the chairmen and the potential leaders, than the people who are working with the committee chairmen?
>
> Fraser: If I may speak bluntly—and it might be unwise to do so—some of the chairmen of whom I believe there has been more criticism than

others would surely be elected by their committee but might not be elected by the Caucus. That is one aspect to be looked at. It is one reason why I have a question about the proposal.[85]

Majority Leader Carl Albert added:

> The gentleman is talking about taking power away from the Caucus. It would also be taking power away from the House, the power to approve the committee.[86]

The only leading DSG reformer actually to endorse the Schwengel amendment was the adroit Phillip Burton. He seems to have viewed the Schwengel amendment as something of an electric shock that might jolt the Hansen Committee on which he served, and the Democratic Caucus come January, into taking action on seniority. Of course in the interim, there was the temporary transfer of discretion to the individual committees, which in all likelihood would not have arisen since the sitting chairmen would continue.

Still, the seniority debate on the House floor afforded members an opportunity to express their various attitudes and convictions on various sides of the subject. Majority Whip Boggs borrowed from and adapted Churchill to describe seniority as "the worst system on earth until you examine all the others."[87] He gave a rather unorthodox justification of seniority:

> Let me give you another example. There is the distinguished chairman of the committee on the Judiciary, the revered Manny Celler. He is 82 years old, I believe. He happens to be a member of the Jewish faith, a minority faith. There was a time when, believe it or not, in the days of the know-nothings in this country, when a Jew, if he happened to be elected, could not have become a chairman of a committee. So I say to my fellow reformers—and I consider myself one—that in these amendments you seek to tear down this institution, not to build it up. And I trust that these amendments will be resoundingly defeated.[88]

Thus seniority could be justified for many reasons: it was universally applied; it was accorded legitimacy; and most of all, it was known. Any new system would be arbitrary, experimental, and of course, the great unknown.

To close the debate, in much the same place that it began, Charles Gubser reiterated the grave danger of a "loaded" bill:

> . . . long ago as a youngster, I learned that it was the last breath of air which burst the balloon, and the last 10 pounds of weight which capsized the boat. I now know that it is the last well-meaning amendment that kills the bill.[89]

There were teller votes on both amendments. The Schwengel substitute was overwhelmingly defeated 28–196. Reuss's amendment was soundly rejected 73–160.

The Legislative Reorganization bill was approved by the full House on September 17, 1970 and by the Congress on October 8, 1970; it went into effect immediately before noon January 3, 1971.[90] The record teller was by far its most important feature. The Congress's decision to halt production of the SST was arguably a direct result of the enforced openness and accountability to the public ensured by the record teller. The added staffing and information facilities provided needed assistance to congressmen deluged with constituency cases and legislative business. Of course, the decision to adopt the record teller would have profound implications for special interest influence. Secrecy could protect members from the consequences of their actions. But public disclosure would end the opportunities for "closet" liberals or conservatives to say one thing and vote another. It also was the first step toward detailed tabulation and monitoring of votes by special interest and public interest groups on a host of votes and issues hitherto shielded from public view.[91]

But the reform effort, and particularly the clarification in debate of some of the issues that were on the political horizon, should not be underestimated as factors in the evolution of reform. The record teller had a strong political motive, at least from the point of view of DSG liberals. DSG's leaders saw the opportunity to wrap their campaign in the cloak of "anti-secrecy" (which of course was an issue, and one which they sincerely sought as a goal in itself). However, the overriding aim was to enhance liberal legislative prospects in Committee of the Whole votes. Similarly, the DSG activists withheld support for Reuss's amendment because the time was not right and it could have jeopardized their precious gain on the record teller and other provisions. DSG (and almost everyone else) opposed the Schwengel amendment because it represented a total change in the way the House, and parties, selected their committee leaders—and in so doing, posed a threat to even a most truncated version of "party responsibility." Indeed, from DSG's standpoint, the Schwengel amendment may have served a salutary effect, i.e. to focus attention on the prerogatives and power of the Caucus. It elicited ringing defenses of the powers of a Caucus which had hardly been used for sixty years, and of which DSG members had shown little comprehension only a year and a half earlier when O'Hara polled them. Rep. Bob Eckhardt of Texas, a DSG activist, stated in unequivocal language:

I would respectfully submit to the House that I believe that anything that is done in the rules themselves to widen the authority of the Caucus implies the power of the House to restrict the authority of the Caucus.

I speak for the power of the Caucus. I think the Caucus of the majority party, and its opposition on the minority side, is the ultimate basis of Anglo-American effectiveness in a legislative body.[92]

It was this emerging attitude that would underlie the continuing effort within the Democratic party (and to a lesser extent, within the Republican Conference),[93] to assert the role of the Caucus. However, this begged several larger questions, namely, how to use the Caucus, how to select chairmen, and perhaps more obliquely, if reformers were to take power away from the chairmen in whom should they vest that power? Once again the intricacies of the reform process obscured the conflicting implications for power relations. More attention was placed on the immediate goal of wresting power from the chairmen than on thinking through the precise dynamics of the new power structure—or its institutional consequences.

NOTES

1. Bolling worked with Rayburn on the 1961 move to enlarge the Rules Committee from 12 to 15. He also authored two books and articles on House reform. See Richard Bolling, *House Out of Order, op. cit.* Richard Bolling, "A Congressman's View of the Problem, It's Up to the Democrats," *New Republic,* November 21, 1964, pp. 13–14 and Richard Bolling, *Power in the House, op. cit.* especially Chapter 7, "To Restore the House," pp. 255–271.
2. Conlon planned to hire more staff, develop a weekly legislative information service and increase the number of special reports on issues.
3. Interview with Richard Conlon, Staff Director, Democratic Study Group; August 27 and 28, 1975, Washington, D.C.; also October 9, 1975, Cambridge, Massachusetts. Hereafter cited "Conlon Interview."
4. *Ibid.*
5. *Ibid.*
6. Interview with Rep. James G. O'Hara, September 10, 1975, Washington, D.C.
7. See Davidson, Kovenock and O'Leary, *Congress in Crisis, op. cit.,* pp. 131–142. In January, 1969 a similar fate would befall Rep. John Rarick of Louisiana who had supported Alabama Governor George Wallace in the 1968 Presidential Election.
8. See "Adam Clayton Powell Excluded from House . . . ," *CQ Almanac,* 1967, pp. 533–549.
9. Udall did challenge Speaker McCormack in what was seen as a largely symbolic effort. On January 2, 1969, McCormack defeated Udall handily 178 to 58.
10. Of course, the party leadership posts, Speaker, Majority Leader, i.e. when the Democrats are in the majority, and Caucus Chairmen were—and are—elective posts. The office of Majority Whip remained appointive—by the Majority Leader—although there were murmurings about making it elective as well.
11. Conlon Interview.
12. DSG does not release an official number of members. At this time, there were slightly more than 100.
13. O'Hara Interview.
14. This is oft-quoted but of unascertainable origin. See John V. Lindsay, "The Seniority System," in Mary McInnis, ed. *We Propose: A Modern Congress* (New York: McGraw Hill, 1966); also in *Congressional Record,* July 28, 1970, pp. H26034–H26039.
15. Conlon Interview.
16. O'Hara Interview.

17. O'Hara, Conlon Interviews.
18. Conlon Interview. Wilbur Mills of Arkansas was the Chairman of the Ways and Means Committee, and Judge Howard Smith of Virginia was Chairman of the Rules Committee. Smith was defeated in a primary election in 1966 and hence, was not in Congress at the time of the DSG session. However, his reputation as a conservative and obstructive chairman lived on in House lore.
19. Speaker Rayburn's after-hours sessions with his political allies, mixing legislative strategy, conversation, and bourbon.
20. See Richard L. Lyons, "McCormack Beats Back House Revolt," and David S. Broder, "House Moves Forward—But Ever So Slightly," both in *Washington Post*, January 3, 1969, p. Al.
21. In addition, in an accompanying move which received little attention, the Caucus was empowered to ratify Committee on Committees nominees. Prior to 1969, the nominees of the Democratic Committee on Committees were sent straight to the House floor. From 1969 onward, at DSG's instigation, their nominees would have to be ratified by the full Caucus. This was also a key change. Conlon Interview.
22. In perusing files generously made available to me by individuals in groups in no way affiliated with DSG—including some unconnected with the Democratic party—I would often discover DSG materials.
23. "Voting in the House," DSG Special Report, March 10, 1969. See Richard Bolling, Extension of Remarks, *Congressional Record*, March 18, 1969, pp. H6749–H6752.
24. *Ibid.*
25. *Ibid.*
26. *Ibid.*
27. Conlon, O'Hara, Bolling Interviews.
28. See pp. 85–89.
29. "The Seniority System in the U.S. House of Representatives," DSG Special Report, February 25, 1970. See Donald M. Fraser, Extension of Remarks, *Congressional Record*, February 26, 1970, pp. H5169–H5172.
30. DSG Seniority Study, February 25, 1970, *op. cit.*
31. *Ibid.*
32. The amendment sponsored by Charles S. Joelson (D.–N.J.) increased Education appropriations by $894,547,000 and was passed on July 30, 1969 by votes of 242–106 on the teller, and 294–119 on a roll call. *CQ Almanac*, 1969, p. 549.
33. See "Congressional Votes on Indochina War: 1966–1972," *CQ Weekly Report*, January 27, 1973, pp. 119–120.
34. U.S. Congress, Organization of Congress, *Hearings Before the Joint Committee on the Organization of the Congress*, 89th Congress, *op. cit.*
35. This was written into the rule under which the bill was considered in order to preclude any amendments separating the Education and Labor Committee or seeking any other jurisdictional changes.
36. Conlon Interview.
37. DSG Voting Study, *op. cit.*
38. See *CQ Almanac*, 1970, p. 454.

39. Conlon, O'Hara Interviews.
40. Conlon Interview. Also see "Record Votes on Amendments," DSG Internal Memorandum, June 16, 1970.
41. See description in Andrew J. Glass, "Legislative reform effort builds new alliances among House members," *National Journal*, August 25, 1970, pp. 1608 and 1611. Also see Norman Ornstein and David Rohde, "Congressional Reform and Parties in the U.S. House of Representatives," in Jeff Fishel and David Broder (eds.), *Parties and Elections in an Anti-Party Age* (Bloomington: Indiana University Press, 1976).
42. Rep. Barber Conable, quoted in Glass, "Legislative Reform," *National Journal*, August 25, 1970, *op. cit.*, p. 1608. However, Minority Leader Gerald Ford apparently thought otherwise. In a personal letter to Rep. Paul McCloskey, February 9, 1970 Ford stated: "I believe House Republicans can take advantage of the current situation among the Democrats and I most emphatically believe we should." Later in the letter, he added, *"In my opinion Republicans should use this in the 1970 campaign, particularly among our youth and in the academic community.* It is a legitimate campaign issue." (emphasis in original). I am grateful to the office of Rep. Barber Conable for making available to me their file on Republican reform, particularly the Bipartisan Campaign of 1970 (hereafter cited "Republican Member's File").
43. Bipartisan Amendments, Republican Member's File.
44. By which members would receive less pension benefits the longer they remained in Congress, after a certain age—e.g. 70.
45. The distinction between these two aspects was first noted by Nelson Polsby in his study of the 1962 Majority Leadership contest between Carl Albert and Richard Bolling. However, in this context it was a distinction between two different strategies: inside (Albert) and outside (Bolling). In that contest, Polsby portrayed a triumph of the inside strategy. In the eyes of DSG and the bipartisan reformers, these were two aspects of the same strategy. See Nelson Polsby, "Two Strategies of Influence: Choosing a Majority Leader, 1962," in Robert L. Peabody and Nelson Polsby, *New Perspectives on the House of Representatives*, (Chicago: Rand McNally, 1969) (paperback edition), pp. 325–358.
46. The Republicans, typically, were in the minority with 15 active members. Republican Member's File.
47. James M. Shannon, "Thomas P. O'Neill: A Study in Leadership," unpublished Johns Hopkins University Senior Honors Thesis, 1972.
48. *Congressional Record*, July 27, 1970, p. H25796.
49. Letter from Rep. Charles Gubser to House Colleagues, June 2, 1970. These letters are commonly referred to as "Dear Colleagues."
50. *Congressional Record*, July 27, 1970, p. H27799.
51. Gubser, "Dear Colleague," June 2, 1970, *op. cit.*
52. See Glass, "Legislative Reform," *National Journal, op. cit.*, pp. 1610–11.
53. Letter from Reps. O'Neill and Gubser to House Colleagues, July 20, 1970.
54. Conlon Interview.
55. For example of communication, see Letter from Andrew Biemiller, Legislative Director, AFL-CIO, to House members, July 10, 1970.

56. Glass, "Legislative Reform," *National Journal, op. cit.* p. 1612.
57. For example "Project Pursestrings" and "Continuing Presence in Washington."
58. Glass, "Legislative Reform," *National Journal, op. cit.* p. 1612.
59. Conlon Interview.
60. Eleven of each party including the key tacticians on each side.
61. Letter from Bipartisan reformers to Newspaper Editors, July 2, 1970.
62. *Ibid.*
63. July 13–16, 20, 27–29, and September 15–17.
64. *Congressional Record,* July 13, 1970, p. H23918.
65. Mahon of Appropriations, Morgan of Foreign Affairs, Perkins of Education and Labor, Freidel of House Administration, Garmatz of Merchant Marine and Fisheries, Dulski of Post Office and Civil Service, Colmer of Rules, Miller of Science and Astronautics, and Price of Standards of Official Conduct. Colmer was a surprising supporter; he had been an arch-conservative and obstructionist as Judge Smith's sidekick—presumably including on the 6–6 vote in the Rules Committee.
66. Mills of Ways and Means, Aspinall of Interior and Insular Affairs, and Teague of Veterans' Affairs.
67. *Congressional Record,* July 13, 1970, p. H25797.
68. *Congressional Record,* July 27, 1970, p. H25803.
69. Quoting Rep. John Moss, *Congressional Record,* July 28, 1970. p. H26039.
70. Mills made an abortive run for the presidency in 1972. Shortly thereafter he was beset with back trouble which curtailed his activity. Finally, alcholism and a series of highly publicized incidents in 1974 regarding Mills and a dancer named Fanne Fox damaged irreparably Mills' position of power on Capitol Hill.
71. Mills had been promising tax reform for years; but always other business took precedence. 1973 came and went without tax reform legislation. Moreover, there were liberals on Ways and Means: Vanik, Corman, Green, Gibbons, Carey—who backed tax reform. However their support was not enough to overcome the resistance of Mills and others.
72. The point of order was that it altered the jurisdiction of the Rules Committee. The rule under which the bill was being considered (because of the Education and Labor furor) had expressly forbidden revision of committee jurisdictions.
73. On the House floor, See *CQ Almanac,* 1971, p. 16.
74. See H. Allen Smith comments in Glass, "Legislative Reform," *National Journal, op. cit.,* p. 1607.
75. *Congressional Record,* July 27, 1970, p. H25831.
76. For instance, the Hansen Committee, see pp. 73–77.
77. Conlon Interview.
78. *Congressional Record,* July 27, 1970, p. H25831.
79. *Ibid.*
80. *Congressional Record,* July 28, 1970, p. H26028.
81. *Congressional Record,* July 28, 1970, p. H26023. The Hansen Committee (on Organization, Study and Review of the Democratic Caucus) and the Conable Task Force of the Republican Conference were delegated the tasks of studying these issues.

82. *Ibid.*
83. *Ibid,* p. H26039.
84. *Congressional Record,* July 28, 1970, p. H26024.
85. *Ibid.*
86. *Ibid.*
87. *Ibid.*
88. *Congressional Record,* July 28, 1970, p. H26025.
89. *Congressional Record,* July 28, 1970, p. H26043.
90. The Senate approved it on October 6 and the House on October 8. Hence PL 91–510 became effective for the 92nd Congress.
91. See "Legislative Reorganization Act: First Year's Record," *CQ Weekly Report,* March 4, 1972, pp. 485–491.
92. *Congressional Record,* July 28, 1970, p. H26029.
93. The Conable Task Force of the Republican Conference held hearings in 1970 and recommended that GOP ranking members on Committees not be selected on the basis of seniority. Technically, then, the Republicans departed from strict seniority before the Democrats. Of course, less was at stake. Also, in the first major test of this in January 1973, Rep. John Erlenborn challenged the ranking member of Government Operations, Rep. Frank Horton. He was easily defeated 100–36. Seniority, for the Republicans as well, was not easily defeated.

Three

Party Reform II: A Coordinated Effort to Reform the Democratic Caucus; Pincer Movement on the Chairmen, 1970–1973

3:1 *A PARTY APPROACH: THE HANSEN COMMITTEE AND THE CAUCUS, 1970–1971*

Political Background

The first major breakthrough in re-establishing the Democratic Caucus had been the January 1969 authorization of monthly meetings. But the DSG leadership resolved to proceed cautiously, aware that careless selection of the issues to be raised in Caucus could damage their credibility and effectiveness. For if the Caucus became merely a soapbox for anti-war liberals, many Democrats would stay away, making it difficult to maintain a quorum and increasing the risk of alienating Democrats from future party projects.

Moreover, the early months of 1970 were times of disquiet and frustration among liberal Democrats. The Nixon Administration was becoming more adept at wielding its power while Congressional Democrats were proving no more effective in organizing their opposition. The perceived incoherence and listlessness of the Democratic Congress was typically blamed on the party leadership, and particularly on the 78-year-old Speaker McCormack, who had always voted liberal but was criticized as weak and deferential in his relations with committee chairmen. His most outspoken critic, Rep. Jerome Waldie of California, sponsored a motion of "no confidence" in McCormack in the Caucus on February 18, 1970, which was promptly tabled (i.e. killed) by a vote of 192-23. The move mustered less than half the number of supporters of Udall's abortive challenge to McCormack in the Democratic Caucus the year before. This did not, however, indicate any widespread support for McCormack's leadership; it implied only that a mere handful of liberal Democrats were willing to resort to what many considered "confrontation" tactics.

This motion was another example of what pragmatic liberals on the DSG Executive felt were the excesses of their more aggressive fringe members. They saw little to be gained in what most members viewed as a gratuitous attack on the elderly Speaker, and an effort which might further undermine the already unfavorable reputation of the liberal wing of the party.[1] In any case, the "no confidence" approach seemed peculiarly unsuited to the weak-party, dispersed structure of Congressional politics. It was accusatory without being specific (indeed, there was little in the way of specific grievances), in a constitutional system which authorized impeachment as the recourse for removing officials. It was thoroughly negative, leaving McCormack little opportunity for response, and apart from embarrassing him, served only to elicit a groundswell of support for the Speaker. Moreover, the exercise did nothing to point out the systemic forces which hindered both the Speaker and the liberals from exerting more influence in the Congress and country.

Yet this was not to say that the liberal dissatisfaction with the leadership could not be channelled in a more constructive direction. According to Conlon, the DSG staff director, this was precisely what he was thinking as he sat in his living room on the afternoon of February 8 watching the televised Democratic "State of the Union" broadcast.[2] The challenge to McCormack, and the more generalized frustration it expressed, presented DSG strategists with "a perfect chance to move something else—another kind of proposal that would be acceptable."[3]

Conlon's idea was that the Caucus should commission a special party committee to assess various proposals regarding reform, and to report their recommendations back to the Caucus for action. Conlon's proposal would transfer the responsibility for reform to a legitimate party organ, providing credibility to the issue and insulating DSG from its exposed position as the agitator for reform. Conlon presented his idea to DSG Chairman Fraser, who enthusiastically approved. A hastily arranged meeting with Bolling at the National Democratic Club in the Congressional Hotel was followed by a DSG

Executive meeting to draft and re-draft a resolution to submit to the Caucus.

The proposal called for the establishment of a Committee on Organization, Study and Review which would consider various proposals concerning the reform of the seniority system as well as other suggestions concerning party rules. The DSG Executive supported the plan as a useful means of insuring consideration of alternatives to seniority. Although the Executive was in agreement, others, even within DSG, were less sanguine: Meetings of the full DSG were marked by acrimonious exchanges between anti-seniority reformers and some senior and conservative DSG members who feared a seniority study committee. Two of the latter were Rep. Chet Holifield, a founder and former chairman of DSG who by this time was Chairman of the Government Operations Committee, and Rep. Ed Edmondson, a capable Oklahoma Democrat who was reluctant to tamper with the traditional Democratic power structure.[4]

Outside the DSG camp, there was little discernible enthusiasm for the proposal, although the leadership, in the person of Carl Albert, offered typically muted encouragement. Most senior Democrats were suspicious, but were willing to follow the leadership in a policy of accommodation—at least as long as there was no overt broadside against seniority in the offing. "The establishment," wrote Richard Lyons, the Capitol Hill reporter for the *Washington Post,* "may not wish to deny the democratic appearance of a study. In fact, Albert virtually embraced the idea Friday. But the leadership will probably do what it can to see that not much comes of it."[5] Privately, Albert continued to doubt the viability of proposed alternatives to seniority.[6] However, the open-ended "study" approach, rather than a frontal attack on seniority (and implicitly, on the chairmen themselves), provided him with enough room to maneuver. With a few changes, the committee proposal would be acceptable to the leadership, especially since it might take the wind out of the sails of reformers, at least for a while.

The original draft proposal had included a clause urging the committee to encourage chairmen to work more closely with the party leaders. Albert asked the DSG sponsors to delete this clause because it might antagonize committee chairmen. Fraser readily consented; the change did not affect the mandate with regard to seniority. But the fact that the Majority Leader felt compelled to remove such a modest suggestion indicated both the sensitivity of the issue and a pronounced reticence about assailing chairmen. Nevertheless, Albert once again deserved credit for forging a reformist plan into a "leadership proposal." Lacking enough support within the party to succeed on their own, DSG had hoped that the leadership would "take on" its proposal. The Caucus adopted the resolution—a "compromise" sponsored by Albert—on a voice vote on March 18, 1970. DSG had achieved its goal: a Caucus-mandated committee on seniority, comprising a "broadly representative" task force of eleven members, which was to be appointed by Caucus Chairman Dan Rostenkowski of Illinois.

The "Report Back Date"

There was one additional problem arising from the pace of the committee's work. DSG's leaders had hoped to require the committee to report back to the Caucus by May or June. They felt that this would allow a reasonable period for the committee to reach agreement while guaranteeing that the Caucus would have enough time to act on seniority before the summer recess. Since 1970 was an election year, they reasoned, members might find the inevitable diversion of re-election politics unconducive to detached consideration of the seniority question. Moreover, liberal reformers suspected that the committee might drag out its work so that no action could be taken during that session, and it was anyone's guess how the 1970 election would affect the composition of the Democratic Caucus convening in January 1971. While no one at that point publicly alleged that the committee might produce a "whitewash," there was a general feeling among anti-seniority forces that only an early "report back date" would assure an opportunity for dialogue on the committee's recommendations at a monthly Caucus meeting, and action—one way or the other—during that session.

Wayne Hays, the mercurial congressman from Ohio with power bases on both Foreign Affairs and House Administration, and, implicitly, the leadership opposed an early report back date, arguing that seniority should not be allowed to become an election issue. This was not an ill-founded worry inasmuch as Republicans showed signs of laying claim to the Congressional reform issue (as indicated in Ford's letter to McCloskey and murmurings from "Rumsfeld's Raiders"[7]—who would form the Republican side of the bipartisan coalition on the Legislative Reorganization amendments). One threat was that Republicans would use the Congressional reform issue against a Democratic party that had refused to take action on seniority. Another danger in the eyes of "regular" Democrats was that the small group of hard-core anti-seniority liberals (those colloquially known as "bombthrowers") might be so alienated from the Democratic chairmen as to withhold their support when it came to organizing the House in January. In the event of a close election, it was conceivable that these fifteen to twenty-five members[8] might try to bargain with the leadership in exchange for procedural concessions. Reformist liberals settled on support for a June report back date. Hays advocated that the committee report to the new Caucus in January. In a Caucus vote immediately following the voice vote approving the Committee, the June date was defeated 110 to 46, reminding ardent reformers of their very limited core of support.

The reformers, then, had achieved their goal of a committee, but had been rebuffed on the timetable. After the vote, Fraser lamented the decision, alleging that it "seriously undercuts the likelihood of meaningful action."[9] Bolling still regarded it as "significant progress,"[10] but nineteen other liberal reformers reacted with vehement hostility. Led by Rep. Jerome Waldie and Rep. Allard Lowenstein of New York, the group called a press conference and predicted that the January report back date would postpone reform another two years, since there would not be time to mobilize a reform effort in the fleeting Caucuses in January. Their dissatisfaction was accompanied by a warning (from Waldie): "We're saying, 'Don't count on us anymore to go along automatically.'"[11] "We are not prepared to provide the margin of victory for those not representative of the national Democratic party,"[12] added Lowenstein. While these spokesmen were also critical of Minority Leader Ford, and unlikely to cast their votes to elect him Speaker, approximately half of the 19 would not rule out the possibility of voting with the Republicans in the event of a situation in which they held the balance of power.

Activity

The Hansen Committee

Caucus Chairman Rostenkowski appointed a committee which fulfilled the mandate for a "broadly representative"[13] composition. DSG liberals O'Hara, Thompson and Burton were flanked by such pillars of orthodoxy as Wayne Hays, Joe Waggonner of Louisiana, Olin "Tiger" Teague of Texas, and Phil Landrum of Georgia, all Southern Democrats and active members of the "conservative coalition." Neal Smith of Iowa was a diligent Midwestern moderate and Shirley Chisholm of New York shored up the far left of the party.

Julia Butler Hansen of Washington state, a respected senior figure in the party and an influential Appropriations subcommittee chairwoman, was named to chair the panel, thereafter known as the Hansen Committee. So representative were the eleven members that observers agreed that any proposal this group deemed acceptable would undoubtedly be accepted by the Caucus. It was questionable, however, whether there was anything on which such a committee could agree.

The disparity in views, as well as the representative quality of the Committee, was unusual for Capitol Hill; but perhaps even more surprising was the comity with which they set about their work. Most House committees are stratified on rather formal lines, with hierarchical distribution of responsibilities and power and with the chairmen and senior members wielding disproportionate power. In addition, virtually any meeting, hearing or "mark-up" session of a House committee is the product of substantial background work and briefing by committee personnel, as well as varying levels of participation by members' personal aides. The chairmen's control over staff, information, and agenda was yet another means of exercising power over their committees' work. The Hansen Committee, by comparison, possessed none of these Congressional characteristics and accoutrements. Instead, the structure of this *ad hoc* party committee was informal, much more egalitarian than regular House committees and markedly different in its *modus operandi*. It had no permanent staff, no set rules, and only an informal understanding that they would strive for consensus rather than dwell on their differences.

Members of the Hansen Committee stressed the beneficial effect of the "cross-section" and "broad-based" representation on the committee, "an idea which was novel in itself." "The idea was to use the committee as a filter," i.e. a panel that was interested in finding solutions that members could "live with, instead of trying to ram through something on a 16-14 vote like in a regular House committee."[14]

In order to eliminate the tendency for overt "vote-trading," the Committee adopted the highly unusual practice of not having any formal votes. Instead, if someone objected to a particular provision, the members would seek ways to accommodate this view. Although there were a number of hotly debated subjects, Committee members were surprised to see how successfully the procedure facilitated acceptable compromise between the committee's informal coalitions. The Committee held no formal hearings but individual members did consult with their Democratic cohorts outside the Committee. Inside, they followed their improvised non-voting policy of "majority accommodation." Reflecting back on the experience, one Committee member expressed the view that "it couldn't have been done any other way."[15]

Rep. Julia Butler Hansen was by all accounts a fair-minded chairwoman who performed a vital mediating role, but she made no attempt to dominate the Committee. Instead, the awareness that each member represented a more broadly-based point of view within the Caucus fostered a spirit of accommodation extending power and legitimacy to every Committee member, even if Burton, Hays, Landrum or Waggonner might emerge as the pivotal figure in engineering a compromise around key points of contention.

Beyond the glaring disparities in ideology and regional base, the Committee members were joined by a common pragmatism. Burton, Hays and Waggonner probably had more in common with each other in terms of temperament and style than they did with many members of their own sections of the party. Each had earned a reputation as among the House's better "head counters," and was keenly aware of what his own allies and adversaries would and would not approve.

The options the committee considered included different ways to provide the full Caucus with a means of participation in the selection of chairmen. Bolling's idea that the Speaker should nominate chairmen subject to ratification by the Caucus was apparently never seriously considered by the Hansen Committee. Nor did they discuss altering the existing arrangement by which the Democratic members of the Ways and Means Committee, serving as the Democratic Committee on Committees, nominated all Democratic committee members—as well as the chairmen—on the basis of seniority. But significantly, the tried and true Congressional option of "doing nothing" does not appear to have been seriously entertained either. The Committee was going to recommend some sort of change; how sweeping this reform would be remained to be seen.

The Committee focused on specific methods of obtaining a Caucus vote on individual chairmen. The original Fraser goal expressed within the DSG Executive was to have automatic "up or down" votes on each chairman. If the senior Democrat on a committee was defeated, the next-in-line would be subject to a vote, and so on down the list until a majority approved a chairman.[16] However, there was heavy opposition to this idea, notably from DSG reformer Burton as well as the Southerners. In opposing the automatic vote, this bloc felt that committee chairmen "should know who their accusers are."[17] They saw the automatic vote as a potential weapon by which anonymous members (through secret ballots) could "gang up" on individual chairmen from motives of spite and petty jealousy. In seeking to extend the power of the rank and file in the Caucus, this "automatic vote" procedure was an attempt to build into the selection process an accountability of committee chairmen to the full Caucus. It increased the power of every Democratic member, even though the votes were to be allowed only on "nominees" of the seniority system. However, Burton and Waggonner felt that the proposed alternative was too drastic and was unfair to the chairmen; they maintained that chairmen were entitled to know who their opponents were, and their reasons for opposition. Only then would they be able to defend themselves.

The point was discussed thoroughly, and the Committee was anxious to accommodate the objections of such powerful members. After various other proposals had been discussed, Burton put forward the idea that there should be a Caucus vote on a chairman only when ten members of the Caucus stood up and demanded it. Under these circumstances the accusers could be identified.

Although this emerged as the consensus plan, it had considerable drawbacks; the ten members would risk retribution from the chairman, which might have a chilling effect on the whole procedure. However, outnumbered and interested in establishing some means of demanding a vote on chairmen in the next January Caucus, the "automatic vote" supporters conceded the point. At least the Hansen Committee recognized the widespread unpopularity of chairmen. Another Hansen proposal further chipped away at the chairmen's power, stating that "no member can be chairman of more than one legislative subcommittee."[18] It had long been the practice of a full committee chairman to hold two or more subcommittee chairs within the committee. Many members also served on more than one full committee and held subcommittee chairs on two or more of these. The reform, originally proposed by Thompson and enthusiastically supported by Burton,[19] was designed to "spread the action" to the middle echelon Democrats who were in line, again by virtue of seniority, for the subcommittee chairmanships. The Hansen recommendations could, according to one calculation,[20] affect as many as 16 sitting subcommittee chairmen, on committees including Government Operations, Armed Services (3 members affected), Foreign Affairs (4 affected) and other moderately influential House committees. The new rule would force these members to choose between subcommittee chairs and give way to younger, oftentimes more liberal, members.

These subcommittee reforms would have immediate effects. As for the ten member challenge, it was a small step away from seniority although hardly a renunciation of it. Finally, as a concession to the liberals on the Committee who had been over-ruled on the "automatic vote," the Hansen Committee added a clause which—like the Reuss proposal on the House floor—stated that seniority need not be the only criterion used for selection. This was euphemistic: the procedure for challenging chairmen on demand of ten members implied that, if the senior Democrat was rejected, the next member to be considered would be the next-in-line according to seniority. But this was largely an academic exercise since, in the 1971 Caucus, even if ten brave souls did challenge a chairman it was unlikely that reformers would have nearly enough votes to defeat him.

Challenge to a Chairman

Despite the awkwardness of the ten member challenge procedure, DSG reformers were intent on trying to use it in a selective way to warn chairmen that the Caucus would be watching them closely. They decided to focus on a chairman notorious for his abuse of the pre-rogatives of the chair, John McMillan of South Carolina, a 77-year-old Southerner known for his extreme conservative views on race. As Chairman of the District of Columbia Committee, he controlled half of the Congressional jurisdiction on the District, which was 67 per cent Black. Moreover, the peculiar position of Washington, D.C. as a Federal "District,"—or as bumper stickers proclaimed: "D.C., Last Colony"—deprived residents of Washington of any real autonomy. Instead, they remained at the behest of Congress, and especially the House and Senate Committees. The fact that the House committee was chaired by a Southerner whom many Blacks deeply mistrusted only fueled the movement for Home Rule.

McMillan, then, was a symbol of the seniority system, Southern Democratic conservatism, and old-style Congressional obstructionism. In addition, the D.C. Committee was most important to D.C. residents themselves, and to the residents—especially the many suburban Washingtonians—of the adjoining states of Maryland and Virginia who wanted to make sure that D.C. did not pass measures that would offend their own state interests (e.g. a commuter tax). But few others cared greatly about the District, so that McMillan could be attacked without upsetting the internal dynamics of House committees of more general importance.

On February 3, the Caucus met to vote on chairmen. When the

District of Columbia Committee came up, a core of liberal Democrats sprang to their feet demanding a vote. A series of speeches on each side followed, with various invocations of the advantages—and evils— of seniority that had been hurled back and forth in previous debate. When the votes were tallied, the Caucus had renominated McMillan by only 126 votes to 96, a very respectable showing for the re- formers—although also demonstrating that Southern Democrats had the support of many who were wary of setting an anti-seniority prece- dent.

The operation broke new ground for a generation of congressmen brought up on the "universalistic"[21] seniority criterion. Although DSG obviously would have preferred McMillan's outright rejection, they had won a spiritual victory. They had challenged a sitting chairman for the first time. In so doing they had put chairmen on notice that they should treat junior members with respect. Furthermore, the chairmen now knew that they could ignore their committee members' demands only at their peril.

3:2 AN INSIDE-OUTSIDE APPROACH TO PARTY REFORM, 1972–1973

Political Background

DSG had made progress in the 1969 and 1971 Caucuses, but it had only scratched—not dented—the seniority system. While the McMil- lan challenge probably would have an impact, and the new subcom- mittee chairmen would assure a more liberal approach to the work of some of the subcommittees,[22] a major inroad into the existing power structure had remained elusive. When it came to substantive policy positions, the liberal anti-war forces had still been unable to persuade the House or the Democratic Caucus to take a position against the war in Indochina.[23] Moreover, domestically Congress was providing mea- ger resistance to President Nixon's increasingly overt campaign to dismantle Democratic social programs through his use of the veto and the impoundment of Congressionally appropriated funds.[24]

The frustration which had long plagued liberals in the House was equally felt by the cluster of outside groups who lobbied for liberal measures on Capitol Hill and who constituted the "liberal commu- nity" in Washington. Some of these groups had grown out of opposi- tion to the war;[25] others were more established national liberal organi- zations, like ADA, the National Committee for an Effective Congress, a few liberal unions—particularly the UAW—and various religious organizations. Still others were outgrowths of the increasingly influential consumer movement led and symbolized by Ralph Nader. The League of Women Voters had established a reputation for their interest in "good government" issues, and a new force on the scene, the brainchild of former Secretary of HEW John Gardner, was the citizens' action lobby, Common Cause. There had previously been like-minded liberal groups inside and outside the Congress which shared a disenchantment with Congress's inhospitability to liberal aims. Unfortunately, that disenchantment and reputations for ineffectiveness were about all they shared. Aside from the Legislative Reorganization Amendments campaign and a few other issues, these groups had rarely worked together. If the DSG had for years been characterized inside the House as a band of well-intentioned "do-gooders" but legislative "losers," the liberal groups outside had been spoken of in even less admiring terms in many quarters of Congress.

During the 1971 Majority Leadership contest, members had mentioned in interviews[26] that they did not pay attention to letters that were part of a Common Cause "letter campaign" because they didn't think Common Cause was representative of anyone but a small group of liberals. One member, after ranting about Common Cause and Ralph Nader and his associates (both of which he saw as nuisances) rhetorically challenged Nader to "come up here and run for Speaker if he thinks he knows what's best for us,"[27] alluding to the fact that the Constitution does not specify that the Speaker be a sitting member of Congress. Rep. Hays referred to the organization as "Common Curse," and added that anyone who contributed money to Common Cause possessed "more money than (they) know what to do with."[28] The liberal groups in the late sixties and beginning of the seventies were the object of mistrust and ridicule in many circles. And for a so-called "community"—liberal or otherwise—the groups tended towards fragmentation and an inability to coalesce on programs. Like the anti-war groups before them, they had often been prone to competition and petty bickering, partly as a result of their dependence on the same sources of "liberal money." Personality clashes between members of rival organizations often reduced the opportunities for communication—and resulted in duplication of effort, overlap of projects, and a lack of coordination between their similar campaigns. Indeed, the anti-war groups had appeared at some points to care more about making sure that it was they who received credit for ending the war—were it miraculously to end—than in developing a concerted effort designed to end it. And the performance of the liberal groups was showing only slight improvement.

However, forces both inside and outside were changing. Conlon of DSG, John Gardner and David Cohen of Common Cause, John Isaacs of ADA, Russell Hemenway of the National Committee for an Effective Congress, Nader, and others were starting to demonstrate a level of political *savoir-faire* which required congressmen to take notice. The DSG "inside" operation was by now respected and well-established. Nader, who was about to embark on an ambitious study of Congressional procedures and members called the Congress Project, had by now become a folk hero around the country. By virtue of his numerous appearances before Congressional committees and in the media, he had established himself as a virtual "Good Housekeeping Seal of Approval" on consumer issues. Indeed, his credibility was seen to be transferable to other subjects, including the quality of representation in Congress itself. Other groups and individuals—especially Common Cause and ADA—were also increasing their clout on Capitol Hill and their national followings. Moreover, the Legislative Reorganization amendments and in particular the record teller had taught DSG's leaders and the outside groups who had participated, that their strength lay in "inside-outside" co-operative action.

Activity

The Committee for Congressional Reform

On July 20, 1972 representatives of liberal groups gathered at the United Methodist Building in Northeast Washington to hold an "exploratory meeting on Congressional reform."[29] The meeting had been suggested by Stewart Mott, the liberal philanthropist,[30] and Dudley Ward, the General Secretary of the United Methodist Church Board of Christian Social Concerns, a liberal church organization. Representatives of other groups included Jack Conway and David Cohen of Common Cause, Russell Hemenway and Susan King of the National Committee for an Effective Congress, DSG's Conlon, and representatives of the League of Women Voters and various religious associations. The meeting elicited what had been fairly well known: Congressional reform was seen as a top priority issue by virtually all of these organizations, but there had been little common effort in this direction between them. Conway said that Congressional reform remained the primary goal of Common Cause and had been its "first major national issue." With Cohen as the strategist, it was about to launch a campaign to "focus public attention on the evils of the system" (with an attack on the "seniority system as (the) major objective"). Hemenway described some of the problems he had witnessed in the Congressional reform effort—particularly, that it was difficult to sustain interest in the seniority issue, especially among Congressmen who had liberal tendencies but who were beginning to reap the benefits of seniority. He thought freshmen would probably be more receptive. Stewart Mott asked about the logistics of a campaign, perhaps wondering how much of his money might be required.

Conlon thought a coalition of groups could alert the public "as to how (the) present seniority system works against public interests." However, he warned against the outside groups trying to be too specific in their prescriptions. The minutes record a summary of his remarks: "Should explain weakness of the system—let Congress work out details of solving the problem. DSG will be working on this issue, but doesn't know the focus yet." Two main conclusions were reached at the first exploratory meeting. The first cited the need to establish a smaller "representative committee" to outline "strategy and tactics" and the second was that "DSG could do the quarterbacking and feels they are inside and the one to do the job. The outside groups cannot draw up plans and programs and expect members to accept it."[31]

At the July 31 meeting of the Coalition, in response to a question from Mott, Conlon zeroed in on DSG's prime issue: "a record vote on the selection of Committee Chairmen."[32] Conlon also suggested a "checklist for candidates" in the forthcoming election, which would seek commitments on key items on the reform agenda. These priorities developed by the small working group were outlined in a memo entitled "Proposal for Organizational Efforts on Behalf of Congressional Reform," which proposed four items: (1) Openness in committees, subcommittees and Party Caucuses, (2) Public record votes in committees, subcommittees and Party Caucuses, (3) "To substantially modify the Seniority System . . . and replace it with a system which elects Committee chairpersons and ranking members on the basis of energy, and sensitivity to the needs of the time as well as length of service," and (4) full disclosure of financial interests of members. The group established itself as a "Committee for Congressional Reform (Ad Hoc)" which would "assist groups working on Congressional reform and help to coordinate activities when appropriate and useful."[33] The United Methodist Board assumed responsibility to underwrite costs, although other organizations were encouraged to contribute as well.

Provision Number 6 of the statement said that "the ad hoc committee will work in close liaison with the Democratic Study Group, various Republican offices and organizations, the National Committee for an Effective Congress, Common Cause, and others who have historically devoted considerable attention to the issue of Congressional reform."[34] The goal of the Committee was to "light a fire under Congress."[35] The Committee also made provision for hiring a staff, which was eventually directed by Mike Beard. The Committee for Congressional Reform had a projected budget of approximately 32,000 dollars for a 5 month period.

The Committee for Congressional Reform was unusual in its integration of numerous different kinds of organizations behind an issue of common concern. And although Congressional reform itself was a many-faceted subject, the coalition[36] was able to narrow its focus to a few obtainable goals, largely because of the "inside" element of the "inside-outside" strategy. The DSG Executive, and particularly Conlon, played an important guiding role by advising the Committee as to which issues the inside reformers considered politically practicable. The first activity of the coalition was to solicit support from Congressional candidates at a time when they were historically most responsive: i.e. immediately before an election. This "Checklist for Candidates" contained four specific provisions:

- open meetings of Congressional Committees except in instances involving national security and invasions of personal privacy
- recording of key votes in Committee, on the floor and in Caucus, and to make those votes available to the public
- selection of Committee leadership by recorded vote on the basis of ability, fairness and sensitivity to national needs rather than solely on the basis of seniority
- separate recorded ballots for each Committee Chairperson[37]

Common Cause, ADA and other organizations did separate mailings. The returns, which were fragmentary, indicated that shortly after the election 91 members for the first session of the 93rd Congress responded favorably, including 19 of the 76 freshmen, and 72 of 359 incumbents. This tally was supplemented by individual comments from members who had special comments on the questions.[38]

The Committee for Congressional Reform, then, served an internal educational function by narrowing the broad focus of Congressional reform to four main issues. In addition, the Coalition performed a crucial "outside" educational task by sending out newsletters and information sheets to over 150 organizations and 1,000 newspaper editors. Their public relations campaign included advice on advertising from a New York public relations firm, Ruder and Finn—arranged through Mott and Samuels—and a limited advertising effort.[39]

The Common Cause Campaign: "Open Up the System"

Meanwhile, organizations beneath the coalition umbrella were continuing to mobilize their own campaigns as well. Common Cause, under David Cohen, launched its "Open Up the System" Operation, urging their supporters to confront candidates on "issues that go directly to the need for accountability: the seniority system, campaign financing, conflicts of interest, lobbying disclosure, secrecy, and Congressional reform."[40]

By this time Common Cause had developed a well-organized Washington operation, including three experienced, full-time lobbyists. They had also organized increasingly active chapters around the country which coordinated local and regional activities and mobilized support for their national campaigns. The Common Cause Operation hoped to inspire local branches initially to bring pressure to bear on local Congressional candidates, and later, after the election, to flood Washington with mail urging reform.

Common Cause had grown out of the Urban Coalition, the national organization which sought to focus public attention on the problems of the cities in the 1960s. Gardner, the former HEW Secretary, had been its chairman, directing its membership of liberals and Civil Rights activists: whites, blacks, businessmen, and academics on urban redevelopment issues. By 1970 the war in Vietnam, along with the unsolved domestic problems, had re-awakened that recurring theme among middle class Americans: alienation from traditional party politics. This spurred the rise of ostensibly non-partisan, anti-partisan or even anti-political new movements such as "consumerism" as championed by Nader; environmental organizations, and on a local basis, various community action groups.

Perhaps the most ambitious of the lot was Common Cause—an organization which was reminiscent of the Progressive movement in the early part of the century; it was predominantly middle-class, painstakingly bipartisan, and intent on "cleaning up" the unsavoriness of politics-as-usual. Gardner was a registered Republican who had served in the Democratic Johnson Administration, while other Common Cause officials had ties to the Democrats and the labor movement. Cohen, the tactician of the "Open Up the System" campaign, had been a lobbyist with both the Americans for Democratic Action and the United Auto Workers under Walter Reuther.

Common Cause came to the issue of Congressional reform because of a realization that the way in which the system operated determined the kinds of issues to which it was likely to respond. "The key to public interest lobbying," said David Cohen, who later became the Common Cause president and chief Congressional reform strategist, "is anticipated reaction; you have to know what's happening, including how you're likely to be screwed."[41] Cohen described Common Cause as a "new breed lobby" which "lobbies the issue as much as the member."[42] The important role of his organization, Cohen contended, is to "put issues on the agenda, to get them considered, get them to the stage where they're seen as realistic."[43] It is in this context that outside mobilization becomes important, and Common Cause came to play a vital role in the "educative function" that the DSG Executive had identified four years earlier.

Common Cause also conducted research, advanced arguments for their positions in the press and on public platforms, and continued to work with "inside contacts." Cohen called Conlon "the key player" in the Congressional reform effort, the link between the inside and the outside forces. He was the "bridge" between the more prominent outside groups and the inside DSG figures: O'Hara, Fraser, and Burton as well as Bolling, who by this point was not quite as close to DSG but remained the leading authority on matters of Congressional procedure and reform.

ADA: A Special Project

Americans for Democratic Action was founded in 1947 by a group of liberals including Hubert Humphrey, Joseph Rauh and Eleanor Roosevelt. Since that time it has been a leading force in liberal causes from Civil Rights to the anti-war movement, exerting influence through an active Washington-based lobbying operation and regional chapters across the country. The National Director, Leon Shull, an attorney who had made the jump from Philadelphia reform politics to national liberal politics, ran a Washington operation which included two full-time lobbyists on Capitol Hill, John Isaacs and Lynn Pearle. They also had numerous national and regional ad hoc committees, including a special Washington "Legislative committee" chaired by

Linda Kamm, who had worked as a staffer in the House, including a stint with DSG. Kamm became the director of ADA's early 1973 "special project" on Congressional reform

Hatched in the Autumn of 1972, the ADA special project was designed "to force a vote on the election of every House committee chairman . . . [and] . . . to use the reform rules adopted in January 1971 to establish the precedent that all committee chairmen shall be voted upon."[44] The campaign was part of the overall plan of DSG and the Coalition; but because of its reliable and experienced lobbyists with established ties on the Hill, ADA had been selected to take responsibility for this crucial reform item. The reformers were unsure about the prospects for changing the Hansen Committee's ten member challenge procedure in time to affect the votes in January 1973. They decided that they would work to insure that there were at least ten members who would challenge every chairman. Ideally, they hoped to recruit considerably more than ten in order to diminish the awkward "accusatory" nature of the process and the accompanying risk of retribution by the chairmen.

ADA made clear that they were not "waging a campaign against any particular chairman. Rather, we are trying to establish the principle that these significant party assignments should be subject to Caucus action instead of automatic succession."[45]

Their first task was to contact members who had been receptive to ADA schemes in the past, especially those with known reformist leanings. Kamm, Isaacs and Pearle set about this, informing Democratic Congressmen of their intentions and seeking commitments from them for the new Caucus. The responses provide a useful glimpse at the varying attitudes and styles within the reform bloc. The contacts and discussions with members took place throughout December 1972. By late December, the ADA trio had received some sort of response from most of the members they had approached.[46] On December 28, ADA compiled a list of members who had agreed to challenge the chairmen when they were nominated in the Caucus.[47] "Definites" included DSG leaders O'Hara, Fraser and Thompson, veteran DSG members Bob Eckhardt of Texas, Don Edwards of California, Frank Evans of Colorado, Spark Matsunaga of Hawaii and Lloyd Meeds of Washington. Other Democrats who had taken part in reform efforts, especially the more provocative projects, were Rees and Waldie of California. Waldie went so far as volunteering to make the motions for votes on Wilbur Mills and Wayne Hays—a chore seen as being beyond the call of duty. In addition, there were members of the left of the party who were also very low in seniority, and who had previously spoken out against seniority: Bella Abzug of New York, Father Robert Drinan and Michael Harrington, both of Massachusetts, and John Seiberling of Ohio. Other members who agreed to make the challenge but who were in middle seniority positions were Ken Hechler, the West Virginian congressman who had written a book[48] about the 1910–1911 insurgency in Congress, Lee Hamilton of Indiana, and Benjamin Rosenthal, both liberal Foreign Affairs Committee members, the latter of whom had become a subcommittee chairman as a result of the Hansen reforms[49] during the previous Caucus.

Four members told ADA that they were in favor of the move, but wished only to endorse it privately at that point, three of whom entertained present or future leadership hopes.[50]

Five more were listed as "hesitant," including Henry Reuss, Brock Adams, Les Aspin, David Obey and Peter Kyros. Reuss was a senior member of Banking and Currency who did not want to offend Wright Patman, the chairman with whom he had to work. Aspin was one of the tiny band of dovish liberals,[51] a "Trojan Horse" of sorts, inside the Armed Services Committee.

Perhaps most interesting among the reformers canvassed were the three flat refusals: Richard Bolling, Ron Dellums, and James Corman, the last two from California. The three represented divergent styles although all were nominally "liberal Democrats": Bolling, the proceduralist, a student of House history and skillful legislative tactician; Dellums, the Black radical; and Corman, the liberal and junior member of Ways and Means who had adopted the collegial ways of that Committee. Bolling, the third-ranking Rules Democrat had various reasons for demurral, one of which was simply that confrontation was not his style. More important was the fact that Ray Madden of Indiana, a liberal, would be succeeding Colmer as the Chairman of Rules. A third reason was that Bolling continued to favor the idea of a strong Speaker. He had always advocated that the Speaker should have the right to appoint chairmen; and he distrusted almost as much as the existing system of unaccountability and diffusion the possibility of a powerful but chaotic Caucus, ineffective on its own and worse, a bar to the exercise of power by the leadership. Dellums at the time was jockeying for position in (successful) hope that the leadership and the Committee on Committees might find a seat for him on the Armed Services Committee; and Corman—at once a liberal and Ways and Means member—probably decided that the latter characteristic should take precedence—especially since there was no good reason for a sitting Ways and Means member to alienate Wilbur Mills.[52]

In some cases, members were unreachable after the election, and therefore did not present their views to ADA. Phillip Burton is on a list of "possibles" but does not appear on any lists of those who expressed a view.

By late December the ADA project had produced 25 members[53] who had agreed to challenge the chairmen. But by this time DSG strategists had formulated another plan to try to avoid having to use this tactic. A DSG task force under the leadership of Frank Evans had outlined a procedure which would replace the ten member challenge scheme with the long-awaited automatic vote on each nominee, with the added guarantee of a secret ballot. This was the first of a series of far-reaching DSG proposals presented to the Caucus when it convened at the beginning of the session.

Maneuvering Outside the Caucus

The Committee on Congressional Reform, Common Cause, and ADA had mobilized unprecedented external pressure which drew considerable public attention to the reform issue.[54] But the real test would come in the Democratic Caucus in early January, and at the subsequent Caucuses where the other reform proposals were to be considered. The Executive of DSG had been working on a reform package to bring to the Caucus, including the Evans proposal for an automatic secret ballot vote on chairmen, and a number of other important planks which had emerged from the usual DSG postelection strategy sessions. These included an attempt to reconstitute the Steering Committee of the Caucus,[55] a new "open committee" initiative, a move to make the Caucus votes and Journal available to the public, as well as an attempt to make it more difficult to use a "closed rule" on tax and other major bills.[56]

The Caucus action once again can only be understood in the light of the machinations which preceded it. The organizing Caucus was scheduled to meet on January 2, 1973. Before this meeting, Speaker Albert told DSG leaders that this Caucus would not take up any of the reform proposals because there would be too much business. To bring up the reform proposals then would be too "confusing."[57] This business included nominating the Speaker and Majority Leader. Albert faced only token opposition, again from Conyers; and O'Neill was unopposed in his bid to replace Majority Leader Hale Boggs who was presumed dead after having disappeared on a campaign trip to

Alaska. Other business included adopting the rules for the session and passing an "end the war" resolution by Rep. Nedzi, the latest in a series of attempts to get the Caucus to take a stand against Vietnam.

The DSG reformers, most of whom were supporters of the Nedzi effort and who were generally disposed to abide by the party leaders' wishes, accepted the decision of the leadership. Moreover, the new chairman of DSG, Phillip Burton, had maintained close ties with his Hansen Committee colleague, Olin "Tiger" Teague, the Caucus Chairman. At the January 2 Caucus, Teague announced that there would be another meeting on January 10 at which the reform proposals would presumably be discussed. On January 6, Teague cancelled the January 10 Caucus owing to "mechanical problems."[58] The same day Teague, in his capacity as Caucus Chairman, hastily convened the Hansen Committee to consider the package of reforms which DSG had been circulating. The Hansen Committee met on January 8 and 9 and devoted most of their attention to the plan proposed by Evans for an automatic secret ballot. They were no doubt conscious of the larger reformist contingent in the Caucus—given credence by the majority for the Nedzi anti-war resolution on January 2—and also the pro-reform pressure exerted by the external liberal groups. They realized that the Evans proposal might have the votes to win in Caucus, and that ADA probably had enough firm commitments to challenge each chairman using the old 1971 procedure. Therefore, on January 9, the Hansen Committee recommended a new procedure for selecting chairmen which included the usual Committee on Committees nomination with the new automatic vote provision: "The Caucus shall vote on each nominee."[59] This was a major step forward by the Hansen Committee, much further than they had been willing to go the previous session. However, their proposal differed in one crucial way from Evans'; the Hansen version did not specify how the vote should be taken, thus leaving open the possibility of voice votes, which could result in the deferential and continued "unanimity" of the old seniority system. In the eyes of a liberal strategist at the time, it was a "modified watered down version of Evans which doesn't preclude a voice vote which would be worthless."[60]

In addition, the Hansen Committee recommended a "sweetener" for freshmen: Burton proposed that all freshmen be given a major assignment, a belated House corollary to the Senate's "Johnson rule."[61] Hansen also proposed that no member of Rules, Ways and Means, and Appropriations—the three most important House committees—could serve on any other committees. The Hansen Committee adjourned on January 9, but arranged to reconvene on the 18th.

On January 11th, Common Cause issued a press release entitled, "Common Cause Charges that House Leadership Does Not Dare to Hold Caucus on Reform."[62] David Cohen and two other Common Cause lobbyists alleged that "deliberate delay and perpetual postponement is the last ditch effort being used by the House establishment which dreads reform and does not have the votes to stop it."[63] They called on the leadership to schedule Caucuses for the consideration of reform during the week of January 22. If they refused, Common Cause urged Democratic members to force the leadership's hand by using the original 1969 process by which 50 Democrats could call a Caucus meeting.

Two days later, the Committee for Congressional Reform sent telegrams to every Democrat asking them to urge the party leadership to "secure a date certain for a Caucus on House reform proposals," suggesting that "further delay in Caucus consideration of much needed reform measures will be a disservice both to the Democratic party and the House of Representatives." In addition, Dudley Ward noted that his committee had "received written commitments from a clear majority of the Democratic Caucus for open meetings of committees except in matters of national security and invasions of personal privacy. They ought to be given the opportunity to make good on that pledge."[64]

On January 17, Teague announced that there would be a Caucus on January 22, at which only the proposal for an "automatic vote" on chairmen would be considered, with the strong likelihood that the Hansen recommendation for a vote of unspecified kind would be given priority.

The next day, ADA sent out a short letter to every Democrat reminding them that the January 22 Caucus would consider the Hansen Committee automatic vote plan "as well as a possible modification to be offered by Representative Frank Evans if the Hansen proposal does not specify how the vote is to be taken."[65] They went on to say that if some form of the automatic vote were not adopted, "Representative Jerome Waldie is again prepared to demand votes for each chairman under the 1971 rule that would still be in effect."[66]

The Caucus was scheduled to take up the automatic vote issue, then proceed to the Committee on Committees nominees, and then adjourn. Reform leaders feared that there might be an indefinite delay until the next Caucus, placing in doubt the bulk of the ambitious package of reforms developed by DSG and endorsed by the outside groups in limbo. Although it would be possible to demand the Caucus meeting under the 50 member provision, DSG leaders, especially Burton, knew that a meeting called under strained circumstances would diminish the likelihood of success.

Developments

The January 22–23 Caucuses

When the Democratic Caucus convened on January 22, the only item of business was consideration of the Hansen Committee recommendation providing for an automatic vote on all chairmen. It did not specify how this vote should be taken. Evans, after his two month effort inside and outside DSG working for a secret ballot, intended to propose an amendment requiring a secret ballot vote on each chairman. Reformers agreed that the secret ballot was vital since it provided the political insulation likely to insure that the procedure would be used.

A clear split between the reformers and the rest of the Caucus emerged over what they perceived to be a divergence of interests. Reformers saw that only the secret ballot would guarantee the intended operation of the reform. Chairmen, moderates, conservatives, i.e. most of the "regulars," wanted to keep the door open for a more leisurely pace towards reform—or perhaps no pace at all. The two sides were at loggerheads because the leadership had not this time worked out a pre-Caucus compromise which would "fix" the Caucus debate, and smooth the way for uncontroversial passage. Although the leadership had engaged in negotiations, the two sides insisted on their own versions. Thus for the first time since DSG initiated its cautious attempt to revive the Caucus in 1969, the battle over reform shifted from the cloakroom, hallways, and offices of the principals on each side, or the chandeliered offices of the Speaker and Majority Leader. On January 22, it spilled out onto the Caucus floor.

During the morning session, Hansen advocates sparred with proponents of the Evans plan, often in heated debate. In the afternoon session, Rep. Chet Holifield offered a third alternative. Holifield, the Government Operations Chairman and estranged former DSG chairman, correctly perceived that he would be challenged for his chairmanship by Rep. Rosenthal. Like the Hansen Committee, Holifield also was willing to concede the "automatic vote" on chairmen. However, instead of leaving the vote procedure unspecified like Hansen, or else requiring secret ballots like Evans, he proposed that all votes be "recorded" and "open."[67] Holifield opposed Evans' secret ballot by arguing, "If I'm going to be stabbed in the back, then I want it to be done openly."[68]

Rep. John Young of Texas, a conservative Democrat who had no great enthusiasm for any of the reforms, moved to table Holifield's amendment. Reformers feared that if the Holifield proposal was tabled, the other versions might be tabled as well, precluding any reform of the selection process for the entire session in the process, and perhaps endangering the entire DSG-ADA-Common Cause "package." Young's motion to table was overwhelmingly defeated. Next Holifield's amendment was considered, and was also easily defeated. The reformist Evans "secret ballot" proposal was similarly rejected. This left only the Hansen proposal. Jonathan Bingham of New York, a shrewd DSG reformer, hurried over to Tip O'Neill on the chamber floor and suggested a plan to salvage the automatic vote and, without offending the Hansen backers, to provide what the reformers wanted. Bingham suggested adopting the Hansen plan, and then for O'Neill to propose a resolution providing that there would be a secret ballot vote on each chairman "on demand of 20 per cent of the Caucus." This last provision maintained the illusion of a victory for the Hansen plan—along with the discretionary aspect of the 1971 ten member challenge process. However, it was operationally a triumph for the reformers since they knew that they had the votes to produce a 20 per cent (48 members) demand on every chairman. Thus, with the Bingham-O'Neill plan immediately on the horizon, the Hansen version was proposed and approved 204-9. O'Neill promptly offered his "20 per cent" resolution, which was accepted 117–58.

The leadership had once again played a decisive role by tilting toward the reformers in a pinch, but only after insuring at least the appearance of concessions. The leaders' sponsorship of the 20 per cent resolution was responsible for winning over many members who would not have voted for the same provision had it been proposed by a reformer. If there was any question about the leadership's position on reform, Speaker Albert provided the answer the next morning when Congressman Stratton of New York moved to reconsider the previous day's reform. In a rare intervention, Speaker Albert himself made the motion to table the Stratton motion to reconsider. Albert's motion was approved by voice vote, sealing approval of the reforms. The automatic vote had prevailed, with the secret ballot provision that presumably would make the process viable. However, establishing the procedure and using it effectively were two different matters, something the reformers quickly came to realize.

The reformers had now achieved their goal of reforming the process but they lacked an obvious target. They desperately needed a suitable symbolic "sacrifice."

Ever since the McMillan challenge during the previous Congress, reform strategists had figured that, with an upsurge in reformist support within the Caucus—combined with McMillan's continued obstinacy against Home Rule for D.C.—they could add to the 96 votes against him in 1971 and depose him. Reformers calculated that with a bit of luck in the election—taking into account retiring and defeated Democrats—an anti-McMillan majority in the Caucus was imaginable. However, the Democratic voters of South Carolina had robbed them of their prime target: McMillan was defeated in the primary, and consequently preempted from re-election.[69]

Now that McMillan had been defeated, the reformers found themselves groping around for a replacement. Mendel Rivers had died,[70] William Colmer of Rules had retired, Wayne Aspinall of Interior had also been defeated in a primary. Indeed, after years of decrying the outrages perpetrated by the seniority system, reformers were embarrassed to find such a dearth of examples. Where were yesterday's "ogres"? There were chairmen who the reformers would dearly have loved to have "taken on," but no-one so objectionable enough to insure his defeat by the Caucus. All the possible "candidates" possessed positive qualities that would undermine the reformist case. Poage of Agriculture was seen as lacklustre and very close to organized agricultural interests but not well-known around the House. F. Edward Hebert had just taken over Armed Services from Rivers and was not yet seen as an entrenched, and thus vulnerable, target; a move against him would be premature. Richard Ichord of the House Internal Security Committee was not personally unpopular, although his committee was. Liberals could not very well attack a chairman simply because they did not like his committee. Instead, they would have to wait and continue efforts to abolish the committee.[71] Indeed, the one chairman who combined domestic policy conservatism with extreme "hawk" views on Vietnam was the unassailable Olin "Tiger" Teague on Science and Astronautics, one of the less important House committees. As Caucus Chairman and one of the most popular men in the House, he was not even considered.

The two most effective and powerful committee chairmen, Mills on

Ways and Means and Mahon on Appropriations—both conservative and masterful legislative operators—still possessed unimpeachable reputations within the Caucus because of their mastery of their sub jects, control of their committees, and wide respect within the House. Indeed, the two men who might have "qualified" as objects for re formist attack on the basis of age turned out to be Ray Madden, 81— the liberals' new hope to represent their interests as Chairman of Rules, and Wright Patman, 79—the Banking and Currency Chair man—who was sometimes criticized for autocratic rule or cantanker ous behavior in the chair, but was a consistent liberal of the old South ern Populist school. Indeed, Patman had offended banking interests enough to have made all the right enemies in the eyes of liberals.

The reformers, then, were on the verge of successfully challenging a chairman, but having opened the seniority cupboard, they found it disappointingly bare. This was partially due to turnover and partially due to resentment of the institutional power of chairmen generally, rather than notably abusive individual chairmen. It also raises the point that seniority was probably a more popular target in conceptual, rather than specific, terms.

Consequently, on the next day, January 22, when the Caucus con vened to receive the nominations of the Committee on Committees for chairmen and committee members, the reformers were able to insist on secret ballot votes[72] on every chairman, but there was no intensive campaign against any one of them. The only organized opposition came in a move against Holifield, the chairman of the Government Operations Committee, perhaps the best indication that liberal reformers had been driven to distraction.

The challenge by Rep. Benjamin Rosenthal of New York, the middle-level, liberal Foreign Affairs subcommittee chairman and a member of Government Operations committee, against Holifield was based on the Chairman's alleged insufficient commitment to con sumer action and uninspired performance of Congressional over sight. The 69-year-old Holifield had, in fact, become the most reluc tant of reformers. He had previously tried to circumvent the 1971 Caucus rules limiting chairmen to service on one legislative subcom mittee by arguing that one of his own subcommittee chairmanships was in fact "investigative" and thus not subject to the Hansen guidelines. Albert and O'Neill had quietly intervened and Holifield had relented. Rosenthal, a consumer advocate and Congressional ally of Ralph Nader, had been distressed at Holifield for removing a clause which would have expanded Congressional subpoena powers from a consumer protection bill. Holifield responded by alleging a "Nader-Rosenthal vendetta against me."[73] Rosenthal broadened his attack by assailing Holifield's reluctance to pursue oversight more aggressively. But the Caucus was apparently not in the mood for an assault on a chairman. When Holifield spoke in defense of his record he received a standing ovation, followed by speeches of endorsement by the Speaker and O'Neill themselves, as well as by Wilbur Mills and Jack Brooks, who as the second ranking Democrat on Government Operations, would have been Holifield's likely successor. In the secret ballot vote, Holifield was re-nominated by a hefty 172-46 margin.

Seniority had once again triumphed in 1973,[74] although the precedent of a vote on every chairman—along with other reforms—was bound to have its democratizing effects on chairmen in the conduct of their committees. The "automatic vote experiment" had revealed a pronounced unwillingness to oppose the sitting chairmen. The most votes against any one chairman were the 49 cast against (versus 108 for) Ichord; and even this was generally thought to be more out of opposition to the committee than to Ichord himself. Poage had 169 for—48 against; Hebert 154-41; Patman 155-41. The challenge to Holifield brought out 172 in favor as opposed to the 46 against. Wayne Hays was approved 117-39. Charles Diggs, the Black who would succeed McMillan as chairman of the D.C. Committee received a 154-36 endorsement, presumably being opposed by those who did not favor his likely liberal positions in favor of Home Rule and on other D.C. issues. Eleven,[75] or just over half of all chairmen, were opposed by less than ten votes. The lowest cast against any were the two opposing Melvin Price for Chairman of the Committee on Standards of Official Conduct, the so-called "Ethics" committee which had been established in 1970 to monitor such questions as Congressional malfeasance, conflict of interest and campaign money irregularities. And when it came to approving members of committees as recommended by the Committee on Committees, they were all approved *pro forma*.

Even though reformers had still not achieved a tangible victory over seniority, reform leaders felt that they had made important headway in democratizing the process by which chairmen were selected. The more practical liberal leaders were satisfied with the initial success, realizing that incremental change was the best hope. Phillip Burton's comment after the two late January Caucus meetings was one of unrestrained delight: "I'm wildly happy at what we've done. We're finally getting somewhere."[76] Others in the reformist camp were less buoyant about the modest achievement, but pleased that they had at least set the stage for a further assault on the chairmen. Reformers also saw hopeful signs for the rest of the "reform package" that they would be bringing up in future Caucuses, whenever they might take place.

3:3 PUTTING TOGETHER A REFORM PACKAGE: THE CAUCUS AS FORUM, OBJECT, INSTRUMENT

The automatic vote on chairmen with the secret ballot provision was only the first goal of 1973 for DSG and its coalition of outside backers. The remaining items on the reform agenda for 1973 included proposed reforms which were of equal—and often greater—tangible impact. The "reform package" included three main themes: (1) continued strengthening of party; i.e. increasing the role of the Caucus as in the selection of chairmen, but also using the party to assure broader distribution of positions, especially subcommittee chairmanships; (2) furthering anti-secrecy reforms; and (3) altering House rules to provide more discretion for the House leadership, particularly vis-a-vis committee chairmen.

These three points were instances of the Democratic Caucus being used as a forum for the consideration of reform, as an object of reform, and as an instrument of reform. The first—i.e. strengthening party—was part of the continuing effort by liberals to assert a "majority of the majority" and, in so doing, to skew power alignments more in their favor. The second included moves to make the Democratic Caucus reform itself, but the major thrust of all three was to use the Democratic Caucus to effect redistributive change in the House of Representatives as an institution.

Party Reform: "Both Directions at Once"

The first theme of Party reform included two distinct, divergent sub-themes: the consolidation of power in the leadership and the dispersion of power to each Democratic member in his capacity as Caucus and House committee member, and to a smaller number of middle-echelon members in the form of subcommittee chairmanships. These two strains of the reform movement evidenced a deep split in the reformist camp over the direction the reforms should ideally take. The school of thought, articulated by Bolling, championed a strong Speaker and assertive party leadership. The emphasis on party leadership represented an attempt to "spread the action" to younger, middle-seniority members, as well as to each Democrat in the form of certain guaranteed "rights" as committee and subcommittee members. Thus, the "democratization" of the party and House was a classic trade-off between democracy and efficiency, participation and consolidated leadership. While virtually all of the self-proclaimed "pragmatist" DSG leaders possessed at least a theoretical affinity for the idea of "strong leadership," they recognized the demand for short-term concessions to the ascendant middle level members—which in many cases included themselves and their closest colleagues. While few were willing to go as far as Bolling in ceding vast power to the Speaker, there did exist a "conventional wisdom" in favor of endowing the leadership with greater discretion and control over the Caucus and House. This was particularly striking in that Albert himself had personally sought no new powers; in fact, a few reformers knew that privately he did not want enhanced "tools" for the leadership.[77] These factors aside, the reform movement itself never bothered to project exactly where its reforms would lead. The House, as a general rule, is inclined to move incrementally. This certainly held true for internal reform. But more than just incrementalism, the reform movement also suffered from ambiguous—or divergent—goals. When it came to Party reform, the DSG strategists "could never agree on exactly which direction" in which to move, reflected O'Hara, "so we went in both directions at once."[78]

The first sub-theme of enhanced leadership capacities was embodied in the plan for the Steering and Policy Committee of the Caucus. Party reformers had persuaded the Caucus to reconstitute the Democratic Steering Committee in 1962, but McCormack had never shown any interest in using it. McCormack, a longtime member of Rayburn's informal "Board of Education," had little time for institution-building or grandiose reformist schemes. He concentrated instead on trying to work with the Congress, warts and all—the sitting committee chairmen and "conservative coalition" leaders—in order to pass Democratic programs. Albert, while expressing interest in exerting stronger leadership as demands for it began to reverberate through the Congress, had made no overt efforts to consolidate his personal position; he too was concerned with working with the existing power brokers. Consequently, the Democratic Steering Committee had remained inactive from 1962 to 1973.

During the summer of 1972, Jonathan Bingham led a DSG task force on Congressional reform which concentrated on developing a plan to revive the Steering Committee. DSG reformers thought the Caucus might become much more effective if it had "an Executive committee of the Caucus,"[79] much as DSG was successfully led by its own Executive committee. Moreover, this was an opportunity to provide the leadership with an enduring instrument of control over party matters, part of the larger goal of building the party caucus into a forum for the "programmatic" function of responsible parties, i.e. formulation of policy. All but the most radical reformers conceded that the full Caucus was an unwieldy and unsuitable place for detailed consideration of policy. It was much the same proposition as Wilbur Mills' argument for "closed rules" on tax bills. "The floor" of the Caucus, it was generally agreed, was not the place for open-ended policy formulation. Most DSG reformers, however, were enthusiastic about endowing the leadership with the capacity to plan policy in this smaller committee of the Caucus, or in "task forces" of the Caucus, and then to bring the proposals in more manageable form to the Caucus for consideration. The formation of these committees was a corner-stone of the idea of reassertion of party; and DSG liberals saw this as a potential means of circumventing entrenched conservative committees on important issues.

During the summer of 1972, the Bingham Task Force met on Wednesday mornings at eight o'clock for breakfast,[80] and discussed possible compositions of the committee and ideas for its future role. The Task Force produced a proposal for a Steering and Policy Committee which would include the Speaker, Majority Leader, Majority Whip and Caucus Chairman, with some members appointed by the Speaker and others elected by the full Caucus. The Task Force sought to assure the Speaker a firm means of control while at the same time providing for upward-flowing Caucus election of members. This would create the potential for stronger leadership and more creative use of the Caucus, and at the same time answer any critics who might see this as a move favoring leadership aggrandizement at the expense of the rank and file.

After the election, DSG's Executive decided to include the Steering and Policy Committee proposal in their 1973 reform package. The first problem, as usual, was to sell it to the leadership and then, to steer the proposal through the Caucus. The Bingham proposal had provided for election by the Caucus using a regional representation formula. However, Southern members, especially prominent Hansen Committee members, wanted to make sure that the Steering and Policy Committee would not be dominated by Northern liberals, just as younger members sought to avert its control by their seniors. Hence, the proposed committee would include 12 members including the Speaker, the Majority Leader, the Majority Whip and the Caucus Chairman, and 12 members elected from 12 different regions.[81]

DSG described the plan as one which would assure fair regional representation and would give Members with under twelve years of service—representing nearly 60 per cent of the Democratic membership—a voice in leadership and policy decisions:

> We believe the proposed Committee would strengthen the leadership and the role of the Caucus. If Congress is to meet the direct challenge to its constitutional responsibilities now in progress, it is necessary that our party have the capacity to present a comprehensive and broadly based legislative program.[82]

The Subcommittee Bill of Rights.

The "other direction" of Party reform was a continuation of the dispersive intent of the 1971 reforms affecting subcommittee chairmanships. This action had opened up a possible 16 subcommittee chairs.[83] The 1973 effort was an attempt to expand and to institutionalize guarantees of broader participation in committee and subcommittee business. One provision aimed at establishing "Committee Caucuses" of Democrats on each committee that would select subcommittee chairmen, oversee party ratios on the subcommittees,[84] and monitor subcommittee budgets. This was part of the larger strategy of creating "majority of the majority" opportunities, in this case on full committees—as against the tendency towards committee microcosms of the "conservative coalition." The power of committee caucuses to appoint subcommittee chairmen (again, implicitly on the basis of seniority) built accountability to committee members into a system where subcommittee chairmen had previously served at the behest of the full committee chairmen.

The "Subcommittee Bill of Rights" was the most sustained challenge to the prerogatives chairmen had previously enjoyed, included in the second sub-theme of Party reform.

The movement for the enhanced power of subcommittees had been building since the 1971 reforms designed to recognize the new authority of subcommittees (limitation of the number of chairmanships one member could hold and increased staff under the control of the subcommittee chairman). New specific proposals were developed by DSG and particularly by Peter Barash, DSG's Conlon and Linda Kamm as well as Rep. Richard J. Hanna (D.-California). Particularly important in setting forth the intellectual justification for new subcommittee reforms was a memorandum from Barash to Conlon. Barash's main point was that it was not enough simply to democratize the selection of full committee chairmen or even to curtail their power over the day-to-day functioning of the committees. Instead, it was necessary to shift substantial autonomy to subcommittees and their chairmen. Barash's memorandum, which in revised form went out on December 27, 1972 to DSG members with proposals for a "Subcommittee Bill of Rights" merits quotation at length, in that it is one of the few elaborations on the "inside" motives of those seeking to "spread the action"[85]:

> The thesis of this memorandum is that meaningful Congressional reform is impossible without a major restructuring of the entire committee system; and that such a restructuring is inadequately accomplished by changes only in the method of selecting committee chairmen. Reform reaching down into and democratization of the entire committee structure is essential.
>
> A substantial portion of the blame for Congresses' inability to legislate in the public interest is attributable to the fact that too much power rests in the hands of a few men, most notably the committee chairmen. *The goal of reform is not accomplished merely by taking autocratic powers from reactionary chairmen (selection by seniority) and giving them to benevolent or progressive committee chairmen (elected by their peers).*
>
> Three practical considerations advise against putting all reform efforts into an attempt to elect committee chairmen:
>
> (1) We have too often seen how a progressive, enlightened legislator becomes tyrannical or despotic at the moment a committee chairmanship is assumed. Lord Action's dictum "power corrupts and absolute power corrupts absolutely," comes to mind;
>
> (2) It is conceivable that incumbent chairmen or an individual seeking the chairmanship, could maintain autocratic control of a committee by making promises or offering rewards to committee members having little to do with public interest considerations: a trip authorized here; an extra staff member there; a juicy investigation or bill offered for home consumption, etc., might be the bargaining tool with which committee chairmen could retain autocratic control. Meaningful responsiveness to the public interest urgings of committee Democrats might thus play second fiddle in a chairman's fight to maintain powers;
>
> (3) Even if the Democratic caucus were successful in requiring the election of committee chairmen, very few if any changes could be anticipated. Moreover, the defeat of a W. R. Poage could be offset by the defeat of a Wright Patman. If a major rationale for committee reform is to "spread the action around" (or even to give northern and western Members a continuing voice in the committee process), *then that objective can only be achieved by guaranteeing the autonomy of the subcommittee chairmen.*

The essential roadblock to major Congressional reform is the nature and extent of a chairman's power, not the method of selecting who will wield that power. Accordingly, the election of committee chairmen cannot possibly remove that roadblock.

Recommendation for Reform

What is most likely to make the committee process and, thereby, the Congress more responsive to the public good would be reform aimed at creating more new subcommittee chairmanships *and the insulation of those subcommittees from the iron rules of the chairmen.* I strongly urge that reforms be offered in the Democratic caucus which would require the following for all House Committees:

- Incorporation in the rules of each committee by majority vote of all committee members, of the name, jurisdiction and budget of each subcommittee. (See, for example, rules 4 and 19 of the House Committee on Education and Labor; and rules 16 and 23 of the House Committee on Interior and Insular Affairs);
- Substantial autonomy by subcommittee chairmen over the hiring, firing and direction of subcommittee staff, expenditure of budget and direction of investigative and legislative priorities (see for example Rules 10 and 11 of the House Committee on Education and Labor);
- Automatic referral of bills, resolutions, etc., to the appropriate subcommittees (see rule 18 of the House Committee on Education and Labor and Rule 14 of the House Committee on Interior and Insular Affairs).

The practical advantages of vesting substantial autonomy in subcommittee chairmen can be readily seen in the Senate. Consider, for example, the independent work of Senator Hart's Anti-Trust and Monopoly Subcommittee, Senator Kennedy's Administrative Practices Subcommittee and Senator Ervin's Constitutional Rights Subcommittee on the Senate Judiciary Committee, chaired by Senator Eastland; the progressive work of Senator Ribicoff's Executive Reorganization Subcommittee of Senator McClellan's (now Ervin's) Committee on Government Operations.

Under present committee arrangements in the House, and even with the election of chairmen, such independence would be unlikely, if not impossible.

In summary, the most meaningful House reform and the one which should receive the highest priority, is the right of autonomous action by the various subcommittee chairmen. In the 92nd Congress, there were 118 Democratic subcommittee chairmen out of 256 House Democrats. While not all of these individuals could be counted on to support this kind of reform, a majority would. Together with the new members and others who are 2 to 4 years away from subcommittee chairmanships, success is a distinct possibility.

These proposals were refined and put forward by DSG, who then worked with the Hansen Committee to include the "Bill of Rights" in its package of reform proposals. Burton and Conlon were key players in the integration of these provisions to strengthen subcommittees and particularly their chairmen. Burton was important in shepherding the proposals through the Hansen Committee, from which they emerged as "Hansen Committee Resolution #3" regarding Committee and Subcommittee Organization and Procedure.[86] This initiative provided the first recognition of certain basic rights of subcommittee members and corrected what were by now viewed as abuses of the full committee chairmen's power in the past. Among the rights included were a requirement that a bill be referred to the appropriate subcommittee within two weeks of receipt by the committee, foreclosing a chairman from "sitting on" a bill; and assuring adequate subcommittee budgets, mandating party ratios on subcommittees in accord with the ratio of the full committees; and finally, authorizing subcommittees to perform their duties[87] expeditiously and then to report to the full committee. In addition, in 1973 the Democratic Caucus established a bidding process by which subcommittee chairmen were approved by the Democratic committee members in Caucus, as opposed to the previous system which gave committee chairmen discretion over who became subcommittee chairmen. As for subcommittee membership, there was also established a new bidding process to fill subcommittee vacancies.

The sum total of the 1971 and 1973 provisions regarding subcommittee rights amounted to the first formal acknowledgement of the increased importance of subcommittees, especially as they had developed since the Legislative Reorganization Act of 1946. In effect, they further diluted the authority of the full committee chairmen, and increased the opportunities for participation by all members. One final provision required that all Democratic members of a committee have at least one subcommittee position before anyone received a third, closing off the possibility of a capricious chairman "packing" subcommittees with favorites while excluding others from important subject areas.

This was a critical development. And while much of the emphasis of the subcommittee reforms was framed in terms of "rights" for the rank and file members, as the Barash memorandum reveals, an overriding intention was to imbue subcommittee chairmen with new power.

Anti-Secrecy

If the Party reform measures were designed to shift power upwards and outwards, the anti-secrecy moves were aimed at assuring that those who would be exercising that power would be accessible and accountable to the public. Expanding on the "record teller" triumph of three years before, reformers sought first to open House committee meetings by making it politically unappealing to close them. The Eckhardt-Foley-Fascell "open committee" proposal in the Caucus sought to require committees to have a separate record vote at the beginning of a committee meeting in order to close it. This was an attempt to put teeth into the "open committee" provision of the 1970 Legislative Reorganization Act.

More controversial was the Matsunaga proposal to make the Democratic Caucus Journal available to the public. This would make Caucus votes a matter of public record, something which aroused opposition within the party, including from liberals who continued to regard the Caucus as a special case where privacy was justifiable as a guarantee of candid intra-party decision-making.[88]

The Speaker's Power in the House

The last theme of the reform package involved persuading the Caucus to mandate the House to provide the Speaker with greater control over House business. Proposals in this category included a move against the much-maligned closed rule. This provision imposed a layover[89] of four legislative days before a closed rule could be granted, required the committee requesting a rule to notify the House of their intention in the *Congressional Record,* and provided that 50 Democrats could sponsor an amendment—and call a Caucus to consider whether the Caucus should "instruct"[90] the Rules Committee to make such an amendment in order. This move was obviously aimed at the Ways and Means Committee, and its closed rule on tax bills.

Finally, there was a move to increase the Speaker's power over floor proceedings by giving the leadership two more days in which they could schedule suspension bills, i.e. bills under which the normal rules of the House are suspended and the process made less unwieldy. This proposal would increase the number of days per month allowed for use of the Suspension Calendar from two to four.

3:4 ACTING ON THE REFORM PACKAGE

The Caucus was scheduled to meet again on February 1. DSG forces mobilized for the internal effort. Common Cause and ADA once again cranked out letters urging passage from outside. On January 30, ADA sent letters to all House Democrats soliciting support on their four top priorities: the Eckhardt-Foley-Fascell open committee meeting plan, the Matsunaga provision to open the Caucus Journal, the limitation of the closed rule, and the Steering and Policy Committee.[91]

On February 1, the Caucus convened to consider the reform proposals, specifically the Matsunaga "Caucus Journal" provision, as well as another anti-chairmen move, this one by Rep. Charles Bennett of Florida and not part of the DSG package. The Bennett plan would limit to six the number of years that any chairmen could serve.

The Matsunaga amendment was the first to be considered. Matsunaga made a speech to the Caucus introducing his proposal to amend Rule 11 of the Caucus which he claimed would simply "clarify the existing Caucus rule," i.e. specify that the Journal is intended to be open to the press and any other interested observers. Matsunaga quoted the early twentieth century Speaker of the House, Champ Clark, to the effect that the Caucus Journal was intended to be open. Reaching out for a traditional ploy of reformers meeting resistance, he—as O'Neill had done in 1970—denied that it was actually reform:

> Mr. Chairman: Just about a week ago, I was taken aback, when a member of this Caucus approached me and said, "Sparky, I received your letter on your proposed amendment and I am surprised that you would make such a radical proposal . . .
>
> Because there may be others among my friends here who may have been misguided in their thinking, let me assure you, Mr. Chairman, and all fair-minded Democrats, that my amendment is intended merely to clarify the existing rule, except for minor additional requirements such as publishing the Journal within twenty-four hours after the Caucus meeting.[92]

The Hansen Committee, however, saw matters differently. They supported the interpretation that kept the Caucus Journal closed to outside scrutiny, and drafted an alternative motion which specifically "clarified" the question of access to the Caucus Journal by limiting it to members of the Caucus. As Matsunaga branded the Hansen version, "it would shut the door, which is now open, to all except Caucus members. It would replace the sign over the door reading 'Open to the Public' with a sign reading 'Private: For Members Only.' "[93]

Within the Caucus, Hansen members Waggonner, Hays, and Hansen herself spoke against the Matsunaga amendment. It was "washing the party's dirty linen in public,"[94] and it was commonly feared that positions taken in Caucus or changed on the floor might eventually come back to haunt the Democrats if the Republicans had access to them. Indeed, switches of position from Caucus to the floor might provide the Republicans with ready ammunition. With this in mind, Tip O'Neill had privately expressed his reservations about the Matsunaga language. The Majority Leader was worried that the open Journal might inhibit members from expressing their true feelings in Caucus, or perhaps more important in O'Neill's mind, it would make it even more difficult for him to persuade Democrats to support the leadership position if they were already on record against it. Of course, the first issue was the more fundamental: if a Caucus is indeed a place where members of a party hammer out policy, is it not their right to do so unimpeded by the watchful eye of the press, lobbyists, and perhaps even the public? O'Neill did not speak against the Matsunaga amendment, but the leadership did not express any enthusiasm for it either. Their public silence and private reluctance, the outspoken opposition by Hansen Committee members, and the existence of the Hansen Committee alternative all converged to bolster the anti-Matsunaga forces.

One of the more thoughtful DSG reformers, Rep. Tom Foley, a key backer of the open committee proposal scheduled to come up shortly after the Matsunaga amendments, best summed up the case against the Matsunaga "reform." In a private letter explaining his position to Common Cause, Foley noted:

> Many reform groups make no distinction between party caucuses and Congressional committee meetings. Here again, I disagree with this confusion of two very different areas. A party Caucus can legitimately have a confidential character. I do not believe that Democratic members have any inherent right to participate in the discussions of the Republican Conference where party strategy might well be the subject of discussion. To suggest that all party caucuses be open to the press is to remove any possibility of confidentiality as to the opposition party and will only serve to move discussions to more confined and limited participation in more informal settings. This may well have the effect of denying all members of the party an opportunity for participation, and, therefore, could be regressive in effect.[95]

When the Matsunaga amendment came up for a vote, the Caucus rejected it 57-72. Matsunaga did not press the issue by asking for a record vote on it, sensing that it was not wanted, and would not be appreciated by the leadership—of which he was by now a part.[96] The Caucus quickly accepted by voice vote the Hansen plan which specifically limited access to the Caucus Journal to members of the Caucus itself.

The Caucus then recessed for lunch, with an afternoon session scheduled to consider the Bennett proposal limiting chairmen to three terms—six years—and perhaps any or all of the remaining "package" of proposals. However, it was not to be. They had barely mustered a quorum for the morning session; in the afternoon a quorum never materialized, perhaps demonstrating a lack of enthusiasm for the Bennett proposal and a general disposition to proceed gingerly on the impending reforms. There is no evidence of a "campaign" to prevent a quorum; in fact, the leadership had issued a Whip call for the afternoon session. Common Cause, without citing any hard evidence, later alleged that Waggonner had orchestrated a very low-key boycott. But whatever the reason, the reform movement was once again stalled.

This was not to say that the reformers did not have the votes. Indeed, Fascell who along with Foley and Eckhardt was mobilizing support for the open committee meetings proposal stated: "If we can ever get recognized to offer our proposal I think we can pass it . . . but I have my doubts about whether we will ever be recognized."[97]

The reformers finally got an opportunity on February 21 to discuss the Eckhardt-Foley-Fascell plan and the other key ingredients of the package. The resolution stated that House committee meetings shall be open unless there was a record vote to close them on the same day. The leadership was for it and the Hansen Committee remained uninvolved, but the problem was maintaining a Caucus quorum. Caucus members who were not enthralled with the prospect of reform simply could stay away as they had done on the afternoon of February 1. No precise attendance figures are available for these Caucuses, but it is possible to gauge enthusiasm for reform proposals based on a comparison of vote totals on different questions before the Caucus. There were officially 240 members of the Caucus; DSG unofficially numbered 150. On previous votes within the 1973 Caucus, the number of members present and voting had varied: on the Holifield challenge, 218; on the controversial Nedzi "end the war" resolution, 229; on the Hansen Committee "automatic vote" on chairmen, 213, but on the immediately ensuing O'Neill amendment for a secret ballot upon request of 20 per cent of the Caucus, only 175. The Matsunaga attempt to open the Caucus Journal to the public elicited only 129 [total] votes cast, and was decisively rejected, while the first attempt to consider the Bennett proposal failed to produce a quorum. Now, on the Eckhardt-Foley-Fascell open committee meeting proposal, the total Caucus vote was only 120, exactly half the Caucus. It was adopted 83–37, after limited debate and only token opposition by Rep. Sikes of Florida. But there was little enthusiasm among members who were present in the chamber but did not vote.[98]

In other business on February 21, the Caucus passed the DSG anti-"closed rule" provision. Led by Phillip Burton, the DSG-backed plan demanded that any chairman seeking a closed rule should give notice in the *Congressional Record* and that the Democrats on the Rules Committee should wait four days before taking action on the request. Upon the written demand of 50 Democrats who wished to introduce a specific amendment to the bill, a Democratic Caucus would be called within three days to consider whether that amendment should be allowed. Although there was no express "binding" of the Rules Committee on these matters, it was presumed that Democrats on Rules would abide by the mandate of the Caucus. This provision was a "compromise" worked out by Burton and Mills, another example of Burton's shrewdness and willingness to deal with those whom liberals commonly shunned. Burton explained the elaborate procedure necessary to get around a closed rule when he said it was designed to "stop every wing ding proposal from reaching the floor."[99] When the proposal came up on the Caucus floor, it was adopted by voice vote. The Bennett proposal to limit chairmen to three terms was rejected, also by voice vote. It had attracted the support of only a few individual liberal reformers, and was generally ignored by DSG and opposed by the leadership.

The Steering and Policy Committee proposal was taken up the next day, although the significant action on it had taken place earlier in private consultations between DSG leaders, the leadership, and Hansen Committee figures. The DSG-backed resolution constituted a Committee which included the Speaker (or Minority Leader, if the Democrats were in the minority), the Majority Leader, the Majority Whip, the Chairman of the Caucus, eight members appointed by the Speaker, and twelve additional members elected from twelve different regions. It would meet at least once each month while the House was in session and at the request of the Speaker or four of its members. The Speaker and Majority Leader would serve as Chairman and Vice-Chairman respectively. The Committee's functions would include:

- recommendations to the Caucus or the leadership regarding 'party policy, Legislative priorities, scheduling and other matters;'[100]
- review of matters 'noticed by Members for action by the Caucus and, when appropriate, make recommendations with respect thereto;'

• recommending to the Committee on Committees nominees for Chairmen of House standing committees.[101]

The key item for most members was the nature of the regional representation on the committee. The country was divided into 12 "compact and contiguous regions"[102] each containing approximately one-twelfth of the members of the Democratic Caucus. Provision was made for adjustment at the beginning of each Congress to allow for electoral fluctuations. The Steering and Policy Committee resolution was adopted by voice vote. Also adopted by the Caucus in 1973 was a provision putting the Speaker, Majority Leader, and Majority Whip on the Democratic Committee on Committees *ex officio.* Albert reportedly demurred at first but was convinced by reformers that this would be an effective method of assuring leadership participation in the nomination and selection of chairmen and members.[103]

Outside the bounds of the Caucus—but related to the Party reforms—the Speaker appointed the Select Committee on Committees to investigate possible changes in House committee jurisdictions. This was a bipartisan move, approved by Minority Leader Gerald Ford. The committee would be chaired by Richard Bolling, and the House appropriated 1.5 million dollars to conduct their study. There had been substantial progress on Party reform—although it was not clear exactly what would be the overall effects of reforms which sought to move *simultaneously* toward greater subcommittee autonomy, against secrecy *and* toward presumed strengthening of the leadership via the Steering and Policy Committee. While these Party reforms moved in several directions at once, it was clear that committee chairmen were the main objects of attack. But this attack came through the party apparatus. As activity in this sphere subsided for a while, there developed a direct attempt to rationalize the committee system. The debate would now shift to Committee reform.

NOTES

1. For example, see "DSG, A Winner on House Reform," *CQ Weekly Report,* June 2, 1973, pp. 1366–1371; this describes the liberals' and DSG's reputation for ineffectiveness throughout most of the 1960s. Also, for background, see Geoffrey Drummond, "Democrats in Trouble in Congress Because They Badly Misjudged Nixon," *Washington Post,* February 7, 1970, p. A15.
2. This was the Democrats' response to President Nixon's official State of the Union Message to Congress. The President's Message is required by the Constitution. The Democratic answer was a political innovation. See Richard L. Lyons, "Democratic 'State of the Union' Blames GOP for problems," *Washington Post,* February 9, 1970, p. A1.
3. Conlon Interview.
4. Edmondson was a good example of an unlikely DSG member who participated in DSG affairs while at the same time failing consistently to vote for DSG positions. It was members like Edmondson whom DSG sought to protect by not releasing their membership lists.
5. Richard L. Lyons, "Seniority Rule Stirs Discontent in Congress," *Washington Post,* March 16, 1970, p.A6.
6. Mary Russell, "Carl Albert, Winning with a Waiting Game," *Washington Post,* January 10, 1971, p.B3.
7. The reform group led by Donald Rumsfeld, Republican of Illinois; Letter from Gerald Ford to Rep. Paul McCloskey, *op.cit.* February 9, 1970.
8. This was thought to be approximately the number of "bombthrowers" in the Democratic party. It proved to be fairly accurate based on ensuing events. See "House Seniority Study," *CQ Weekly Report,* March 20, 1970, p. 783.
9. Richard L. Lyons, "Democrats Set Study of Seniority," *Washington Post,* March 19, 1970, p.A3.
10. *Ibid.*
11. Richard Lyons, "19 in House Threaten Revolt Over Seniority," *Washington Post,* March 20, 1970, p.1. The 19 were Waldie, Lowenstein, Brock Adams, Thomas Rees, Abner Mikva, John Culver, Robert Leggett, Lionel van Deerlin, James Scheuer, William F. Ryan, Don Edwards, Patsy Mink, William Hathaway, Ken Hechler, James Howard, Shirley Chisholm, Edward Koch, William Clay and John Conyers.
12. *Ibid.*
13. For details of the characteristics of the Membership, see Norman Ornstein, "Causes and Consequences of Congressional Change: Subcommittee Reforms in the House of Representatives, 1970–73," in Norman J. Ornstein, ed. *Congress in Change* (New York: Praeger, 1975), p.94.
14. Interview with Rep. Neal Smith, September 5, 1975.

15. Interview with Rep. Wayne Hays, September 10, 1975.
16. Udall had earlier suggested an automatic contest between the top three seniority Democrats; but the Hansen Committee started with a consideration of the original Fraser idea. Interestingly, as early as 1970 the Democratic "filter" committee had flirted with the long-range DSG goal of an automatic vote on each chairman.
17. Hays and Conlon Interviews both included this phrase.
18. Rules of the Democratic Caucus, 1971.
19. Ornstein records the observation (of an unidentified member): "The limitation of subcommittee chairmanships to one per member was Burton's thing. He pushed it vigorously, and he, for whatever reason, opposed the automatic election of chairmen. Whether the two were tied together, I don't honestly know." This raised the question of whether Burton's two positions—on subcommittee reform and seniority reform—were part of a larger strategy. In any event Burton can be seen as a prime mover behind the drive for increasing the power of subcommittees and their chairmen; he was less concerned with increasing the power of the leadership or the rank and file in the Caucus. Ornstein, "Subcommittee Reform," *op.cit.* p.96.
20. This was the estimate of *CQ Weekly Report,* January 22, 1971, p.179. According to a private DSG estimate, a total of 19 members became subcommittee chairmen who would not have done so without the reform. Unpublished DSG background material; undated, probably February, 1975. Cf. Ornstein, "Subcommittee Reform," *op.cit.* p.102. Ornstein concludes that "the reform itself brought in a minimum of sixteen new subcommittee chairmen."
21. See Polsby, "Institutionalization of the House," *op.cit.*
22. Particularly on the Foreign Affairs Committee. See "New Leaders, Staff Changes Stimulate House Foreign Affairs Committee," *National Journal,* June 19, 1971, pp.1314–22.
23. On April 20, 1972 on a motion by Rep. O'Neill—as in 1970 on the record teller, at the urging of DSG—the Caucus instructed Democratic members of the Foreign Affairs Committee to prepare and report legislation setting a date certain for termination of U.S. military involvement in and over Indochina. This was highly unusual, using the Caucus' power to instruct. It had been used only twice in the previous 48 years (on January 18, 1961 instructing the Democrats on Rules to report a bill enlarging the Committee from 12 to 15. See p.12, and on June 21, 1949 on Banking and Currency's handling of a housing bill.) Note that to *instruct* is not to *bind.* See "Caucus Instruction and Binding Actions," *DSG Special Report* 93-12, June 4, 1974. The provision stipulated by the Caucus was included in the Foreign Military Aid Authorization Bill in 1972, but was stricken from the Bill on the House floor.
24. See pp. 133–134.
25. For example "Project Pursestrings" and "Continuing Presence in Washington."
26. Interviews conducted in a project under the direction of Professor Robert L. Peabody regarding the 1971 Majority Leadership Contest.
27. This quotation from a middle-level Western Democrat was not for attribution.

28. "Report from Washington," *Common Cause, Pamphlet,* Vol. 2, No. 9, September, 1972, pp. 1–2.
29. Minutes of the Committee For Congressional Reform, hereafter cited as "Reform Minutes." I am grateful to the staff of Americans for Democratic Action for making these available to me, as well as to ADA, Common Cause, DSG officials and others for discussing aspects of the reform campaign.
30. Mott, an heir to a fortune which includes substantial holdings of General Motors stock, is a well-known contributor to a wide range of liberal causes and candidates.
31. The above quotations are cited from Reform Minutes, July 20, 1972.
32. Reform Minutes, July 31, 1972.
33. *Ibid.*
34. *Ibid.*
35. *Ibid.*
36. The Committee was commonly referred to by its members as the "coalition."
37. *Ibid.* It is interesting to note that a previous draft (Reform Minutes, undated) had included 6 provisions rather than 4. The two excised concerned making Congressional committees "responsive to national needs and the will of the majority of the Caucus members" and to "vote to discipline committee members, including chairpersons, who fail to comply with Caucus directives." Both were removed as containing the seeds of criticism, i.e. trying to bring back "King Caucus."
38. Internal ADA Memo, undated, ADA File.
39. See Advertisement, *Washington Post,* January 2, 1973, p.C18.
40. Common Cause Pamphlet, Vol. 2, No. 9, September, 1972, *op.cit.*
41. Interview with David Cohen, President, Common Cause, September 17, 1975.
42. *Ibid.*
43. *Ibid.*
44. Letter from Leon Shull, President of ADA to ADA Officers National Board and Chapters, November 27, 1972.
45. Letter from John Isaacs and Lynn Pearle, ADA lobbyists, to Democratic Members of Congress, December 21, 1972.
46. ADA File, and Interview with John Isaacs, September 16, 1975.
47. Internal ADA Memo, December 28, 1972. ADA File.
48. Kenneth Hechler, *Insurgency: Politics and Personalities of the Taft Era, op. cit.*
49. See pp. 102–103.
50. John Brademas, Morris Udall, Sam Gibbons, and Jonathan Bingham. The first three had all been mentioned as leadership aspirants.
51. The others being Rep. Michael Harrington, and after Harrington moved to Foreign Affairs, Rep. Patricia Schroeder and Rep. Ronald Dellums.
52. See John Manley, *The Politics of Finance* (Boston: Little Brown; 1970) for a good description of the collegiality of Mills' Ways and Means Committee.
53. By early January, they claimed 30.

54. To an extent that even their critics, like Rep. Hays, took notice. See p. 79.
55. The Steering Committee was set up in 1962 by Speaker McCormack but had been almost completely ignored.
56. See p. 120n.
57. "House Reform: Easy to Advocate, Hard to Define," *CQ Weekly Report,* January 20, 1973, p.6.
58. *CQ Weekly Report,* January 20, 1973, *op.cit.,* p.6.
59. Hansen Committee Recommendation, Democratic Caucus, January, 1973.
60. Internal ADA Memorandum; undated, most likely early January 1973.
61. The 1953 Rule instituted by Senate Majority Leader Lyndon Johnson by which every Democratic Senator was guaranteed one "major" committee assignment.
62. Common Cause Press Release, January 14, 1973. I am grateful to Common Cause and particularly David Cohen for making available a complete set of Common Cause statements on Congressional Reform.
63. *Ibid.*
64. Committee on Congressional Reform Press Release, January 19, 1973, ADA File.
65. Letter from Isaacs and Pearle of ADA to Democratic Members, January 18, 1973.
66. *Ibid.*
67. "Seniority Rule: Change in Procedure, Not in Practice," *CQ Weekly Report,* January 27, 1973, p.136.
68. *Ibid.*
69. The victor over McMillan in the primary, John Jenrette, was in turn defeated in the general election by Republican Edward Young. However, in 1974 Jenrette defeated Young.
70. In March 1971.
71. See "House Abolishes Un-American Activities Committee," *CQ Almanac,* 1975, p.31.
72. There was a motion for a secret ballot vote on Poage, Chairman of Agriculture, which received the required 20 per cent support. After the vote on Poage, Poage moved a secret vote on Mahon of Appropriations, and so on—so that effectively the Bingham 20 per cent solution achieved Evans' original goal.
73. Marjorie Hunter, "House Democrats Pick Chairman: Seniority Wins," *New York Times,* January 24, 1973, p.20.
74. *Ibid.*
75. Morgan of Foreign Affairs, Staggers of Interstate and Foreign Commerce, Rodino of Judiciary, Sullivan of Merchant Marine and Fisheries, Dulski of Post Office and Civil Service, Blatnik of Public Works, Madden of Rules, Teague of Science and Astronautics, Price of Standards of Official Conduct, Dorn of Veterans Affairs, and Mills of Ways and Means.
76. *CQ Weekly Report,* January 27, 1973, *op.cit.,* p.136.
77. This emerged in interviews, and later in Albert's public statements, for example in opposing reformers' efforts to give Albert more power over

Steering and Policy, and Rules Committee, see, for example, p.267.

78. O'Hara Interview. On this point, it is worthwhile to note that at least one political scientist has seen this movement in opposite directions simultaneously as intentional, a calculated balancing act of sorts. See Gary Jacobson, *The Politics of Congressional Elections* (Boston: Little, Brown, 1983), pp.163–164. My evidence leads me to the conclusion that while there was clearly an effort to accommodate reformers of different orientation there was little articulation of goals or recognition (at least publicly) of the implications for power relationships. If this was all part of a larger "plan," I have been unable to uncover evidence of it.

79. Interview with Rep. Jonathan Bingham, September 25, 1975.

80. One source described this time of meeting as designed to keep Rep. Burton away. "Phil never would get up for an 8 o'clock meeting of knee-jerk liberals," said a fellow reformer.

81. DSG Internal Memorandum, January 16, 1973.

82. *Ibid.*

83. See Ornstein, "Subcommittee Reform," *op.cit.* especially p.102.

84. These ratios were subject to variation from one session to another, the result of negotiations between Majority and Minority.

85. Barash memorandum to Conlon, undated, probably early December, 1972, in DSG files, followed by December 27, 1972 Memorandum to DSG members, "Congressional Reform of House Committees: The Need for Subcommittee Autonomy" which is a revised version of the earlier Barash memorandum. Also to be found in DSG files of this period is a lengthy draft of proposals regarding subcommittee reform by Richard T. Hanna. In addition, Hanna sent a "Dear Colleague" on December 20, 1972 outlining a package of subcommittee-oriented reforms. In this letter, Hanna stated: "I am optimistic that this Congress shows great promise and that we can accomplish constructive reforms which will strengthen the Congress by insuring the active involvement of our less senior members in the legislative process. I believe we have an opportunity to benefit as never before from the extensive talent and expertise from one of the largest classes of freshmen Congressmen as well as one of the most junior House of Representatives in recent years." Hanna "Dear Colleague," December 20, 1972, in DSG files.

86. Undated, probably February, 1973 of Hansen Committee proposals, 1973, in DSG file.

87. That is, to conduct hearings, draft, mark-up and report bills, conduct oversight, etc.

88. See pp. 22–23 and 104–105.

89. A period of delay so that members would be aware of the motion for a closed rule.

90. This was a Caucus device less drastic than "binding" Democrats to follow a particular course. See p. 78n.

91. Letter from Leon Shull of ADA to Democratic Members, January 30, 1973. This was his order of presentation.

92. Statement in the Democratic Caucus by Rep. Spark Matsunaga; press release, February 1, 1973.

93. *Ibid.*

94. "House Democratic Caucus Rejects Reform Proposals," *CQ Weekly Report*, February 10, 1973, p. 277.
95. Letter from Rep. Thomas Foley to Jack T. Conway, President of Common Cause, December 20, 1972.
96. Matsunaga was named a Deputy Whip by Majority Leader O'Neill in January 1973.
97. "Democratic Caucus Rejects Reform," *CQ Weekly Report*, February 10, 1977, *op cit.*
98. For description of the unenthusiastic mood, see "House Reforms: More Moves Toward Modernization," *CQ Weekly Report*, February 24, 1973, p. 419.
99. *CQ Weekly Report*, February 24, 1973, *op.cit.* p.419.
100. Resolution, Democratic Caucus. In DSG Internal Memorandum, January 16, 1973, *op.cit.*
101. From DSG Internal Memorandum, January 16, 1973, *op.cit.*
102. *Ibid.*
103. Conlon Interview.

Four

Committee Reform I: The Bolling Select Committee on Committees, 1973

4:1 DEVISING CONSOLIDATIVE COMMITTEE REFORM IN THE HOUSE

Institutional Background

Although reform efforts inside the House Democratic Caucus had by now made headway, a few reformers, and others, notably the leadership, were convinced that the House was in need of more fundamental reform. Party reform had been in large part an indirect attempt to redistribute power away from oligarchic sectors of the committee system. The ensuing moves were a direct assault on that committee structure itself. The new procedures in the Caucus to make chairmen more accountable and to create more openings for subcommittee chairmanships were important Party reforms with significant institutional implications. However, neither change did anything to alter the maze of committee jurisdictions given official recognition by Rules X and XI of the House. This committee structure was the ultimate expression of the institution's dispersive essence. Although the 1946 Legislative Reorganization Act had ostensibly consolidated committees—indeed, had reduced the number from 48 to 19—the inevitable rise of new subcommittees, along with the appetites for jurisdiction of committees generally, had inhibited much of the coherence intended by the 1946 Joint Committee.

For one thing, a diffuse system was bound to evolve in a similarly diffuse fashion. The Speaker, upon the advice from the Parliamentarian of the House, referred bills to committees based on the jurisdictions outlined in the rules. But these provided only the most slender of guidelines. When new issue areas received widespread public attention it was natural for committees claiming the slightest jurisdiction to seek an active role. For example, "energy" was embraced by various far-flung committees and subcommittees, all deeming the subject to be within their purview. By 1973 when the energy crisis precipitated by the Yom Kippur War and Arab oil boycott had descended upon an unsuspecting America, no less than fourteen different House standing and joint committees shared responsibility. These included six committees with so-called "primary" responsibility, and eight "secondary" committees.[2] A survey of bills introduced during the 92nd and the first part of the 93rd Congresses revealed that 172 bills had been referred to these fourteen panels and that in the first eight months of 1973, 49 bills covering 77 different energy-related topics had been referred to nine different committees. In typical Congressional fashion, the overwhelming majority of these were left to die quiet deaths in committee. In fact, of these 172 bills only 16 were "reported out," from seven different committees. Of these, only 7 were enacted into law.[3]

Admittedly, energy had experienced an unusually meteoric rise and provided a rather extreme example of band-wagon jumping by committees. However, it highlighted both the strengths and weaknesses of the overall system. At best, a fragmented committee structure allowed the flexibility for autonomous committees to respond to the same problems in different ways. But it also militated against development of coherent policies. Overlapping jurisdictions and disproportionate allocation of responsibility produced an uneven quality of performance. Some areas suffered from too much conflict between rival committees, others from the unaccountability flowing from their monopoly on a particular jurisdiction.

Complicating the matter further was the growth of subcommittees, an entirely new layer of fragmented power. Indeed, most full committee chairmen recognized the increased importance of subcommittees by claiming the chair of their most prestigious subcommittee.[4] Hitherto, they had exercised authority by appointing allies to chair subcommittees, and by controlling subcommittee staff allocation and agendas. However, these prerogatives of full committee chairmen had been swept away by the Subcommittee Bill of Rights in the Democratic Caucus in 1973. Full committee chairmen could still exert influence through informal interventions, but the trend was toward more autonomous subcommittees. Increasingly, these subcommittees performed the real work of the House: writing legislation, conducting mark-ups, holding hearings and conducting such oversight of administration as was performed.[5]

Full committees were still important, but now mainly served to confirm or reverse decisions made in subcommittee, much the same relationship as the House floor to committees.[6]

Perhaps the most convincing testimony to the dispersive effect of subcommittees lay in the example of the three most powerful committees: Ways and Means, Rules, and Appropriations. The first two did not have subcommittees (although Rules had had temporary subcommittees on occasion), and had each developed a unified, collegial ethos. In the case of Ways and Means, the chairman, Wilbur Mills, upon assuming the chair in 1958, had immediately consolidated his personal position by abolishing all subcommittees. On the other hand, Appropriations had devolved its actual appropriations function to subcommittees arranged by departmental and subject areas; hence the full Appropriations Committee was not equal to the sum of its parts.

Of course, the importance of subcommittees varied according to issues, personalities, and political circumstances. But subcommittees provided potential power bases for middle seniority members. Particularly ambitious or adroit subcommittee chairmen could carve out niches for themselves in the House and among the public. In short, subcommittees catered to the American cult of specialization and constituted the most recent expression of Congressional individualism and diffusion. By 1973 the 21 committees[7] had spawned 132 subcommittees.[8] This development was not without attendant complications, one being seemingly insurmountable scheduling conflicts. Since many members served on more than one full committee and often up to three or four subcommittees they were often expected simultaneously to attend two or more subcommittee or committee meetings. In response, congressmen tended to develop priorities favoring committee work which fulfilled specific constituency or special interests. This produced too many of what Rep. Robert Leggett would later call "think alike" committees,[9] referring to the tendency of the Agriculture Committee to be dominated by members responsive to farming interests, Education and Labor to education groups and organized labor and so on.

These were the structural characteristics of the committee system in

1973, a rich source for those looking to find deficiences such as the innumerable anomalies, conflicts and overlaps that hamstrung Congressional performance. However, unlike other issues of reform which often involved the prerogatives of party, this issue demanded an institutional, and possibly bipartisan, solution. Still, no solution would be easy, since any realignment of committees would affect the core of the Congressional power structure and individual members' careers. Indeed, criticisms of the committee system concerned its existing distribution of power. The dispersed system ensconced the committee chairmen. If reformers could rationalize the committee structure—by streamlining its jurisdictional alignments—this might dove-tail with the Democratic Caucus reforms to increase committee accountability. Moreover, a consolidated committee system might enhance the possibilities for stronger House leadership. All this, argued a few thoughtful reformers,[10] was surely what the House reform movement had been working towards all along.

Political Background

Although these were tempting prospects, Committee reform was widely recognized as political "dynamite." The slight brush with rejurisdiction by the 1965–1966 Joint Committee on the Organization of the Congress—the separation of the Education and Labor Committee—had helped stall the entire plan in the House for four years.[11] Even then it was only after the offending item had been excised by the Sisk Subcommittee of the Rules Committee that the rest of the bill received serious consideration and passage. A more positive precedent was the sweeping consolidation of committees in the 1946 Legislative Reorganization Act, which had significantly reduced and consolidated committees. However, even that herculean achievement had been facilitated by exogenous political factors: in many cases lopping off committees which were of negligible consequence on arcane or outdated subjects.[12] In addition, partisan change was in the air in 1945–1946; a widespread belief, soon to be vindicated, was that the Republicans would win a majority in the 1946 mid-term elections. This rendered less potent the immediate threat of lost chairmanships and committee positions. Moreover, despite occasional criticism, since 1946 the structure of committees and subcommittees had earned broad acceptance.

As Fenno has observed,[13] committees serve as a means for members to fulfill various personal goals, one of which is re-election.[14] But committees provided many other opportunities as well; such as the chance to formulate policy, influence the content of legislation, conduct hearings on important issues, investigate and inform. Indeed, in the American system, Congressional committees were where congressmen did many of the things that had compelled them to go into politics in the first place. As Woodrow Wilson had noted long before,[15] committees were the workplaces of the House. Though there were certainly defects, the pockets of criticism were strongly counterweighted by a reservoir of appreciation. Some even extolled the virtues of a "messy"[16] House, viewing it as a befuddling but accurate reflection of the diffuse American society. Its defenders, like the parents of an unmanageable but sprightly and creative child, were reluctant to impose discipline on Congress lest they stifle its imagination. Thus a visceral objection to plans for rational reorganization was that rigidity would replace flexibility. This might pose a threat to such revered qualities of the present system as member specialization and sophistication, the opportunity for individual initiative, and easy accessibility for relevant interest groups. Fragmented power assured diversity of view and maintained the potential for minority opposition to even the most popular President. In short, it made for an institution resistant to any single source of external domination. In some circles, Congress's organizational irrationality was seen as a virtual guarantor of democracy itself.

Aside from the odd outside observer who spied a Gaullist cloud ascending over Capitol Hill, those most fearful of Committee reform were those inside the House who had the most to lose. The disproportionate allocation of work and responsibility was bound to be vigorously defended by the small group of committee leaders to whom great power had accrued. Over the years since 1946 the committee system, and its self-sustaining preservative—seniority—had conferred legitimacy on its top-ranking members. For example, it had become *de rigueur* for the adjective "powerful" to accompany any mention in the press of Wilbur Mills' name. But then, for the great majority of members Mills was powerful not only by virtue of his position as Chairman of Ways and Means but also through the myth of invincibility which his skillful use of his position generated.

It was perhaps for a combination of these reasons that there had been no systematic attempt to alter the committee system in twenty-seven years. Party leaders encountering intractable committee chairmen found it easier to placate them than to confront them in a contest over the source of their power. Throughout the rest of the House, although many individuals had personal opinions on the weaknesses of their own committee's performance, the system militated against any comprehensive, institution-wide analysis of the problem.

By 1973 however, the changed composition and mood of the House had created a situation in which, for a number of reasons,[17] a few important figures were becoming convinced of the need for a thorough-going reassessment. In response, the Speaker decided to establish a committee to try to put the House in order. The original proposal for a committee to study Rules X and XI came from Congressman John Culver in a "Dear Colleague" letter.[18] But the initiative clearly lay with the leadership, specifically the Speaker and his confidant and co-strategist, Bolling. Albert consulted Minority Leader Gerald Ford and senior members of the Rules Committee, the panel most involved in the subject of internal procedure. Emerging from these discussions, against the background of the reformist efforts inside the Democratic Caucus at the beginning of 1973, was the announcement by the Speaker on January 15 that he supported H.Res. 132 authorizing the establishment of a Select Committee on Committees, to be chaired by Bolling, with Dave Martin of Nebraska, the Ranking Republican on Rules, as Vice-Chairman. The Committee would be painstakingly bipartisan—five members of each party—and would have up to $1.5 million to conduct its study.

There was initially scattered opposition to the idea of setting up a special Select Committee to undertake this task. Republican Conference Chairman John Anderson and others argued in favor of using the existing Joint Committee on Congressional Operations. Others disapproved of the hefty price tag. Bolling opposed the Joint Committee approach, in part because he strongly favored a unicameral approach that emphasized the uniqueness of the House. More to the point, he and the Speaker wanted a bipartisan committee whose composition and character could be tailored to their own intentions.[19]

In order to assure unamended approval of their resolution, H.Res.132 was reported out of the Rules Committee under a closed rule, a somewhat inauspicious start for both the new, liberal Chairman of Rules, Ray Madden (who had only recently announced that he favored limitation of closed rules),[20] and the reformist credentials of Bolling's Select Committee. The firm support of Albert and O'Neill, however, combined with the endorsement by Minority Leader Gerald Ford, assuaged much of the discontent. The resolution passed a key vote on the "previous question" on the rule 205-167. The resolution itself carried 282–91.

Despite mild disagreement over the creation of a completely new

Select Committee, its cost, and the unpopular "closed rule," there was little publicly-stated opposition to the basic idea. There were sporadic, private grumblings in a few quarters of the House about the possible implications. Most of it was to be expected: chairmen and senior committee members were fearful of what a rejurisdiction might hold in store for them and their personal empires. But others harbored doubts as well, for a number of reasons—some of them involving personalities. The choice of Bolling to chair the committee elicited a mixed response. In many ways, Bolling was a natural choice to lead such an investigation: he possessed a deep knowledge of House rules and history, long-standing interest in reform, and a powerful intellect. He had also recently developed a close working relationship with the Speaker. Yet for all his experience and competence, Bolling had also accumulated his share of detractors over the years. His sometimes blunt demeanor, his unabashed ambition, his reluctance to suffer fools gladly, and perhaps even the rigor of his intellectual approach itself had all made him controversial, somewhat mistrusted and not altogether popular with his colleagues.

Suspicion, then, was not limited to the "barons" of the committee hierarchy Bolling had criticized in his books.[21] Some of the most audible murmurs, in fact, emanated from the heart of the Party reform movement, the DSG Executive.[22] Bolling, never a mainstay of DSG during his association with Rayburn, had gravitated toward them during his period in the wilderness after his failure to challenge Albert successfully for Majority Leader in 1962. But by the early 1970s he was seen to have "moved away"[23] from the DSG mainstream, opting for his resurrected relationship with Albert and his new role as the "Speaker's Agent." What bothered the DSG leaders more, however, was the carefully balanced bipartisanship of the Committee. DSG was first and foremost a group of liberal and moderate Democrats intent on implementing national Democratic party policies. Its more aggressive leaders—while not adverse to pragmatic maneuvering on an ad hoc basis—were suspicious of the "even-even," five of each party, composition of the Select Committee. They noted with apprehension the solid support of Ford. Perhaps most unsettling of all was the selection as Vice Chairman of Dave Martin, one of the most conservative members of the House. DSG had developed fairly clear ideas about Party reform, but they were less united on—and convinced of— the need for institutional reform, especially if it meant unnecessary concessions to the Republicans.

Bolling and Select Committee members vigorously strove to assure open-mindedness as they undertook their study. Indeed, Bolling stressed repeatedly over the course of the hearings and again in an interview[24] that the committee devised their plan only after hearing all the evidence. The changes the Select Committee made at various stages confirm this. However, from the very beginning, there was scuttlebutt around the House that the Speaker and Bolling had had a few specific ideas in mind; e.g., cutting Ways and Means and Wilbur Mills "down to size,"[25] looking seriously at splitting Education and Labor, abolishing a few of the lesser committees like Merchant Marine and Fisheries, and Post Office and Civil Service, and perhaps finally getting around to what civil libertarians had been trying to do for years—abolishing Internal Security. On the Republican side, they presumably would insist on "being thrown" a few "bones," among them increased funds for minority staffing, the split of the notoriously liberal Committee on Education and Labor, and the abolition of proxy voting—which Republicans viewed as bolstering Democratic influence in committee. The committee sought to avoid pre-conceived notions; however, perhaps more powerful was the mischief of rumor. Fears of what the Bolling Committee might produce were most pronounced among members of committees mentioned in the rumors: Ways and Means, the minor committees—like Merchant Marine, and Post Office—and the much-maligned Education and Labor Committee. The overlapping membership of the last-mentioned committee and the DSG Executive made it such that staunch Party reformers, in a few cases, were the most reluctant Committee reformers.

Composition

One DSG activist who was a Committee reformer was the new DSG Chairman, John Culver. It had originally been Culver's idea expressed in his "Dear Colleague" letter, that the Select Committee should be created. A large and formidable former Harvard football player, scholar at Cambridge University and lawyer, Culver had been one of the first to point out the inefficiency of the labyrinth of committees. He described committees as "catch-basins for miscellaneous or tenuously related subjects" and "archaic or too narrowly focused when viewed against modern public policy issues."[26] Moreover, Culver's experience on both the Foreign Affairs and Government Operations Committees had nurtured a strong conviction—almost an obsession—that Congress was derelict in performance of its oversight function. In addition, Culver had become intrigued by "futurism," and was challenged by the prospect of organizing the national legislature to meet tomorrow's needs. Culver was an obvious choice for the Select Committee, and his DSG chairmanship was a "bonus," an interlocking link with the established reform camp

The Speaker officially selected the Democratic members, but it is widely accepted that the Democratic members were "nominated" by Bolling. Other Democrats selected included Robert Stephens, 59, a canny Georgian on Banking and Currency; Lloyd Meeds, 45, a conscientious Education and Labor, and Interior and Insular Affairs member from Washington state; and Paul Sarbanes, 39, a cerebral second-term member of the Judiciary and Merchant Marine and Fisheries Committees who had complemented his Princeton, Oxford, and Harvard Law School background with a host of governmental positions prior to his election to the House in 1970.

Republicans in addition to Martin included Peter Frelinghuysen, 57, of New Jersey, a Princeton-educated scion of an old political family and member of Foreign Affairs; Charles Wiggins, 44, of California, an articulate and respected conservative on Judiciary; William Steiger, 34, of Wisconsin, the boyish-looking Education and Labor member who was hailed as a rising star among House Republicans, and who had shown an interest in reform going back to the Legislative Reorganization Amendments of 1970; and C. W. "Bill" Young, 42, of Florida, another Republican, a member of the Armed Services Committee, soon to switch to Appropriations.

The composition was fairly representative of each party according to ideology, age, seniority, and region. As far as committees represented, there were a few glaring omissions: the Select Committee included no members of Ways and Means, Agriculture, or Interstate and Foreign Commerce, among others. There was a slight overrepresentation of several committees, most notably at the top: Bolling and Martin were both senior members of Rules. However, the most striking characteristic of the committee was its considerably "above average"[27] intellectual calibre. This characteristic of the Select Committee membership was not widely discussed or criticized early on, but it would come to be a factor as opposition to the Committee's plan mushroomed. Members of the committee tended to be slightly more intellectual (not necessarily a compliment in the House) and more conscientious than the average member. In one cynical section of the House they were branded "Boy Scouts." This characterization by a few Democrats of their five member contingent reflected the view that the Democrats on the committee "looked at the House in the same way as Bolling." Indeed, a few Select Committeemen, as members of

"The Group,"[28] were commonly to be found at Bolling's Wednesday morning coffee sessions long before the Select Committee's establishment. The committee lacked "operational types"—the kind of hard-driving political brokers epitomized by Burton, Waggonner and Hays.

Activity

Bolling appointed a Majority staff which included a range of members with Capitol Hill and academic experience. Bolling chose Dr. Charles Sheldon of the Library of Congress to be his staff director. Sheldon, a senior economist and specialist in scientific matters, had worked for Bolling on Joint Economic Committee business. Other Majority appointees came to the job with legal training, previous work in Congress or in the Congressional Research Service, and some with academic political science backgrounds. Martin's Minority appointees included experienced Republican staffers as well as a political scientist, Roger Davidson, co-author of a book[29] on Congressional reform in the middle 1960s.

The Select Committee was an unusual case of Majority and Minority staffs being encouraged to work as one, a tangible indication of its bipartisanship. As the Select Committee set about its work, hardly anyone outside it delved into the characteristics and orientations of the staff. However, later it too would be assailed by critics of the Bolling plan as overly "academic" and out of touch with the realities of Capitol Hill politics. In fairness, Bolling and Martin selected exactly the staff they desired: bright, efficient, conversant in social science techniques, and likely to be creative in helping members to weigh alternatives to the existing committee system. Bolling expressly wanted the politics left to the members, and even then, only when it was time to "sell" the plan to the House. Only Linda Kamm, the ex-DSG aide and the ADA Legislative committee chairwoman with close ties to the liberal reformist wing of the party, was considered to be a "politically oriented" staff member. The staff received strict instructions to steer clear of politics, a dictum which remained in force throughout the period of drafting the plan. For his part, Sheldon, a Congressional Research Service senior specialist, was the apotheosis of the Bolling staffer: a hard worker and sophisticated analyst, an apolitical technician.

Within the self-centered enclave of the House other institutions are suspect. Even the Senate just across the Capitol Mall is greeted with a mixture of jealousy and disdain. But "academia" evoked an even more pronounced "love-hate" response. Congressmen talked to academics and frequently hired staff at least partly on the basis of academic credentials. Yet the alleged isolation of the "ivory tower," compounded by the fact that many academics seemed to have little feel for the politics of the place, caused some congressmen to distrust visiting scholars. When the Select Committee was later branded by critics as too "academic" in its approach, it was clear that the term was not intended as a compliment.

The Select Committee at Work

The Select Committee set about their task from their sprawling complex of connected offices on the sixth floor of the old Congressional Hotel—now a House office building annex. The staff aggregated information from the available literature on the House committee system. After working out a *modus operandi* and work schedule, the Select Committee decided to solicit maximum "input" from members and outside groups. Although House procedure and functions—oversight, for example—were within the terms of reference of the Committee, there was a consensus that the main thrust of their work would be rejurisdiction. Consequently, the Bolling Committee was especially concerned with soliciting the views of everyone who might be affected by shifts of responsibility, or who might have worthwhile suggestions. The Select Committee scheduled three sets of public hearings over the course of ten weeks in the middle of 1973. The first set was for all House members who wished to testify, beginning on a precedent setting note with the Speaker as lead-off witness, the first testimony by a sitting Speaker before a Congressional committee in over 100 years.

The Speaker noted the importance of the Select Committee's work, offered a few procedural suggestions, but basically proffered the view that there were no easy answers. If there had been, he noted, he would not have had to appoint the Committee. Minority Leader Ford followed the next day with general words of encouragement, along with a few specific recommendations, among them the separation of Education and Labor. The party leaders were followed by other members of the House—ultimately totalling 63—spanning every House committee, though tilted toward their upper reaches: the committee chairmen, ranking members and other senior members. The second set of hearings sought the views of academic experts on specific subjects: policy areas, oversight, staffing, information facilities, and more adventurously, "futurism."[30] The third set of hearings provided an opportunity for representatives of outside groups to express their views. Andrew Biemiller of the AFL-CIO, Ralph Nader, John Gardner of Common Cause, Clarence Mitchell of the NAACP and others appeared.

In addition to the formal hearings, the members of the Select Committee divided the House membership into ten sections with each member given a list of colleagues to contact for informal conversations about particular problems and suggestions. Also the Select Committee staff conducted their own discussions with staff members of the various House committees. Other informal consultations took place, the Select Committee sounding out various affected interest groups.

All of this activity was what Bolling described as "the pleasant part"—the opportunity to discuss problems and possible correctives. The more difficult job, one which many argued was an impossible or thankless task, was "to make the trip from what would be ideal to what would be practical."[31]

The way that the Select Committee proceeded to consider the possible alternatives itself is a complex and fascinating study which merits more attention than is presently possible.[32] But even a brief description of the developments of the Bolling plan will contribute to an understanding of its aim and ultimate recommendations, as well as the stormy reception it later encountered in the Democratic party and House. The hearings and informal discussions had produced an interminably long list of proposals covering a wide range of conflicting assumptions, goals, and specific proposals.[33] In order to isolate the disparate set of alternatives, the Select Committee staff retreated into seclusion to consider the varying suggestions and hoped to return with a clarified set of options.

The August Study and the October 3 Alternatives

In early June of 1973, Bolling asked the staff director, Dr. Sheldon, for the staff to prepare a memorandum for reorganization "based on what was thought acceptable to him and Mr. Martin."[34] The staff set themselves up in a large room in the Cannon House Office Building for a series of intensive meetings to isolate "organizing principles," objectives, and specific ingredients of a proposed reorganization. The project involved 11 Select Committee staff members. From July 10 to 16, the special task force worked on arrangements for the project. Between July 16 and August 3, 1973, the project members met three

days a week in morning and afternoon sessions. They divided themselves into subcommittees and observed pre-arranged procedural
guidelines including strict confidentiality, rotating responsibility for
writing summaries of their meetings and taking votes on contentious
issues. The staff of a committee studying committees was particularly
mindful of the impact their own organization might have on their
plan for reorganization.

The group employed "game theory"[35] to arrive at their basic objectives, and perhaps as a result, tended to start with first principles. For
example, their list of aims included "To have standing committees"[36]
and, in other instances, evidenced indecision or disagreement, for
instance: "To be aware of subcommittees but not deal with them directly—although this in fact was done" and "To be conscious of the
role of the Speaker and the leadership but to tread lightly here."
However, sandwiched in the same list were a few fundamental tenets
that would affect everything else: "To minimize jurisdictional overlap,
but to provide some mechanism for coordinating the inevitable overlap that occurs in any configuration of standing committees," "To
equalize committee workload," and "To eliminate the distinction between major and minor committees."[37]

The recognition of the problem of subcommittees was only the first
mention of a continuing quandary for Select Committee strategists
who realized that subcommittees had become extremely salient sub-
institutions. And their brief reference to the Speaker and party leadership quickly followed by the halting decision to "tread lightly here"
acknowledged the abundance of opinion favoring stronger leadership. Yet at the same time it concluded that a major initiative in this
area would have to come from within the Democratic party.

The next stage was pivotal: the identification of more specific goals.
The staff dubbed them "policy objectives" which would have to be
resolved before they could usefully proceed to anything else. There
was disagreement among the staff, as well as among the committee
membership, over the precise nature of these broad objectives. In a
section entitled "Procedural lessons," the task force recognized this
when they observed, "Organizing principles should be thoroughly
discussed, agreed upon, and clearly stated at the beginning." After
they had proceeded to the specifics, they noted: "No 'right' or 'logical'
outcome exists. A variety of committee schemes can be drafted."[38]

A variety of schemes is exactly what the August study and ensuing
staff work produced: four detailed alternative proposals for commit-

tee rejurisdiction—each with conflicting underlying assumptions or "organizing principles," and each "rational," or at least internally consistent, in its own way.

The first plan included twenty committees, roughly the same as the existing system, and started from several novel and significant new "organizing principles" that "in most instances a Member would be limited to one committee assignment," and that "each committee have an oversight subcommittee, a budget subcommittee, and no more than three other subcommittees."[39] This "one-tier" approach would assure all members one committee assignment in a major policy area, and would eliminate scheduling conflicts by requiring that each member serve on only one committee, except for those sitting on three special "minor" committees (Standards of Official Conduct, House Administration, and Budget). The subcommittee provisions attempted to assert the House over its subcommittees in order to reverse the present drift. Oversight and budget subcommittees would provide the means for subcommittees to perform two functions that most observers agreed were not being done in the existing system— overseeing executive agencies and weighing the impact of committee actions on the overall budget. The twenty proposed committees amalgamated old jurisdictions and abolished six committees whose jurisdictions would be integrated into new panels. Singled out for oblivion under the plan were the powerful Appropriations Committee (to be replaced by the new Budget Committee) and Education and Labor (which would be separated). There would be substantial rejurisdiction to new committees from Banking and Currency, Interstate and Foreign Commerce, Merchant Marine and Fisheries, Post Office and Civil Service, Public Works, and Veteran Affairs. The Ways and Means Committee would be retained under the plan, but would lose large chunks of its jurisdiction, including trade, Social Security (except for specific tax aspects), debt level, and medical programs.

The enormity of the task and the difficulty of the decisions ahead was evidenced by the committee's inability to find definite solutions, even in this open-ended atmosphere. For example, on the subject of the District of Columbia Committee they stated: "While this committee was not actually abolished by the staff, the staff could not agree to retain a D.C. Committee."[40] Still, this staff working plan for twenty committees provided the first, consolidative alternative for the members to ponder. Other staff memoranda containing possible models would soon provide a broader array of options. After a period of internally circulating memoranda expressing various staff preferences—preceded interestingly by a very futuristic "ideal" plan from the pen of Bolling himself[41]—the staff produced another set of complete committee reorganizations. They unveiled on October 3 three schemes at variance with each other. The first two were polar opposites, presenting the alternative directions carried to their extremes. Both were unrealistic, but together they brilliantly evoked an almost unlimited range of possibilities.

The first was entitled "A Plan for Multiple-Interest Committees"[42] and was rigorously consolidative in approach. Drafted primarily by Terry Finn and Roger Davidson, both staff political scientists, this plan would reduce the number of standing committees from 21 to 12. Seeking to rationalize the committee structure and to bolster it in ways the 1946 reorganization had failed to do, the plan included as its overarching aims:

- A reduction of committees.
- Committees that are broad in jurisdiction and representative in membership.
- Single assignments to committees of relatively equal importance.
- Flexibility in effectuating changes in committee and subcommittee structures.
- Strong central leadership through the Office of the Speaker.[43]

The rationale behind this scheme was to eliminate the "think-alike"[44] character of special interest-oriented House committees and to replace them with broad policy-centered groupings. These "multiple interest committees" would assure "coherent consideration . . . not only for individual bills, but also for interdependent policy issues and related government agencies."[45] The plan also included a strict adoption of the "one-tier" system; and most significantly of all, quite unabashedly sought to equip the Speaker and party leadership with the institutional tools necessary for strong leadership. "Firm leadership is necessary in any institution, and especially one as large as the House," went the rationale. "Under this plan, the Office of the Speaker would be expanded to include the agenda-setting role now performed by the Rules Committee, the house-keeping role now performed by the House Administration Committee; and a more active role in coordinating committee consideration of legislation."[46]

These proposals, combined with "subcommittee controls," whereby committees would establish their own subcommittees subject to review by the Speaker, amounted to a sustained and detailed endorsement of a reasserted Speakership. The approach followed on sentiment within the party reformist bloc about the need for stronger leadership—a line most persistently espoused by Bolling. This model had been presaged in a few of the academic presentations, in one case, an old form under a new name: "integrative capacity."[47] But the Finn-Davidson draft sought to do something that the Party reformers had never faced squarely; it set forth a plan for unequivocal re-institutionalization of powers of the Speaker. This notion had not been seriously considered since Speaker Cannon's demise in 1910, and would wrest control over agenda from the Rules Committee and housekeeping from House Administration which Rep. Wayne Hays had only recently transformed into a veritable political canteen. This proposal for "multiple interest committees" had as one of its linch-pins a vastly expanded role for the Speaker. Of course, this was only an internal staff exercise in plotting alternatives, but it had identified possible prerogatives for a Speaker that some members considered necessary for a more cohesive Congress, although Speaker Carl Albert had made it plain that he was not one of them.

The alternative plan was directed in exactly the opposite direction, providing for "Organizing the House into a Large Number of Committees."[48] This memorandum was drafted by staffers Joan Bannon, Gerald Grady, Linda Kamm, and Walter Oleszek, with contributions from the rest of the staff. This plan would set up thirty-six committees and six select committees, bringing the total back to a number only slightly less than the pre-1946 structure. It was intentionally disper-sive, arguing that a number of specific functional objectives of the institution would be served by the adoption of such a structure. These desirable by-products of a larger number of committees included "specialization and expertise"—allowing "greater opportunities to become knowledgeable in specific policy areas"[49] and "oversight"—increasing the "probability for more effective legislative review of agency performance." This would also provide more "opportunities for leadership": "A committee system larger in number than today's will afford Members—Democrats and Republicans alike—greater opportunities to assume committee leadership positions, either as full or subcommittee chairmen or ranking members."[50] Other salutary effects would be "many more points of entry . . . for citizens and interest groups"[51] and increased importance of the floor as a result of the presumed increase in productivity of each of these new committees. This plan also included one rationale which was the only mention in all of the staff drafts of anticipated political problems in getting a plan accepted by the full House. The overall model was justified on the grounds that,

> increasing the number of committees would be less disruptive to members and staff than adoption of a plan with a few committees. With more committees than the present system, greater opportunities exist to accommodate the interests of members as far as assignments, staff positions, and physical arrangements are concerned.[52]

This alternative model was in striking contrast to the equally blunt, Speaker-led consolidative option. It included some imaginative mechanisms for handling the large House committee work-load. The committees would be separated into 22 "A"—(major committees) and 20 labeled "B" (secondary committees) including all of the Select Committees. Scheduling conflicts would be eliminated by having A and B committees meet on different days. A mandatory rotation system would prohibit members from serving more than six years consecutively on a committee. And in order to place a limit on intricate subcommittee possibilities, no member could serve on more than one subcommittee on each of his committees. The committee system under this plan would be "multi-track" and the plethora of committees presumably would foster greater participation, more equal distribution of power, and better productivity. The obvious difficulties with coordinating such a system would be handled by the Rules Committee, which would have the option of referring bills to more than one committee in "joint, split, or sequential"[53] order. The Speaker was not to be totally ignored in the scheme. He, in "consultation with the Steering and Policy Committee,"[54] would control the "timing" of measures when they came up for floor consideration.

This dispersive plan proposed breathtaking confirmation and expansion of a tendency that had been abroad in the House since the 1946 reorganization. It was interesting for its presentation of the case in terms of the various individualistic strains of behavior it would allow. The two "extreme" proposals taken together provided useful end-points on a continuum of dispersive versus consolidative models on which the House could choose to gird its committee structure.

The Plan for Minimal Changes

These two proposals leading in opposite directions were worthwhile intellectual exercises, especially useful in mapping out the logical extremes of possible reorganization and in clarifying the issues involved. But even a committee bent on far-reaching reorganization had to recognize political realities. The House was likely only going to move incrementally: hence the plan for "minimal changes."[55] This experience provided clues to the main items of contention which would arise in the Select Committee's deliberations and again later, after the Bolling Committee had reported their resolution.

The staff's minimal plan contained a two-step scheme for re-jurisdiction "developed to indicate the flexibility with which jurisdiction can be realigned without excessive change in the existing committee structure."[56] Both parts of the plan kept twenty-one committees, the same number as the existing House, but sought to rationalize their jurisdictions and integrate old jurisdictions into new committees. (In the first proposal of the two-pronged plan, the staff eliminated Internal Security, Post Office and Civil Service, and Appropriations, and split Education and Labor; the second proposal axed Merchant Marine and Fisheries.) The jurisdictions of the rest of the committees would be streamlined and to some extent made more equal. All health and social security measures would be placed in a new committee—supplanting Ways and Means and Interstate and Foreign Commerce on these matters. The second step of the plan would be to create new committees on Energy and Policy Planning, and to improve the Government Operations Committee's oversight performance. The staff, in suggesting a phased abolition of existing committees and the gradual introduction of new committees, implied that this would be politically more acceptable. Moreover, this lack of boldness on jurisdictional matter was accompanied by an ambitious compensatory set of procedural proposals. In other words, one way to shake up the House was to re-work the actual distribution of jurisdictions; another was to devise new mechanisms by which the existing jurisdictional alignments could be more easily manipulated. Thus the non-jurisdictional part of the plan proposed a bill referral device similar to that of the previous staff plan which would have reduced the number of committees and consolidated broad procedural power in the Speaker. Once again, procedural assertiveness by the leadership—perhaps through the Rules Committee—was seen as a means of expediting business, not just on the House floor but concerning the work of committees as well. For example, the Speaker could refer bills to committees which he knew to be receptive to a certain position, rather than to one where he knew there would be obstruction. Or he could authorize more than one committee to consider bills at the same time ("split referral") or one after the other ("sequential").

Other procedural reforms focused on oversight of the administration, that much-talked-about but little-acted-upon function of Congress which had first been identified in the 1946 Reorganization Act. The staff envisioned a Government Operations Committee with enhanced responsibilities. Finally there was a proposal that was perhaps the most radical of the lot and that embraced both procedure and jurisdiction. The staff proposed abolition of the House Appropriations Committee, and thereby, the dissolution of the existing division between the authorizing and appropriating functions. Legislative committees normally authorized funds; the Appropriations Committee (in most cases, actually the specialized subcommittees of Appropriations) reviewed the authorizations and recommended appropriations to the full House. This role had earned the Appropriations Committee a reputation for being cold-hearted budget slashers, even though their miserly scrutiny derived primarily from the lack of accountability built into the rest of the Congressional budgetary process. The system of divided authority over authorization and appropriation had been established in 1921 to correct the deficiencies of the previous method whereby authorizing committees also determined appropriations. The staff plan proposed a return to the pre-1921 practice, suggesting that fiscal accountability could be expected from committees which had to authorize and appropriate with an eye toward attaining passage of their measures on the House floor. Committees would have to be more responsible than in the existing system where they knew that the austere Appropriations Committee would intervene.

This change would have transformed the entire Congressional budgetary system, a subject of particularly intense interest at the time in the wake of President Nixon's extensive impoundment of funds.[57] Nixon was boldly seeking to over-rule Congressional policies on the grounds that they were inflationary; thus he was using impoundment as a virtual absolute veto—indeed, a recourse that could be used after the constitutionally prescribed veto had been overridden. This enraged congressmen, even those who sympathized with Nixon's economic aims. However, outrage at the President was necessarily blunted by a recognition that Congress's own budgetary procedures were hardly in a state which allowed them to be overly critical of others. Congress possessed no mechanism to relate revenues to expenditure; there was hardly any accountability built into the authorizing functions (performed by the various subject-matter legislative committees); and there existed no procedure to establish overall spending ceilings. In the practical politics of the House, it fell to the Appropriations Committee to cover for Congress's collective lack of a coherent budgetary system.

Thus the Congress was in a weak position to cast stones at the White House, even if the impoundments were affronts to Congressional prerogative. The budget information that congressmen relied upon most often came from the Executive's own Office of Management and Budget. Internal disorderliness and a general feeling of dependence on the Executive branch led many congressmen to conclude that wholesale reform of Congress's budgetary apparatus was in order. Indeed, Bolling, as a member of Rules and the Joint Economic Committee, was a leading proponent of Budget reform, but there was already a Joint Study Committee which was examining this precise subject,[58] and it would hardly have been politic for the Select Committee to give the appearance of trying to upstage them. Bolling himself and Vice-Chairman Martin were both high-ranking members of the Rules Committee which had laid claim to House jurisdiction on the matter. Hence Bolling was already positioned to take an active role in the debate. He would later play a leading part as floor manager of what became the Budget and Impoundment Control Act of 1974, and so it made little sense for the Select Committee to seek another contentious item.

Aside from this proposed radical surgery on Appropriations, the plan for minimal changes showed that there were numerous potential reforms which might provide far-sweeping change, and at the same time, keep the same number and ambiance of existing committees. The staff proposal had charted out a "workable" realignment. But the interconnection of each aspect of the plan revealed the sensitivity they must bring to their work. Each shift affected almost every other, and even a relatively modest restructure might so upset those who were uprooted that the entire plan would be placed in jeopardy. But by this point, in the late Autumn of 1973, the Select Committee—especially Bolling—was intent on producing a plan that would dare to be controversial, if that was necessary to rationalize the structure. Culver was convinced the Committee should set its sights high, and others were anxious that their enormous efforts would not result in trivial, piecemeal reform. They aimed to produce a plan which as Bolling would later describe it, restructured committees "the right way"[59]—placing emphasis on coherence and rationality. But the right way was not necessarily the uncontroversial way.

4:2 SEEDS OF CONTROVERSY

During the course of the Select Committee's hearings, Richard Fenno, a prominent political scientist, at one point referred to the difference between "wholesale" and "retail" reform.[60] The former would be a major transformation of practice, and would be extremely difficult to achieve; the latter and probably the more fruitful course would be practical, gradual changes. Certainly witnesses had offered a number of suggestions which constituted truly radical departures. For example, Rep. Bella Abzug had suggested dismantling the entire system of standing committees and replacing them with ad hoc committees.[61] This and some of the more starry-eyed musings of the "futurists" were intriguing reflections of both the broad scope of the Committee and fertile imaginations of the witnesses. However, never far from the minds of the Select Committee members, no matter how committed they were to producing daring and sweeping change, was the reality of having ultimately to "sell" the plan to their fellow members. This imperative called into question even some of the more sensible items which might have conceivably fit Fenno's "wholesale" reform category. For example, the staff proposal to abolish Appropriations and reunite the authorizing and appropriating function in legislative committees received relatively short shrift in the Select Committee's deliberations. Rep. Culver thought the idea had merit, but no one else in the Committee saw it as a plausible goal. If nothing else, the fifty-five members of the sitting Appropriations Committee would pose a formidable phalanx of opposition. Another far-reaching change which received a chilly reception at an early stage was the suggestion of a "rotation" system, a plan in which members and chairmen of committees would be periodically rotated to prevent the "think-alike," clientele-centered syndrome that Rep. Leggett and others had noted. Rotation, argued its advocates, would pump fresh air into allegedly stuffy committees. Specialization and security-of-tenure (through seniority) had fostered cosy relations with interest groups. Culver was intrigued by this idea as well; but rotation—whether mandatory or voluntary—also was dismissed peremptorily. Quite apart from serious substantive objections, it was an item unlikely to attract any support in the House. Perhaps a more pivotal item was the decision by the Select Committee to reject any alteration of subcommittee practice. This was partly a recognition of the potency of the newly endowed sub-committee satraps. But this decision also demonstrated a keen awareness of the intractability of the existing subcommittee system. The Committee concluded that it would be better to stick to the full committee system itself, to make the proper changes there and hope that the rest of the subcommittee structure would somehow take care of itself.

All of these were potentially sweeping departures. But each had received only fleeting consideration before disappearing from the reform landscape. Surely one reason was that there were clear disagreements over the practicality or desirability of the substance of each proposal, but a more significant consideration for the Select Committee was the fact that they all were sure vote-losers. And while the Bolling Committee had set out with an open mind to identify the problems and propose answers, it consisted of ten politicians who had politicians' instincts for the possible. As a group they were perhaps less yielding than many, but they still saw little to be gained in undertaking a suicide mission. They were looking for proposals that were worthwhile reform, that would pass, and most of all, that would work.

The Modified One-Tier Structure

But what if, to achieve reforms both worthwhile and workable, the House required fundamental reform? One recurring subject mentioned by committee members and witnesses at the hearings was the monstrous problem of scheduling committee meetings. Members often had two (and occasionally even three) assignments, each with the added demands of subcommittee work. It was physically impossible to contribute in any worthwhile manner to all of these jobs on more than a spasmodic, eclectic basis. This untenable situation gave rise to basic questions about the allocation of responsibility and work-load which inevitably focused on the number and size of committees.

The scheduling problem was inherent in the existing committee system. While members' time and energies were finite, their commitments—including all the demands not involving committees—were seemingly endless. The existing committee structure squandered members' talents and time and often left congressmen dashing between committee rooms. Oftentimes the detailed work was left to committee and subcommittee chairmen and staff who could give it closer attention. Scheduling, then, was a fundamental problem, and one which Select Committee members focused on early in their hearings.

At the second hearing, during the testimony of Minority Leader Gerald Ford, Bolling had broached the scheduling subject:

> We should . . . try to devise a system in which a person, until he got to the leadership level where you end up with any number of assignments inevitably, would have one assignment instead of a proliferation of assignments that he could do only partly.[62]

Minority Leader Ford was generally receptive to Bolling's suggestions, but he added a note of caution: it would probably be necessary to add a "grandfather clause"—protecting sitting members from displacement under a new system.

Members' lines-of-questioning revealed that, although they had not settled on an exact solution, it was clear that they were keen to do something about this question of workload and scheduling. The suggestion which kept cropping up in hearings and discussions was to move toward equalization, what some called a "one tier" or "one track" system in which every committee member would have a "major" committee assignment. The jurisdictional alignments would be revised to assure that each committee was in fact "major," encompassing a broad field of public policy. Major committees—and exclusive assignments—would assure "multi-interest" representation, as opposed to the clientele-oriented tendencies of the present system.

There was little opposition in principle to the desirability of the one-tier approach. However, after pondering its practical implications Sarbanes began to express reservations. The more he thought about it, the more troubled he became about likely opposition from members who would be dislocated. Sarbanes concluded:

> I wrestled with exclusive assignments, and it just can't be done. Two thirds of the members are now on two committees, and these assignments are important to them. But it's not necessarily bad—*if* you can schedule so as to avoid conflicts. This plan opens up a range of alternatives for members. Their personal political goals can be served while business is being taken care of.[63]

Sarbanes' plan sought to increase the number of committees to 26, and to institute a "two-tier system" of 12 major committees and 14 secondary ("non exclusive") committees. Each member would serve on one of the 38-member major committees. The scheduling would be done on a carefully constructed "modular" basis—as in American high schools—so that there would be a time set aside for major committee meetings, another for their subcommittees, another for minor committees, and so on. Sarbanes' position was that everyone ought to have the opportunity to participate, but he felt strongly that no system could make lazy or distracted members diligent. Moreover, the Select

Committee might never know if the one-tier plan could work, if it ran into such fierce opposition that it doomed the whole reorganization enterprise. His plan sought to solve the scheduling problem without trampling on the dispersive web of committees and subcommittees.

The Majority of the Select Committee favored the one-tier approach, although there were still reservations, especially on the part of Sarbanes. Sarbanes and Steiger, the youngest members of the Committee, were appointed by Bolling to form a task force to draft a working plan. They, along with the staff, were to draw up a draft, which could serve as the basis for detailed points of discussion. In the process, it was hoped, they would be able to work out a compromise on the one versus two-track approaches. This bone of contention, the basic question of organizing principles, in the event, was resolved by a "modified one-tier" system. This sought to eliminate the overlaps of the major committees by making them more equal. But it was also flexible enough to preserve such politically potent minor committees as D.C., Merchant Marine and Fisheries, Veteran Affairs, House Administration and Standards of Official Conduct. These minor committees had developed close working relationships with clienteles which had grown used to having special committees dealing with their domains: the shipping industry and seafaring trade unions with the Merchant Marine and Fisheries Committee; Veterans Affairs with Veterans organizations such as the Veterans of Foreign Wars and the American Legion. And of course, a District of Columbia Committee was necessary at least until Home Rule for the District came fully into effect (and politically, had the only black committee chairman, a fact not lost on the Select Committee). Standards of Official Conduct had only recently (established in 1970) carved out a place for itself as the internal "ethics" committee, and while some argued that its functions should, like the suggestion for the House Internal Security Committee, be transferred to the Judiciary Committee or Government Operations—there was also strong outside support for its maintenance as an independent entity. House Administration under the shrewd chairmanship of Wayne Hays, and subcommittee chairmen such as Brademas and Thompson, had become a bastion of patronage—and power—in the dispensing of House offices, supplies, printing, and the coveted "junkets" (otherwise known as fact-finding trips during the recesses).

In addition, the modified one-tier plan included the new Budget Committee as a minor assignment—not because it was anticipated to be of minor importance but because it was slotted to a secondary position in the House system, to be held on a rotating basis for a fixed period by members selected from other committees. Under this arrangement, members could take positions on the Budget Committee without losing seniority on their regular assignments.

This decision was of key importance. Sarbanes had conceded the point[64] accepting a modification; but he still worried about the political implications. The modified one-tier plan was finally adopted by the Select Committee. But this begged one other related question: how to ease the transition so as not to alienate the mass of members who would be dislocated under the plan? Sarbanes had calculated that approximately 50 relatively junior members would be displaced under the modified one-tier, and there would have to be some mechanism for assuring them a reasonably attractive alternative. This was the point that Minority Leader Ford had made about a "grandfather clause." But the Select Committee decided that the most they could do to assuage potential opposition was to give an assurance: members who had served on a committee vitally concerned with a certain subject would be given preferential treatment for the new committee dealing with that subject. Other possibilities were considered,[65] but the standard division between institutional and party prerogative inevitably appeared. Assignment to committees was the province of the two parties; and a Select Committee of the House could not tell the party leadership or the two party Committees on Committees how to conduct their business. And of course Bolling had long before gone on record as a champion of the rights of the Caucus, a notion firmly respected by the other Majority members as well. So the most they could do was to write into the final plan this recommendation about transition, and hope that the good faith of the party committees in dispensing assignments, and the overall merit of their plan would supersede members' doubts.

The Ingredients of Rejurisdiction

The Select Committee had reached consensus on the desirability of the modified one-tier approach. With the organizing principle in hand, they set out to rearrange jurisdictions so as to fulfill its goals: relative equality between major committees, more broadly based "multi-interest" representation, and elimination of overlap. This task would no doubt involve scuttling some of the smaller, more clientele-oriented committees and integrating their functions in one of the new committees. It would also mean removing jurisdictional anomalies. Equalization would require a paring down of the jurisdictions of the few committees which had monopolized the most important subjects.

Constituency Committees: Merchant Marine and Fisheries, and Post Office and Civil Service

Two committees which the early staff plans had earmarked for extinction, and which Select Committee members agreed were expendable, were the House Committees on Merchant Marine and Fisheries, and Post Office and Civil Service. Both catered to specific interest group constituencies, although the Merchant Marine committee actually had three prime areas of activity: the shipping industry, the outdoor sport ("field and stream") axis, and environmental quality. Post Office and Civil Service was concerned with public employees, and issues such as salaries, benefits and pensions. All of these areas could easily be assimilated into broader committees; and in the case of the environmental quality aspect, the various subcommittees which had competed for attention (and the distinction of getting their bills to the Rules Committee before the other) could all be integrated into a new energy or environment committee. On the grounds of coherence and one-tier rationality, these two committees were slated for abolition under the Bolling plan. As we shall see, these provisions especially regarding Merchant Marine provoked instant hostility in the affected constituencies, and among committee members themselves. The Chairwoman of Merchant Marine and Fisheries, Mrs. Leonor K. Sullivan, was particularly resentful of this untoward gesture by her Missouri colleague, Bolling. Ultimately, the Select Committee would relent and "refloat" Merchant Marine and Fisheries, after having experienced the fierce opposition it had engendered. This was a small issue on which the Select Committee felt it could compromise and still preserve the overall integrity of the plan. But as we shall see, the initial opposition of trade unions in the shipping industry would be of greater consequence than simply gaining the reinstatement of the Merchant Marine Committee. For, in addition, the Bolling committee was also proposing another reshuffle of vital concern to organized labor.

Splitting Education and Labor

The separation of Education and Labor was a long-time target of rationalist reformers; it had been the contentious item that had hamstrung the reorganization plan of the Joint Committee of 1966. But it was not its rationality which was the main reason for its prominence in these circumstances. The prime reason was political. As the most outspokenly liberal and rambunctious committee (continually having its bills overturned on the floor), Education and Labor was a prime target of Republicans and conservatives. Moreover, its conferees were suspected of being too cozy with their Senate colleagues. The chairman and staff were not held in high esteem in the House. Perhaps most significant of all, Minority Leader Ford was particularly anxious to split the Committee. Going back to the origins of the Select Committee itself, this item was probably Ford's *sine qua non* for support of the Select Committee. There was no logical or natural connection between Education matters and labor-management relations. However, historical forces had wedged them together.[66] And, at least in the eyes of outside liberals, and the Washington-based labor lobby, the fusion had been successful. Both were "bread and butter" issues for liberals, and placing both subjects in the same committee afforded activist liberals the opportunity to concentrate on one, and dabble in the other. Indeed, several members—among them the prominent DSG tacticians—chaired subcommittees on Education and Labor and had become acknowledged experts on their subjects; Brademas on education; O'Hara and Thompson on labor matters. Moreover, the AFL-CIO and representatives of the big international[67] unions had developed close ties with members of the committee, and saw the committee as the linch-pin of their influence in Congress. Liberal educationalists could pay obeisance to the labor cause and at the same time continue their good works in education. In addition, some labor sources believed that the combined labor and education jurisdiction served to dull the edges of a potentially acrimonious labor versus management conflict. To labor then, education was an insurance policy against "right to work"[68] anti-labor advocates flocking to a polarized committee.

The attractiveness to liberals of service on Education and Labor was confirmed by the character of its membership. Ratings of voting patterns showed Education and Labor members to be consistently among the most liberal in the House.[69] And their liberalism had been marked by an equally liberal dose of unruliness, a prime example of Fenno's "dispersed" committee.[70] Not unexpectedly, this liberalism and its proclivity to fractious internal conflict had augured a poor record of getting its bills approved on the House floor. It had also marked Education and Labor as a target for conservatives for substantive policy reasons, and of rationalists on process grounds.

Conservative Select Committee Vice-Chairman Dave Martin was an ardent proponent of splitting Education and Labor, as was Minority member Peter Frelinghuysen, both harboring less than fond memories of their service on the committee early in their careers. In his testimony before the Select Committee Minority Leader Ford had suggested separating the two subjects, as had Education and Labor ranking Republican Rep. Al Quie and Southern Democratic Ways and Means member, Rep. Phil Landrum. Liberal-leaning Democratic members of the Bolling committee recognized the incongruity of the existing jurisdiction and were receptive to its alteration in their quest for coherence. They felt that if they could win the support of organized labor, such a move would make for a more rational committee system.

With this in mind, Bolling had consulted his old friend and ally in innumerable liberal-labor campaigns, Andrew Biemiller, a former congressman from Wisconsin and veteran Legislative Director of the AFL-CIO. Bolling and Biemiller discussed the implications of an Education and Labor split; and Biemiller gave his consent on condition that the separation be effected in a way that did not materially diminish Labor's position on Capitol Hill. Later, in testimony before the Select Committee, Biemiller repeated that he was not averse to a separation.[71] Indeed, from Labor's perspective, given the right reshuffle of members, they might actually emerge in an even stronger position. For instance, if labor-oriented members of the present committee stayed with a new Labor Committee, labor might find the sympathetic Thompson as chairman of the new Labor Committee with such stalwarts as O'Hara, Burton, Meeds, and others looking out for labor's interests. Biemiller was willing to defer to his trusted ex-colleague Bolling. In Bolling's view, this was the "green light" of labor approval. Hence Bolling was able to back up politically what he believed personally: that he ". . . couldn't conceive of a rational proposal that would involve keeping the Labor and Education Committee together . . ."[72]

Diluting Ways and Means

As Ways and Means members had suspected, the Bolling Committee was taking a hard look at the jurisdiction of their jurisdictionally well-endowed committee as well. Because Ways and Means was the revenue raising committee, it swallowed up and jealously guarded virtually everything remotely connected with revenue. This included taxes (and thus the popular issue of tax reform), foreign trade, and other aspects of fiscal policy. It also embraced such weighty issues as the welfare system, food stamps, unemployment compensation, pensions, revenue sharing, health care and a number of related areas. One estimate was that 17.9 per cent of House bills in the 92nd Congress were referred to the Ways and Means Committee;[73] and when weighted according to relative importance of the legislation, it was no wonder that Wilbur Mills' legend in the House had prospered. Indeed, it was well within his power to postpone tax reform (as indeed he did) year after year. And when Mills or other Ways and Means members would contend that they had not had the time to deal with one pressing issue or other, this was legitimate. But then it was also an argument for reducing their work-load.

In the December 7 "Sarbanes-Steiger" working plan, Ways and Means was to have its jurisdiction diluted in the following areas: foreign trade would be given to Foreign Affairs (later to be re-named International Relations); substantial control over health insurance bills would go to a new Commerce and Health committee (which would take over much of the jurisdiction of the old Interstate and Foreign Commerce Committee). In the final plan proposed by the Bolling panel a balance sheet of the details of Ways and Means' losses and gains had them ceding maternal and child health jurisdiction to Commerce and Health; Public Debt matters to the new Budget Committee, Renegotiation (of currency agreements) to the Banking Committee (to be re-named Banking, Currency, and Housing), Revenue Sharing to the Government Operations Committee and WIN—the Work Incentive Program to re-train and re-employ workers—to the proposed new Labor Committee. As a small compensation for their considerable losses, Ways and Means would take over the Food Stamp Programs from the Agriculture Committee, and Foundations and Charitable Trusts from the Banking and Currency Committee.

Merging Energy and Environment

Energy was another area which seemed to cry out for rational realignment. The dispersed jurisdiction had diminished the capacity of Congress to develop a coherent policy that balanced energy needs and environmental constraints. Moreover, influential oil companies and increasingly active environmentalist groups added a dimension of conflict which would have to be considered in any reshuffle. And of course, the one-tier, exclusive committee approach suggested either a single energy committee and a separate environment committee, or the consolidation of all energy and environmental issues into one overarching committee. In the latter case, the new multi-interest panel would take over the functions of the various competing sub-committees and committees. The Bolling Committee answer—which came after a key endorsement by Ralph Nader's Congress Watch group—was to rename the Interior and Insular Affairs Committee the Energy and Environment Committee, and to give it control over the bulk of energy and environmental legislation. Some of the jurisdiction of the old Interior committee—such conservation issues as forests, national parks, public lands, and wild-life sanctuaries—would be shifted to the Agriculture Committee. But the new Energy and Environment Committee would become the focal point for the range of energy-related and ecology issues. A multi-interest committee would likely pit the oil industry against the environmentalists. But it seemed a good bet to produce a more coherent policy than did the existing scattered structure. As for the fears of domination by "big oil," the Bolling Committee figured that Nader was behind the joint jurisdiction. Hence, as with labor and the Education and Labor split, key political support had been marshalled behind the Bolling rationalization.

Little Jurisdictional Difficulties

There were other provisions of the rejurisdiction which were the source of immediate or potential difficulty. In the case of narrow interest groups, the burden was heavily on the side of the *status quo*. These groups had built up working relationships with the committees and subcommittees in the existing structure: Howard University, for example, is a Federally-funded, predominantly black educational institution in Washington, D.C. In the existing House structure, Howard University had been under the jurisdiction of Education and Labor, which had adopted a "hands off" approach to it. The Select Committee, having given the matter only brief attention, had (probably inadvertently) shifted Howard to the District of Columbia Committee, and suddenly found itself inundated with letters from Howard University officials and outside black groups who feared that the switch might carry with it an implicit threat of more active Congressional supervision (or interference). The Select Committee had not really given it enough attention for there even to have been the possibility of such a motive. It was a simple "mechanical" problem which the Select Committee quickly rectified, returning Howard University to the new Education Committee in their plan.

But there were other jurisdictional wrinkles which did not go away so easily. In a few cases, conflict could not be avoided. One such case was the jurisdiction for campaign spending legislation, including the issue of campaign finance reform which was increasingly topical in post-Watergate Washington. House Administration under its crafty Chairman Wayne Hays had control over the subject under the old structure. The Bolling Committee planned to transfer it to the Committee on Standards of Official Conduct, the so-called "Ethics" committee. Bolling and Hays were long-time antagonists; it came as no surprise to Hays that the Select Committee would include a provision which diminished his power.[74] The shift had provoked controversy during the Bolling deliberation; in fact, within the committee, Sarbanes had opposed placing this patently political subject matter in an ostensibly non-partisan committee.

There were other jurisdictional implications which cut innumerable different ways. And while those members affected adversely (or else, potentially threatened) quickly made known their dissatisfaction, those whom the plan might have benefited were hesitant to offer public support. In addition, there were enough ingredients in the plan to provide ammunition for those seeking reasons to oppose it.

A Rules Wrinkle

Much of the controversy surrounded the jurisdictional aspect of the plan. However, a jurisdictional matter which also touched on the Select Committee's procedural reforms was a provision giving more authority to the Rules Committee on bill referral matters (the role envisioned for the Speaker under earlier plans). The idea was to provide this committee, the "traffic controller" of legislation, a discretionary role to hear appeals from committees which had claims for particular pieces of legislation. Ideally this problem would be diminished somewhat by the over-all consolidation of jurisdictions. Nonetheless, the provision was destined to arouse suspicion since both Bolling and Martin were leading members of Rules. A plan which stripped other powerful House committees of substantial portions of their jurisdiction but actually extended Rules' power looked like a "power grab," especially in the view of those who were not Bolling admirers to begin with.

In Select Committee deliberations, this potential problem had been recognized. Sarbanes pointed out that there might be political problems. Bolling was frankly embarrassed.[75] However, the rest of the committee insisted that Rules was the logical place for the bill referral appeals mechanism. Moreover, Bolling had reportedly been considering giving up his Rules seat and devoting attention to Budget matters and his Joint Economic Committee assignment.[76] He also was contemplating another try for his long-coveted goal of party leadership. Hence he felt that the "power grab" charge had little force. But then, that did not stop people from mentioning it. And in fairness, those who were likely to give currency to the idea were not those who were likely to know Bolling's personal thinking on the matter. In any event, Dave Martin, the ranking Republican on Rules, decided to retire; so it was an argument doubly wide of the mark. But it was still another political lapse that served to undermine the Select Committee.

The Bipartisan Concessions

Two provisions particularly worrisome to Democrats were plans to increase Minority staffing and to abolish proxy voting. The five-five bipartisan composition of the Select Committee had already raised a few Democrats' eyebrows and elicited backroom grumbles. This reaction was most prevalent among those who tended to mistrust Bolling, and especially those who saw Dave Martin to be an intensely conservative, partisan Republican. Moreover, there had been a conventional wisdom from the committee's inception that the Minority members of the Select Committee were looking for a few minimum concessions out of a reorganization package, e.g. the long-awaited opportunity for more money to hire Republican staff and the abolition of proxy voting. Under proxy voting rules a committee member could leave a card authorizing another member—often the chairman or ranking member—to cast a vote on his behalf. Since the Majority had more members of each committee, to the extent that Congressional committees divide on party lines, this obviously favored the Majority. Thus Martin and the Minority side of the Bolling Committee steadfastly demanded these provisions and received backing from Committee Democrats. There was the issue of fairness, and the Majority of the Bolling Committee saw the merits of more staff support for Republicans and abolition of proxy voting. Perhaps, more to the point, these were both "pot sweeteners" to attract Republican support for the reorganization plan. A solid GOP vote might be enough to offset intense opposition from dispossessed Democrats. Thus a few overtures to the Republicans seemed to make sense both substantively and politically. And cooperation with the GOP fulfilled Bolling's desire to ensure that this was an institutional, bipartisan effort, one which would restructure the whole House in a way more enduring and beneficial than the 1946 reorganization, and which could not be alleged to favor the political ends of either part or the whole of the Democratic party.

Notes

1. This and the following chapter owe much to insights offered by participants during the course of the consideration of Committee reform. I wish to thank Rep. Paul Sarbanes for employing me in 1973, providing an excellent opportunity to view the committee's work first-hand—and again in 1975 and 1976 when the experience of Committee reform could be placed in the context of other reform developments. I am also grateful to Select Committee members and staff who spoke to me both informally and in interviews. Finally, I am extremely grateful to three political scientists for discussing with me their own work: David Lowe of the Johns Hopkins University, a Ph.D. dissertation on Organization theory and Committee reform (Lowe MS) *op. cit.* and Roger H. Davidson and Walter J. Oleszek, *Congress Against Itself* (Indianapolis: Indiana University Press, 1977). I also have profited from conversations with Davidson and Oleszek, both of whom were staff members of the Bolling Select Committee on Committees.

2. Figures are taken from the House Republican Conference *Legislative Digest*, Vol. III, No. 34, September 27, 1974, presumably drawn from Select Committee materials. I am grateful to the Republican Policy Committee and particularly Mrs. Martha Phillips for making available to me Republican materials. Also, Interview with Martha Phillips, Director, Republican Policy Committee, August 25, 1975. I am also grateful to the office of Rep. Barber Conable for making available to me additional Republican information on reform.

3. Republican Conference *Digest, Ibid.,* p. 11.

4. Or like Wilbur Mills on Ways and Means, they simply had no subcommittees; or like Vinson or Spence, they had "number subcommittees" without regular jurisdictions. Ways and Means was the prime offender in this regard, and the 1973 Subcommittee Bill of Rights did not deal with the problem. It would have to be dealt with later.

5. Critics and defenders of Congress alike were unanimous in their verdict that the oversight function was one of Congress's glaring inadequacies. See for example, Morris Ogul's testimony before the Bolling Committee: "Committee Organization in the House," *Hearings Before the Select Committee on Committees,* Vol. 2, pp. 701–709. (These hearings are hereafter cited "Select Committee.") Also see John Culver's remarks during the Committee hearings, for example *Select Committee,* Vol. 2, pp. 22–23, and Professor Richard Fenno's explanation on the same pages. By way of amplification, see David Mayhew, *Congress: The Electoral Connection* (New Haven: Yale University Press, 1974). Oversight, it seems clear, is not performed adequately because it does not offer sufficient political rewards.

6. This was the over-all trend, although it proceeded at different speeds and in varying degrees in various committees.
7. The two additions from the 19 specified in the 1946 Legislative Reorganization were Science and Astronautics in 1967 (in 1974 renamed Science and Technology when Space was de-emphasized in favor of other technological concerns) and Standards of Official Conduct in 1970.
8. The number of subcommittees is subject to slight fluctuation during any given session, it being the prerogative of committees to create and abolish them. This figure is for House standing Committees in early 1973 when the Select Committee on Committees began work. Inclusion of special and investigatory subcommittees as well brought the figure to "almost 150," Republican Conference *Digest*, September 27, 1974, *op. cit.*, p. 6.
9. See Rep. Leggett's testimony, *Select Committee*, Vol. 1, p. 234.
10. For example, Culver and Bolling. Bolling and the Speaker had been discussing the possibility for some time.
11. Of course, this precedent was cited more approvingly by those members who were disposed against the Bolling Plan than those for it—and most approvingly by those interviewees who viewed with immense alarm the prospect of splitting Education and Labor. Moreover, this factor was by no means the only impediment to the Legislative Reorganization Act's earlier passage. It was, however, one that "stuck" in the institution's informal history.
12. For example, prior to 1946 there were House Committees on Claims, the Census, Enrolled Bills, Flood Control, Patents, Pensions, Roads, War Claims, World War Veterans' Legislation, and Disposition of Executive papers. *Congressional Directory*, 79th Congress, First Session, August, 1945.
13. Richard Fenno, *Congressmen in Committees* (Boston: Little Brown, 1973).
14. See Mayhew, *Congress, The Electoral Connection, op. cit.*
15. Woodrow Wilson, *Congressional Government* (New York: Meridian, 1956; first published in 1885).
16. Rep. Bolling is fond of this term; see, for example, his statement: "I happen to think that the House is messy, the House will continue to be messy. It was messy under Cannon, under Clay, under Rayburn, under Albert, and it will be messy under whomever comes along. I think there is a very good reason. It is a highly philosophical one but terribly practical. That is that the democratic process is messy, thank God." *Select Committee*, Vol. 2, p. 58.
17. These included the sheer frustration with the unwieldiness of the system, widespread public dissatisfaction with Congressional performance, increasing presidential derogation of Congress, and internal demands for stronger leadership. The perceptual aspect was illustrated by Bolling's remark to Albert: "If you think it's time . . ., then it's time . . ." Davidson and Oleszek, *op. cit.* See, p. 67.
18. Letter from Rep. John Culver to Democratic members, December 29, 1973. Also see Richard L. Lyons, "Albert, Others Ask Reshaping of Committees," *Washington Post*, January 16, 1973, p. A4.
19. See *The Congressional Record*, January 31, 1971, p. H594.
20. See James M. Naughton, "House Rules Chairman Favors Floor Amend-

ments to Tax Bills," *The New York Times,* January 9, 1973, p. 7.
21. See Chapter 4 of *House Out of Order, op. cit.,* pp. 79–115. Bolling begins the chapter with a quotation from George Bernard Shaw: "The worst cliques are those that consist of one man." Also see *Power In the House, op. cit.,* p. 200 and Bolling's rebuke of Schwengel in the Legislative Reorganization amendments debate on seniority; see p. 60.
22. This information regarding mood and murmurs is based on interviews with O'Hara, Conlon, Cable, Cohen and Kamm.
23. Several DSG sources mentioned this.
24. Interview with Rep. Richard Bolling, September 19, 1975.
25. Hays Interview. Hays added, alluding to Mills' subsequent personal difficulties and resignation as Chairman of Ways and Means, "They (the Speaker and Bolling) were out to destroy Wilbur before he destroyed himself."
26. *Congressional Record,* January 31, 1973, p. H602.
27. Used by a number of sources interviewed; Cable, Hays, Conlon. This was generally recognized.
28. This was an informal group of liberal Democrats led by Bolling that met for coffee and conversation, a variation on Rayburn's old "Board of Education."
29. Davidson, Kovenock and O'Leary, *Congress in Crisis, op. cit.*
30. See the paper by Victor C. Ferkiss, "The Shape of the Future," *Select Committee,* Vol. 2, pp. 860–863.
31. A remark by Bolling. *CQ Weekly Report,* November 24, 1973, p. 3084.
32. Happily, the Davidson and Oleszek, and Lowe studies help fill the void.
33. The Library of Congress's Congressional Research Service produced a short summary of recommendations proposed at the hearings. It is by no means exhaustive. The best source is the complete set of *Select Committee Hearings and Panel Discussions, op. cit.*
34. *Select Committee,* Vol. 3, p. 414.
35. *Select Committee,* Vol. 3, p. 416.
36. This may seem obvious. However, see the testimony of Rep. Bella Abzug, in which she advocated abolition of all standing Committees to be replaced by "ad hoc" committees of the Caucuses. *Select Committee,* Vol. 1, pp. 373–375.
37. *Select Committee,* Vol. 3, p. 415.
38. *Ibid.* They also provide a less controversial "procedural lesson": "A large and secure room with a blackboard or chart space is essential."
39. *Select Committee,* Vol. 3, p. 419.
40. *Select Committee,* Vol. 3, p. 427.
41. Internal Memorandum: Bolling's Background Ideal Plan circulated to Select Committee Members and Staff, August, 1973.
42. *Select Committee,* Vol. 3, p. 448.
43. *Ibid.*
44. See p. 117n.
45. *Select Committee,* Vol. 3, p. 448.
46. *Ibid.*
47. See paper by Joseph Cooper and David W. Brady, *Select Committee,* Vol. 3, p. 541–563.

48. *Select Committee,* Vol. 3, p. 460.
49. *Ibid.*
50. *Ibid.*
51. *Ibid.* Of course, in opening up Congress to more outside pressure, via these additional points of access, this particular reform would have moved Congress in a direction it was already heading—mainly through its subcommittees. But there was little direct focus on implications for specific interest groups at this early stage. Of course, this would become more of a factor when abolition of narrow, interest-oriented committees was proposed.
52. *Ibid.* This anticipated the sources of eventual opposition to the Bolling plan. It is testimony to Bolling's quest for a rational plan as well as his emphasis on keeping the staff removed from political second-guessing that their presentations did not contain more of this type of speculation.
53. *Select Committee,* Vol. 3, p. 470. Also see p. 476.
54. *Select Committee,* Vol. 3, p. 462.
55. *Ibid.,* p. 476.
56. *Ibid.,* p. 478.
57. This was a procedure by which funds appropriated by Congress could be withheld if the President determined that an administrative objective would be served. The Anti-Deficiency Act of 1906 had created the precedent for use of impoundment and presidents since that time had used this power on occasion.
58. The Joint Study Committee on Budget Control, composed of 32 members held hearings and recommended changes included in H.R. 7130, passed by the House on December 5, 1973 by a 386–3 vote. Bolling was floor manager of the bill.
59. Bolling Interview.
60. *Select Committee,* Vol. 2, p. 5.
61. See *Select Committee,* Vol. 1, pp. 373–375.
62. *Select Committee,* Vol. 1, p. 32.
63. Davidson and Oleszek, *Congress Against Itself,* p. 135.
64. Although he still insisted that the staff draft an alternative two-tier scheme just in case the Committee reconsidered.
65. Staff member Linda Kamm drew up the set of alternatives.
66. There was a Committee on Education and Labor from 1867 to 1883. The two were severed for 73 years, then put back together again in the consolidation of committees in the 1946 Legislative Reorganization Act.
67. American unions are dubbed "international" because they have Canadian affiliates.
68. A provision requiring "open shops"—forbidding mandatory membership of trade unions—the bane of American trade unionism.
69. For example, in 1973, only four of the twenty-one Democrats on Education and Labor had ratings in opposition to the Conservative Coalition below 65%. See *CQ Almanac,* 1973, pp. 950–951.
70. Fenno, *Congressmen in Committees, op. cit.*
71. *Select Committee,* Vol. 1, p. 223.
72. Davidson and Oleszek, *Congress Against Itself, op. cit.,* p. 172.
73. Republican Conference *Digest,* September 27, 1974, *op. cit.,* p. 7.

74. Hays Interview.
75. Bolling noted during the Select Committee mark-up sessions: "When I first reported to the Speaker on what the committee had produced back until December, (sic) I went up to him and said: 'I want particularly to call your attention to the fact that I am embarrassed by the fact that the Committee on Rules loses nothing and gains a particular function, this one, and that we have invaded your territory because what we gained is some of your power. It institutionalizes your power and, in effect, modifies it.' He was a little startled by this, but he has sense and has had opportunity to examine it and I have heard no great complaint." See "Committee Reform Amendments of 1974 Open Business Meeting," *Select Committee on Committees*, 93rd Congress, Second Session, 1974. p. 253.
76. Bolling and Kamm Interviews. Although Bolling's devotion to Rules, and his subsequent chairmanship of that Committee call all this somewhat into question.

Five

Committee Reform II: Side-Tracking the Bolling Plan and the Adoption of the Hansen Plan, 1973–1974

5:1 A COALITION OF "NATURAL ENEMIES"[1]: MOBILIZING OPPOSITION TO THE BOLLING PLAN

Political Background

A Mixed Reception

When the "Sarbanes-Steiger" draft of the Bolling Plan was released on December 7, 1973 it met with a "wait and see" attitude. The mammoth impact the plan would have if adopted was slow to sink in. Moreover, the oft-mentioned Bolling emphasis on the "concept" of a streamlined one-tier structure with 15 exclusive "major committees" seemed unusually theoretical to an institution noted for its pragmatism. This portent of potentially sweeping change was perceived only by those who were watching closely.

One such member was Rep. John Dingell, whose position would have been particularly disrupted under a one-tier system. Dingell told *Congressional Quarterly*, "The only good thing I can say about (the committee's report) is that it is written on disposable paper."[2] Dingell, perhaps the ultimate example of the havoc rejurisdiction could wreak, was an influential member of the Interstate and Foreign Commerce Committee. He was also a favorite of environmentalists as the Chairman of the Merchant Marine Subcommittee on Fisheries, Wildlife Conservation, and the Environment. Finally, he chaired a subcommittee on the Select Committee on Small Business.[3] The one-tier concept would force him to choose between his Commerce and Environmental specialties, risk not getting a subcommittee chair on his "major" committee and would force him to give up the Small Business post altogether.

Dingell had transparently obvious personal reasons to object to the changes. But in addition to attacking the details of Bolling's plan, he also disputed its conceptual underpinnings:

> This means that members are effectively disenfranchised from broad areas of interest. It means the House has a diminished corps of experts. Let's take energy. You've got three or four committees that have an interest in energy, and when a proposal comes up on the floor, you have a lively, interesting, and intelligent debate. Where you have only one committee working on it, the committee settles its hash before it brings it to the floor, and there's never a really effective test as to the validity of the judgments of the committee. . . .[4]

Dingell's idea of "multi-interest" representation was on the floor of the House, not in committee. However, Dingell was one of the few early critics to focus on theory as well as the practical implications. Most of the initial reactions tended to result from disconcerting answers to the inevitable question of "how will it affect me?"; although for many it was still too early to tell with certainty. The draft plan itself was subject to change in the Bolling Committee mark-up session, and the ultimate effects of a wholesale reshuffle would not be known until members vied for assignments on the new "major" committees. Majority Whip John McFall noted this unresolved problem in a "Whip Advisory" notice issued on December 14, 1973, summarizing the Bolling draft. "Still under study are the questions of how to assign Members of abolished committees to new committees and how much seniority these transferees would retain."[5] This would be a crucial factor in gaining acceptance of any reorganization. It was all very well to construct a grandiose new scheme for rationalization, but not at the expense of members' carefully plotted in-House careers.

The Bolling Committee knew that they could not encroach on the party's right to name committee members, and they rejected a rigid "grandfather clause" as self-defeating. The best they could recommend was that members forced to choose between two or more "A" committees should be guaranteed their choice of assignment. Members who sat on committees which had a "significant portion" of their jurisdiction transferred should be permitted to follow the jurisdiction to the new committee, where their seniority should receive "meaningful recognition."[6] This—even with the good faith of the Speaker behind it—struck many as a rather equivocal pronouncement, and did not allay the fears of members who mistrusted the Democratic Committee on Committees.

For others the handwriting was on the wall. Members of Ways and Means, and Education and Labor had their worst suspicions confirmed. Members of the Post Office and Civil Service, Merchant Marine and Fisheries, and Internal Security Committees were threatened with abolition and transfer of their functions to new "multi-interest" committees.

A few of the dispossessed reacted to the possibility of displacement with an air of resignation: Thaddeus Dulski, Chairman of Post Office and Civil Service for example. Others were not so self-sacrificing. For example, the House Internal Security Committee members were intent on saving their committee,[7] and could rely on a nation-wide clientele of assorted organizations of self-proclaimed patriots.

The most forceful attack on the December 7 draft was that of the Merchant Marine and Fisheries Committee. Mrs. Sullivan, the chairwoman, was quick to make known her displeasure. The Bolling Committee would soon be inundated with letters of protest from Merchant Marine-related outside groups.[8]

The Education and Labor, and Ways and Means camps were surprisingly quiet. Both were expected to be displeased by the plan; and both contained influential House figures who might seek to mount a counteroffensive. However, a possible explanation for the lack of overt activity against the Bolling plan was the fact that these two pockets of potential opposition—composed of members most disadvantaged by the plan—were on opposite poles of the committee system, both in their general demeanor and ideology. Education and Labor was the unruly bastion of liberals, DSG-activists, and social program enthusiasts. Ways and Means was the stalwart center of the House establishment, well-known for its conservative economic policy stances. The two committees were "natural enemies"[9] having lined up against each other on hundreds of substantive and procedural votes in the past. They had also been on opposite sides in the Party reform debate. Even now that they were threatened by the same source, they seemed improbable bedfellows.

Individuals upset by the plan perused it, some making no secret of their disinclination to accept it. Rep. Dingell of Merchant Marine persisted in his early outrage, and continued to lambast the Bolling plan, often vitriolically. Mills of Ways and Means, although in failing health, wrote to Bolling pointing out his areas of disagreement.[10] Wayne Hays was anxious to restore the campaign finance jurisdiction to his House Administration Committee. But when considered individually, those members offended by the Bolling plan seemed unlikely allies: Education and Labor members, and leading DSG figures: Burton, O'Hara, Thompson, Brademas, Eckhardt, and the likes of Sullivan, Hays, Mills, Ichord of House Internal Security, and others. The Bolling Committee, if nothing else, had seemingly isolated and divided its opposition. Hence the Bolling Committee could initially interpret the relative quietude and inchoate character of its opposition as a favorable sign. Moreover, they could envision passage of their plan over the opposition of self-interested Democrats on the Left (Education and Labor) and Right of the Party (Ways and Means), by consolidating the rest of the Democrats with the presumed solid support of the Republicans, thought to have been "bought off" by the minority concessions. What the Bolling people failed to anticipate was a coalition of these "natural enemies."

Activity

The Origins of Opposition

Mrs. Sullivan promptly communicated what she considered to be the ominous news of Bolling's plans to various outside groups intimately involved with her Committee, and encouraged them to make known their own disapproval. Maritime labor organizations, led by Paul Hall of the Seafarers, were especially active. And this was only a small part of what became a massive letter-writing campaign. The Select Committee received 175 communications favoring reinstatement of Merchant Marine and Fisheries[11] from shipping firms, labor unions and trade associations, other groups, and perhaps more surprisingly, from Federal and State agencies who dealt with the subject. That Federal Government departments were offering advice to Congress on how to organize itself was only one more indication of the extent to which clientelism had permeated the existing system.

The Merchant Marine Committee's transportation functions would be shifted to the new Energy and Environment Committee under the Bolling plan. The shipping industry feared that a "multi-interest" panel might prove less committed to the policy of generous subsidies for America's decreasingly profitable merchant marine. Environmentalists, for their part, had become accustomed to a sympathetic hearing from Dingell's sub-committee. The maritime unions catalyzed labor concern about the reshuffle. In response to the outcry over Merchant Marine, the Bolling Committee reversed itself, reinstating the committee as a small concession to expediency. But the incident jolted the rest of the trade union hierarchy to scrutinize the rest of the plan for rejurisdiction. The intensity of feeling engendered by the maritime unions had moved the debate well beyond the informal arrangement between Bolling and Biemiller, the AFL-CIO legislative director. The Maritime Unions had not been placated by the reinstatement of Merchant Marine and Fisheries. Unions of public employees were also concerned about the prospect of losing the Post Office and Civil Service Committee. These specific grievances, and a more general mood of mistrust, awakened fears about the precise implications of a new "multi-interest" membership Labor Committee.

By late February when the AFL-CIO Executive met in Bal Harbor, Florida, Bolling's understanding with Biemiller had been overtaken by political events; the Merchant Marine debacle had scuttled hopes for an accord between Bolling and labor. This was partly because the maritime unions were especially potent in the trade union movement as a ready source of pickets. Their opposition was enough to undermine Biemiller's position on the Education and Labor separation issue.

Two more factors figured prominently in labor's attitude toward a new Labor Committee: its likely chairman and its composition. Labor's clear preference for chairman was Frank Thompson, an experienced and dependable ally of labor and chairman of the Select Labor Subcommittee of Education and Labor. However, Thompson took his time deciding what he would do were he required to choose between new, separate Labor and Education Committees. While he had developed close ties with labor over the years, his New Jersey constituency encompassed both the predominantly blue-collar Trenton as well as the academic community of Princeton. In addition, he had recently become interested in the issue of government support for the arts, a subject which would fall to the new Education Committee. If Thompson took the helm of the Labor Committee, it would mean deserting his education and arts interest, and in addition abandoning his secure political base as Chairman of the House Administration Subcommittee on Accounts. This, along with the potential internal contentiousness of a Labor Committee polarized on labor versus management lines, served to dispose Thompson against the switch. He continued to hedge on whether he would actually make the move were the Bolling plan to be adopted. But he clearly preferred to keep Education and Labor together if possible.

Looking past the reluctant Thompson, labor tacticians focused on the other possible candidates. The next highest ranking members on Education and Labor were Reps. John Dent of Pennsylvania and Dominick Daniels of New Jersey, both viewed as generally pro-labor but neither of whom inspired great enthusiasm in labor circles. Dent was seen as erratic, and Daniels a useful subcommittee chairman but no match for Thompson as full committee chairman. Moreover, another positively unsettling possibility for labor lobbyists was the spectre of David Henderson of North Carolina. Henderson, a conservative Democrat and Ranking Democrat on Post Office and Civil Service, was under certain circumstances[12] a potential Labor Committee Chairman under the new plan. Henderson was as completely unacceptable to labor as Thompson was completely acceptable. This dearth of possible chairmen—were Thompson to demur—heightened labor's appreciation of the familiar arrangement of the existing Education and Labor Committee.

By February of 1974 it was clear that most of the Education and Labor liberals like Thompson were anxious not to have to make a choice between the two. Brademas clearly did not want to abandon Education; O'Hara would undoubtedly opt for Labor (although he was also weighing a possible Senate candidacy) but he became a zealous opponent of the Bolling plan in hopes that he would not have to choose. Phillip Burton became increasingly critical as well. Moreover, both strong personalities, ambitious for internal House power, and commonly accused of abrasiveness, he and Bolling had never been allies. In addition, Burton was a Party reform man, the DSG Chairman who had steered the Caucus reform movement through its hitherto most productive period. As a key figure on the Hansen Committee, Burton had worked to hammer out compromise, all the while carefully respecting the balance of power in the Caucus. Perhaps most glaring of all, Burton was an advocate of "spreading the action" to middle-range members, even if he also eventually seemed a likely candidate for the role of a forceful party leader. Far from being an autocrat, Burton was the consummate broker. Bolling, on the other hand, had always championed strong leadership—soundly rooted in the party, but the institution-wide dominant force as well. His insistently bipartisan, institutional orientation had disturbed Burton from the Select Committee's inception.

By late winter 1974 with the draft plan unveiled, Burton viewed

Bolling's apparent concessions to Martin as unnecessarily ceding too much to the Republicans. This issue of concessions to the Minority was particularly salient in the late Winter and early Spring of 1974. By then, the political atmosphere in Washington had been transformed. When Albert, Bolling and Ford had concocted their bipartisan committee in the Winter of 1972 and 1973, Richard Nixon was riding high after the biggest Presidential landslide since 1936. The Republicans in Congress were characteristically able to coalesce effectively with Southern Democrats, and had been extraordinarily successful in sustaining Presidential vetoes.[13] Thus in January of 1973, a bipartisan, institutional approach seemed a perfectly reasonable means for the leadership to attempt to consolidate its power, aiming to knock down a few sources of obstruction in the committee system. However, the Summer of 1973 had witnessed the revelations of Watergate, fanned by the Ervin Senate Select Committee on Presidential Campaign Practices. By the Spring, Nixon was fighting to save his presidency; impeachment was in the air; and the Congressional Republicans were seen by most commentators to be courting electoral disaster in November 1974. This was no time, argued partisan Democrats, to enact a reform that the Democrats might have to live with for another 27 years (since the last reorganization). The Bolling plan "at its maximum was the minimum Dave Martin would accept."[14] This would become a refrain of anti-Bolling plan Democrats, seeking to delay consideration of H. Res. 988: Better to wait until after the new Congress convened in 1975 and to reform the institution under more favorable conditions. Bolling, on the other hand, was anxious to bring a bill to the floor. It was against this background that a strategy to oppose the Bolling plan crystallized.

Summoning the Hansen Committee

The relative absence, meanwhile, of overt anti-Bolling plan activity on the part of the Education and Labor members veiled intense anxiety in that committee. One member described their reaction to the December 7 Bolling draft: "We wondered what the hell they were doing over there." Another source close to key Education and Labor figures remembered: "They looked at it and began to go through the goddamned roof."

Education and Labor staffers were dispatched to sit in on the Bolling Committee mark-up sessions in February and early March, 1974, especially William Cable who soon became Education and Labor's inside expert on the Bolling plan. What was now a monitoring operation might later become the basis for a counter-attack to avert separation of the committee. The open mark-ups went ahead under the watchful scrutiny of Cable and other potential opponents. In fact, on a few occasions, Lloyd Meeds actually consulted Cable for his views on aspects of the Education and Labor rejurisdiction. Cable prepared daily summaries keeping his Committee apprised of developments. The controversy would be carried over to the Democratic Caucus,[15] where Bolling had pledged to send his plan before it went to the Rules Committee and House floor. From outside the Congress organized labor was now resolutely in favor of retention of the existing Education and Labor Committee; and inside, members of the affected Committee, especially after issuance of the final Bolling resolution on March 16, 1974, were quietly assessing ways to defeat the entire plan.[16]

In late April 1974, three men ate lunch together in the National Democratic Club in the old Congressional Hotel (the same room where the plan to set up the Hansen Committee had been hatched in 1970, with Bolling present). The three were Richard Conlon, Ken Young—Biemiller's top assistant at the AFL-CIO—and Don Baker of the Education and Labor staff. They blended in with the usual crush of congressmen, staff, lobbyists, and journalists who frequented the dining room. However, on this particular occasion, the gathering was enough to evoke visions of conspiratorial anti-Bolling Committee scheming in the eyes of Linda Kamm of the Select Committee staff who happened to notice the trio. Indeed, at this time when DSG was becoming more and more deeply divided over the relative merits of the Bolling plan, and when the Education and Labor forces had vowed to work for its defeat, here was the chief DSG reform architect chatting over lunch with a key labor lobbyist and a staff member of the threatened committee itself. Of course, these three were perfectly logical luncheon companions, all veterans of numerous common legislative efforts. Indeed, Conlon maintains that the timing of this particular lunch was "a coincidence."[17]

Still, when the subject of the Bolling plan came up, there was little hesitation to decry the scheme that was racking Conlon's organization, challenging the carefully cultivated influence of AFL-CIO—making life more difficult for Young, and threatening to dismember Baker's committee. They acknowledged that Bolling had said all along that the plan would be sent to the two party caucuses. Intent on doing it the "right way," Bolling sincerely believed that the parties had a right to review the plan, assuring full hearted consent of the parties and institution for such a thorough-going revamping. Of course, Bolling was aware that this would provide an opportunity for the plan's opponents to organize, but he felt that this was a risk that would have to be taken. Focusing on this very point, Conlon, Young and Baker turned to the inevitable question of what the Caucus should do with (or to) the Bolling plan. Conlon was in a ticklish position. DSG was officially neutral and its membership was hopelessly split on the issue. Further, Committee Reform was not an issue—like Party Reform—upon which the DSG Executive had devised a strategy behind which its rank and file would fall into line. In such situations DSG's leaders had indulged in behind-the-scenes maneuvers to implement their commonly agreed-upon reform proposals. In the present circumstances, however, the DSG chairman was Culver, the forceful Bolling Committee member and advocate of forward-looking institutional change; and DSG members Meeds, Sarbanes, and Bolling himself were seeking DSG support for their plan—just as they had supported the DSG Caucus reforms. On the other side, many of the veteran leaders of the past DSG reform campaigns, Burton, O'Hara, Thompson, Brademas, Eckhardt and others were now solidly arrayed against what was billed as "Committee reform," but which they did not regard as reform at all. Although Conlon had sympathized with the goal of rationalizing the committee structure, the specifics of this particular plan and its substantive implications which might damage liberal strength had strained his neutrality. He was caught in the middle, a moving force in a group which was unable to agree on which direction to move. Conlon tried to make sure that all DSG reports on the subject maintained a scrupulous objectivity.[18] Still, at the same time he discussed with his old allies Burton and O'Hara possible ways to resolve the issue to their liking.

When the subject of Caucus consideration of the Bolling plan came up over lunch, it concerned the mechanics of Caucus procedure. But there was an implicit understanding that they were all anxious to find a way to alter the Bolling plan. Of course, the ultimate recourse was to amend it on the House floor under an open rule, as DSG had done back in 1970 with their Legislative Reorganization amendments. But this was a risky business to let the plan survive intact until this late in the process. Moreover, the issue at hand was how to get the Democratic Caucus to authorize changes. There were a few possibilities. The plan could be debated on the Caucus floor, but this was likely to create problems of manageability. On the Caucus floor—as on the floor of the House—an open-ended debate might descend into chaos.

And this sensitive issue could easily provoke abusive innuendoes and *ad hominem* attacks. The most attractive alternative was to refer the Bolling plan to a smaller committee of the Caucus, such as the trusty Hansen Committee on Organization, Study and Review.

When Conlon suggested the Hansen Committee alternative, "light bulbs lit up."[19] There was an incontrovertible logic to the idea; the Hansen Committee had originally been set up to review reform proposals; *these* were reform proposals; the Hansen Committee had acquitted itself well in the past; and virtually everyone agreed that it represented the various cleavages in the full Caucus. It seemed perfectly sensible to send the Bolling plan to the party committee that had experience with reform. Of course, there were obvious political motives at work as well. The Hansen Committee included such notable foes of the Bolling plan as O'Hara, Burton, Thompson, Hays, and Waggonner and Landrum, both members of Ways and Means. The Committee was representative of the whole party, and was unquestionably over-representative of the anti-Bolling factions. When Conlon floated the Hansen Committee idea to Burton and O'Hara, the response in both cases was "Of course."[20] The three set the wheels in motion for a draft resolution requesting that the Caucus delegate to the Hansen Committee the task of reviewing the Bolling proposals.

There was a sizeable body of sentiment in the party, and slightly less so within the Hansen Committee itself, that the Bolling plan should be killed outright. Members of both Education and Labor, and Ways and Means thought this to be their only sure means of keeping their committees intact. And with the end of the session in sight, it was possible that the anti-Bolling forces could delay consideration until the next Congress. Bolling had pushed his Committee hard to bring out their plan in time to get a bill to the floor by sometime in the Spring, in order to pass a reorganization safely before election-year politics intervened. This posed a sensitive political problem for liberal Democrats who had been ardent proponents of DSG's approach to Congressional reform. However, that was Party reform, designed to enhance liberal fortunes. Suddenly they found themselves branded as anti-reform by Bolling proponents. Beyond the fractious debate among Democrats this was another instance where the Republicans might try to embrace the Congressional reform issue, especially if the Democratic Caucus were to bottle up the Bolling plan in what looked like a cynical pre-emption of consideration on the House floor.

The question was whether or not to kill it by referring the plan to

Hansen without a "report back" date. Some sectors of the anti-Bolling alliance—Ways and Means, Post Office and Civil Service, and a few Education and Labor members—were quite prepared to withstand charges of anti-reformism in order to preserve their domains. Others favored an early report back date which would allow Hansen to re-draft a Committee reform and give the House a chance to consider it before the end of the session. This would both rescue reforms (mainly procedural ones) that Party reformers could accept, and undercut the Republicans' charge of Democratic coolness to reform. It is a matter of speculation whether there were enough votes in Caucus to refer the plan to Hansen without a report back date. (A DSG "quiet Whip check" implied that there were not.)[21] In the event, Mills and his supporters did not press the point.

On May 1 and 2, the Democratic Caucus met to discuss the plan. Emotions ran high on all sides. Bolling, Sarbanes and Meeds ex-plained the rationale behind it. They favored a Caucus vote to en-dorse their plan, followed by sending the bill to the Rules Committee and promptly to the floor, so as to pass it before the Nixon impeach-ment issue monopolized attention. The anti-Bolling forces had staked their hopes on delay and detour to the Hansen Committee. On May 2, Phillip Burton spoke out against the plan, and gave notice that he would ask the Caucus to refer H. Res. 988 to Hansen.

On May 9, Burton introduced his motion[22] calling for recommenda-tions within about sixty days, and with an added proviso to prevent Bolling Committee supporters from circumventing Hansen and the Caucus by getting a rule and sending it straight to the floor. The Rules Committee, where both Bolling and Martin wielded considerable power, technically had the power to do so; only Bolling's conviction that the parties should participate had sent the bill to Caucus in the first place. While Bolling was extremely unlikely to renege on his pledge, another advocate of the Bolling plan could always present a privileged motion to take the bill to the floor; perhaps Martin, or Republican Conference Chairman John Anderson who also served on Rules. The Bolling Committee asked for a vote to reject this motion, and then to pass a motion referring the plan to Rules and the floor. Bolling and the Speaker canvassed support for a straight referral to Rules while Burton and the diverse collection of foes worked to gain a majority for referral to Hansen. While this anti-Bolling coalition in-cluded most of the powerful committee leaders whom DSG had sought to undermine in their Party reform efforts, the House establishment had found a reformer, Burton, to spearhead the campaign to defeat Committee reform—which, he contended "really isn't reform."[23] Other DSG reformers agreed.

Shortly after Burton introduced his motion, William Clay of Missouri—another vigorously anti-Bolling Education and Labor member—made a motion that the vote be conducted by secret ballot, which carried 98–81. Bolling quickly demanded a roll call vote. However, amidst considerable disarray on the floor, Teague somehow misconstrued Bolling's motion, and questioned whether it was in order under Caucus rules. Obviously confused, Teague (the Caucus Chairman) recessed the Caucus temporarily, while he consulted a member of the House Parliamentarian's staff. (This was Caucus session, so no parliamentarian was on duty.) Teague's muddled re-telling of the facts of the Bolling motion (requesting a roll call vote on the Clay motion to conduct a secret ballot vote on the Burton motion) was phrased in such a manner as to cause the parliamentarian to agree that Bolling was out of order. In fact, Bolling was perfectly justified in his action.[24] However, Teague returned to the chamber, reconvened the Caucus, and then—incorrectly—ruled Bolling's motion out of order under Caucus rules. The vote on Burton's motion would proceed by secret ballot.

Now insulated by the secret ballot, Democrats who harbored misgivings about the Bolling plan but who might have felt obliged to support it because it was "reform," responded by voting their fears. When the secret ballots were counted, the Caucus had voted 111–95 to refer the Bolling plan to the Hansen Committee. But the idea of demanding a recount, especially after it had been made clear that Teague had erred in his ruling disallowing the Bolling motion, was rejected by Bolling himself: even if he could now overturn the vote, it would be a pyrrhic victory. He would prefer to let the plan go to Hansen and hope for the best. Once again Bolling was unswerving in his belief that it must be done "the right way," even when the other side had profited from an obviously unparliamentary device to sidetrack his plan.

In the middle of May, the Democratic Caucus Committee on Organization, Study and Review convened to review the plan. The eleven members: Mrs. Hansen, O'Hara, Thompson, Burton, Hays, Waggonner, Landrum, Neal Smith of Iowa, Frank Annunzio of Illinois, Ed Jones of Tennessee, and Barbara Jordan of Texas reportedly included a solid anti-Bolling majority, nine to two by one estimate.[25] No major defender of the Bolling plan served on the Committee. Its recommendations might prove substantial.

The Hansen Committee at Work

On May 13, the Hansen Committee gathered for its first meeting in the ornate old "Board of Education Room" in the Capitol not far from the House floor, which had been Speaker Rayburn's meeting place for his legendary after-hours strategy sessions. There, over bourbon, the Speaker and his lieutenants would devise legislative strategy. Now in the same room, the Hansen Committee began poring over the plan produced by Bolling—one of Rayburn's few surviving political proteges—and plotting its undoing.

The Hansen Committee's approach contrasted markedly with that of the Bolling Committee. Certainly the Hansen Committee had benefited from the Bolling Committee's earlier research; indeed, their starting point for discussion was a copy of Part II of the Bolling Committee print, H. Res. 988. Their terms of reference, as in the official title of their Committee, were to study and review the proposals. But even then, the composition, assumptions, *modus operandi*, and style of the committee assumed that their review would yield conclusions worlds apart from those of the Committee whose work they were studying.

If the Bolling Committee was slanted toward an intellectual approach which disposed it toward "organizing principles" and ultimately the modified one-tier approach, the Hansen Committee's orientation was intensely political and anti-theoretical in orientation. They were substantially unmoved by the Bolling Committee's plea for conceptual coherence. Burton, Hays and Waggonner were among the House's more noted fixers and bargainers, and the rest of the Committee from Mrs. Hansen, to Landrum, Smith, Annunzio, Jones and the impressive first-termer Barbara Jordan, a graduate of the rough-and-tumble of Texas politics, was heavily weighted toward political pragmatism. If the Bolling Committee had been branded "Boy Scouts" by their critics, the Hansen Committee included the nearest equivalent to a Congressional Mafia. They had earlier been able to engineer deals to achieve carefully balanced incremental Party reform. Now they were dealing with the very basis of internal power, and while the Bolling Committee had adopted an essentially "let the chips fall where they may" approach, Hansen members remained acutely aware of the personal ramifications of Committee reform.

The difference in orientations was manifested in divergent assumptions and methods. The Bolling Committee had started from an ideal plan; the Hansen Committee started from the standpoint of existing political alignments. From there they examined the Bolling report to see what alterations it made. Moreover, with two members of Ways and Means, three of Education and Labor, and three on House Administration who wanted to maintain their own existing jurisdictions, compounded by a disposition toward the "spread the action" approach symbolized by Burton during the drive for Caucus reform, it was not surprising that the Committee viewed jurisdictional change as profoundly disruptive. Whereas the Bolling Committee was a one-year investigation drawing on its own staff of trained academics and professionals, the Hansen Committee held a series of fifteen meetings over the course of two months (including the recesses), relying only on the "volunteer" staff assistance of two men, Mrs. Hansen's aide Joe Carter, and the Education and Labor staffer Bill Cable, who had been monitoring the Bolling Committee's mark-up sessions. The Bolling Committee may have been long on research power, but the Hansen Committee was lean and focused on political implications.

The Substance of the Hansen Plan

The Hansen Committee divided their work into two main areas, the procedural, and the jurisdictional. From the beginning, many Hansen members expressed private hostility to the Bolling rejurisdiction. A few on the Committee were personal adversaries of Bolling as well. But perhaps more significant was the Hansen Committee's mistrust of theories applied to Congressional practice. One Hansen source described the Bolling Committee as "a little too bright, a lot too theoretical."[26] Hence the one-tier concept was dismissed almost out of hand as unrealistic and profoundly disruptive; better to focus attention on the procedural questions which involved using power, rather than shifting it.

There was deep disagreement within the Committee over how to deal with the sensitive question of jurisdictional changes. O'Hara, a steadfast opponent of splitting Education and Labor, favored producing a report in two sections, one on procedural matters and another on jurisdiction. This way they might introduce some attractive procedural reforms while at the same time scuttling the Bolling proposals for realigning jurisdictions. Burton favored a full-scale Hansen Committee reshuffle of jurisdictions. Mrs. Hansen, while not necessarily favoring an elaborate rejurisdiction like Burton, did concur with the necessity of producing a unified report on the entire Bolling plan. They must honor the Caucus request to report back by July Caucus, she argued, and this meant a verdict on the Bolling package once-and-for-all.

It was mainly the realization that the jurisdictional angle would be the most prickly problem, however, that caused the Hansen Committee to take up procedural issues first. Moreover, procedural reform might provide the Hansen Committee the means to dispel rumors that they had been set up as "a political graveyard"[27] of reform. These charges of anti-reformism had rankled, especially with Mrs. Hansen, who was about to retire from the House and was proud of the reform record of this party committee associated with her name. The charges made some Hansen members more determined to produce a plan which was at once worthwhile reform *and* also completely different from the Bolling plan. In anticipation of a bruising battle between the two camps, Mrs. Hansen even went to the trouble of holding up her Appropriations Interior Subcommittee appropriations bill just in case it was needed later as a bargaining chip.

The Hansen Committee's concentration on procedural issues also stemmed from a sincere belief that procedural reforms could work, whereas the jurisdictional ones would only cause problems. Their starting point in this enterprise was the Bolling plan's most politically vulnerable item, the Rules Committee bill referral provision allowing the Rules Committee to review jurisdictional disputes between committees. Bolling had claimed that he was embarrassed by this provision[28] and the fears of his Committee members that it might be seen as self-aggrandizement by Rules members Bolling and Martin had surfaced in anti-Bolling propagandizing. Now the Hansen Committee fixed on this provision. The Rules Committee was a prime target of reformers early in the Sixties but had been substantially reformed since then. Still, there was continuing prejudice against Rules, which the Hansen Committee cunningly set out to exploit. They deleted the Bolling Bill referral provision, and instead invested this discretionary power in the Speaker. In addition, they introduced a device to circumvent the Rules Committee altogether. The so-called "Rules By-Pass" provision would allow the Speaker to recognize the chairman of a committee or his designated member to offer a motion resolving the House into the Committee of the Whole to consider a piece of legislation which had not been approved by the Rules Committee. These recommendations deftly tapped the sentiment abroad in the House favoring strong leadership and at the same time gently detracted from the oftentimes criticized 15 Member Rules Committee—despite the fact that Speaker Albert and Majority Leader O'Neill had recently developed a close working tie to Rules.[29] And with the receptive Rules Chairman Ray Madden, and most ironically of all, Bolling himself, Rules was not the ornery impediment to the Democratic leadership it had been in the 1950s and early 1960s. Finally, the currency given to Bolling's and Martin's alleged "power grab" was perhaps belied by the contention that Bolling entertained thoughts of leaving the committee, and Martin contemplated retirement. But these points were not given wide currency at the time. And in any case these Hansen Committee changes were only the first of a series of crafty political moves. On other procedural matters, the Hansen Committee proposed a few minor changes, each differing slightly from the Bolling Plan equivalent:

- An "early organization" provision allowing House party Caucuses and Conferences to convene after December 1. (The Bolling plan had specified after November 15.)
- A Commission on Information and Facilities (rather than two Commissions set up by Bolling, one on Information, one on Administration Services and Facilities).
- Compilation of Precedents within two years.[30] (There was no provision for this in Bolling.)

This disposition in favor of procedural reform colored the Hansen Committee's attitude toward virtually all of the major jurisdictional shifts prescribed in the Bolling plan, and in the first place separating Education and Labor. O'Hara had always opposed the separation, and now was quite prepared to scuttle the entire Committee Reform in order to stop it. Thompson and Burton had originally supported the separation—in fact, as late as 1973 when the Bolling Committee began work. Thompson, like Biemiller and others in the labor movement, had entertained hopes that organized labor might actually strengthen its position with its own Labor Committee, including in its ambit all issues involving industrial relations. But he had reconsidered. He took into account his own attitude toward chairing such a committee and the fact that a shift would provide him fewer opportunities to work on his other varied interests such as education and the arts. He would also lose his small, but useful, power base as Chairman of the Subcommittee on Accounts of the House of Administration Committee. This led him finally to oppose separation, convinced that training young people—education—and watching out for the interests of working people—labor—were, in fact, quite closely related.

Burton was a veteran of the California legislature's Labor and Public Welfare Committee[31] and as a recognized expert on welfare matters (resident in Ways and Means) he initially leaned toward a new House Committee embracing these subjects. But he never got over his first impression that the bipartisan approach gave too much away to the Republicans; and in any case the separation would require him to choose between his Labor interest and his Interior subcommittee (and risk not getting a chair on the new Energy and Environment Committee). By the time the Hansen Committee sat down to consider this issue, the three Education and Labor members—O'Hara, Thompson and Burton—were staunch advocates of retaining the original committee.

Ways and Means members Phil Landrum had experienced some personal revisionism as well. Landrum had spoken publicly in favor of splitting Education and Labor in his testimony before Bolling's Select Committee, and had even conceded that a reshuffle might be in order in Ways and Means as well.[32] But now he fell into line for retention of the existing Education and Labor jurisdiction. His fellow Ways and Means member Joe Waggonner had never seen any reason to split it.

Indeed, the only Hansen members who supported separating the committee were Mrs. Hansen herself and Neal Smith, both former members of the Education and Labor Committee, who like Martin and Frelinghuysen on the Bolling Committee, remembered their days there with something less than relish. Both were now members of Appropriations, from which they could see the sometimes overblown and often erratic authorization bills which came to their committee from Education and Labor. And they were particularly sensitive to the turmoil which often greeted Education and Labor bills on the floor. In the only actual "show of hands" vote in the entire Hansen consideration, the separation of Education and Labor was defeated 6–2, beginning the almost total unravelling of the carefully constructed Bolling modified one-tier plan.

Also returned to their original homes were most of the Ways and Means jurisdiction[33] and federal elections and campaign spending to Hays' House Administration Committee. Internal Security, which Bolling had sent to Government Operations, was redirected to Judiciary, after the Chairman of Government Operations, Holifield, had said he did not want it. On another key issue, after a series of presentations from sources as diverse as Harley Staggers, the sitting Chairman of Interstate and Foreign Commerce, all the way to Ralph

Nader and a number of Environmental groups, Hansen also discarded the Bolling Plan's Energy and Environment Committee. Staggers preferred the existing arrangement, and, more surprisingly to the Bolling Committee, Nader and the Environmental groups had switched their position on the advisability of placing the issues of production and consumption, i.e. energy and environment, in the same committee. This was one more reason for consternation in the Bolling Camp, as the issue moved—haltingly—toward resolution.

5:2 BOLLING VERSUS HANSEN: THE DENOUEMENT

Political Background

The Remnants of the Reformers: Outside Groups

Inside the House, then, the Party reform forces had been fractured. The movement for reform within the Democratic Caucus was now tipped slightly in favor of the pro-Hansen, anti-Bolling position on Committee reform. DSG itself was "split down the middle." Culver, the present Chairman, was perhaps the most unstinting Bolling supporter; but the DSG Executive was divided, and its wily veterans Burton, O'Hara, and Thompson were not only anti-Bolling, but key architects of the Hansen plan.

DSG had necessarily adopted a painstakingly neutral official position. And this robbed the Bolling plan of the "outside" component of the previous successful "inside-outside" strategy and its crucial source of direction: DSG, and more specifically, Conlon. Not only was Conlon not playing the role of the pro-reform field general in this battle. As we have seen, he was instrumental in propounding the idea to refer the Bolling plan to the Hansen Committee. He too was having problems trying to keep the ill-feeling engendered by the Committee reform issue from undermining DSG's cohesiveness on other issues. Moreover, he was encountering criticism from Bolling proponents who spied bias on the part of DSG toward the Burton-Thompson-O'Hara axis, now spearheading the Hansen cause. Conlon spent time insuring that DSG issue briefs dealing with the alternative plans were assiduous in their objectivity. Still, there were inevitable allegations of bias; so much so in fact that Conlon took the unusual step of letting a Bolling Committee staffer write the section describing the Bolling plan in one DSG information sheet.[34] The disharmony and tension was symbolized by one Bolling Committee member's revocation of his "clerk-hire"[35] authorization to DSG in exasperation over an alleged

DSG tilt toward the Hansen position. DSG, it was clear, was in no position to rally the outside public interest "White Hat" groups behind a pre-agreed reform position. And on this issue, there was no such consensus to begin with. Indeed, after mid-July, there were two alternative plans, both proudly dubbed "reform" by their progenitors. The cross-cutting internal cleavages had produced a ripple effect on the outside clientele groups, splitting the hitherto solidly reformist public interest groups.

The labor movement, including liberal unions such as the United Auto Workers which had been linked with reform efforts in the past was now uniformly behind the Hansen plan in order to preserve the Education and Labor Committee. The Committee for Congressional Reform had by now disbanded,[36] although they had earlier expressed their enthusiasm for the Select Committee's work. Common Cause, ADA, and the League of Women Voters[37] remained steadfastly in favor of Committee reform as presented in the Bolling plan. But when it came to support from their old allies, Ralph Nader's Congress Watch, and the web of Environmental Groups, there had been a curious transformation in the ecologists' attitude toward reform. The Nader and Environmental Groups had switched their support to Hansen, a development which one source close to the Hansen camp described as a fortuitous "split in the White Hat groups,"[38] an important boost for their cause. The Bolling Committee, and in particular Bolling personally, was waging a persistent press campaign which portrayed the Bolling plan as reform, and the Hansen plan as something considerably less than that. Common Cause, ADA, and the League of Women Voters, were taking the same line. But when the unimpeachably reformist figure Nader, and such well-known Environmental groups as the Sierra Club and Friends of the Earth had come out for Hansen, this legitimized the Hansen position as a credible one for self-respecting reformers.

The "Public Interest" and Private Pragmatism

Nader had testified at the Bolling Committee hearings, contributing a wide-ranging set of recommendations such as mandatory rotation of committees, sacking the House Parliamentarian Lewis Deschler, and going a bit far afield into Party reform: shifting the Democratic Committee on Committees function from the Majority Members of the Ways and Means Committee to a Committee of the Democratic Caucus. This last proposal was clearly outside the terms of reference of the Select Committee since it was a prerogative of the parties to decide how they select their committee members. Bolling had been perhaps the leading educator on this point in his books and statements on the House floor. Still, Nader's broadside had made for a provocative and lively hearing on the House's ills. He and the other witness that day, John Gardner of Common Cause (who also showed interest in the idea of mandatory rotation), provided useful outside reformist perspectives.

The question of a multi-interest or single interest committee dealing with Energy and Environment issues did not arise during the course of Nader's testimony to the Select Committee. However, later on November 28 in response to a request from the Bolling Committee staff, Nader's Congress Watch Organization submitted a memorandum[39] emphasizing many of the points Nader had mentioned (including rotation and a new Caucus-based Committee on Committees), and containing a new suggestion—placing all energy and environment issues in one committee. Inside the Bolling Committee, this recommendation was given great credence as an important outside endorsement of the "exclusive" major committee idea fundamental to the one-tier concept. Here was the reflected legitimacy of Ralph Nader marshalled on the side of putting both energy and environment in one big "multi-interest" committee. Nader's support was a significant factor[40] in the Select Committee's decision—buoyed by support inside the Committee from Wiggins and Sarbanes—to construct the new Energy and Environment Committee out of the existing energy hodge-podge.[41] Moreover, the Congress Watch memorandum had helped convince Bolling himself of the wisdom of an Energy and Environment Committee; he had originally favored the half-step of another committee to arbitrate and resolve the Congress's own "energy crisis" of jurisdictions. After the Select Committee had reported their final plan, H.Res.988, they had received an eight page letter[42] from Congress Watch addressed to Bolling complimenting him on the Committee's work. They wrote: "The Select Committee has recommended a number of overdue reforms, in large measure meeting its goals of rationalizing jurisdictional lines between committees, balancing workloads . . ." There were a few minor areas of disagreement which Congress Watch felt could be "cured by floor amendments." However, "other problems require substantial action in the near future by the majority Caucus and by the House."[43] The latter areas were the previously mentioned necessity of taking the Committee on Committees function away from Ways and Means, noting the impending problem of transition and the possibility that the

Bolling Committee's halting attempt at a quasi-"grandfather clause" might result in a committee stacked against Nader-style "public-interest" positions. In addition, the letter continued, ". . . the Select Committee's report does not address itself to the dual problems of the seniority tradition and special interest influence over stagnant committee memberships. . . ,"[44] a lead-in to a reiteration of the mandatory rotation suggestion. However, in recognition of the political obstacles to rotation, they admitted:

> Apparently, broad based endorsement of mandatory rotation does not exist within the House at this point and we reluctantly conclude that this very basic essential reform has not attracted sufficient support to be part of the Select Committee's package. We nevertheless urge the Select Committee and individuals concerned with Congressional reform to place this issue at the top of the agenda for future action.[45]

Nowhere in this letter was there any mention of opposition to the proposed Energy and Environment Committee.

However, as the anti-Bolling forces worked to divert the plan to the Hansen Committee, the Nader people and the environmental groups studied the Bolling plan and began to reconsider their position. In one large multi-interest committee, the big oil companies would try to insure that the new Energy and Environment Committee was stacked with congressmen from oil producing states. This was where the Committee on Committees factor entered in. Were future energy policy to be decided by friends of the environmental movement, of course the groups would favor the proposal. However, they feared that pro-environmentalist members would opt for other committees, or would be given other assignments by a Ways and Means Democratic contingent responsive to big business and presumably, to oil interests.

In a Sierra Club memorandum[46] dated May 30, circulated to fellow environmentalist and "public interest" groups, Linda Billings of the Sierra Club described a meeting the previous Wednesday, May 22 to discuss possible changes in the Committee reform proposals. Five alternative plans provided for some form of re-dispersal of Energy and Environment responsibility to existing Committees and subcommittees. The Billings letter solicited views on how to maximize the advantage of the environmentalist position. Rather than risk the high stakes of a multi-interest committee on which they might face a committee dominated by oil interests, the environmentalist public interest groups opted for the familiar dispersed system.

Nader himself shortly thereafter adopted this position and, along with environmentalist organization representatives, took part in negotiations with Burton of the Hansen Committee about desirable ways to re-allocate the Bolling energy and environment jurisdiction. In the middle of July the Hansen Committee, in response to a last minute plea from Chet Holifield,[47] returned legislative jurisdiction over non-military nuclear energy to the Joint Committee on Atomic Energy which Nader regarded as a captive of the Atomic Energy Commission; Nader threatened that unless the non-military nuclear energy jurisdiction were returned to Interior, "the (Hansen) committee's proposal on energy and environment will be as insupportable as that portion of the Select Committee's proposal."[48] But that was a hollow threat, and the Nader-Environmentalist camp preferred the Hansen version to Bolling's and energized their Capitol Hill lobbyists on its behalf. As the environmentalists told Speaker Albert: the Hansen version ". . . essentially maintains the status quo with respect to energy jurisdiction. While this is not reform, it is preferable to H. Res. 988."[49]

Nader too wrote a letter to the Speaker on September 30, 1974 in which he stated: "With respect to energy and environment jurisdiction, the Hansen Committee proposal will serve the public interest better than the Select Committee proposal." He went on to add that "both plans suffer from an underlying failure to attack the seniority system by adopting mandatory rotation between committees."[50] The letter ended on a note of begrudging support:

> It is regrettable that the current round of House reorganization activity has not brought forth more fundamental reforms to the operation of the committee system. Yet many of the structural and procedural proposals by both the Select Committee and the Hansen Committee will be useful improvements. However, the Select Committee's proposed energy and environment committee presents a grave danger to the public interest and should be rejected by the House.[51]

Another section of the reformist bloc had fallen into line with the pro-Hansen forces. It was a terrific blow to the spirits of Bolling supporters. Indeed, Sarbanes of the Select Committee was moved to comment in a conversation with a representative of Nader's Congress Watch, that the development of Congress Watch's position on this matter raised questions as to whether he could rely on their representations in the future. He further suggested that Congress Watch had "flim-flammed" on the issue.[52] Congress Watch answered this charge in a letter written on October 3, the eve of House consideration of the alternative plans which concluded:

Our difference, as I understand it, is that we view consolidation of energy and environment jurisdiction—absent fundamental reform of the mechanisms which determine committee membership—as an invitation to domination by the oil, coal, and utility lobbies and that this danger outweighs any possible advantage. You, on the other hand, believe that the advantages of the consolidation outweigh the risk of domination.

I trust that this review restores your confidence in the integrity and consistency of our representations and refutes your allegation of any "flim-flam" on our part.[53]

The characterization of the trade-off between possible advantages of consolidation versus the risk of domination by the oil industry was a fair assessment of the situation. Certainly, there was a possibility that the new Energy and Environment Committee would be "loaded" with pro-oil industry members. Of course, contrariwise, oil companies risked having a committee stacked with members friendly toward the ecology movement. Still there was reason to suspect that the existing Democratic Committee on Committees might tilt towards the oil interests, although it was probably more likely that screening by the leadership might well have insured a relatively balanced, truly "multi-interest" committee. However, even if one accepts that the new panel would be dominated by one or the other, this was a question of low-stakes versus high—keeping the dispersed system of competing committees and subcommittees, and the comfortable pockets of access, as against the possible benefits of both a pro-environmentalist committee and a better chance of a uniform energy policy—and the risk of a committee that would produce a pro-oil industry, coherent energy policy. The Nader and Environmental forces opted for the low-stakes solution.

All of this made political sense, a case of so-called "public interest" groups quite justifiably seeking to protect their own interests. Select Committee members could understand that. However, what was more difficult to accept and what inspired the "flim-flam" allegation was the contention by Congress Watch that they had maintained a consistent position. Mandatory rotation was politically unfeasible;[54] everyone knew such a recommendation would have been political suicide, as well as encroaching upon the right of the parties to decide committee assignments. Moreover, rotation had been briefly discussed by the Select Committee, at which time only one member (Culver) expressed enthusiasm. It was dismissed peremptorily as unrealistic. In any case, in their letter of May 7, even Congress Watch recognized that rotation was a political impossibility. As for moving the Democratic Committee on Committees, this beyond a shadow of a doubt required action by the Democratic Caucus, and was clearly beyond the jurisdiction of the Bolling Committee, a bipartisan Select Committee of the House expressly considering changes in House Rules X and XI.

The Hansen Committee, which was a party organ, *could* have recommended changes on these subjects, especially the shift of the Committee on Committees. However, they steadfastly refused to become embroiled in this sort of Party reform at a time when they were grappling with their own procedural and jurisdictional alternative to the Bolling plan and its attendant political intrigue. This point should have been obvious to the Nader-Environmentalists axis since they were consulted by Burton of the Hansen Committee on their attitudes toward the possible shifts of energy and environment back to the existing committees. Moreover, if Congress Watch had really placed top priority on a move to dislodge the Committee on Committees function from Ways and Means, they should have known by then that the best time would be at the beginning of the next Congress and that the group to look to for direction was DSG. In fact, Conlon, pending the outcome of the Bolling versus Hansen battle (and, of course, of the 1974 election) was putting that issue high on the likely reform agenda.[55]

These reformist "public interest" groups sought to have it both ways. They favored radical reform in principle, but opted in practice for the less reformist plan—which perpetuated old jurisdictions and the established clientele relationships. They regretted that there had not been more far-reaching reform, but when an unusually sweeping attempt at consolidation, the Bolling plan, appeared—indeed, a plan which had based its recommendation for an Energy and Environment Committee largely on the strength of Congress Watch's November 28 memorandum—Congress Watch and the others retrenched. Like labor before them, these groups changed their position when their ties to the existing order were threatened and had proved unwilling to take the risks involved in fundamental reform.

Moreover, by holding up unreasonable—and seemingly misperceived—prerequisites for support, Congress Watch justified the switch in their position while, to the end, claiming consistency. It was no wonder that Bolling Committee sources were bitter about what they considered to be irresponsible gyrations and opportunism. The outside support for the Bolling plan was in ruins. The "White Hat" reform bloc was now divided. Coupled with the disastrous turn of events with labor, two outside sectors that might have contributed vital support were now avid opponents. Organized labor alone might not have been able to defeat the Bolling plan. But the impeccably reformist Nader and his cohorts had rendered the Hansen alternative more respectable to reformers. It was now more plausible to cast the battle as between two juxtaposed reform plans rather than, as Bolling had sought to portray it, reform versus anti-reform. And now the defenders of the *status quo* were not only the entrenched committee barons, or even the added assortment of the newly empowered subcommittee chairmen; they also included the "public interest" pillars of the outside reform community who responded to disruption of their contacts just as self-protectively as private interests.

Effective outside support for Bolling had almost evaporated. The remnants of the reformers were ADA, the League of Women Voters, and Common Cause, all respectable enough groups but also middle-class "do-gooder" groups with tenuous ties to key blocs of House members. These organizations, sensing the formidable support mobilizing behind Hansen, initiated an all-out hard-hitting campaign in favor of the Bolling plan. Common Cause, launching a press campaign, attacked the Hansen formula as containing "little real reform."[56] However, they must also have reluctantly noticed by now that this was apparently what many, inside and outside, actually wanted.

The Rule

Since April, the Bolling Committee had been canvassing support for their plan. They sought Caucus approval to send H. Res. 988 to the Rules Committee. There Bolling would ask for an open rule (i.e. allowing amendments) and request that the bill be sent expeditiously to the floor. In fact, Bolling had written to the Rules Committee requesting a hearing on the rule; and had been told that there would be a meeting on July 23. However, intrigue inside the Caucus intervened, and the Rules Committee meeting did not take place until September 12.

In between, there was considerable activity. At the July 23 Caucus, O'Hara offered a resolution instructing the Democratic members of the Rules Committee to "report a resolution making the consideration of H. Res. 988 in order under an open rule, and providing for the reading of the resolution section-by-section."[57] More significantly, O'Hara's motion authorized introduction of the Hansen Committee proposal "as an amendment in the nature of a substitute immediately following the reading of the first section of H. Res. 988."[58] O'Hara's tactic was to insure that the Rules Committee provided ample opportunity for the Hansen proposal to be considered as a completely separate alternative. Indeed, his motion sought to establish the Hansen plan (H. Res. 1248) as a reform plan on an equal footing with the Bolling H. Res. 988. O'Hara's resolution was adopted by voice vote.

The Hansen strategy was to make their plan as attractive an alternative as possible. They would have preferred a vote in Caucus actually recommending the Hansen plan over the Bolling resolution, but that would have provoked an acrimonious conflict in the July Caucus. And while there is disagreement as to whether the Hansen forces could have carried a vote at that time (there is also a story that Burton had thought Mrs. Hansen was rising to move a vote in favor of her plan but was actually only straightening her skirt[59]), the Hansen tacticians reconsidered, and reasoned that time and the opportunity for delay was on their side. At least for some of them, no action on Committee reform was far preferable to adoption of the Bolling plan. Indeed, Burton was on record as having said that they should wait until the next Congress when the expected infusion of young, reformist Democrats would make the timing more propitious for his brand of party-based reform.[60]

The upshot of the July Caucuses was to bind the Democratic members of the Rules Committee into making the Hansen plan in order as a substitute immediately after the Bolling plan had been introduced. The integrity of Bolling once again was evident, and he strongly insisted that there could be no compromise of the essentials of his Committee's plan. Attempts by Caucus Chairman Teague, and ultimately the Speaker, to prod Bolling into meeting with Hansen leaders to engineer a compromise were rejected out of hand by Bolling. He felt strongly committed both to the plan itself, and to his formal obligation to comply with House rules which require committee chairmen to seek passage of bills reported by their committees.[61] Moreover, Bolling had developed a profound contempt for the attitudes of liberals who were ostensibly reformers but who had become entrenched supporters of the status quo in the committee system. These middle-level subcommittee chairmen, a few of whom also happened to be Bolling adversaries and rival aspirants to House leadership, were clearly putting their own interests above that of the institution. For Bolling, the reformer, this was cowardly. Moreover, it violated Bolling's sensibilities which placed a high value on conceptual coherence. In his view, there could be no compromise.

Bolling then was prepared for a fisticuffs on the House floor between the two plans. Despite severe setbacks, particularly the labor and Nader-Environmentalist defections, the more optimistic members of the Bolling camp still hoped that with a sustained press campaign and the intellectual superiority of their plan they might still triumph. Bolling, a fatalist by temperament, felt that in any case the House should be given the opportunity to adopt this plan that would significantly improve its performance. If they spurned the plan, so be it; in that case, Bolling was confident that history would prove him right. Unfortunately for him, there was still one more disastrous defection to come, this time from within his own Committee. Vice Chairman Dave Martin had been increasingly alienated from the Bolling strategy for some time. There had been a few specific provisions that he had disliked; he had resented Bolling's unilateral choice of co-drafters of the December 7 document; and he disagreed profoundly with Bolling's insistence on giving the party caucuses ample opportunity to debate the plan, certain that it would only provide time and a forum for the opponents. The May Democratic Caucus and the subsequent referral to Hansen had confirmed his suspicions. He and Frelinghuysen, both on the eve of retirement from the House, were now convinced that the Bolling plan was doomed. They had allowed their adversaries to mobilize. In their view, it had been folly to send it to the parties.

In August, as Rules Committee Chairman Ray Madden began what would become a marathon series of postponements, cancellations, and general dilatory activity over when the Rules Committee would schedule the hearing on a rule, Dave Martin decided to bolt, drafting his own third version of Committee reform. This was to be H. Res. 1321, a bill very much like the Bolling plan but which included a few procedural innovations[62] from the Hansen resolution. It was intended as a compromise, an attempt to eke out an acceptable middle way. However, Martin's action was received fitfully by the Bolling camp as yet another blow to their hopes. It was seen as a willful act to undermine Republican support of the Bolling plan, but more, an ill-considered blunder that played into the hands of the Hansen proponents. As for the Hansen tacticians, the Martin plan had appeared as a gift from an unexpected donor. Indeed, it had filled the one major gap in their developing strategy to win adoption of their plan. In making their plan in order as a substitute, the Hansen members would be ready to accept amendments under the open rule. If the Bolling strategists persisted in their resolve to keep their plan intact, the Bolling plan would in effect be "frozen." In fact, Bolling did not mind his plan being put in this position; his scenario was to have the

House consider the Hansen plan, defeat it, and then move on to the Bolling plan. The Hansen strategy, on the other hand, was to tailor their plan to the preferences of the House by adding "perfecting amendments." They—including even Burton who had attacked the Bolling Committee's bipartisanship—would also be prepared to make some concessions to the Republicans on Minority staffing and proxy voting themselves if it would win GOP support. But the flaw in the Hansen strategy was that there would probably be enough time for both plans to receive a full hearing. In this situation, the Hansen plan might run out of steam, and then attention would turn back to the Bolling plan. In a straight fight, the Bolling plan might triumph over the Hansen plan, even if it were sweetened with a variety of unrelated amendments from the floor. This was why the submission of the Martin plan came as such a pleasant surprise for the Hansen camp. It provided a third option that would take up more time, be subject to additional amendments from the floor, and generally aid in the Hansen mission of relegating the Bolling plan to temporary—and perhaps permanent—oblivion. Thus the Hansen plan would be made more attractive to the rest of the House by virtue of its amendments, and the Martin plan—without a serious possibility of attaining passage—helped to bottle up the Bolling plan. One Hansen source observed somewhat bemusedly, "if we had pulled the strings, we wouldn't have had Martin do anything differently. He couldn't have been more effective for us."[63] The Hansen Committee had acquired a secret weapon; it was the Bolling Committee's Dave Martin.

The Rules Committee, when it finally convened to discuss Committee reform, became embroiled in protracted debate. It took them two weeks to hear from all the members wanting to testify, and finally to find their way to adoption of a rule. Witnesses before the Rules Committee ranged from the acerbic Dingell who sought to deny a rule altogether: "the most charitable thing to do is to inter it gracefully with some kind words for the author,"[64] all the way over to Bolling who was trying to get the resolution to the floor as quickly as possible in order to assure a vote before the end of the Session. In between were Hansen members who were rounding up support for their plan, and hoping to make sure it went to the floor in the most favorable circumstances. O'Hara, Smith and Waggonner of the Hansen Committee testified, as did Sam Gibbons of Ways and Means. Interestingly, both O'Hara and Gibbons suggested deferral of action on the bill, showing that there were still widespread fears that the Bolling plan might yet carry the day.

After an elaborate set of moves and counter-moves inside the Rules Committee, on September 24, Bolling finally demanded a vote. He and Gillis Long, who had been a key Bolling operative on Rules, had determined that they could probably win a narrow victory, especially if Committee Members absent at the time did not appear. Finally, after a period of waiting for absent members to return, Madden ordered a call of the roll. The vote was on Bolling's motion to report the rule which authorized consideration of H. Res. 988, made H. Res. 1248 (the Hansen plan) in order as an amendment in the nature of a substitute, complying with the Caucus requirement, and also made H. Res. 1321 (the Martin plan) in order as a compromise as well. At this point, Bolling simply sought to get the issue to the floor before it had to be postponed until the next Congress. With eleven out of fifteen members present, the Bolling motion carried 6–5. Moments later, Rep. John Young of Texas—an anti-Bolling man who had missed the vote—walked in the room and became enraged that he had been unable to cast his vote. The next day Young offered a substitute amendment which resolved that the Rules Committee "defer action." After both John Anderson and Dave Martin endorsed the Bolling motion on the rule, the Young motion was defeated by a voice vote. Upon demand of a roll call vote, this verdict was sustained 8–5. The key to the victory was the solid support of the five Republicans on Rules, whereas the Democrats split 3–5 (the Chairman, Madden, and Clem McSpadden of Oklahoma not voting). The debate on Committee reform, almost twenty-one months after the Select Committee on Committees had been created, now went to the floor.[65]

The Floor

The Bolling Committee set about mobilizing support through their Whip system, and by enlisting the support of the three main outside groups still supporting the Bolling plan—ADA, Common Cause, and the League of Women Voters. Of greater significance to the development of a strategy was the consideration of whether they should prepare their own substitute resolution which could be used to add Bolling plan provisions to the Hansen plan. This substitute would tailor the Hansen plan more to the Bolling version, thereby salvaging some of their plan in the event the Hansen plan looked like it would pass. This was a practical option that they had to face—especially if the Hansen strategy was seen to be working. The Hansen approach was to offer H. Res. 1248 as a substitute to the Bolling plan immediately after H. Res. 988 had been introduced. Then they would gleefully watch Martin introduce his H. Res. 1231. House rules required that a substitute amendment to a substitute amendment must be disposed of before entertaining any amendments to the second substitute.[66] Translated to the present situation, this meant that after the Hansen substitute was introduced, and then the Martin substitute after it, a Hansen backer could then offer an amendment to the Martin resolution. This would, in effect, freeze the Martin resolution until the entire Hansen resolution had been dealt with. Hence, all amendments thenceforth would be to the Hansen plan, until there was an "up and down" vote on both H. Res. 1231 and H. Res. 1248 as amended. What the Hansen strategy called for was to keep the Bolling plan in limbo by turning all attention to the Hansen plan. Seizing on the resolution conveniently provided by Martin, the Hansen backers could solicit and pass amendments which would make their plan more acceptable to the House, while the Bolling plan would sit quietly by, unchanged.

The question for the Bolling strategists then was whether to set up an alternative set of amendments which would make the Hansen plan more like the original Bolling plan. Meeds thought that this made sense. However, Sarbanes and Steiger felt that they had come this far insisting on the interrelationship of the various aspects of their plan; they should see it through with its organizational integrity intact. Bolling agreed. Moreover, he espoused the view that they should allow the Hansen plan to be debated, and revised; it should then be voted upon and defeated. Then they would work to gain passage of their own H. Res. 988.

On September 30, the House took up H. Res. 988. The first order of business was the adoption of the rules for consideration of H. Res. 988.

On a vote of 326 to 25, the rule carried, and the House now adopted Committee of the Whole procedure. Rep. Natcher, who had also presided over the 1970 Legislative Reorganization debate, now assumed the Chair. Four hours of debate had been allotted, and there was an informal understanding that the time would be split roughly equally between the three. Speeches in support of the various alternatives ensued.

On the next day, October 1, H. Res. 1248 (Hansen) was offered as an amendment in the nature of a substitute. Next Martin introduced his substitute for the Hansen resolution. Bolling rose to oppose the Martin substitute, and stated the Select Committee position: they would put forward no amendments to other plans. They would ask the House to reject both the Martin and Hansen substitutes, and then to approve the Bolling Plan, perhaps with perfecting amendments.

Next, Mrs. Sullivan took the floor to offer an amendment to the Martin substitute which would reinstate jurisdiction lost by Merchant Marine and Fisheries under the Martin proposal (which was the same as the Bolling plan on this). It was virtually a foregone conclusion that the Martin plan would be overwhelmingly defeated; but Mrs. Sullivan was not taking any chances. Moreover, by offering an amendment to Martin's substitute, she paved the way for fulfillment of the Hansen strategy.

Shortly thereafter, Thompson offered an amendment to the Hansen substitute, providing for minority staffing—one staff member for each Ranking member of a subcommittee. This was a classic example of a "pot sweetener" to win the support of Republicans. A series of parliamentary moves and counter-moves ensued; but the Hansen strategy had now been successfully executed, with the effective—and apparently unwitting—assistance of Martin. Now with both the Sullivan and Thompson amendments to the Martin and Hansen substitutes respectively on the floor, House rules required disposition of one or the other. The Hansen forces could marshal attention to the Thompson amendment—even though it raised the ire of some partisan Democrats distrustful of giving anything away to the Republicans. In the event, the Thompson amendment was adopted 218–180, with 63 Republicans voting in favor. This set the tone for the ensuing consideration. While the Hansen plan would be molded and shaped, the Sullivan amendment to Martin would lie dormant. And the Bolling plan was left in the background, its proponents virtual innocent by-standers.

At one point, on October 2, Bolling tried to seize the initiative by shifting attention back to the merits of his own H. Res. 988. The opponents of his plan, he argued, should move to strike the resolving clause on the resolution (in effect, moving to kill it). This would be a fair test of sentiment on Committee reform. But the anti-Bolling tacticians were not having any of it. Their strategy was working, and Bolling's invitation constituted an admission of that.

In the meantime, outside and internal lobbying was taking place at a frenzied pace. The AFL-CIO—reportedly George Meany personally—was applying pressure to defeat the Bolling plan and stall Committee Reform. The Nader and Environmental groups were pressing for adoption of Hansen. ADA, Common Cause, and the League of Women Voters were mobilizing their supporters on behalf of the

Bolling plan. Inside the House, "Dear Colleague" letters on specific amendments blanketed congressmen's desks. In a more generalized attack on the Bolling plan, Chet Holifield prepared a memorandum for all House members which alleged that the one-tier concept would force large numbers of Democrats off committees of their specialized interest. The Bolling Committee promptly issued a rejoinder. But it was clear that this was no ordinary legislative contest. Outside interests and congressmen alike realized that the result would have profound implications for future substantive issues and enduring power alignments.

The debate took place at an inopportune time. The exhausting Session had included Nixon's demise and the accession to the Presidency of their old colleague, Gerald Ford. Their own election campaigns competed for their attention. No wonder Committee reform was widely viewed as an irritating diversion. Bolling knew this, and had hoped to clear the way for an early decision. On October 7, he asked the House to limit debate on amendments in the Committee of the Whole, and to proceed to discuss all three plans. Dingell, in another of his dilatory tactics, objected. Bolling then asked for a five-hour limitation on debate.

The hapless Martin reacted strongly against this, but was squashed, 295–39, and Bolling then got his five-hour limitation adopted 274–56, on October 7. A resolution of the issues would not be far off, in that after expiration of the five hour limit, there would be votes on first, the Martin substitute, then the Hansen substitute. Only if both were defeated would the House proceed to the Bolling Resolution.

Rep. Natcher called the question on the Martin substitute on October 8. Martin's support was as shallow as had been expected: the substitute was rejected 319–41. Later that night, after the Hansen Committee had ascertained that they possessed the votes to win, the House voted on the Hansen plan. Even John Dingell was ready to let the House work its will on Committee reform. This was not a comforting sign for the Bolling proponents.

The Coalition of "natural enemies" had enlisted broad support. When the fifteen minute period in which to vote expired, the tally was 203 for the Hansen substitute, 165 against.

H. Res. 988, as amended with the "amendment in the nature of a substitute"—i.e. the Hansen plan supplanting it was then adopted without controversy, 359–7. Of committee chairmen, only two voted against the Hansen plan—Mahon of Appropriations and Morgan of Foreign Affairs; thirteen supported it. Of the crucial core of Democratic middle-echelon members, those holding subcommittee chairs, 77 opted for the security of Hansen, 25 voted against it—presumably favoring the Bolling plan—and 16 did not vote. More to the point, the subcommittee chairmen and members of the committees most directly affected by the Bolling reshuffle—and unscathed by the Hansen plan—were almost unanimous in their support for Hansen. Only one member on Ways and Means voted against the Hansen plan; the Republican reformer, Barber Conable. On Education and Labor, every subcommittee chairman voted for Hansen, including such reform veterans as Burton, O'Hara, Thompson, Brademas and Eckhardt. On House Administration, Hays, as well as Thompson and Brademas, were Hansen supporters.

Of the subcommittee chairmen who did vote against the Hansen plan, most served on committees either not adversely affected by the Bolling plan, or in a few cases, positively advantaged by it. Thus of the original DSG Party reform architects (other than Bolling), the only staunch supporter of the Bolling plan was Don Fraser—a subcommittee chairman on the Foreign Affairs Committee, which was slotted to take over Foreign trade jurisdiction under the Bolling plan. Fraser was joined in opposing Hansen by his Foreign Affairs colleagues: Rep. Thomas Morgan, the chairman, subcommittee chairman Rep. Fascell and Rep. Lee Hamilton of Indiana.

Other subcommittee chairmen who opposed Hansen were from such unaffected preserves as Appropriations (Boland, Pike), District of Columbia (Mazzoli), Banking and Currency (Reuss), and Judiciary (Kastenmeier, Edwards). Other subcommittee chairmen to vote against Hansen included Culver and Meeds of the Bolling Committee, for obvious reasons. Indeed, of these subcommittee chairmen who did oppose Hansen—one is hard-put to find one clearly disadvantaged by the Bolling Plan.[67]

An unusually high number of Bolling Committee members were known to be leaving the House. Martin and Frelinghuysen had announced that they intended to retire. Culver was in the process of running (successfully) for the Senate in Iowa. Sarbanes was thought to be seriously contemplating a run for the Senate from Maryland. Thus four out of ten Select Committee members were known to have less than a direct stake in future House alignments: not necessarily reason to question the wisdom of their plan; but another marketable line for the anti-Bolling forces. By comparison, of the Hansen Committee only Mrs. Hansen was planning retirement.

Despite their considerable labors, and the rather unsatisfying na-

ture of their undoing, the Select Committee took its defeat philo-
sophically. Bolling, the fatalist, felt that they had made a deep impression that could not be ignored. And while he would continue to
harbor bitterness toward the potential allies who had deserted him—
for instance: labor, Nader, and some of the DSG Reformers—he was
confident that some of the provisions of his plan would one day pre-
vail, perhaps even as soon as the December Caucus. He was, of
course, correct. But that did not deter him from reaching for some
provocative imagery when describing what the Hansen Committee
had done to his plan:

> If you used a mirror to take a picture of a landscape, the mirror
> would register the image . . . It was as if they (the Hansen Committee)
> broke the mirror, and then took the picture again.[68]

Bolling viewed the Hansen plan, even with some of its procedural
innovations, as utterly destructive of all that his Committee had
hoped to accomplish. As for Hansen's procedural reforms:

> The only worthwhile things in the Hansen version were bad images of
> the Select Committee's. They were broken images. . . .[69]

A different reflection on the same experience came from Bolling's
antagonist, and the Hansen strategist, Wayne Hays:

> The Bolling Committee was like the drunk at the county fair. This
> was the fellow who said that he could knock the block off any man in the
> city. No one said anything. He then said he could punch out any man in
> the *County*. Still, no one said anything. Finally he said he could beat any
> man in the whole state.
> Suddenly a man stepped forward and flattened the drunk. The prob-
> lem was that he took in too much territory.
> That was the Bolling Committee's problem; they took in too much
> territory. It's not as though the House was against each and every of the
> reforms. It's just that there was enough in there to offend an awful lot
> of people a little bit.[70]

Of course, Hays well knew that there were many members who had
been offended "an awful lot" as well. But these two lingering images
from leaders of the opposing camps tell much about both the result
and the orientations of the principals.

The Bolling plan was intentionally consolidative in its aims. It was
an expression of Bolling's affinity for strong leadership, coherent
organization, and generally, his wish to put right a "House Out of
Order." Bolling sought a thorough-going institutional reform, and it
constituted a direct challenge to the dispersive proclivities of the

House. However, by 1973 and 1974 the people wedded to the old order were not only the oligarchic full committee chairmen with their grey hair, conservative views, and oftentimes Southern accents. Instead, the prior form of fragmented power had been fragmented further—to the subcommittee chairmen. And these new members—young, moderate or liberal, and spanning a cross-section of Northern and Western Democratic electoral support—had developed the same affection for the *status quo*. Moreover, the reforms inside the Democratic Caucus of 1971 and 1973 had, in Burton's phrase, "spread the action" to new forces in the party—one of DSG's two major directions of reform. Provisions such as the limitation on the number of subcommittees any chairman could hold and the Subcommittee Bill of Rights had actually strengthened the House's dispersive and individualistic tendencies.

When faced with an attempt to consolidate power—with unknown effects on personal careers—the new subcommittee chairmen allied with the old guard to defeat it. Even key sections of the outside clientele of the liberal reform camp rushed to cover their own flanks as well. Party reform, then, was one thing. It had served to devolve power to younger, more liberal members—and hence, to some extent, had improved liberal fortunes in the House. In addition, it provided some semblance of, or at least the potential for, greater exercise of power by the Speaker. This also was consolidative reform. However, with Speaker Albert in the chair, there was no attempt to use it. In these circumstances, Party reform was *de facto* dispersive reform. It was for this reason that it was popular. The Bolling plan had been defeated because by 1974 consolidative reform had become offensive to the mainstream of middle-seniority members. While the general idea of strong leadership was still lauded, reforms designed to facilitate it had become manifestly unappreciated.

Hence, especially with the expected influx of reformist, new Democratic members in 1974, it was logical to expect that any future reform would take place within the Democratic Caucus. After November 1974, momentum had swung back to the Party reform approach and to DSG. In the most favorable climate for reform since the DSG had first broached the issue, it was this combination of DSG and the new reform Democrats who would launch a full scale reform attack in the Caucus.

Notes

1. Phrase used by Richard Conlon; Conlon Interview. An interesting prediction that such a coalition would not form, precisely due to the incongruity of the opponents, was included in a *Wall Street Journal* article: "I don't see the opposing elements finding each other," said a DSG aide. See "House Reorganizers Offer Plan to Assign Members to Only One Major Committee," *Wall Street Journal*, March 20, 1974, p. 12. On page 1 the same day, the *Journal* summarized: "Opposition will come from two quarters, conservatives who want to keep Ways and Means powerful, and liberal Democrats who'd have to choose between more than one assignment. But they may not combine to fight the plan." This, of course, was the Select Committee's, and especially Bolling's, design—i.e. to keep the likely opponents divided.
2. "House Committee Reform Proposals Drawing Opposition," *CQ Weekly Report*, February 2, 1974, p. 195.
3. An unusual House panel which possessed no legislative jurisdiction but which conducted oversight of the Small Business Administration and served as a convenient "minor" post for members anxious to aid constituents.
4. *CQ Weekly Report*, February 2, 1974, *op. cit.*, p. 195. Dingell was known as one of the feistiest legislative tacticians and "gut-fighters" in the Congress, as were some other of the leading opponents of the Bolling Plan—particularly Burton, Hays, and Sullivan.
5. Whip Advisory Notice from John McFall to Democratic Members, Number 274, December 14, 1973.
6. *DSG Fact Sheet*, 93-22, April 18, 1974, p. 10.
7. Father Robert Drinan, civil libertarian and a former Dean of Boston College Law School, had campaigned for abolition of HISC long before entering Congress. He was assigned to the Committee in 1971 and continued to advocate its abolition.
8. Inside the Select Committee, Sarbanes, along with Bolling, had spoken up for the committee, and had only grudgingly acquiesced to its abolition, Sarbanes feeling that he could not press the case since he sat on the affected committee.
9. Conlon Interview.
10. Bolling Interview.
11. For a breakdown of the organizations contacting the Committee, see Davidson and Oleszek, *Congress Against Itself, op. cit,* p. 159.
12. If the entire Post Office and Civil Service jurisdiction went to the new Labor Committee, and especially if Thompson demurred, it was conceivable that Henderson would outflank either Dent or Daniels—another example of the uncertainty caused by rejurisdiction.

13. See "Nixon Vetoes 16 Bills in Second Session of 92nd," *CQ Almanac* 1972, p. 28.
14. This phrase turned up in a number of interviews: Conlon, Hays, O'Hara, and Interview with William Cable, Staff Member, Education and Labor Committee, September 18, 1975.
15. The plan would also be considered by the Republican Conference where smooth passage was expected—not least because of the Minority staffing and Proxy voting provisions, as well as the separation of Education and Labor which remained popular with the GOP.
16. This included attendance by Education and Labor Chairman Perkins and Thompson at a meeting of committee chairmen and others opposed to the Bolling plan. The secret meeting took place on March 27, 1974, see Davidson and Oleszek, *Congress Against Itself, op. cit.*, p. 193.
17. Conlon Interviews.
18. Conlon, Cable, O'Hara, Cohen Interviews. Also, Interview with Linda H. Kamm, Counsel, Bolling Select Committee on Committees, August 5, 1975.
19. Conlon Interview.
20. Conlon, O'Hara Interviews.
21. This was a rumor spread by DSG forces to make Mills and others who wanted to kill it outright think that there was not sufficient support to do so, showing that at least one section of the anti-Bolling DSG element also worked to facilitate an alternative Committee Reform.
22. Democratic Caucus Resolution by Phillip Burton, May 9, 1974, Photocopy of draft proposal. Democratic Caucus Notebook.
23. Prudence Crewson, "House Reorganization Faces Stiff Opposition," Jefferson City, Mo. *Post-Tribune*, April 30, 1974, p. 2. Also see Open Business Meeting, *Select Committee, op.cit.*, p. 350 for mention of Burton's position.
24. As Teague later admitted; see David Nyhan, "House Structure Reform Dodged by Democrats," *Boston Globe*, May 10, 1974, p. 58.
25. *ADA Legislative Newsletter,* Vol. 3, No. 10, June 1, 1974, p. 2.
26. Smith Interview.
27. A quotation of David Cohen of Common Cause. An ADA lobbyist called the referral to Hansen "a cruel hoax." See Richard C. Madden, "Democrats Block House Overhaul," *New York Times,* May 10, 1974, p. 1.
28. It should be noted that this was strictly a "procedural" issue; however, its "jurisdictional" dimension was the politically attractive argument that it was a power grab by the Rules Committee.
29. In 1971 and 1973 the leadership had placed members responsive to it on the Committee: Gillis Long of Louisiana, Clem McSpadden of Oklahoma, and Morgan Murphy of Illinois.
30. This had not been done since 1936. Precedents since then were kept in scrapbooks with clippings from the *Congressional Record* and annotations. Deschler had been appropriated 80,000 dollars to compile them but had yet to do so. See Ralph Nader's testimony, *Select Committee*, Vol. 3, p. 282.
31. In the California State Assembly. The United States Senate also had a committee of that name until 1979, now re-named Human Resources.
32. Landrum suggested that "there is no real justification for the Ways and

190   Reform Roots

Means Committee having jurisdiction over welfare legislation." *Select Committee*, Vol. 1, p. 282.

33. Except general revenue sharing, work incentive programs, and health care that is supported from general revenues as opposed to payroll deduction. On the other hand, the Bolling plan would have given Ways and Means jurisdiction over Food Stamps, from Agriculture; Hansen did not.
34. Conlon, Kamm interviews.
35. Individual DSG members allocate the DSG some of their official House allowance for hiring staff.
36. They closed their doors in early 1973. Committee on Congressional Reform Minutes, ADA file.
37. It is worth noting that two of the remaining pro-Bolling groups—Common Cause and the League—were typical progressive, middle-class, procedure-as-opposed-to-issues "mugwump" organizations not known for their clout with Democrats. And the third group, ADA, was seen as being to the left of many Congressional Democrats. This array of support could hardly encourage Bolling supporters.
38. Cable Interview.
39. November 28, Memorandum from Congress Watch to Select Committee on Committees Congress Watch File. I am grateful to Congress Watch for access to their Congressional reform file.
40. Bolling, Sarbanes, Kamm interviews. Also conversation with Walter Oleszek of the Select Committee Staff.
41. Including Interior, Agriculture, Interstate and Foreign Commerce, Merchant Marine, and the Joint Committee on Atomic Energy. See p. 152n.
42. Letter from Joan Claybrook and Nancy Chasen of Congress Watch to Rep. Bolling, May 7, 1974.
43. *Ibid.*
44. *Ibid.*
45. *Ibid.*
46. Letter from Linda Billings of the Sierra Club to other Environmental and Public Interest Groups, entitled "Working Draft—Not for Circulation," May 30, 1974.
47. Holifield in addition to being Chairman of Government Operations was also Chairman of the Joint Committee on Atomic Energy.
48. Letter from Ralph Nader to Rep. Julia Butler Hansen, July 16, 1974.
49. Letter from Linda Billings of Sierra Club and leaders of 6 other Environmental Organizations to Speaker Carl Albert, September 24, 1974.
50. Letter from Ralph Nader to Speaker Albert, September 30, 1974.
51. *Ibid.*
52. Letter from Mark Lynch of Congress Watch to Rep. Paul Sarbanes, October 3, 1974.
53. *Ibid.*
54. It is one of these ideas which sounds appealing but is a political "nonstarter" in that it runs into House norms of specialization and career advancement through expertise. The incentive system in Congress is geared toward accruing power, and service on one or two committees over time nurtures that incentive system. See Norman J. Ornstein, "Toward Restructuring the Congressional Committee System," in *Changing*

Congress: The Committee System, The Annals, Vol. 411 (Philadelphia: American Academy of Political and Social Science, 1974) especially pp. 154–155. Also see "Report from Washington," Common Cause, Vol. 4, No. 4, March–April, 1974, p. 7.

55. As would be borne out two months hence.
56. "Quick Congressional Action Needed on Important Reform Legislation," Common Cause, Editorial Memorandum, September, 1974, p. 5.
57. Democratic Caucus Resolution, July 22.
58. *Ibid.*
59. See Davidson and Oleszek, *Congress Against Itself, op.cit.,* p. 217 and Interviews.
60. Burton was reported to have said: "This product (the Bolling plan) can hardly be called an improvement . . . it ought to be sent back to the drawing board." Conlon, Bolling interviews; Burton was known also to be less than an admirer of Bolling himself.
61. Rule XI, Section 713(a)(1)(1)A states: "It shall be the duty of the chairman of each committee to report or cause to be reported promptly to the House any measure approved by the Committee and to take or cause to be taken necessary steps to bring the matter to a vote." *Rules of the House of Representatives, Constitution, Jefferson's Manual,* and *Rules of the House of Representatives* (Washington, D.C.: U.S. Government Printing Office, 1975), p. 428.
62. Requiring subcommittees on all committees with more than 15 members; subpoena power would be extended to all committees; and the precedents of the House would be compiled within two years—and every two years thereafter by the Parliamentarian (not the Speaker, as in the Hansen proposal). See Patricia Goldman, "Background on the Martin Resolution for Committee Reform," House Wednesday Group, September 19, 1974; and *DSG Legislative Report,* Week of September 30, 1974, p. iv.
63. Cable Interview.
64. Davidson and Oleszek, *Congress Against Itself, op.cit.,* p. 228.
65. See Appendix, p. A1–A5 for a summary of the differences between the Bolling, Hansen and Martin plans. More detailed descriptions can be found in "The Bolling Committee Recommendations," *DSG Fact Sheet* 93-23, April 18, 1974; "The Hansen Committee Recommendations," *DSG Fact Sheet* 93-33, July 16, 1974; "A Comparison of the Bolling and Hansen Committee Recommendations for House Committee Reform," House Wednesday Group, August 5, 1974. The full report of the Bolling Committee was "Committee Reform Amendments of 1974," Report of the Select Committee of Committees, 93rd Congress, Second Session, Rept. 93-216, March 21, 1974. The Hansen recommendations were printed in a "Staff Draft," July 18, 1974 and later in the so-called "Red book": "Summary of Major Changes in Rules X and XI of the Rules of the House of Representatives" (Washington, D.C.: U.S. Government Printing Office, October, 1974). These pamphlets appeared immediately after the Hansen victory. Jurisdiction over such printing matters remained in House Administration, chaired by Rep. Wayne Hays.
66. Rule XIX, Section 823 states: "An amendment in the nature of a substitute may be proposed before amendments to the pending portion of

original text have been acted on, but may not be voted on until such amendments have been disposed of." *Rules of the House, op.cit.,* p. 536.

67. Udall perhaps is a possibility; but then, without calling into question his reform credentials, his Interior subcommittee might well have reappeared on the new Energy and Environment Committee with him at the helm. And even then, there was a good chance Udall would not be in the House much longer. Instead he hoped to be influencing energy and environment matters from the White House or the Senate.

68. Bolling Interview.

69. *Ibid.*

70. Hays Interview.

Six

Party Reform III: The Triumph of the Party Reformers in the Democratic Caucus, 1974–1975

6:1 ORCHESTRATING CAUCUS REFORM: OUTSIDE ENCOURAGEMENT AND INSIDE MANEUVER

Political Background

"The election next month will quicken an evolution on Capitol Hill that, in the view of many members of Congress and others, could have revolutionary consequences. Congress, the nation's oldest institution, is getting younger. As a result, it could be entering a period of reform."[1] That assessment of the possible impact of the forthcoming 1974 Congressional elections was obviously based on more than actuarial projections. It was also a product of the political tumult of the intervening period which included the unfolding of the Watergate scandal, the resignation and disgrace of Vice President Spiro Agnew, and the collapse of Richard Nixon's presidency—culminating in his own resignation on August 9, 1974. The advent of Gerald Ford required that pundits make only minor adjustments of their predictions of a Democratic landslide. Whether out of distrust of the Republicans, frustration with the faltering economy, or in response to the positive attractions of fresh-faced Democratic challengers, the electorate seemed ripe for the rhetoric of reform. On November 5, 1974, the voters registered their judgment: a massive Democratic majority in the House of 291 to 144[2] including 75 new Democratic members, and 92 freshmen altogether.

The infusion of new Democrats provided veteran reformers with a presumptive majority for both liberal policies and DSG-style Congressional reform. After six years of incremental gains, the reformers appeared to be on the verge of a major breakthrough. Shortly before the election, *Washington Post* columnist Mary Russell had described the reform movement as "generally half finished, leaving the House like a caterpillar in its chrysalis, no longer crawling, but unable to fly."[3] With the election behind them, reformers outside and inside now began plotting the other half.

Activity

Outside Groups

The October imbroglio over Committee reform had divided reform-minded outside organizations. But the Democratic landslide and its accompanying prospect of major Party reforms served admirably to smooth the rift. Organized labor, ADA, Common Cause, Ralph Nader's Congress Watch and the League of Women Voters all rallied behind various ingredients of the developing "reform package." The differences that remained concerned emphasis more than substance.

The AFL-CIO, relieved at having preserved the Education and Labor Committee, sought to undo one aspect of the Hansen plan they had been forced to accept in order to save their patron committee. The Hansen plan had reinstated almost all of the Ways and Means jurisdiction, tampering with it only in requiring it to establish four subcommittees. AFL-CIO had, for years, opposed the conservative economic legislation produced by Ways and Means. Now through Party reform, they saw their chance to make Ways and Means more receptive to liberal, labor-backed policies. A week after the election, the AFL-CIO sent a letter to every Democratic congressman endorsing reform of Ways and Means:

> Among the major issues coming before the new Congress will be: tax justice, national health insurance, trade, and improvements in unemployment insurance. All this legislation falls within the jurisdiction of the Ways and Means Committee. Therefore, the AFL-CIO is convinced that, among other changes, the Democratic Caucus must make modifications in this committee's structure.
>
> We strongly support two necessary changes . . . 1) a party ratio that reflects the make-up of the 94th Congress, and 2) a substantial enlargement in the total number of members of this important committee . . .[4]

The AFL-CIO also favored reform of the closed rule which would provide for germane amendments from the floor if they were sponsored by a "significant"[5] number of members

The United Auto Workers wrote members endorsing the same provisions, and added some important additions beyond the liberalization of Ways and Means: shifting the Committee on Committees function from the Democratic members of the Ways and Means Committee to the Steering and Policy Committee of the Democratic Caucus,[6] opening Conference Committee meetings to the public, and requiring distribution of copies of all record votes in the Democratic Caucus to each Democratic member (virtually assuring their availability to the press).

Common Cause quickly followed with their advice for Democrats: 1) transfer the Committee on Committees' function to Steering and Policy, 2) reform closed rule procedure, 3) open Conference meetings, 4) record Caucus votes and 5) limit the tenure of committee chairmen to four terms.[7] Only the last point was a Common Cause addition to the reform package, a resurrection of the Bennett proposal—versions of which had been introduced (and defeated) off and on since 1970. On November 15, ADA called for adoption of the same set of proposals, although in different order, stating that the previous reforms "were only a continuation of a process which had far to go."[8]

Finally, Ralph Nader weighed in with a letter to all Democratic representatives on November 25 mentioning all the previously stated Common Cause-ADA proposals, and adding one more for the benefit of the freshmen: an assurance that freshmen members be guaranteed representation on Ways and Means, and Appropriations.[9]

The outside groups had been advised of proposals by their DSG Executive contacts, who were anxious to develop an effective "outside" staging operation. Meanwhile, the inside component, DSG and its reform tacticians, put the finishing touches on their reform package as swarms of reformist freshmen descended on Washington for the December 2–4 "early organization" Caucuses.

Inside: The DSG Reform Package

The DSG Chairman Tom Foley, Conlon, and the DSG Executive Committee had been holding their usual post-election meetings. The mood could not have been more different from the glum 1968 meetings when they had launched the first halting attempt to revive the Caucus. Now in late 1974 Nixon was out of office; an un-elected

Gerald Ford was President; and there was a liberal majority in the House for the first time since 1964–1966.

The DSG reformers planned their attack carefully, seeking to take full advantage of the propitious circumstances. The proposals advocated by the various outside groups—with the exception of the term limitation for chairmen—were all proposals DSG was planning to put forward at the December Caucus. The reforms were designed to "improve the responsiveness and effectiveness of the Democratic majority and the House itself in the 94th Congress,"[10] and were the basis of a special DSG reform meeting on November 26 and a briefing for freshmen on December 1. The DSG package called for:

- Shifting the Committee on Committees to the Steering and Policy Committee from the Democratic Members of Ways and Means.
- Enlarging the Ways and Means Committee from 25 to 37 members.
- Mandating the Party leadership to negotiate party ratios "not less than 62.2%," the proportion of Democrats in the full House.
- Requiring that the Majority Whip be elected at the start of the 94th Congress, and providing that no member serve as Whip for more than two consecutive terms.
- Distributing Record Votes to Caucus members.
- Opening Committee meetings, extending the existing open meeting provisions by requiring a vote at the start of each separate meeting rather than permitting one vote at start of consideration of a bill.
- Opening House-Senate Conferences, extending anti-secrecy reform.
- Amending the Caucus rule of filling subcommittee vacancies, providing that all subcommittee positions be filled by bidding in order of full committee seniority. "This would give junior members and freshmen a better chance of getting subcommittee assignments of their preference."
- Permitting committees to use proxies (restricted by the Hansen plan, H.Res.988, as amended) but tightening up their use: proxies must be authorized in writing, signed by the member, designated to a member authorized to execute the proxy, limited to a specific matter, assert that member is absent on official business or is otherwise unable to attend, and contain the date and the time proxy was issued.[11]

By the day before the Caucus, DSG had added one more provision: requiring that subcommittee chairmen of the Appropriations Committee—like full committee chairmen—be voted upon by the full Caucus. This was a recognition of the almost total autonomy of those subcommittees, and of the grip each subcommittee held over appropriations in their special fields. A December 1 DSG Special Report[12] provided a summary of the reform package, including detailed rationales for each provision. Unlike 1964 when the new Democratic majority had arrived in Washington poised for action but there had been no concerted effort for procedural reform in the January organizing Caucus, this time DSG was prepared. Moreover, the "early organization" in December, originally suggested by Speaker Albert in his testimony before the Bolling Committee and included in the Hansen substitute, H.Res.988, now sustained the momentum of the election victory. The "outside" and "inside" forces had been mobilized.

The Caucus, December 2–4

The Democrats caucused on the House floor at noon on December 2. The first order of busines was the election of a new Caucus Chairman to replace Teague, who was stepping down after two terms.[13] The contestants were Phillip Burton, the liberal reformer and architect of both DSG Party reform and the more recent Hansen victory over the Bolling Committee, and B. F. Sisk, the moderate Rules Committee member and unsuccessful candidate for Majority Leader in 1971. Burton had staked a claim to the mantle of the reformers, skillfully cultivated during his days as DSG Chairman and in his earlier advocacy of an elective Whip (with himself in mind as the candidate). A pragmatic liberal, Burton was the candidate of the reformist left wing of the party, although his reputation as a power broker attracted the support of Wayne Hays and others not associated either with reformism or the left. Sisk was the candidate of the center and the right, a founding member of DSG whose conservative policy stances and procedural traditionalism had led him to part company with DSG on their recent projects. In late 1973 he had organized a group of moderates and conservatives, the United Democrats of Congress, in an attempt to counter the increasing influence of DSG. UDC attracted 100 members and had held meetings but had yet to find a more positive *raison d'être*. Now the mild-mannered Sisk was running with support of senior and conservative committee potentates, unenthusiastic about reform and even less enamored with an activist Caucus led by the Machiavellian Burton.

Most observers agreed that it would be a close race, and that, had it taken place in the 93rd Congress, Sisk would have been the favorite. However, the 94th Congress's 75 freshmen, elected on a platform of reform and courted by DSG—by Burton personally, in his capacity as chairman of DSG's campaign committee—had tipped the scales in favor of Burton. One informed estimate was that 85–90 per cent of the freshmen would back both Burton and the DSG reform package.[14] Assuming that the veteran members were approximately evenly divided—perhaps slightly anti-Burton and anti-reform—overwhelming freshman support would supply the margin of victory. In a secret ballot vote, Burton won 162–111, an indication of a solid reformist majority, and confirmation of the pivotal role of the 75 new members.

The Caucus then considered the first item of the DSG package, the shift of the Committee on Committees function to the Steering and Policy Committee. Don Fraser offered a resolution to remove this role from Ways and Means, a move particularly attractive to freshmen, the ones most directly affected. They would shortly be seeking assignments to committees and were encouraged by veteran reformers to believe that they could expect more favorable treatment from the Steering and Policy Committee. Ironically, Speaker Albert, the man who would be the major beneficiary of the reform, opposed the shift. He was quite satisfied with the existing arrangement by which the Speaker and Majority Leader sat on the Committee on Committees as non-voting *ex officio* members. But reformers were not to be dissuaded. David Obey summed up the reform position: "It ought to be a function of the leadership, and if the leadership doesn't want it, I want them to have it anyway. I want members to owe their committee assignments to the leadership, not to the Ways and Means Committee."[15]

The Committee on Committees shift passed 146–122, a relatively narrow 24 vote margin, probably reflecting hesitance on the part of veteran members rather than a crack in the solidly reformist freshman bloc.

Further DSG proposals were submitted to the Caucus, and—one by one—the old order succumbed to the new majority. By voice vote, the Ways and Means Committee was enlarged from 25 to 37. Appropriations subcommittee chairmen were made subject to Caucus approval, on a vote of 147–116. Subcommittee autonomy was increased on two voice votes, the first authorizing Democratic Caucuses of full Committees—rather than Chairmen—to set subcommittee jurisdictions, and a second requiring that subcommittee assignments be done by a bidding process based on seniority on the full committee, opening up more desirable assignments to junior members. On other voice votes, committees were required to have a Democratic majority of not less than two-thirds plus one; "open committee" provisions were tightened; and all dual committee chairmanships were barred. This last rules change affected standing committee chairmen of joint, special, or select committees. On a motion by Bolling, the Caucus adopted 106–55 a provision giving the Speaker the authority to appoint all

Rules Committee members, a move not included in the DSG package but which was part of Bolling's quest to strengthen the speakership.

Finally, in a provision which anticipated challenges to chairmen in the January Caucuses, the Democratic Caucus passed a procedure for contests between rival candidates. In the event that the senior member was rejected, they would be asked for a second nominee. However, the second nominee could be opposed by members nominated from the floor. The provision also required a five day campaign period when there were contests.

The only DSG reform proposal to fail was the elective whip, overwhelmingly rejected 32–108. This was in marked contrast to the 114–123 defeat two years before. One key difference was that Burton, the prime supporter of an elective whip in 1973 now was Caucus Chairman and had no interest in creating a more legitimate "rung on the ladder" to party leadership. Other (non-DSG) reforms which were rejected involved limitations on the tenure of chairmen: the first, mandatory retirement at 70—defeated by voice vote—the second, a six year limit on service as chairman—defeated 63–131. Minority staffing and proxy voting, both controversial partisan items, were held over until the January 13, 1975 Caucus, the day before the Congress convened.

The dominant impression left by the December Caucus was the totality of the reformers' victory. The new majority, led by an experienced and prepared DSG, had demonstrated its mastery. By December 4 the "rules of the game" had been quietly transformed.

6:2 USING THE REFORMS: INSURGENCY AGAINST SELECTED CHAIRMEN

Activity

Between December 4 and January 13, the reformers inside and outside plotted their campaign to make use of the recent reforms. Their preoccupation was, once again, seniority and the deposing of chairmen. While the DSG and outside reformist tacticians pondered various vulnerable targets, the freshmen initiated their own method of assessing the incumbent chairmen.

The Freshman Caucus

Representatives Timothy Wirth of Colorado, Gladys Spellman of Maryland, and Ned Pattison of New York had organized meetings of freshmen during the first Caucus period. Wirth raised money for a staff and an office, and Richard Ottinger, a former member and previous freshman in the 1964 intake, was elected temporary chairman of the new "freshman caucus." On the recommendation of Floyd Fithian of Indiana, the freshmen organizers invited all full committee chairmen to come before them to discuss their committees' work. This was a complete turnabout from the days when freshmen would come hat-in-hand to the august Ways and Means member for their region and seek favorable treatment in the parcelling out of committee assignments. Now the chairmen were called before the freshmen, 75 strong and respectfully looking over the chairmen to see whether they merited continuance.

The meetings, held on January 9, 10, 11 and 13, were closed and informal, with chairmen answering questions about specific legislative business or grievances about their conduct. The chairmen responded in different styles: Mahon of Appropriations deferential, Hebert of Armed Services condescending, Poage evasive about issues before his Agriculture Committee such as food stamps and school lunches, and Patman of Banking and Currency "unresponsive."[16] Wayne Hays impressed the freshmen with his blunt but refreshing candor. Judiciary Chairman Rep. Peter Rodino, whom freshmen had seen on television chairing the Impeachment hearings, entered to a standing ovation. On the other extreme, Hebert was reported to have perturbed the new members by addressing them as "boys and girls," although his office denies that he said this.[17] The meetings exposed freshmen to various aspects of committee work, the prerogatives—and potential abuses—of the chair, and standards on which to judge the incumbent chairmen. Freshmen now had impressions that would influence whom they would and would not support in the January Caucuses. Meanwhile, a joint force of DSG, Common Cause, and Nader's Congress Watch was developing a more formal set of criteria for evaluating chairmen.

The Common Cause Report on Committee Chairmen

The reformers laid out three standards:

- Compliance with Caucus Rules, Committee Rules, and House Rules
- Personal and Procedural Fairness
- Use of Power[18]

They assessed the extent to which chairmen had observed the various rules governing the conduct of committee business. Particularly interesting were the sections examining implementation of recent Caucus guidelines on subcommittee autonomy, staffing and party ratios.[19] The groups then took into account personal demeanor in the conduct of committee work. Finally, they dealt with more political considerations: use of the chair to advance personal policy or constituency objectives, voting record, and other factors summed up by the question: "Does he abuse or misuse (power) in any manner?"

The reformers proceeded to assess 14 chairmen on this basis, and released their findings on January 13 under the imprimatur of Common Cause. The original plan had been to attribute jointly the report to Common Cause and Nader's Congress Watch, but on the day before its release Congress Watch pulled out of the project because of the report's unflattering treatment of Wright Patman, whom Nader had decided to support.

The document began by noting that "for the first time Members are giving serious consideration to evaluating the performance of incumbent chairmen rather than simply reinforcing the seniority system by rubber-stamping the ranking member."[20] After outlining the criteria, they summarized their findings: three chairmen—Madden, Patman, and Staggers—showed "significant shortcomings," three others—Mahon, Poage, and Hays—were responsible for "more serious abuses," and one, F. Edward Hebert of Armed Services "flagrantly violates all three standards."[21]

The report went on to cite abuses of individual chairmen, ranging from George Mahon's alleged packing of four of his eight Appropriations subcommittees with conservatives, to Ray Madden's use of his position on Rules to hold up bills in aid of his own "pork barrel" legislation. Common Cause leveled a series of allegations against their old nemesis Wayne Hays. The House Administration chairman was described as "ultimate controller of staff payrolls, allocator of offices and furniture, overseer of the House Information System, and now even dispenser of parking spaces."[22] They went on to cite Hays for his threats to cut staff salaries to settle "purely personal scores" and a conflict of interest in being Chairman of House Administration and Chairman of the Democratic Congressional Campaign Committee, which put him in charge of both writing legislation on campaign spending and doling out money to Democratic campaigns. Patman was faulted for "directing the Committee in an incoherent and haphazard manner."[23] Others mentioned for less serious flaws were Diggs of the District of Columbia Committee, Sullivan of Merchant Marine and Fisheries, Staggers of Commerce and Health,[24] Perkins of

Education and Labor, Morgan of Foreign Affairs, Haley of Interior and Insular Affairs, Ichord of House Internal Security, and Teague of Science and Technology. The report was sent to all Democrats on January 13, three days before the first January Caucus, and two days before the Democratic Steering and Policy Committee would decide on their own recommendations for nominees to be presented to the full Caucus.

Steering and Policy as the Committee on Committees

Although the 24 member[25] Steering and Policy Committee was now making the recommendations, the leadership had no intention of departing from the traditional practice of recommending the senior Democrat on each Committee. Hence O'Neill offered a motion that the ranking members be recommended by the Committee on Committees *en bloc*. However, Jonathan Bingham of New York, the man who two years earlier had suggested to O'Neill the compromise solution for the secret ballot vote on chairmen, now objected to O'Neill's motion. Bingham favored an individual secret ballot vote on each senior member. A majority of the Steering and Policy Committee concurred. They proceeded down the list of committees in alphabetical order. The first three committees: Armed Services, Agriculture, and Appropriations produced nominations of Hebert, Poage, and Mahon—but all by surprisingly close margins of 14–10. By the fourth vote members of the Committee realized that seniority was not being treated as inviolate. Secrecy and the rapid-fire succession of votes precluded calculated conspiracy, but not individual intrigue. When the votes were tallied on Banking and Currency Chairman Wright Patman, he had been refused renomination 11–13. They then voted on the next two ranking members, William Barrett of Pennsylvania and Mrs. Leonor Sullivan, both of whom were rejected by the same margin. Finally, the fourth ranking member, Henry Reuss, who was present and voting as a member of the Steering and Policy Committee, was approved 15–9.

When the Steering and Policy Committee came to the "H's" (for House Administration) there was a tie vote, 12–12, on the controversial Hays. Two more votes each yielded the same deadlock. Finally on the fourth vote, Hays was denied renomination, 11–13. Members of the committee—including Albert and O'Neill—expressed surprise at his defeat, although Hays soon thereafter alleged that O'Neill had had a hand in it.[26] If Hays suspected that the committee preferred the next ranking member, Frank Thompson, he was quickly given reason for having thought so: Thompson was recommended by a resounding 20–4. The rest of the incumbent chairmen (except Wilbur Mills who had stepped down in late 1974) were recommended for renomination.

Immediately after the adverse vote on Hays in Steering and Policy, Hays and Burton swung into action to try to reverse the decision. Perhaps the most talked-about "unholy alliance" or "odd couple" in the House, Burton and Hays respected each other as pragmatic, tough-minded legislators. Between Burton's carefully nurtured support in the reform, liberal, and freshmen camps, and Hays' backing from the moderates and others whom he had ingratiated through perquisites or campaign hand-outs, the duo had a wide base. Moreover, they both viewed the Steering and Policy vote as a preemptive strike inspired by O'Neill against a potential opponent—probably Burton—in a contest to succeed Albert. O'Neill denied this; nonetheless, the rumors circulated that someone on the Steering and Policy Committee, half-chosen by the leadership, was out to get Hays. Burton and Hays counter-attacked with a barrage of telephone calls to members on January 15.

In making their case to give Hays a second chance, Burton and Hays invented a new concept, the "fairness doctrine for incumbent chairmen." This held that every sitting chairman had a right to an up-or-down vote in the Caucus. The Steering and Policy Committee, they maintained, had denied chairmen the opportunity to put their case to the full Caucus. Although the new nomination and approval procedures had been adopted in the December Caucus, their use in displacing Hays (and Patman) had nudged Burton and Hays back to the 1971 and 1973 practice where the senior member on each committee was the *pro forma* first choice of the Committee on Committees.

The Burton-Hays position was a shrewd appeal to members' sense of fairness, as well as to the notion of an expanded role for the full Caucus. In terms of the initial debate in the DSG Executive in 1968, the Burton-Hays line pulled the method back toward the original Fraser up-or-down vote, with a second vote contest similar to the 3-way race originally envisioned by Udall. But it was directly opposite the Bolling idea of a "strong speaker" influence on selection. But then, Burton and Hays were concerned with getting Hays back his chairmanship, not with conceptual niceties or historical progress. Indeed, their creation of the "fairness" concept was a clever mask of the intensely political character of what was actually at stake. Burton and Hays were fighting to maintain the Hays side of the alliance. Burton was now Caucus Chairman and the premier liberal in the House. If Hays were able to deliver additional support, Burton would be a strong claimant for a higher party leadership post. Some reformers took a dim view of Hays, and of the alliance; for example, DSG's Conlon, Bolling, Meeds, and Abner Mikva of Illinois rallied behind Thompson. But the political clout of Burton and Hays—especially important in converting freshmen who had looked early to Burton for leadership and had been favorably impressed with Hays' candid performance at the Freshman Caucus—were receptive to the "fairness to incumbents" idea. When the Caucus met on January 16, the Burton-Hays campaign had already had its effect.

The Caucus received the list of chairmen submitted by the Committee on Committees, but it quickly became clear that their recommendations would not be treated as sacrosanct. Poage of Agriculture, cited for serious abuses by the Common Cause report, was rejected 141–146. The Appropriations Chairman, Mahon, was approved 193–94. Then Hebert, the key target of the Common Cause pamphlet, was rejected 133–152. Both Poage and Hebert had been weakened further by poor performances at the Freshman Caucus. Poage accepted his defeat gracefully; Hebert did not. He blamed his rejection on the Common Cause campaign, and threatened to fight the decision on the House floor.

Next the Committee on Committees considered Henry Reuss, whose nomination would serve as the first test of the Burton and Hays "fairness" doctrine. Patman, for his part, had circularized members with a "Dear Colleague"[27] letter alleging that "thirteen members of the House Steering Committee have secretly voted to deprive all other members of the House Democratic Caucus of the right to decide whether to retain me. . . ."[28] Reuss was backed by many liberals and reformers, but Patman—the cagey old populist—received the strong endorsement of Nader from outside, and inside, from liberals such as Thomas L. Ashley of Ohio. Moreover, if the Burton-Hays notion of fairness applied to Hays, it presumably held for Patman as well. Hence both non-incumbents, Reuss and Thompson, should be rejected, argued Burton, in order to facilitate a vote on Patman and Hays in the Caucus, scheduled for January 22. The case apparently had force: Reuss was rejected narrowly 141–146.

The next four chairmen (Diggs, Perkins, Morgan, and Brooks of Government Operations, in succession to Holifield who had retired) were all approved without difficulty. In the vote on Thompson, the Burton-Hays strategy triumphed easily, the Caucus rejecting Thompson 109–176. The remaining incumbents were nominated by decisive margins. The seniority system had been successfully challenged in Caucus, in the defeat of Poage and Hebert. However, it had also been

temporarily resurrected as a basis for Committee on Committees recommendations in the form of the "fairness to incumbents" doctrine,
buoyed by the rejection in Caucus of Reuss and Thompson.

The Steering and Policy Committee reconvened the next day, January 17, to make new recommendations. Under the new rules, nominations from the Caucus floor were in order. Thompson hedged for
most of the week on whether he would make the race against Hays.
The *New York Times* and the *Washington Post* both ran editorials
strongly critical of Hays, urging his defeat.[29] Nader and Common
Cause expressed similar sentiments. On January 21, the day before
the Caucus, Thompson decided to risk the ire of Hays, and announced that he would run. However, by this time Burton and Hays
had corralled the support of such diverse members as Charles Rangel,
the Harlem liberal, Walter Flowers of Alabama, liberal Ed Koch of
New York City and many others. Conlon, Bolling and other Thompson supporters tried to recoup the defections of the last week; but the
superior campaign of the Burton-Hays forces, compounded by
Thompson's indecision and late entry, produced a sizeable Hays victory, 161–111.

The Patman-Reuss contest was complicated by the entry into the
race of Robert Stephens of Georgia, the seventh ranking member of
Banking and Currency and ranking Democrat on the Bolling Committee. Stephens was more conservative than either Patman or Reuss,
and it was unclear exactly what impact he would have on the outcome.
In the three-way vote, Reuss tallied 130, Patman 90, Stephens 58. In
the run-off Reuss beat Patman 152–117.

The remaining item on the agenda was the vote on Appropriations
subcommittee chairmen, in accordance with the December rules
change. There had been speculation about possible challenges to Rep.
Jamie Whitten of Mississippi, the conservative chairman of the Subcommittee on Agriculture, Environment and Consumer Protection.
However, after he had been criticized for his positions on environmental and consumer bills, and in anticipation of opposition in
Caucus, Whitten announced that he would give up the environment
and consumer protection aspects of his jurisdiction, successfully
averting the challenge. The remaining Appropriations chairmen
were approved without controversy.

Developments

The 1974–1975 organizing Caucus, then, had witnessed the most
sustained assault on the existing order in the House since 1910–1911.
The party Caucus had been strengthened, three chairmen had been

deposed, and the insurgent reformers and freshmen had given every indication that they stood for an invigorated Congress, asserting itself against the presidency. The freshmen received the lion's share of credit for the reform successes in much of the press coverage, a fact mildly irritating to the DSG veterans who had spent six years of incremental plotting and maneuvering. Without question, the overwhelmingly reformist 75-strong freshmen contingent had provided an impetus—and the votes—for the breakthrough. However, they alone would have been hard-pressed to implement any of the reforms—or even to know what was likely to be in their interest—without the guidance provided by the DSG Executive and by the influential outside reform groups. For their part, the Republicans attacked the assertive reformist Caucus as irresponsible and unrepresentative. Warning of a return to the days of "King Caucus" as he had done during the Bolling-Hansen wrangle, John Anderson, the GOP Conference Chairman, reminded Democrats that a majority of the majority caucus was still a minority of the full House.[30] Republican Congresswoman Marjorie Holt of Maryland, focusing on the overthrow of Hebert of Armed Services, attacked the move as "a blow against our national defenses,"[31] although Melvin Price, Hebert's successor, was widely acknowledged to be as pro-Pentagon as Hebert, only more democratic and judicious. Republicans did have two specific reasons to be angered by the Democratic Caucus: minority staffing and proxy voting. During the previous October's consideration of H.Res.988, Thompson had added his "pot sweetener" of minority staffing additions to lure Republican support for the Hansen plan. Now the Democratic Caucus peremptorily modified that provision. In Caucus on January 13, in a compromise after Jack Brooks had moved to nullify that provision, Thompson agreed to a plan allocating 42 staff members to each Committee, the majority numbering 26, the minority 16, an increase of 6 for each party. Proxy voting, banned under the Hansen H.Res.988 (as it had been by the Bolling version), was reinstated with more stringent guidelines. On both issues, the Republicans emerged slightly better off than they had been before passage of H.Res.988 in October, but less well off than they would have been had the Democratic Caucus not reneged.

Apart from the Republicans, the deposed chairmen and their sympathizers—including one Democrat, John Jarman of Oklahoma, who switched to the Republicans in protest at the Caucus coups—the response to the successful insurgency was overwhelmingly favorable. The media, hitherto unlikely to investigate the vagaries of the sprawling lower house, suddenly found that their headline stories were coming from the House rather than the Senate. Moreover, reform had become more than a lame, vague hope of disgruntled junior liberals and habitual malcontents. It had been plotted, battled over, implemented, and used—and in doing so, had shifted the dynamics of Congressional power and possibly of American politics. The events had been dramatic. However, there was a lingering question about the six-year reform experience, taking on greater significance after the euphoria of the first weeks of the 94th Congress had subsided. In which direction had the reforms moved internal power in the House? What would be the short and long-term implications?

Notes

1. James Naughton, "Younger Congress Viewed as Reforming Procedures," *New York Times,* October 3, 1974, p.1.
2. Rep. John Jarman of Oklahoma switched to the Republican party in late January—in protest over the Caucus reforms—bringing the ratio to 290–145.
3. Mary Russell, "Hill Change: Slow Motion," *Washington Post,* September 15, 1974, p.B 1.
4. Letter from AFL-CIO to Democratic Members, undated, unsigned copy from ADA file.
5. Probably 50, but DSG had not yet decided.
6. Letter from Jack Beidler, UAW lobbyist, to Democratic members, November 12, 1974.
7. Letter from John Gardner, Chairman of Common Cause, to Democratic members, November 13, 1974.
8. Letter from Leon Shull, ADA National Chairman, to Democratic members, November 26, 1974.
9. Letter from Ralph Nader to Democratic members, November 25, 1974.
10. DSG Memorandum from Tom Foley, Chairman, to DSG members, November 26, 1974.
11. A summary of proposals contained in the DSG Memorandum, November 26, 1974.
12. "94th Congress Reform Proposals," *DSG Special Report,* No. 93-15, December 1, 1974.
13. A Caucus rule passed in 1973 required that no Caucus Chairman serve more than two terms.
14. "94th Reforms: House Dems Lead," *ADA Legislative Newsletter,* Vol. 3, No. 21, December 15, 1974, p. 2.
15. "December 2 House Caucuses: Preparing for the 94th," *CQ Weekly Report,* November 16, 1974, p. 3119.
16. "Reform Marches On," *ADA Legislative Newsletter,* Vol. 4, No. 2, February 1, 1975, p.1.
17. *Ibid.*
18. "Report on House Committee Chairmen," Common Cause, January 13, 1975.
19. *Ibid.*
20. *Ibid.*
21. *Ibid.*
22. *Ibid.*
23. *Ibid.*
24. Formerly the Interstate and Foreign Commerce Committee.
25. Albert, O'Neill, Burton, McFall, Brademas, Wright, Matsunaga, Fulton,

Davis, Metcalfe, Jordan, Brodhead ("leadership"—either *ex officio* or appointed). Moss, Udall, Reuss, Price, Bolling, Patman, Bevill, Stephens, Thompson, Dent, Bingham, Giaimo (elected on a regional basis by members).

26. See *ADA Legislative Newsletter*, February 1, 1975, *op. cit.*, p. 2.
27. Letter from Rep. Wright Patman to Democratic Members, January 15, 1975.
28. Patman "Dear Colleague," January 15, 1975.
29. The *Times* noted that the Caucus had "a second chance to vote down Representative Wayne Hays. . . . They ought not bungle this opportunity again." "Caucus: Second Round," *New York Times*, January 22, 1975, p.38. The *Post* added that Hays had been "autocratic, petty, secretive, and vindictive in a thousand ways," although in courting the freshmen, he had been "friendliness personified." "The Trouble With Mr. Hays," *Washington Post*, January 22, 1975, p.A20.
30. See, for example, John Anderson's remarks: "King Caucus as Kooky Monster or Two-Thirds Equal One Third," *Congressional Record*, March 3, 1975, pp.E834–835.
31. *ADA Legislative Newsletter*, February 1, 1975, *op. cit.*, p.3.

Seven

The Upshot of Party and Committee Reform by the Middle 1970s

7:1 THE DIRECTION OF REFORM: THE POTENTIAL FOR CONSOLIDATION, THE PRACTICE OF DISPERSION

"There's change," commented Richard Bolling after the flurry of Caucus reforms in December 1974, "but I don't know what it all means."[1] The conflicting criticisms and contradictory goals produced reforms similarly rife with inconsistencies. Surely it would be some time before the reformed House sorted itself out; only then could the actual effects of the reforms be assessed. Nonetheless, observers offered some preliminary speculations. For example, Michael Malbin of the *National Journal* wrote in December:

> It is clear that the committees lost something. But who gained is not as clear. The leadership got some of it, and junior members who will get better subcommittee assignments got some of it. The performance of the House is bound to be affected by the shifts. But it will take some testing and a few confrontations before it can be said precisely who got how much, or what it all means for policy.[2]

The upheaval of January made it clear that a significant redistribution of power had taken place. Some observers, suddenly noticing the shakeup on the less well-known side of Capitol Hill,[3] had dubbed it a sort of revolution, incited and executed by the freshmen.[4] This observation, however, overlooked the complicated series of reform events over six years of which 1975 was only the crowning achievement. For those who had thought that there had been a Congressional *coup d'etat,* it was only a matter of time before they discovered, to their disappointment, that it had only been a changing of the guard.

More realistic observers simply hoped that the removal of some of the "dead weight" from the committee system would manifest itself in greater Congressional productivity and effectiveness. Political science commentary reflected this quandary over reform's implications. For example, in late 1975, a book of essays[5] appeared which included one chapter discussing "The Dispersion of Authority in Congress," immediately followed by another entitled "Central Policy Organs in Congress," each article tracing these divergent trends of recent Congressional behavior. Of course, there was evidence to be found for both tendencies, which only compounded the confusion. Two other political scientists reviewed the reforms, with special emphasis on their implications for parties, and observed that most of the reforms were "explicitly aimed in part at making the majority party and its leaders effective instruments of decision-making." But they hastily appended this note of caution: "(That they simultaneously moved to diffuse power into subcommittees clouds somewhat our picture of the future role of party in Congress.")[6] A parenthetic cloud, indeed, hung over optimistic forecasts of the reassertion of party. While in the heady atmosphere of early 1975 it seemed just plausible that there might be a DSG-led assertion of the Caucus and realization of an American-style "party responsibility," the experience of the six years of incremental reform contained much more evidence to the contrary. It was certainly true that many of the instruments necessary for party rule were in place: monthly Caucus meetings, new powers for the Speaker, a revitalized Steering and Policy Committee and the political ingredient of a swollen Democratic majority. However, a close examination of the reform experience between 1969 and 1975 reveals that the instruments of party, in fact, simply shifted power further outward in the committee system, not draw it into the party caucus.

The Democratic Caucus served as the instrument of "spreading the action," i.e. shifting power to subcommittees, their chairmen, and to rank and file committee members, rather than consolidating it in the leadership. The reconstruction of events suggests that reform created the potential for consolidation, but in practice resulted instead in dispersion.

There was a compelling political reason for this. Just as in 1967, Lewis Froman had concluded that "the decentralization of power in

Congress . . . generally favors conservative interests. . . ," by the early 1970s *further* decentralization worked to the advantage of liberals. The old regime was dominated by a small number of full committee chairmen who, especially after 1946, had been able to impose their views, usually conservative, on the rest of the House. Party reformers were aided by attrition;[7] the departure of key chairmen and a broader turnover in composition—especially the intakes of 1958, 1964 and 1974—boosted the reform movement. But for most of the period the reformers relied on guile more than dependable numbers to achieve their aims. The DSG Executive deftly cultivated the support of the leadership; together they molded reform to what was thought to be acceptable to the Caucus. The key Party reforms passed because DSG and the leadership had successfully minimized conflict. Reform inside the Caucus was orderly and incremental. Ironically, the "centralized" reform leadership provided by the DSG Executive and Democratic leadership was responsible for reforms which devolved more power to subcommittee chairmen and the rank and file of each committee: making future centralized leadership all the more difficult—and perhaps improbable. By the time the Bolling plan for Committee reform appeared in 1973 and 1974 the middle seniority stakes in dispersion were already firmly implanted. The 1971 Caucus reform limiting members to one legislative subcommittee chairmanship, the creation of Democratic Caucuses on Committees, the Subcommittee Bill of Rights and the transfer of the seniority precedent outward to the selection of subcommittee chairmen all served to expedite the shift in the locus of the House's power to subcommittees. Liberals, many of whom were elected in the years of big liberal gains—1958 and 1964— had already assumed or were in line for subcommittee chairs.

The Bolling plan threatened these carefully nurtured subcommittee riches. It was consolidative reform striking directly at the heart of the most recent resting place of dispersed power. It was perceived as a serious threat and thus was vigorously opposed and defeated. The upshot was that Party reform was effectively dispersive reform, and was implemented and made tangible. Committee reform was an attempt at consolidative reform, and ran headlong into the superior claims—and member preferences—of the House's individualistic tendencies.

Analysis of the reform experience reveals how and why this occurred. Out of the multifarious internal maneuvers and "inside-outside" campaigning emerged a few major reform developments. To assess them in more detail, I shall seek to explain six aspects of the experience: the first three involve the process of reform; the last three involve the results of reform. The areas covered are:

1. Why reform was raised as an issue.
2. How the various proposals for reform were dealt with; i.e. the configuration by which they were considered and decided upon.
3. Who supported and opposed reform, particularly its two major variants: Party reform and Committee reform.
4. In which direction the reforms shifted power in the House: consolidation or dispersion.
5. Why reform took place at all.
6. Why the reforms which did take place shifted power in the direction they did.

7:2 THE PROCESS OF REFORM: CONSIDERING REFORM ISSUES, MINIMIZING CONFLICT, AND CATERING TO EMERGING POLITICAL VALUES

Raising Reform as an Issue: Changed Political Circumstances

Between 1946 and 1968, Congressional reform was a minor issue, its advocacy limited to a handful of academics, editorialists and liberal congressmen. The Joint Committee on the Organization of the Congress of 1965–1966 broached many of the reform issues which would later be taken more seriously. But the political circumstances of the time did not seem to warrant the investment of liberals' time and energies in battles over structure or procedure. Instead, Lyndon Johnson provided the leadership Congressional liberals themselves lacked; liberals devoted their attention to passing Johnson's Great Society legislation. Such interest in Congressional reform as there was in the middle 1960s was limited to relatively non-controversial items such as increased staffing, better information facilities, and other "housekeeping" reforms. It ignored issues of greater salience for power relations firstly, because liberal frustration with Congress's conservative tendencies had been temporarily assuaged, and secondly, because—the spate of Great Society legislation aside—the House oligarchy remained predominantly hostile to change, particularly where its own affairs were concerned. Influential senior members were especially mistrustful of attempts to modify existing practice. Three political scientists concluded a study of attitudes toward reform in the middle 1960s by observing: "The most pervasive damper on reformist thought and action is the known hostility of the seniority and elective leadership in Congress to many crucial kinds of change."[8]

Such was the state of Congressional reform prior to 1968. In order for a reform movement to become aroused there would first have to be a new political impetus, and secondly, enough turnover in composition (and concomitant internal dislocation) for reformers to dislodge the oligarchs who remained. The election of Richard Nixon provided the political jolt which forced liberals to come to terms with their limited base on Capitol Hill and to resolve to do something about it. The internal circumstances facilitating reform were the steady gains by Northern and Western liberals and moderates in the Democratic Caucus and the parallel slight decline in Southern representation.[9] While geography was not a perfect indicator of political leaning— there are always the liberal Bob Eckhardts, Andrew Youngs and Barbara Jordans from the South (perhaps increasingly so), and the James Delaneys[10] from the North, the growth of the non-Southern share of the Democratic Caucus and the decline of the senior Southern representation[11] stirred restiveness and a desire for a greater share of power from the middle seniority Northerners. Perhaps more significant was the new political effectiveness of DSG, especially its pragmatic Executive members. Finally, the party leaders, Speaker Albert and especially Majority Leader Tip O'Neill, evidenced a new receptivity to reform which was in direct contrast to the attitudes of the previous leadership.

Since 1911, and particularly since 1946, power in the House had been largely in the hands of its conservative committee chairmen. The Legislative Reorganization Act of 1946 had given the chairmen of the 19 committees the power which had previously been apportioned amongst 48 committees. The Act also spurred a steady rise in the number of subcommittees. By the time liberals came along to reform the reforms which had given power to the full committee chairmen, the growth of subcommittees provided a sector of potent claimants for that power: the subcommittee chairmen. Unarticulated but implicit in the reform movement was a quest for a greater share of the Democratic majority's considerable power—commensurate with liberals' increased numbers and seniority status in the party—and a desire that power be redistributed in a way which produced demonstrable gains in the individual power of liberal members. The instrument and the forum was the party Caucus; the new locus of power was subcommittees. The precise manner in which this occurred becomes clearer as we reconstruct the process of reform's consideration.

The Consideration of Reform

The process by which reform was considered formed a complicated web of proposals, objects, forums and decisions. Table 7:1 reviews these points in chronological order, and shows that the main objects of reform were the Democratic Caucus and House procedure (the latter category includes both procedure in the full House and within committees). It is also clear that the bulk of reform activity took place within the Democratic Caucus. Two trends become apparent: first—of the reform proposals which actually emerged out of the potpourri of "ideas" there was a remarkably high rate of passage, which leads to the conclusion that reform proposals which found their way to resolution were generally acted upon favorably; and secondly, most of those enacted—even those affecting House or Committee practice—were passed by the Caucus of the majority Democratic party. Despite the fact that parties are often seen as the lamentable weaklings of the American system, it remains a fact of Congressional life that the majority party dominates Congress (a fact painfully obvious to the minority).

In the present study, the majority was not only responsible for "organizing" the Congress: i.e. electing the House's committee leaders; it was also the main locus of successful moves for reform. Thus even the major attempt at bipartisan, institutional change during this period, the Bolling plan, found its way to the party caucuses. In fact, its referral to the Hansen Committee of the Democratic Caucus, followed by the victory of the Hansen plan, illustrates the profound impact the majority Caucus can have on reform of the whole House.

The extremely high rate of acceptance liberal reform proposals enjoyed provides a clue to another aspect of the reform process. The impressive record of the reformers in winning acceptance for their proposals might lead one to conclude that reform was extremely popular in the House, i.e., that selfless members rushed to embrace reform proposals for the overall good of the House! Of course, the reality was somewhat different: the various stratagems of reformers, the elaborate campaigns to mobilize outside support, and the ploys of reformers and anti-reformers alike made reform far from a foregone conclusion. The hostility to reform so apparent in the middle 1960s remained a prominent—if less frequently articulated—characteristic of the House virtually throughout the period under study. Only after 1974 was reformism the clear preference of the Caucus. It is difficult to reconcile this impressive streak of reform successes with the known

TABLE 7:1

Selected Reform Issues, Objects, Forums and Actions, 1965–1975

Year	Reform Proposal	Object	Forum	Action Taken
1965	21 Day Rule	House Floor procedure (to circumvent Rules Committee)	Caucus House	Adopted
1966	"Housekeeping" Reforms, Staffing Congressional Research Service etc.	House Facilities	Joint Committee	Stalled for four years, Adopted 1970
	Seniority Reform	Party Selection of Committee Leaders	Joint Committee	None
	Committee Re-jurisdiction: Separation of Education and Labor Committee, etc.	House Committee Structure	Joint Committee	None
1969	Monthly Meetings of the Democratic Caucus	Party Caucus	Democratic Caucus	Adopted
	Ratification of Committee Lists by Democratic Caucus	Party Caucus	Caucus	Adopted
1970	Committee to Study Seniority and Recommend Changes (Hansen Committee)	Party Selection of Committee leaders	Caucus	Adopted
	Legislative Reorganization. Anti-Secrecy Amendments, particularly Record Teller	House floor and Committee of the Whole	House	Adopted
	Legislative Reorganization. Anti-Seniority Amendments	Party Selection of Committee Leaders	House	Rejected
	Seniority Task Force and Reform (Conable Task Force)	Party Selection of Committee Leaders (Republican Ranking Members)	Republican Conference	Adopted
	Electronic Voting	House Floor Procedure	House	Adopted
	Guarantee of Debate Time	House Floor Procedure	House	Adopted
1971	Ten Member Challenge to Chairmen Provision (Hansen Committee)	Party Selection of Committee Leaders	Caucus	Adopted

TABLE 7:1—*continued*

Year	Reform Proposal	Object	Forum	Action Taken
	Seniority Modification (no longer the sole criterion)	Party Selection of Committee Leaders	Caucus	Adopted
	Committee Membership limitation (no Democrat could serve on more than two committees with legislative jurisdiction)	Party Service on Committee	Caucus	Adopted
	Subcommittee Chairmanship limitation (no Member may chair more than one legislation sub-committee)	Party Service on Subcommittees	Caucus	Adopted
	Subcommittee Staff allowance (each subcommittee chairman could appoint one staff member)	Party Service on Subcommittee	Caucus	Adopted
	Party ratios (should be negotiated at rate of 3 Democrats to 2 Republicans on Committees)	Party Composition of Committee	Caucus	Adopted
	Committee Membership Nominations (allowing nomination of a Democrat to a Committee if 50% of members' state delegation support claim—more to circumvent Democratic Committee on Committees)	Party Selection of Committee Members	Caucus	Adopted
	31 Day Rule	House Floor procedure (to circumvent Rules Committee)	Caucus House	Adopted by Democratic Caucus, Overturned on House floor: Rejected
1973	Reconstituted Steering and Policy Committee	Party Decision-making	Caucus	Adopted

TABLE 7:1—*continued*

Year	Reform Proposal	Object	Forum	Action Taken
	Automatic Secret Ballot on Committee Chairmanships (Evans Proposal)	Party Selection of Committee Leaders	Caucus	Rejected
	Automatic vote on Committee Chairmanships, Unspecified Voting Arrangements (Hansen Proposal)	Party Selection of Committee Leaders	Caucus	Adopted
	Secret Ballot on Demand of 20% of Caucus Members	Party Selection of Committee Leaders	Caucus	Adopted
	Committee Designations (as "exclusive," "major," or "non-major")	Party Selection of Committee Members	Caucus	Adopted
	Guarantee of a Major Committee Assignment	Party Selection of Committee Members	Caucus	Adopted
	Establishment of Democratic Caucuses on Committees	Party Decision making on Committees	Caucus	Adopted
	Subcommittee Bill of Rights	Party Rules regarding Subcommittee Practice	Caucus	Adopted
	Subcommittee Chairmen approved by Committee Democratic Caucuses	Party Rules regarding Subcommittee Practice	Caucus	Adopted
	Subcommittee Membership Bidding Process (on Subcommittee Vacancies)	Party Selection of Subcommittee Members	Caucus	Adopted
	Expansion of the Committee on Committees to include Party Leaders	Party Membership of Subcommittee Members	Caucus	Adopted
	Closed Rule Restriction 4 day layover	House procedure through a Caucus Rule	Caucus	Adopted
	Term Limitation on Caucus Chairmen and other Caucus officials	Party Leadership posts	Caucus	Adopted

TABLE 7:1—*continued*

Year	Reform Proposal	Object	Forum	Action Taken
	Open Committee Meetings (Eckhardt-Foley-Fascell)	House Committee procedure	Caucus House	Adopted
	Open Up Caucus Journal (Matsunaga Provision)	Democratic Caucus Rules	Caucus	Rejected
	Scheduling of Suspension Bills (2 more days)	House Rules Change	House	Adopted
1974	Budget and Impoundment Act. Establishment of a Budget Committee	House Rules Change	House	Adopted
	Adoption of Special procedures for nomination and election of Budget Committee Members	Party Selection of Budget Committee Members	Caucus	Adopted
	Refer Bolling Plan to Hansen Committee	Party Review of House Committee Reform	Caucus	Adopted
	Bolling Committee Reform Plan	House Committee Structure	House	Rejected by House
	Martin Committee Reform Plan	House Committee Structure	House	Rejected by House
	Hansen Committee Reform Plan	House Committee Structure	House	Adopted by House
1975	Shift of Democratic Committee on Committees function to Steering and Policy Committee	Party Selection of Committee Members	Caucus	Adopted
	Enlargement of the Ways and Means Committee from 25 to 37	House Committee Structure	Caucus House	Adopted
	Party Ratios (2 Democrats to every 1 Republican)	Party Composition of Committees	Caucus House	Adopted
	Automatic Vote on Chairmen	Party Selection of Committee Leaders	Caucus	Adopted

TABLE 7:1—*continued*

Year	Reform Proposal	Object	Forum	Action Taken
	Nominations from Caucus floor on Contested Chairmanships	Party Selection of Committee Leaders	Caucus	Adopted
	Appropriations Subcommittee Chairmen Voted Upon same as Full Committee Chairmen	Party Selection of Subcommittee Leaders	Caucus	Adopted
	Speaker nomination of Rules Committee Members	Party Selection of Committee Members	Caucus	Adopted
	Subcommittee Selection of Assignments— Bidding Process	Party Selection of Subcommittee Posts	Caucus	Adopted
	Open Committee Meetings	House Rules (vote to close on same day as meeting)	Caucus	Adopted
	Open Conference Meetings	House Rules	Caucus House Senate	Adopted
	Limitation on number of chairmanships (of Joint, Select and Standing Committees)	House Committee Structure	Caucus	Adopted
	Abolition of HISC	House Committee Structure	Caucus House	Adopted
	Ways and Means Vacancies filled by Special procedure for 94th Congress	Party Selection of Committee Members	Caucus	Adopted
	Caucus Votes (all record votes in Caucus distributed to members)	Party Decision Making	Caucus	Adopted
	Minority Staffing	Party Allocation of Staff	Caucus	Adopted
	Subcommittee Jurisdiction (set by Democratic Caucus on Committee)	Party decision making on Subcommittee	Caucus	Adopted

skepticism toward reform, but the answer, to a large extent, lies in the fact that the important decisions often took place before formal consideration in the official forums, the Caucus or House. There was typically a conscious well-orchestrated attempt by the reformers and party leaders to minimize conflict over reform. Reformers understood that it was in their interest to present the reform proposals in the most favorable circumstances, preferably with the public support of the leadership. The Speaker and Majority Leader sought to maintain party harmony while veering toward the liberals, who presented increasingly strong claims to a greater share of the party's power. Thus many of the key reform proposals were presented to the Democratic Caucus or House as *faits accomplis,* as is borne out by Table 7:2 which describes the DSG position on proposals, the position of the Democratic leadership, and the vote on adoption.

Minimizing Conflict: DSG, the Leadership, and the Hansen Committee

The DSG Executive was the major force behind the Party reform movement. The DSG chairmen, O'Hara, Fraser and Burton provided pragmatic and effective leadership. Staff director Richard Conlon added his personal political acumen and produced many of the DSG's best ideas, shrewd tactics, and skillful execution. At their biennial post-election sessions, the DSG Executive formulated their reform goals for the next session's opening Caucuses. They surveyed the political landscape, assessed the state of the reform effort, and developed proposals which the Caucus might be realistically expected to accept. They understood clearly that their success depended, in large part, on timing. In addition, they realized that the less controversial reform was made to appear the better the chance of passage. The DSG Executive had no wish for symbolic victories. ("It's always been a marriage of the pragmatic types and the ideologues, but it's dominated by the pragmatists," observed James O'Hara.)[12]

The Executive devised the strategy, and the DSG membership was generally expected to fall into line behind it. Consequently, almost all of the important decisions regarding reform took place within the DSG Executive, in negotiations between the DSG Executive and the leadership, and later, within the Hansen Committee (and its discussions with others, including DSG's leaders and the leadership).

O'Hara's original idea for monthly meetings of the Caucus in 1969 was only the first successful attempt by DSG to win the leadership's backing and parley that into a concerted reform campaign. The DSG Executive decided that monthly meetings were their prime goal for the 1969 Caucus; they approached Speaker McCormack and Majority Leader Albert with the idea. After McCormack's initial hesitancy, both he and Albert assented. Shortly thereafter, the Caucus was presented with a "leadership proposal" for monthly meetings which the Caucus promptly adopted by voice vote. One can only speculate as to what might have happened if the Caucus had been presented the same proposal, touted as a bold new DSG-backed reform and intended as the first step in a series of sweeping changes, without the endorsement of the leadership. The DSG activists had no inclination to find out. This tactic of soliciting the leadership's support became the standard practice of DSG, and a key element of their success, as the rest of Table 7:2 reveals. Ten out of the sixteen selected reform proposals[13] were approved by voice vote, having first been worked out by DSG, the leadership, and perhaps third parties, before the Caucus or House considered them. These included many of the most significant reforms of Caucus procedure.

Two other examples of the way in which successful reforms depended on the assiduous minimizing of conflict—both in 1970—were the creation of the Hansen Committee on Organization, Study and Review, and the passage of the Record Teller amendment on the House floor. The idea for the Hansen Committee was Conlon's; he saw it as an effective device to establish an official party committee to study seniority, and to lend reform recommendations on seniority credibility they would lack if supported solely by DSG. In order to win passage, DSG again approached the leadership who, after changing some of the language and transforming it into a substitute in the name of Albert, smoothed the way for its adoption (again by voice vote). The Legislative Reorganization Amendments in 1970 afforded reformers the opportunity for institutional change. DSG, in conjunction with the Republican "Rumsfeld's Raiders," sponsored anti-secrecy amendments, most notably the record teller revision of the Committee of the Whole practice. On this occasion, the reformers enlisted two respected members unassociated with the reform effort, Tip O'Neill and Charles Gubser, to bolster the bipartisan campaign. They also recruited outside support from liberal groups and newspapers. Finally, after this impressive array of inside and outside support had been assembled, Majority leader Albert and Minority Leader Ford endorsed the record teller, which was accepted by the House on a voice vote.

Other proposals which passed after similarly shrewd maneuvers are included in Table 7:2. A revealing contrast between noncontroversial

TABLE 7:2
Adoption of Key Reform Proposals, 1969–1975

Year	Proposal	DSG Position	Leadership position	Vote on Adoption
1969	Monthly Meetings of Democratic Caucus	For	For	Voice Vote
	Approval of Committee Lists	For	For	Voice Vote
1970	Creation of the Hansen Committee	For	For	Voice Vote
	Record Teller Amendment	For (with Republican partners)	For (With Minority Leader)	Voice Vote
1971	Hansen Committee Seniority Modification: Ten Member Challenge, Seniority not sole criterion for selection	For	For	Voice Vote
	Limitation on Subcommittee Chairmanships	For	For	Voice Vote
1973	Reconstitution of the Steering and Policy Committee	For	For	Voice Vote
	Hansen Committee Proposal for an Automatic Vote on Chairmen (without specific voting arrangement)	—*	For	204–9
	O'Neill-Bingham Proposal for a Secret Ballot on Demand of 20% of the Caucus	For	For	117–58
	Subcommittee Bill of Rights and other Committee and Subcommittee Reforms	For	For	Voice Vote
	Eckhardt-Foley-Fascell Open Committee Proposal	For	—	83–37

TABLE 7:2—*continued*
Adoption of Key Reform Proposals, 1969–1975

Year	Proposal	DSG Position	Leadership position	Vote on Adoption
1974	Budget and Impound-ment Control Act	—*	—	House
	Burton Resolution for Referral of the Bolling Plan to the Hansen Committee	—	—	111–95
	Clay Motion for a Se-cret Ballot on the Bur-ton Resolution to refer the Bolling Plan to the Hansen Committee	—	—	98–81
	O'Hara Motion to In-struct the Rules Com-mittee to make the Hansen Plan in Order as a Substitute to the Bolling Plan.	—	—	Voice Vote
	House Acceptance of the Hansen Plan	—	Albert against, O'Neill for.	203–165
1975	Shift Committee on Committees Function to the Steering and Policy Committee	For	—	146–122
	Speaker Nomination of Committee Mem-bers	For	—	106–55
	Enlargement of Ways and Means from 25 and 37	For	—	Voice Vote
	Caucus Approval of Appropriation Sub-committee Chairmen	For	—	147–16
	Subcommittee and Committee Reforms	For	—	Voice Vote

*DSG preferred the Evans proposal for an automatic secret ballot vote. However it was defeated (see Table 7:3).

and controversial reform was the 1971 voice vote passage of the Hansen Committee's proposal for a ten member challenge to chairmen and the use of that provision to challenge McMillan. While the former adoption by voice vote implied "unanimous" support for the reform, the direct challenge to McMillan revealed that only 96 members were prepared to depart from seniority in practice. But while 96 votes against the obstreperous chairman of the District of Columbia Committee was a high-water mark for reformers at the time, it was far from a majority; it pointed out the wisdom of the DSG approach to win support without risking a vote on the Caucus floor.

In 1973 the Caucus passed by voice vote two other potentially far-reaching reforms: the reconstitution of the Steering and Policy Committee and the Subcommittee Bill of Rights. These proposals had been quietly worked out by the Hansen Committee, with participation by prominent DSG figures (including Hansen members Burton, O'Hara and Thompson). In the dispute over the secret ballot addendum to the automatic vote on chairmen, the Hansen Committee and the DSG reformers (led by Rep. Frank Evans) were unable to work out a mutually acceptable agreement. The Evans amendment providing for a secret ballot was defeated, the Hansen provision for an automatic vote without a secret ballot was overwhelmingly approved. But once again a clever orchestration of events allowed the reformers to achieve their objective. DSG reformer Jonathan Bingham suggested to Majority Leader O'Neill that he should sponsor an amendment providing for an automatic vote on demand of 20 per cent of the Caucus, and it carried easily. The link between the DSG Executive and the Democratic leadership became the key to the success of reform. DSG formulated the proposals, rallied its own membership, and cultivated external support from the liberal groups. But it was the prestige and legitimacy of the leadership that enabled DSG to gain support from the sections of the party unsympathetic to reform.

The fate of the DSG proposals which failed to win the support of the leadership can be seen in Table 7:3. The four proposals selected were all easily defeated in votes on the Caucus floor. These included the demand for an early "report back" on seniority from the Hansen Committee in 1970, the Evans proposal for an automatic secret ballot on chairmen, the Matsunaga proposal for an Open Caucus Journal, and the proposal for an elective whip. On all the proposals except the last the leadership took no position, fearful that these reforms were too ambitious. DSG's proposal for an elective whip—supported strenuously by DSG's Phillip Burton—was opposed by the Majority Leader who privately lobbied for its defeat before the 1973 Caucus, and in the Caucus session he asked the Caucus to preserve the Majority Leader's prerogative to appoint his own whip. In 1975 the same plan was proposed; this time a new member of the leadership, Caucus Chairman Phillip Burton, along with the Majority Leader, privately opposed the proposal, and it was decisively defeated again.

The most flagrant example of a reform which defied attempts to limit conflict was the Bolling plan of 1974. Rejurisdiction of committees provoked a storm of political controversy. There were several devices designed to reduce the opportunities for confrontation: review by the original bipartisan Select Committee, screening by the

TABLE 7:3

Rejection of Key Reform Proposals, 1970–1975

Year	Proposal	DSG Position	Leadership Position	Vote on Adoption
1970	Early "Report Back" Date for the Hansen Committee	For	—	46–110
1973	Evans Proposal for an Automatic Secret Ballot on Committee Chairmenships	For	—	67–139
	Matsunaga Proposal For an "Open" Caucus Journal	For	—	57–72
	Elective Majority Whip	For	O'Neill privately Against	110–115
1974	Bolling Committee Reform, H.Res.988	—	Albert for, O'Neill Against	165–203*
1975	Elective Majority Whip	For	—	32–108
	Six Year Limit on the Tenure of Chairmen	—	—	63–131

*This was the vote on the Hansen plan. Its acceptance precluded consideration of the Bolling plan; hence a vote against Hansen was seen as a vote for Bolling.

party caucuses before sending it to the Rules Committee, and examination by the Rules Committee itself before its presentation on the House floor. But the contentiousness of the Bolling plan stretched these devices to their breaking point, and inspired the anti-Bolling forces to resurrect the Hansen Committee as their own device. Finally, the consideration of Committee reform on the House floor revealed a last effort to minimize conflict: through the rule mandated by the Democratic Caucus and accepted by the Rules Committee, the House made the Hansen plan in order as a substitute. In the event, the less controversial Hansen substitute was voted upon and adopted; thus there was never even a vote on the incendiary Bolling plan.

The indications are, then, that the process of reform was characterized by a series of maneuvers which sought to minimize conflict. This was the single most constructive aspect of the reform strategy—and the key variable underlying most of the successes.

Internal Support for Reform: Guile for Reform, Numbers for Dispersive Reform

Reformers, it appears, had often relied upon political guile to achieve their goals. Most of the reforms inside the Democratic Caucus were approved by voice vote after collaboration between DSG and the leadership or after the Hansen Committee had worked out a scheme deemed acceptable to all wings of the party. Those reforms which were put to a vote were usually the ones which had failed to attract the support of House leaders. Controversiality, in these cases, became self-fulfilling: since the leadership did not back them they were deemed controversial. Without the leadership, the reform camp could muster only rather thin support. The four votes which did take place provide the most accurate assessment of the reformers' actual strength, certainly more so than the "unanimous" approval for reforms indicated by the voice votes. Table 7:4 lists the maximum strength of reformers based on reform proposals voted upon in the Democratic Caucus from 1971 to 1975. The 1970 early "report back" date probably yields a low figure since some reformers wished to prevent the Republicans' using Congressional reform as a campaign issue. Only 156 out of 245 Caucus members voted on the proposal, and only 46 supported it. The challenge to McMillan in 1971 was a better showing, yielding 96 votes against. The Open Committee provision of 1973 which passed the Caucus mustered only 83 votes out of 120 cast, less than half the Caucus.

It was only in 1974 that the reformers actually received the support

TABLE 7:4

Maximum Strength of Reformers on Votes in the
Democratic Caucus, 1970–1975

Year	Number of Votes for Reform Proposal	Number Voting	Number in Caucus	Reform Proposal
1970	46	(156)	(245)	Early Hansen "Report Back" Date
1971	96	(222)	(235)	Against McMillan for Chairman of District of Columbia Committee
1973	83	(120)	(249)	Eckhardt-Foley-Fascell Open Committee Proposal
1974	147	(263)	(291)	Caucus Approval of Appropriation Subcommittee Chairman

of a majority of the Caucus (147 out of 291 in the Caucus, and 263 cast) on the provision to require Caucus approval of Appropriations subcommittee chairmen. The reformers, then, were able to succeed with considerably less than a working majority throughout most of the period of reform. Although DSG's ringing phrase was to assert "the majority of the majority party," (this may well have been an accurate characterization of the number of liberals and moderates in the party[14]) there is no firm evidence that a majority of the party was reformist until after 1974.

The "Inside-Outside" Approach: Support for Reform

It was shrewd mobilization of support from "inside" which contributed to the reformers' remarkable success. This was aided by support from "outside." Prior to 1970 Congress's procedures and their possible revision were viewed as largely an in-house matter. DSG's campaign for the record teller in 1970 was the first use of external groups in the reform effort, bringing into the reform fold such groups as ADA, Common Cause, the National Committee for an Effective Congress and the League of Women Voters. A few of these would become fixtures of later reform campaigns. The creation of an umbrella organization in 1972, the Committee for Congressional Reform, consolidated external support while its members, ADA and Common Cause, proceeded with their own ad hoc projects such as ADA's campaign for the ten member challenge provision in 1972–1973 and Common Cause's "Open up the System" efforts. Ralph Nader's Congress Project and its offshoot, Congress Watch, participated in the reform effort, as did a few of the trade unions, notably the UAW. All of these organizations worked in conjunction with the DSG Executive, and Conlon in particular, who informed the groups of DSG's goals and suggested how they might be of assistance.

There was virtually no disagreement over goals between the various external groups from 1970 to 1973, the period of intensive Party reform activity. The aims of the liberal groups were, by and large, what the DSG Executive told them they could achieve. However, on the issue of Committee reform, DSG itself was racked by division. The Executive was officially "neutral," and unofficially split in half, with its most adept members implacably opposed to the Bolling plan. Committee reform proved just as divisive for the external groups; ADA, Common Cause, and the League of Women Voters supported the Bolling plan; the AFL-CIO balked over the Education and Labor separation, and Nader's Congress Watch, along with a coalition of liberal environmentalist groups concerned about the Energy and Environment merger, also vigorously opposed it. The lack of consensus over reform was clear within both the "inside" and "outside" sections of the reform community. The contrast between reforms which met resistance and those which did not provides further clues to the political motives of the reformers, and of the implications of reform for power alignments.

The passage of DSG-backed reforms through 1973, and again in the Caucus after the 1974 election, reflected a general acceptance of incremental Party reform. The reforms were designed to apply pressure to conservative chairmen, and in doing so to endow the leadership, subcommittees, and the rank and file with greater powers. But Committee reform was another matter. This was not incremental and was not only a threat to the small number of committee chairmen but also a direct blow to many subcommittee chairmen (and other middle level Democrats who aspired to these subcommittee chairmanships). Many of the members disadvantaged by Committee reform were those who had supported and benefited most from the Party reforms.[15] Indeed, the Party reforms appear actually to have strengthened the sources of resistance to Committee reform. While Party reform was acceptable to the Caucus when presented in a measured fashion by the leadership in collaboration with DSG, Committee reform defied attempts to reduce conflict. Instead, the Bolling plan positively manufactured internal fractiousness.

Personalities and Politics

Much has been made of the impact of personalities on politics; in this case, it is possible to speculate endlessly. What if Olin Teague, the Caucus Chairman, had not ruled erroneously on Bolling's motion in the May 1974 Caucus which led to referral of the Bolling plan to the Hansen Committee? Was Bolling the right person to steer such a controversial measure through the House? Had Carl Albert been a more forceful Speaker inclined to champion certain reform efforts, might the reforms have bode differently for the House? Such questions suggest that what happened was far from inevitable, even though the trend toward further dispersion did seem to have had a certain historical compulsion about it. Each of these questions can, albeit speculatively, be answered. Had Teague not ruled Bolling out of order, the glare of public votes on reform might easily have switched enough votes (the margin was 98–81) to have reversed the outcome. The Caucus might well have rejected the referral to the Hansen Committee. Without time and a rallying point, the anti-Bolling members might never have coalesced and the Bolling plan might have passed.[16]

There is strong evidence that Bolling was the best person to chair the committee and produce a sophisticated and far-sighted plan, but not the best one to usher it through the Caucus and House. Respected by many but mistrusted as well, Bolling placed his own indelible imprint on the plan. Perhaps it was a mistake not to put a "Burton, Hays or Waggonner" on the Bolling Committee. But then its plan most likely would have been substantially different; and internal incohesion which would have resulted in the Committee might have militated against a coherent, worthwhile plan to begin with.

Finally, the Speaker undoubtedly was a key figure in the reform successes. In his characteristically low-key manner, he gave vital support for reform, especially after the reform-oriented Tip O'Neill became Majority Leader. Those who assailed Speaker Albert for timidity seriously underestimated his behind-the-scenes importance, without which DSG might have had precious little to show for all its ambitious schemes. Those who criticized Albert for not asserting himself on policy matters had a more persuasive point. But then, Albert and O'Neill, viewing leadership from its eye, were probably in the best position to appreciate its fragility, certainly more so than the abrasive junior members who clamored for "strong leadership" while at the same time jockeying for position in the subcommittee and committee hierarchy. The closer to the leadership one gets, it seems, the greater the realization of the limitations upon it, especially in an institution with the individualistic traditions of the House. Albert and O'Neill, perhaps correctly, perceived that no one, and certainly not they, could take the House in a direction it did not want to go, indeed, especially when it was proceeding swiftly in the opposite direction.

7:3 THE RESULTS OF REFORM: THE INSTITUTIONALIZATION OF DISPERSED POWER

Direction: Party Reform as Dispersive Reform

Reform of the House could conceivably have turned out differently. The unforeseen consequences and future implications of reform, especially in new inter-institutional circumstances, may shift power in a different direction. However, during the period under study the trend has been strongly toward further dispersion, which is all the more ironic since it was precisely the opposite of what many reformers had originally hoped.[17] Further, it was directly contrary to what various observers commenting shortly after the reforms thought had occurred. The two main strands of the initial interpretations were first, that the Caucus had assumed broad new power, and secondly, that seniority had unlamentably been dealt a death-blow.[18] These were common interpretations; yet neither proved to be the case. Party became not the instrument of power on policy but the means of transferring power further outward in the committee system. The seniority system had not been destroyed; it merely followed the shift in power to the subcommittees. There the old device found new utility as the guarantor of middle level members' accession to subcommittee chairs and assured most junior members access to at least one subcommittee of their choice.

Rather than enhancing development of even an attenuated "responsible" Democratic party, reform merely advanced a trend toward greater dependence on subcommittees as the workplaces of the House and elevated concomitantly the status of subcommittee chairmanships. It is true that one-half of the reformers' so-called pincer movement on the chairmen aimed to consolidate power in the leadership. This, it appears, proved largely superficial, in part because the leadership lacked the political will, but also because members, including many reformers, preferred to enhance their own individual bases of power, and guarded them jealously. Consequently, consolidative reform was always more nominal than real, more talked about than transformed into workable proposals: in short, more beloved in principle than in practice.

Moreover, there were compelling political forces militating against serious consolidative reform. First, ever since 1911, the power which was divested from the speakership was steadily transferred to the full committee chairmen. This devolution of power to the chairmen constructed a barrier to strong leadership; even an assertive Speaker like Rayburn possessed influence based on his ability to persuade rather than formal institutional powers. The cleavages in the Democratic party strengthened the seniority system and the fragmented committees. The norm of individualism was especially attractive to the committee chairmen who benefited most from it. Since many of these seniors were Southerners—conservative stalwarts in their committees and conservative coalition voters on the House floor—they had no wish to depart from such a congenial system of limited fragmentation. This small group of privileged members would have lost ground by either the reduction of the fragmentation (i.e. consolidating power) or its expansion (dispersion). Moreover, some of their power could be summarily wrested from them by the party Caucus—at whose nominal pleasure they served.

Northern and Western Democrats had an obvious interest in seizing on the Caucus as a means of nudging recalcitrant chairmen into support of "national Democratic" policies. This, in fact, was the main thrust of the initial DSG campaign. However, a funny thing happened on the way to "party responsibility." The ideal of a coherent, programmatic party gave way to "spreading the action." If there was to be Congressional implementation of so-called national Democratic goals, it would most likely come from an assertive liberal subcommittee chairman or diligent committee member. Contrary to the bold new pronouncements, reform confirmed and advanced the House's long-standing dispersive bent. While the Caucus did experience a spurt of activism, the role of party was largely transitory: the Caucus was not the final resting place of power but the vehicle for its transferral. Party reform achieved its goal of diluting the power of full committee chairmen. However, rather than a "pincer movement" or, as in O'Hara's words "both directions at once," close examination reveals it to have been a full-dress march in one direction. Table 7:5 illustrates this point. The reform proposals are divided into two columns—Consolidative and Dispersive—based on their intended or likely effects on power relations. Some of the reforms might have led in either or both directions; for example, monthly meetings of the Caucus were a prerequisite for Caucus-based developments of either use by the Speaker or by the rank and file. Of course, the other possibility was that the Caucus would be used to pass reforms which enhanced the position of sectors of the party outside the Caucus and leadership—i.e. the subcommittee chairmen.

There were actually very few party reforms that increased the powers of the Speaker. Those that did were often mitigated by other provisions within the same proposal; for example, the reconstitution of the Steering and Policy Committee was intended by the Bingham DSG task force as a new base of power for the leadership. In order to insure that the Speaker control the committee, half of it was either part of the leadership itself or appointed by it; the other half was elected by region in the Caucus. But by the middle of 1975 the Steering and Policy Committee was virtually unanimously pronounced a "flop." A large part of this was due to the fact that Speaker Albert remained unconvinced of its utility, and to a lesser degree, to the fact that the half of the Steering and Policy Committee which did not owe its place to the leadership was not necessarily disposed to defer to the leadership. The initial indication of this was the response to the first motion before the Steering and Policy Committee in its capacity as the Democratic Committee on Committees in 1975. Majority Leader O'Neill moved that all senior Democrats on Committees—i.e. in most cases the incumbent chairmen[19] be renominated by the Committee on Committees. This was what the Ways and Means Committee had been doing for years; it was a reassertion of the seniority system, and would have left any insurgencies up to the full Caucus. Jonathan Bingham, the architect of the rejuvenated Steering and Policy Committee, moved for a separate vote on each chairmanship, resulting in the defeat in the Committee on Committees of Hays and Patman. It was clear on this reform issue, and probably many others as well, that the Steering and Policy Committee was not prepared blindly to follow the leadership. The Speaker, ever sensitive to the limitations of his power, remained less than enthused about trying to build the Committee into a new policy panel.[20] The other Party reforms favoring the leadership were the prerogative of the Speaker to nominate members of the Rules Committee and small adjustments of the Speaker's latitude in scheduling bills on the floor: all in all, hardly the stuff of pre-1910 Speaker's powers. Those reforms which led in the other direction, however, were both numerous and tangible—especially those which strengthened subcommittees.

TABLE 7:5

Reform Proposals and Power Relations:
Consolidation and Dispersion, 1969–1975

	Consolidative	*Dispersive*
Year	*Reform Development*	*Reform Development*
1969	—Monthly Meetings of Democratic Caucus	—Monthly meetings of the Caucus
	—Caucus Approval of Committee lists ("ratification" by full Caucus)	—Caucus Approval of Committee lists ("ratification" by full Caucus)
1970		—Legislative Reorganization Amendments Act—open meetings staff additions, Record Teller (House Rules change)
1971		—Prohibit full Committee Chairmen from chairing more than one subcommittee on their full committee (Caucus Rules change)
		—Prohibit any member from serving as chairman of more than one subcommittee with legislative jurisdiction
		—Provide each Subcommittee Chairman with at least one staff person (Caucus)
		—Seniority Modification: selection of chairmen need not follow seniority; ten-member challenge provision (Caucus)
		—McMillan challenge—vote 126–96
		—Appointment to Committees: if 50% of members' state delegation supports nominee, Chairman of Committee on Committees bound to place name in nomination to the full Caucus (Caucus)

TABLE 7:5—*continued*

	Consolidative	Dispersive
1973	—Steering and Policy Committee Speaker, Majority Leader, Majority Whip *ex officio,* appointment of half of committee by Speaker (Caucus)	—Steering and Policy Committee—election of half of committee, 12 members by Caucus member on a regional basis, according to Democratic representation in the Caucus (Caucus)
		—Automatic Vote on Chairmen, 20% request for secret ballot vote (Caucus)
		—Exclusive, Major, Non-major distinction of committee posts, requiring members to relinquish other assignments. Effect to make members choose to serve on one major; one major and one non-major, or two non-major
		—Guarantee of a major Committee Assignment on request of member
		—Committee Democratic Caucuses—consisting of Democratic members of each committee
	—Addition of Speaker and Majority Leader and Caucus Chairman to Committees on Committees *ex officio*	—Subcommittee Bill of Rights: 1) Bills must be referred to subcommittees within two weeks
	—Scheduling of Suspension Bills, allowing leadership two more days (4 from 2) to bring bills to the floor under suspension of the rules	2) Each subcommittee must have an adequate budget
		3) Party Ratios on Committees must be no less advantageous to Democrats than ratio on full committee
		4) Subcommittees must transact business and re-

TABLE 7:5—*continued*

	Consolidative	Dispersive
		port to the full committee on their activities in timely fashion
		—Subcommittee Bidding Process—so that every member of a committee has at least one preferred assignment before anyone else receives a third
		—Closed Rule Restriction—layover of 4 legislative days, circumvention of Rules Committee upon request of 50 members
		—Further requirements of Open Committee Meetings—"Eckhardt-Foley-Fascell"
1974	—Bolling Committee Reform Plan	—Budget Committee, election by full Caucus, rotation of membership limitation on tenure of chairman
	—Hansen procedural mechanism (adaptation of Bolling Committee Plan): Speaker's power to make joint, split, or sequential referrals of legislation to committee, and to appoint *ad hoc* Committees when legislation overlaps jurisdictions	—Hansen Plan, require Ways and Means to form four subcommittees
	Budget Control Act	
1975	—Steering and Policy Takeover of function of Committee on Comittees Speaker controls half of membership	—Steering and Policy Takeover of Committee on Committees function—regional election of half of Committee
	—Speaker takeover of power to nominate all members of the Rules Committee	—Ways and Means Enlargement
		—Party Ratios—Two-thirds

TABLE 7:5—*continued*

Consolidative	*Dispersive*
	plus one Democratic majority on each committee
	—Limitations on dual committee chairmanships (of minor and joint committees)
	—Further strengthening of open committee meetings; Open Conference Committee meetings
	—Record Votes of Caucus available
	—Ways and Means vacancies filled by special procedure
	—Minority Staffing
	—Subcommittee Jurisdictions set by each Democratic Caucus in Committee

Seniority: Shifted Outward

The Democratic Caucus implemented reforms which departed from strict observance of seniority as the criterion for selection of full committee chairmen. In its place they adopted a requirement for an automatic secret ballot on each chairmanship in the Caucus after it had received the nominations of the Committee on Committees. (In 1975, the discretion of the Committee on Committees to nominate someone other than the senior member was somewhat blunted by the success of the Burton-Hays "Fairness to Incumbents" doctrine which reinstated the *pro forma* Caucus vote on each committee's senior member).

Still, the breakdown of the seniority system in selecting full committee chairmen must be seen as one of the most significant accomplishments of the Party reform movement. Seniority had become the symbol of many other Congressional ills: its alleged incrustation was an easy explanation of its alleged ineffectiveness. The reforms of 1971 and 1973 chipped away at it, setting the stage for the 1975 defeats of three chairmen under the new automatic vote procedure. This was a tremendous symbolic victory for reform. But its symbolic importance should not divert attention from less recognized but perhaps more tangible developments. In fact, the very seniority system derided by Party reformers in the selection of full committee chairmen was actually strengthened in another area of party practice: the selection of subcommittee chairmen and the bidding process for assignment to subcommittees. This was the other side of the Party reform movement's attitude toward seniority. As a result of the 1971 limitation of members to one subcommittee chair, the 1973 Subcommittee Bill of Rights, the establishment of Democratic Caucuses on Committees and other reforms in 1975, a new seniority system was put into place, one which employed this criterion to insure a "spreading of the action." Middle seniority members were the beneficiaries of a seniority system which had not been "abolished," but only shifted outward.

Subcommittees: A New Base for Middle Level Democratic Liberals

The ascendancy of non-Southerners was soon reflected in an increased moderate and liberal presence in the middle range of the seniority structure. The best indicator of political coloration still seems to be geography; the rise of non-Southern subcommittee chairmen revealed growing middle seniority strength in this increasingly important sub-institutional section of the House. Graph 7:1 shows the steady rise of non-Southern subcommittee chairmen. It should be stressed that this was a trend which took place primarily as a result of electoral forces: from 1960 to 1971 there was no internal reform regarding subcommittees. It was this change in composition which placed younger, more liberal members in these middle positions; firstly, by the Democrats who were first elected in 1958, then by the 1970s by some of the 1964 and later entrants. At the same time, many Southern full-committee chairmen (who often held prestigious subcommittee chairs as well) had departed. By 1971, these compositional factors, the momentum of DSG's drive against full committee chairmen, and the sheer press of business which made small units more practicable workplaces all converged to form the basis of the subcommittee-centered Caucus reforms.

The reforms passed by the Caucus which affected subcommittees are chronicled in Table 7:6: first, they recognized what had been increasingly the case, i.e. the new dependence on subcommittees, and secondly, they expedited and formalized this trend. In "spreading the action," reforms strengthened subcommittee autonomy, and with it

GRAPH 7:1

The Northern and Western Share of Subcommittee
Chairmanships, 1961–1975

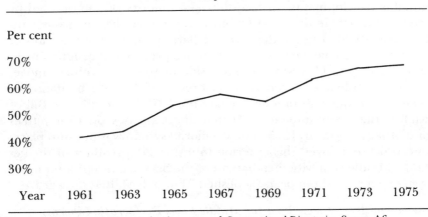

Source: *Congressional Quarterly Almanacs* and *Congressional Directories*, See p. A6.

GRAPH 7:2

The Liberal Democratic Base in the Caucus and House, 1947–1975

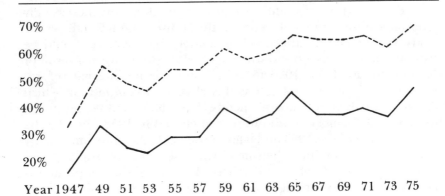

Northern and Western Share of
the Democratic Caucus, 1947–1975 — — — — — — —

Northern and Western Democratic Strength
in the House, 1947–1975 —————

Source: *Congressional Directories*.
    see p. A7 for details.

TABLE 7:6
"Spreading the Action": Reforms Affecting Subcommittees 1971–1975

Year	Reform
1971	*Subcommittee Chairmanship Limitation:* A Caucus rule stating that no member may chair more than one legislative subcommittee.
	Committee Membership Limitation: A Caucus rule stating that no member could serve on more than two committees with legislative jurisdictions.
	Subcommittee Staff: A Caucus rule permitting each subcommittee chairman to select and designate at least one staff person for his or her subcommittee.
1973	*Committee Designations and Membership Limitations:* A Caucus rule designating all House Committees as either exclusive, major or non-major. This required members serving on exclusive committees to relinquish other assignments, permitting members to serve on either one major and one non-major committee or two non-major committees.
	Committee Caucuses: Caucus rule creating a Democratic Caucus on each House committee with authority over selection of subcommittee chairmen, party ratios on subcommittees and subcommittee budgets.
	Subcommittee Bill of Rights: Caucus rules requiring: 1) all legislation referred to a full committee be referred to the appropriate subcommittee within two weeks; 2) guaranteeing that each subcommittee have an adequate budget to meet its responsibilities for legislation and oversight; 3) requiring that party ratios on subcommittees be no less favorable than the party ratio on the full committee; and 4) authorizing all subcommittees to meet, hold hearings, and report to the committee on all matters referred to it.
	Subcommittee Chairmen: A Caucus rule requiring a bidding process for subcommittee chairmen and approval by the Democratic Caucus on the committee.
	Subcommittee Membership: A Caucus rule establishing a selection process for subcommittee positions: i.e. a bidding process for subcommittee vacancies in order of seniority. All members must have one position before any other received a third.
1975	*Appropriations Subcommittee Chairmen:* A Caucus rule requiring ratification of Appropriations subcommittee chairmen by the Caucus.

TABLE 7:6—*continued*

Year	Reform
	Subcommittee Membership: A Caucus rule establishing new procedures for choosing subcommittee members on the basis of seniority; eliminating full committee chairmen from any role in their selection.
	Subcommittee Jurisdictions: A Caucus rule clarifying that the Democratic Caucus on each committee shall set the numbers and jurisdictions of subcommittees.

the independence of subcommittee chairmen. Although by 1975 the formal authority over subcommittee business rested in Democratic Caucuses on each committee, in fact these Caucuses functioned primarily to insure the selection of chairmen on the basis of seniority, and also to prevent the full committee chairmen from interfering with the subcommittee chairmen's conduct of business.

The benefits which accrued to middle range members, many of whom were active liberals and Party reformers, are listed in Table 7:7. The 1971 reforms limiting members to one subcommittee chair did not open a floodgate[21] (in fact, John Moss and Henry Reuss, both liberals, actually had to give up subcommittee chairs as a result of the reform). But the subcommittee reforms did enhance the opportunities for members to wield power through subcommittees; and they had a delayed reaction as seen by the large number of accessions in 1974 and 1976. By 1976 the diffusion of power had reached the unprecedented point of a freshman becoming a subcommittee chairman. Herbert Harris of Virginia took the chair of the Bicentennial, the Environment and the International Community Subcommittee of the District of Columbia Committee (again, technically on the basis of seniority).[22]

The Basis for Party Reform: Increasing Liberal Strength

Although liberal reformers relied on shrewd maneuvering rather than majority support, their increased strength in the Democratic party and House was important in tipping the scales in their favor. Graph 7:2 traces the approximate strength of liberals—using Northern and Western Democrats as a rough gauge of potential liberal strength and the Southern Democrats as the barometer of conservatism. While there is some slippage especially in the latter part of the period when more of the Southerners evidenced liberal "new South" tendencies, this geographical categorization remains the best indicator of ideological cleavages within the Democratic Party.[23]

1946 was a bad year for both the Democratic party and its liberal wing; 1948 was better, 1950 and 1952 not so good and so on. When liberal Democrats fared poorly at the polls it dealt a blow to their future influence in the House based on seniority. Likewise the Democratic booms of 1958, 1964 and 1974 swept into office Northern and Westerners who would become key liberal activists and reformers. The main fluctuation was in the North and West: between 1947 and 1963 the number of Southern Democrats never rose higher than 119 or fell lower than 105. In five of those years the total was either 110 or 111. During the same period the Northern and Western section of the Democratic party varied from the disastrous 74 of 1947 to the resplendent 171 in 1959. The peak years of 1964 (195 Northern and Western Democrats) and 1975 (199) constitute the high water marks: in the former case, the seniority basis of reform and in the latter, its fruition. In the 1964 elections, the Southern Democrats for the first time slipped below the 100 mark, decreasing steadily in the face of Republican gains in the South to a low of 84 in 1973, before rising slightly in the Democratic landslide of 1974 to 91.

The Impediment to Committee Reform: Seniority, Party Reformers and the Defeat of Consolidative Reform

Unluckily for the Bolling Committee, their major effort at Committee rationalization came at precisely the time when liberal Party reformers had made substantial gains in the existing ("irrational") system, as Table 7:7 has shown. Table 7:9 provides a breakdown by seniority on the vote for the Hansen substitute for the Bolling plan. The voting pattern was largely along seniority lines: the higher the seniority the greater the attachment to the *status quo;* and the higher the likelihood for a vote for Hansen. While the Party reformers were able to overcome the resistance of senior sectors of the House through gradualism and shrewd presentation of the proposals, Committee reformers presented a far-sweeping plan which ran afoul of not just the entrenched seniors but also many of the wily middle-range Party reformers themselves.

Table 7:10 lists the members who were active in the Party reform movement and their votes on Committee reform. No member seriously disadvantaged by the Bolling plan voted against passage of the Hansen substitute. As is illustrated by the column describing members' committees, the threat of disruption provoked the most serious opposition from members of Education and Labor, and Ways and Means. Consolidative reform had been overwhelmed by the subtle effects of Party reform's augury of dispersion.

A Problem of Reformism

The desire of consolidative reformers for a more coherent, streamlined Congress was a major underlying theme of the criticism, and the impetus for reform. But the evidence suggests that a combination of institutional trends and Party reform successes actually served to move the House further away from their goal.

This raises a perplexing problem of reformism. In seeking change, reformers aimed to dislodge a ruling elite; i.e. to shift power alignments. In creating temporary dislocation, reformers opened up the possibility that the power wrested from the chairmen could be transferred in either direction. While an aggressive leadership might have been able to consolidate its power and use it on policy matters as it had done so deftly on the passage of Party reform, it seems in retrospect that the likelihood of this happening was slender indeed. Since 1910–1911 the trend has been toward the gradual but steadily increasing dispersion of power. Individualism and a natural inclination to maximize one's in-House and electoral strength infected even the most junior members. This tendency was enhanced by the increasingly active government, the growing complexity of issues and the changing profile of members (i.e. younger, more issue-oriented and active). These values and trends spurred the reform drive and largely preordained its result. The change in composition headed the House in this direction; the Party reforms confirmed and expedited the shift.

The whole period of reform failed to achieve what the handful of consolidative reformers had hoped. In fact, it gave rise to a whole new layer of resistance. While there may be many positive aspects of a system in which members have great opportunity for individual initiative, such a system also predestines the House to remain inchoate, difficult to lead—and undirected. For those who sought to establish a fundamental basis for more rational and effective Congressional performance, a frenzied period of reform activity passed without producing significant benefits. While the party and committee reform experience left the House more open to liberal influence in its middle and upper tiers of power, for those who sought more coherence, it remained preponderantly, in Bolling's words, a "House Out of Order."

TABLE 7:7
The Beneficiaries of Reform: Accession to
Subcommittee Chairmanships, 1970–1976

MEMBERS & SUBCOMMITTEES

1970

Tom Foley
Agriculture
Domestic Marketing & Consumer
Relations

Henry Reuss
Banking and Currency
International Finance, &
Government Operations
Conservation and Natural Resources

Thomas L. Ashley
Banking and Currency
International Trade

John Brademas
Education and Labor
Select Education

Frank Thompson
Education and Labor
Special Labor & House
Administration Accounts

Dante Fascell
Foreign Affairs
Inter-American Affairs

Robert Kastenmeier
Judiciary
Number 3

John Dingell
Merchant Marine and Fisheries
Fisheries, Wildlife Conservation and
the Environment

Morris Udall
Post Office and Civil Service
Compensation

Ken Hechler
Science and Astronautics
Advanced Research

TABLE 7:7—*continued*

George Brown
Veterans' Affairs
Education and Training

1972

Charles Bennett
Armed Services
Number 3

James O'Hara
Education and Labor
Agricultural Labor

Benjamin Rosenthal
Foreign Affairs
Europe

John Culver
Foreign Affairs
Foreign Economic Policy

Don Fraser
Foreign Affairs
International Organization and
Movements

Lee Hamilton
Foreign Affairs
Near East

Phillip Burton
Interior and Insular Affairs,
Territorial and Insular Affairs

Don Edwards
Judiciary
Number 4
(Bankruptcy and Reorganization)

Jerome Waldie
Post Office and Civil Service, Health
Benefits

1974

Otis Pike
Armed Services
Number 5

TABLE 7:7—*continued*

MEMBERS & SUBCOMMITTEES

Ronald Dellums
District of Columbia
Education

Brock Adams
District of Columbia
Government Operations

Thomas Rees
District of Columbia
Revenue and Financial Affairs

William Ford
Education and Labor
Agricultural Labor

Lloyd Meeds
Interior and Insular Affairs
Indian Affairs

Patsy Mink
Interior and Insular Affairs
Mines and Mining

John Conyers
Judiciary
Crime

James Howard
Public Works
Energy

James Symington
Science and Astronautics
Space Science and Applications

Mike McCormack
Science and Astronautics
Energy Research and Development
and Demonstration

1976

Sidney Yates
Appropriations
Interior

Herbert Harris
District of Columbia

TABLE 7:7—*continued*

MEMBERS & SUBCOMMITTEES

The Bicentennial, the Environment,
and the International Community

Augustus Hawkins
Education and Labor
Equal Opportunities

Bella Abzug
Government Operations
Government Information &
Individual Rights

Lester Wolff
International Relations
Future Foreign Policy
Research and Development

Lionel Van Deerlin
Commerce and Health
Consumer Protection and Finance

Joshua Eilberg
Judiciary
Immigration, Citizenship and
International Law

Ralph Metcalfe
Merchant Marine and Fisheries
Panama Canal

William Clay
Post Office and Civil Service,
Employee Political Rights and
Intergovernmental Programs

Patricia Schroeder
Post Office and Civil Service
Census and Population

Teno Roncalio
Public Works
Public Buildings & Grounds

George Brown
Science and Technology
Environment and the Atmosphere

James Corman
Ways and Means

TABLE 7:7—*continued*

MEMBERS & SUBCOMMITTEES

Unemployment Compensation &
Small Business
Government Procurement and
International Trade

William Green
Ways and Means
Trade

Charles Vanik
Ways and Means
Oversight

TABLE 7:8

Seniority of Subcommittee Chairs at the Time of Their Accession

Congress	1–3 terms	4–6 terms	7–9 terms	10–12 terms	13–15 terms
89th	1	6	2	2	1
90th	3	7	5	1	—
91st	1	7	2	1	—
92nd	1	15	3	1	—
93rd	8	17	2	—	—
94th	11	12	7	1	1
95th	19	15	3	—	—
96th	19	10	1	—	—

TABLE 7:9
Seniority and Opposition to Committee Reform, 1974

Support for the Hansen Substitute to H.Res. 988

	First Termers Dems/GOP	Two to Five Termers Dems/GOP	Eight or More Terms Dems/GOP
FOR Hansen Substitute	59%/23%	64%/64%	84%/44%
AGAINST Hansen Substitute	41%/77%	36%/36%	16%/56%
N =	29/39	113/96	75/16

SOURCE: *Congressional Record*, 120 (93rd Congress, Second Session, 1974) pp. H10168–10169, October 8, 1974. See Davidson and Oleszek, Table Three, Chapter Seven providing similar information in slightly different form. Davidson and Oleszek MS, *op. cit.*

TABLE 7:10
Party Reformers' Votes on Committee Reform, 1974

Member	Affected Adversely?	Vote on Hansen Substitute
Brock Adams†		Present
Jonathan Bingham		No
Richard Bolling*		No
John Brademas††	Education and Labor, House Administration	Yea
Phillip Burton†	Education and Labor, Interior and Insular Affairs	Yea
Shirley Chisholm	Education and Labor	No
James Corman*	Ways and Means	Yea
John Culver†		No
Robert Eckhardt	Merchant Marine and Fisheries	Yea
Don Edwards†		No
Frank Evans		Absent
Dante Fascell†		No

TABLE 7:10—*continued*

Member	Affected Adversely?	Vote on Hansen Substitute
Tom Foley†		Yea
William Ford†	Education and Labor	Yea
Don Fraser†		No
Sam Gibbons*	Ways and Means	Yea
Julia Butler Hansen†		Yea
Kenneth Hechler†		No
Spark Matsunaga*	Agriculture, Rules	Yea
Lloyd Meeds†	Education and Labor, Interior and Insular Affairs	No
James O'Hara	Education and Labor, Interior and Insular Affairs	Yea
Thomas P. O'Neill		Yea
Thomas Rees		Yea
Henry Reuss		No
Benjamin Rosenthal		Yea
Paul Sarbanes	Merchant Marine and Fisheries	No
Neal Smith		Yea
Frank Thompson	Education and Labor, House Administration	Yea
Morris Udall	Interior and Insular Affairs, Post Office and Civil Service	No
Charles Vanik	Ways and Means	Yea
Jerome Waldie	Judiciary, Post Office and Civil Service[1]	Absent

NOTE: † = Subcommittee Chairman
    * = Serves on Committee which had no subcommittees
A "Party reformer" was someone active in reform effort, mainly DSG's campaigns.

[1]Waldie was off running for Governor of California at the time, mitigating both the threat or dislocation (none, since he was giving up his seat, and explaining his absence).

SOURCE: *Congressional Directory, op. cit.,* Second Session, 1974 and *Congressional Record* 120 (93rd Congress, Second Session, 1974) pp. 10168–10169, October 8, 1974.

TABLE 7:11

Subcommittee Chairpersons' votes on Committee Reform
(Hansen substitute amendment to H. Res. 988)

Yea	Nay	Not Voting	Voting Present to Indicate Conflict of Interest
75	26	9	4

Notes

1. Michael J. Malbin, "Congress Report/New Democratic Procedures Affect Distribution of Power," *National Journal*, December 14, 1974, p.1881.
2. *Ibid.*
3. For background on this, see Michael Green, "Obstacles to Reform: Nobody Covers the House," *The Washington Monthly*, June 1970, pp.62–70.
4. See, for example, "Congress's Old Order Changeth, Very Quickly," *New York Times*, January 19, 1975, section 4, p. 2.
5. Harvey C. Mansfield, Sr. (ed). *Congress Against the President* (New York: Praeger, 1975) pp.1–34.
6. Ornstein and Rohde, "Reform and Parties," *op.cit.*, p.5.
7. Of course, attrition cut both ways in that attrition would serve to put liberals in positions of power which had by then been weakened by reform.
8. Davidson, Kovenock, O'Leary, *Congress in Crisis, op.cit.*, p.100.
9. See p. 249.
10. Delaney, number two man on the Rules Committee, was a Democrat from New York City but often deserted his liberal fellow New Yorkers and allied with the conservatives.
11. Death, defeat and discreditation played parts in this. Mendel Rivers had died before reformers ever mounted a challenge; Judge Smith of Rules, McMillan of D.C. and Aspinall of Interior and Insular Affairs all were defeated in primaries—as were such less-well-known figures as George Fallon, Sam Freidel and Edward Garmatz: all from Maryland and all in the space of two years (1970 and 1972). Wilbur Mills was felled not by electoral defeat but by personal scandal.
12. "DSG, A Winner On House Reform," *CQ Weekly Report*, June 2, 1973, *op. cit.* p.1268.
13. Selected for their importance in setting out the "consolidation vs. dispersion" alternative directions of reform.
14. See p. 247.
15. See pp. 250–252.
16. Of course, on the other hand, the opponents of the Bolling plan were hardly legislative neophytes. It seems probable that they would have fallen back on another scheme for delay and diversion. Moreover, even if the Bolling plan had passed, there were various ways that its implementation—like that of sections of the 1946 Legislative Reorganization Act before it—could have been blunted, either subtly or overtly. For instance, the sections regarding oversight, which was largely ignored, and the legislative budget which was completely ignored.
17. Especially advocates of stronger leadership, for example, Bolling and the academic "party responsibility" advocates.

18. For example, a *Washington Post* editorial enthused: "The essence of the change is that the Caucus has become both formally and actually the source of power and the ultimate instrument of discipline for all House Democrats." William V. Shannon of the *New York Times* observed that the 1975 actions "shifted the balance of power from chairmen of the legislative committees to the Policy Committee and the Caucus." The *Post* added, approvingly: "The seniority system as the rigid, inviolable operating framework of the House has been destroyed." "The Democratic Caucus in Command," *Washington Post*, January 20, 1975, p.A18 and William V. Shannon, "The Bolling House," *New York Times*, January 21, 1975, p.33.

19. I.e. except for Mills.

20. The first Steering and Policy Committee sub-group to take on a major policy issue was the task force on Energy chaired by Rep. Jim Wright of Texas. Although his panel did manage to produce a plan out of the maze of conflicting energy proposals, Wright's panel was not enough of a success to cause Speaker Albert to appoint similar panels on other issues. See *CQ Almanac*, 1975, pp.174–175 and 194–195.

21. See note 20, p. 109.

22. Of course, there were others of equal seniority who did not get a subcommittee chair. The Committee Caucus took into account Harris' Virginia constituency interest in D.C. affairs. But his selection did not violate seniority. As far as I have been able to determine there have been no seniority violations in the selection of subcommittee chairmen. (Source: *Congressional Directory, op. cit.* for 1973 through 1976).

23. I tried others: notably ADA "Liberal Quotient" ratings and CQ Conservative Coalition ratings. However, the changing issues and the erratic choice of "key votes" prompted my return to geography as the safest indicator.

PART III

The Eclipse of Reform and the Ascendancy of Special Interests

Eight

Requiem for Consolidative Reform: The Failures of the Obey Commission, 1976–77 and the Patterson Select Committee on Committees, 1979–1980

One of the best indications that one sort of reform has taken hold is to examine attempts at different kinds of reform. Two reform experiences in the middle and end of the decade amounted to the last sputterings of the movement for consolidative reform; their failure constitutes confirmation of the strong trend toward structural fragmentation. The following reviews an effort to centralize the House's rambling administrative system and the reformers' last, modest try to rationalize selected portions of the committee system. The inhospitality of the House to these reform attempts signalled the demise of reform generally.

8:1 THE OBEY COMMISSION ON ADMINISTRATIVE REVIEW

The first campaign for reform involved internal House administration. This reform effort originated in both the Bolling Committee's call for greater administrative rationality and a series of Congressional scandals in the middle 1970s. Most prominent among the latter was the revelation in 1976 that Rep. Wayne Hays had employed his mistress, Elizabeth Ray, a secretary who was a self-described non-typist, on the payroll of his committee. This, along with indications of unseemly Congressional conduct by Hays and others, such as junketing and the falsifying of travel reimbursements, led to a call for a general review and overhaul of the House's administrative apparatus. A Task Force on House Accounts (headed by Rep. David Obey) recommended establishment of a bipartisan commission to examine this whole area.

In July, 1976 Speaker Albert appointed a 15-member panel composed of eight House members and seven outside citizens to review existing administrative practices. The panel was composed of the following members:

Members of Congress	*Private Citizens*
David Obey (Chairman)	Ralph Huitt
Melvin Price	Charles U. Daley
Lloyd Meeds	Lucy W. Benson
Lee Hamilton	William DuChessi
Norman D'Amours	William Hamilton
Bill Frenzel	Robert Galvin
William Armstrong	Roscoe Egger
Robert Bauman	

H. Res. 1368 mandated the Obey Commission to "conduct a thorough and complete study with respect to the administrative services of the House of Representatives, including staff personnel, administration, accounting and purchasing procedures, office equipment and communication facilities, record-keeping, emoluments and allowances." Although the mandate did not expressly authorize the report of legislation, it was widely assumed that the study would result in one or more packages of proposed reforms.

The Commission undertook a broad-based set of surveys, public hearings, interviews and consulting studies—which is detailed in the Commission's bulky fourteen hundred page Final Report.[1] Our concern here is not to describe all the findings or recommendations of the Obey Commission but to focus on those aspects of the Obey Commission experience which are relevant to the matter of reform's potential for shifting power in the House and which reflect on the process of reform.

The Obey Commission's main recommendations were in three different areas: Congressional ethics and disclosure of members' personal financial dealings, the administration and scheduling of House business, and the management of the legislative process. The area of ethics reform was the area of greatest success.[2] The Commission recommended—and with strong leadership support, the House later adopted—reforms which banned the use of unofficial office accounts (unreported funds for running House offices received from private sources), placed limits on outside honoraria for speeches, articles and the like, restricted gifts from lobbyists to members, expanded financial disclosure and prohibited foreign "junkets" by lame duck members. Perhaps the strongest immediate impact on members' pocketbooks was to limit to 15 per cent of Congressional salary the amount that a member may earn in honoraria.[3]

The areas of administrative and legislative management reform proved more problematic. The Commission recommended, based on extensive interviews with members focusing on their own frustrations with their jobs, a reorganization of administrative operations including the following:

House Administrator

There should be a new central administrator for the House, appointed by the Speaker and approved by the full House, who would take over a range of housekeeping duties presently dispersed to various other House officials, including the Clerk of the House, the Architect of the Capitol, the Doorkeeper of the House, the House Administration Committee and the House Select Committee on Congressional Operations. The House Administration would have broad management responsibilities of housekeeping matters such as furniture, maintenance, supplies, House accounting and paying bills and the operation of House support service facilities such as the Congressional subway, restaurants, audio and visual studios, garages and barber and beauty shops.

House Auditor

An Auditor would be appointed by the chairman of House Administration with the concurrence of a majority of House leaders (Speaker, majority and minority leaders) who would have responsibility for auditing all House accounts—checked annually by outside auditors—and issue reports in a published annual report.

House Clerk

The Clerk's Office would be substantially stripped of its existing powers in favor of the new House Administrator, and would be given (from the Speaker's office) control over the official reporters who record floor, committee and subcommittee proceedings. The clerk would also play a role in coordinating Congressional information services—such as the Congressional Budget Office, the Office of Technology Assessment, the General Accounting Office and the Congressional Research Service of the Library of Congress.

The Obey Commission's major recommendations concerning legislative business management were as follows:

Information Services

This broad set of recommendations ranged from providing computer terminals as standard House office equipment (and a $12,000 annual allowment for computer services), to requiring better provision of testimony in advance of public committee hearings.

Staffing Limits and Office Resources

The Commission recommended that committee staff increases be limited to three percent over that of the previous Congress. As for individual member offices, members could count part-time staffers as one full time staff member in the overall allotment of 18 full-time staffers (up to a maximum of four part-timers).

Fair Employment Practices

The Commission recommended that the House establish a fair employment practices "grievance" panel, to be composed of two majority and one minority party members, and to serve as a hearing board for allegations of employment discrimination. The Commission recommended no recourse or power to impose sanctions on members, other than to refer matters to the House Ethics Committee. But this was at least a modest step toward applying to Congress itself a modicum of the fair labor practice standards which Congress had imposed on the rest of the Federal government and private industry.

Travel on Official Business

The Commission recommended that members file reports before and after travel on official business to explain the purposes of the travels. This anti-"junket" proposal also required approval for travel from the House Administrator and the publication of quarterly reports in the *Congressional Record* of financial information about each trip taken by members.

A New Select Committee on Committees

The commission also cited continuing scheduling and policy problems due to overlapping jurisdictions of committees and recommended the formation of a new Select Committee on Committees to devise a new plan for realigning jurisdictions before July 1, 1978.

While the Obey Commission package of proposals was clearly intended to consolidate and rationalize the House's administrative structure, and won early support of its "basic thrust" from the leadership, it was destined to run into the entrenched opposition characteristic of "turf" battles.

The House entities (e.g., House Clerk, Doorkeeper, House Administration, Architect of the Capitol) and their Congressional supporters who were to relinquish authority and duties to the proposed new House Administrator obviously had reservations about the plan. Rep. Jack Brooks, Chairman of the Select Committee on Congressional Operations, for example, opposed the Obey plan in part because the House Placement Office (a job search service) would have been removed from the Select Committee's purview. The typical problem with such broad-based legislative reform packages is that there is no single fatal flaw which provokes universal disapproval; instead, there are numerous small items which enable opponents to nibble away at, and coalesce in opposition to, the overall package.

Even prior to formation of the Obey Commission, there was a general feeling that the House had already been buffeted by *enough* "reform." Moreover, there was a sense that the litany of Congressional scandals—along with the fallout from Watergate—had already subjected members of Congress to an unfair level of scrutiny and innuendo. There was, then, a feeling abroad in the House that "enough is enough."

Timing and visceral reactions are always important in politics. But looking at the experience in broader institutional terms, this further attempt at consolidative reform collided with the same dispersive and individualistic tendencies which had undermined earlier reform efforts. Members tended to guard jealously their control over their own staffs, and to be wary of any plans for centralized efficiency on matters as critical to their base and mode of operations as their support staffs. None of the individual proposals—for central control over accounts, regular audits, and a spate of modest efficiency-minded reforms—appeared to pose a great threat to members' individual "turf," but when viewed as a package they took on the appearance of another, potentially disruptive, wave of reform. As such, they were treated with suspicion. This general reaction, coupled with the spectre of another attempt to rationalize the committee system, and the Obey Commission had assembled the "chemicals" of a chain reaction against the proposed reform. It was the prospect of Committee reform with all of its evocations of the earlier, bruising Bolling Committee battles, and now with three more years of "spreading the action" on the one hand, and, on the other, more turnover of membership and hence a lack of awareness of recent institutional history[4]—combined to diminish the allure of yet another study of committees. Even if sensible in principle, the general "climate" precluded a groundswell of enthusiasm for it in practice. A reform effort involving turf had once again become *ipso facto* controversial. This did not augur well for the Obey Commission's likelihood of success.

Scuttling the Obey Package

The fate of the Obey package could probably have been foretold based on the formidable gauntlet of House panels it would have to run in order to win passage. Jurisdiction over the Commission recommendations was jointly vested in the Committees on House Administration and Rules. The Democratic Caucus was also expected to review the proposals—another opportunity for opponents to build a case, and momentum, against it. Of course, the ultimate test would come on the floor, and the outcome would depend largely on the nature of the rule under which the package would be considered. Proponents preferred as narrow a rule as possible to preserve the integrity of the package, and to preclude wide-ranging amendments. Opponents wanted either to defeat the rule (and possibly, in so doing, the package itself) or to consider the bill under an open rule in order to water down—or gut—the package.

The House Administration Committee (which would have had its jurisdiction reduced by the resolution) did not seek to change the legislative proposals made in the resolution. It did, however, vote to give itself the power to adopt rules and regulations implementing the Commission's recommendations. This provided the Committee with effective veto power over the reorganization. More specifically, House Administration deleted the recommendation of a three percent ceiling on committee staff growth and struck several other Commission provisions, involving staff training and education funds and money for transition staff for new members.

The Rules Committee also made changes, including two attempts by Obey himself to make the package more palatable. Obey proposed (and Rules adopted) a costly but politically attractive proposal to allow approximately 140 members to hire a new staff member to specialize on committee work. The other amendment adopted by Rules made the selection of the House auditor subject to unanimous—rather than majority—approval by the Speaker, majority leader and minority leader (a measure designed to placate Republicans).

The treatment of the Obey plan by the Democratic Caucus was a harbinger of opposition to come. The leadership, sensing opposition to the plan and possible moves to amend the plan on the floor of the Caucus, in a carefully orchestrated ploy introduced a Steering and Policy Committee resolution endorsing the Obey package, followed quickly by an announcement that the meeting did not have a quorum. Under Caucus rules, this meant that discussion of the resolution by Caucus members was in order but there would be no amendments or vote. In this way the Caucus prevented a divisive debate over the package, and prevented Republicans from accusing the Democratic Caucus of side-tracking reforms that were aimed at administrative and management efficiency. This was a clever, but cosmetic tactic, providing only temporary diversion from the intrinsic unpopularity of the package; this would quickly become evident from the floor vote on the rule in the full House. Even a strong statement on the floor in support of the package by Speaker O'Neill was not enough to win a favorable vote on the rule.

In a vote on the special rule—to limit the number of floor amendments—on October 12, 1977 the rule was defeated 160-252, with 113 Democrats allying with 139 Republicans to kill the Obey package.

There were several reasons for the speedy death of Administrative reform. Many members were just "fed up" with reform. Others saw it as a "power grab" by the Speaker and the new Administrator, whomever he or she might have been. Obey himself was seen by some as an abrasive and controversial figure. Still other members did not want another divisive in-house tiff over committee rejurisdiction. The vote on the special rule enabled members to vote against the rule on procedural grounds, and shelved the whole package while sparing members from voting on the substantive package.

For these and other reasons, reforms (even some arguably innocuous ones) were greeted with mistrust and apprehension by the Fall of 1977. Once again reform threatened encroachment upon existing turf, and again it encountered formidable opposition.

8:2 THE PATTERSON SELECT COMMITTEE ON COMMITTEES, 1979–1980

The Obey Commission had found that members harbored continued dissatisfaction with the sprawling House Committee system. And while the fate of the overall Obey package—especially when viewed in the context of the Bolling plan before it—was hardly grounds for optimism about a new reform initiative, there were persistent rumblings in favor of another crack at Committee reform.

Much of the impetus to reform is the involvement of people who participate specifically to "watch out" for their group and individual interests. When the Obey Commission suggested a new Select Committee on Committees with an early report back date, others in the House Democratic party recognized the benefits—both offensive and defensive—of themselves becoming involved. Hence at its September 28, 1977 meeting, the Democratic Caucus approved a resolution endorsing the establishment of a new Select Committee on Committees, but it also went on record as approving work on the same subject by two other panels: an ad hoc Rules Subcommittee headed by Rep. Gillis Long and a resurrected Hansen Committee of the Democratic Caucus (Committee on Organization, Study and Review). The fact that three different panels leapt into the fray indicated more than that it was a problem requiring attention. If the Bolling Committee had not otherwise succeeded, it had succeeded in educating members as to the importance of "turf battles," and particularly who did the realigning. The scramble to participate came "early" in the reform process this time.

The Problem as Identified in 1977

The Obey Commission had approached the problem of the committee/subcommittee structure as one of scheduling and legislative management. Its draft report concluded:

> Members have too many assignments, and jurisdictions are too confused for the strains and conflicts members currently endure to be substantially alleviated by piecemeal and procedural reform . . . Only marginal improvements can occur until a basic restructuring of the Committee system takes place.[5]

Finally the Obey group discovered that the jurisdictional overlaps had survived and continued to pose difficulties. They noted as examples that during the 94th Congress nineteen different committees and subcommittees had dealt with some aspect of health-related legislation and that virtually every standing committee of the House had before it some piece of legislation dealing at least tangentially with energy (83 different subcommittees, according to the Patterson Committee). This point, of course, was not shockingly new, but it did indicate support for a post-Bolling Committee push to try to accomplish some consolidation of the committee system which had not succeeded before.

The effort was ill-starred virtually from the start. The impetus from the Obey Commission inspired leadership support for a study commission on Committee reform, but much of the House remained noticeably unenthusiastic. The resolution authorizing establishment of the Select Committee (H. Res. 118 of 1979) passed by a less-than-encouraging margin: 208-200. Opposition came from a broad range of committee chairmen, a strong majority of Republicans (who objected to the 2 to 1 Democratic majority on the committee) and an ample contingent of newly ensconced liberal Democratic subcommittee chairmen (especially on committees such as Interstate and Foreign Commerce and which were probable targets of a reshuffle).

With that dubious send-off, a fifteen member House Select Committee on Committees was established, chaired by Rep. Jerry Patterson, a third-term California Democrat with close ties to Phillip Burton in both the California delegation and the Democratic party in the House. Rep. James Cleveland, Republican of New Hampshire, was ranking member. The members of the Select Committee were:

Jerry M. Patterson, California (Chairman)
William Clay, Missouri
Mike McCormack, Washington
John B. Breaux, Louisiana
Patricia Schroeder, Colorado
Bob Traxler, Michigan
Butler Derrick, South Carolina
Joseph L. Fisher, Virginia
Peter H. Kostmayer, Pennsylvania
Charles Whitney, South Carolina
James C. Cleveland, New Hampshire
Frank Horton, New York
Bill Frenzel, Minnesota
Jim Leach, Iowa
Gerald B. Solomon, New York

The Select Committee membership was notable mainly for its representation of committees which had more than a passing interest in the outcome of possible changes in jurisdiction.

Select Committee on Committees Member's committee assignments were:

> Patterson—Merchant Marine and Fisheries; Banking, Finance and Urban Affairs
> Clay—Education and Labor, Post Office and Civil Service
> McCormack—Public Works and Transportation; Science and Technology
> Breaux—Merchant Marine and Fisheries; Public Works and Transportation
> Schroeder—Armed Services; Post Office and Civil Service
> Traxler—Appropriations
> Derrick—Banking, Finance and Urban Affairs; Budget
> Fisher—Budget
> Kostmayer—Interior and Insular Affairs; Government Operations
> Whitney—Agriculture
> Cleveland—House Administration; Public Works and Transportation
> Horton—Government Operations
> Frenzel—Ways and Means; House Administration
> Leach—Banking, Finance and Urban Affairs; Post Office and Civil Service
> Solomon—Public Works and Transportation

Source: *The Almanac of American Politics,* 1978.

The Select Committee was given a February 1, 1980 report back date (later extended to April 1, 1980) and was mandated to recommend changes in the committee structure, jurisdiction, rules, procedures, staffing, facilities and media coverage of committee sessions. Select Committee concerns also included the overall size of committees and subcommittees, the possibility of a limitation on the number of member assignments and the overall structure, size and alignment of the House committee and subcommittee structure.

The Select Committee set up a series of task forces to review recent House and Senate reform and to explore possible recommendations. These task force reports were undertaken by the Select Committee in order to benefit from the "mistakes" in the past. The major conclusion in terms of strategy was based largely on the experience of the Bolling Committee and the Obey Commission was that any comprehensive package of reform proposals would undoubtedly contain so many "small" encroachments that they would provoke broad-based opposition. The Select Committee resolved to "target" its reform proposals to focus them on specific problems. This approach, they hoped would solve problems narrowly and incrementally, rather than proposing such sweeping reform that the reformers would, in effect, build their opponents' coalition for them. This was seen as the most sensible strategy: to pick and choose the most significant and soluble, problems, and seek to gain passage of each with carefully crafted "piecemeal" reforms. The only problem with this strategy was that by this point the House had become impervious to even this more modest and subtle approach to reform.

The Select Committee produced recommendations in five areas:

Reduction of Committee Scheduling Conflicts

This was an initiative involving scheduling of House committee and subcommittee business to reduce conflicts in committee meeting times. This proposal would have mandated each committee to transact business only on certain days. The proposal[6] drew distinctions between major and minor committees and determined which days each could have business meetings and mark-ups. Many chairmen objected to the extent that this reduced their autonomy and also to the imposition of centralized regulatory authority (and order) over the committee system. Many chairmen objected. This plan, unanimously endorsed by the Select Committee and later approved by the Rules Committee, was kept from even coming to the floor by the outspoken and widespread opposition by chairmen.

"Cubbyholes" in the Capitol

Another modest proposal, recommended by the Select Committee in a 6-5 vote,[7] was to refurbish some balcony spaces in Statuary Hall in the Capitol building as cubbyholes with telephones for members to use when there was not enough time between votes or other floor activity to return to their regular House offices. The Select Committee suggested in the summer of 1979 that money from the contingent fund (estimated to be a relatively paltry $129,000) be used to do the necessary remodeling. In fact, this proposal did not even require formal House authorization; instead it could have been accomplished administratively by the Speaker. But before any action was taken on the matter, Republican Congressman Dan Lundgren of California moved on the House floor to prohibit the plan. His amendment to the continuing appropriations bill of 1980 prohibited use of any federal funds for remodeling Statuary Hall "or any other structure constituting additional office or work space for members of Congress." Lundgren caustically dubbed the Select Committee's idea "a little present for the coming holiday season."[8] Thus did a suggestion for a tiny addition to members' facilities fall prey to Congressional pennypinching—perhaps a reflection of the then-burgeoning movement for government belt-tightening. At a time of public demand for austerity, there was understandable sensitivity to any proposal which might be construed as a vote for Congressional luxury. The vote for Lundgren's amendment was 371-31. Although a small matter, it was an inauspicious start for the Select Committee.

Greater Leadership Authority Over Multiple Referrals

This proposal provided the Speaker with greater authority over the multiple referral process which had grown out of the Bolling-Hansen reforms of 1974. This process allowed the Speaker a degree of flexibility in dealing with bills within the jurisdiction of more than one committee (which is often the case) by referring them jointly, sequentially, or "split"—i.e. separate sections to different committees. After a detailed review of the effectiveness of this system, the Select Committee recommended changes by which the Speaker would be required to designate one committee to have lead responsibility for each bill which was multiply referred, and to establish strict deadlines for action by all other committees handling a portion of the multiple referral.

This proposal was designed to overcome the tendency of the multiple referral process to serve as yet other layer of process—affording access to special interest groups and opportunity for legislative maneuver and delay. The Select Committee's report on multiple referrals had found that the multiple referral process was having the effect of causing "substantial delay" in the legislative process. This was an area where the leadership might gain some leverage over the committees by strengthening the Speaker's authority over the committees—and his ability to affect the substance of bills lying at least tangentially within committee jurisdiction. The Select Committee reported their plan unanimously; it languished in the party caucuses and was never taken up on the floor.

Reduction in Subcommittee Assignments and Subcommittees Themselves

The Select Committee presented another proposal to limit each member to no more than five subcommittee assignments—a gradual move toward limiting each House committee to no more than six subcommittees. This was an attempt to staunch the proliferation of subcommittee assignments which compete for members' attentions.

The plan was unanimously approved by the Select Committee and then referred to the two-party caucuses (as had been previously agreed). The Republican Conference quickly approved the idea, and suggested that it be made a part of House rules. The Democratic Caucus, with the majority's obvious stake in the contours of the committee and subcommittee system, deferred action and finally refused to sanction any limitation. The rejection by the Democrats precluded this matter as well from consideration by the full House.

A New, More Comprehensive Energy Committee

Clearly the most controversial and ambitious proposal of the Select Committee was its attempt to establish a new Energy Committee with more comprehensive jurisdiction over the far-flung elements of national energy policy. It was not to be all-encompassing, but its significant consolidation was in sharp contrast to the existing diffusion to over 80 different subcommittees and committees. The Bolling Committee's experience in this regard provided a reminder of a litany of pitfalls of such a reform attempt: fears of lost power by environmentalists and oil and utility company representatives alike; vigorous opposition from members of committees and subcommittees with existing energy jurisdiction and "unholy" alliances in opposition by groups typically divided on matters of substantive policy. An especially tenacious and formidable foe (as he had been during the Bolling battle) was John Dingell—by this time not only the chairman of the Subcommittee on Energy and Power of the Commerce Committee (a critical energy bailiwick) but also the heir-apparent to Harley O. Staggers as Chairman of the full Commerce Committee. Dingell, along with many others with jurisdiction over small portions of the energy issue, had no wish for a realigned Energy Committee. Once again, significant blocs of members were content with things as they were, particularly as opposed to the uncertainty of things as they might be.

The Select Committee's proposal (H. Res. 549), which was passed by the Select Committee 11-4, would have realigned jurisdictions as follows:

A new committee on Energy would have taken portions of the energy jurisdiction from Interstate and Foreign Commerce (essentially taking Dingell's Subcommittee on Energy and making it into a full committee), and would have taken other pieces from Public Works and Transportation and Interior and Insular Affairs. The new committee would be given jurisdiction over "national energy policy generally."

The jurisdiction on energy matters involving technical aspects of science and technology was to be left in the Science and Technology

Committee and, to assuage environmentalists, to provide the Interior Committee with jurisdiction over environmental aspects of all energy matters, ". . . except those of standing committees with specific jurisdiction over environmental matters under existing laws."

The plan was destined to encounter stiff resistance. It inspired several substitutes, including a more ambitious plan by Rep. Phil Gramm of Texas which would have consolidated all energy jurisdiction and centralized it in one omnipotent energy committee (this was the one plan *more* unpopular than the Select Committee's). There was also a plan by Jonathan Bingham for essentially no change in the existing system (changing the name of Interstate and Foreign Commerce to Energy and Commerce and leaving most of all the other pieces in place). And in view of the strong support indicated for Bingham's substitute, there was a last minute attempt by Reps. Patterson, Cleveland and Frenzel to recommit the bill to the Select Committee with instruction to report out a bill similar to the original Select Committee proposal. The only substantive change in the latter bill was the transfer of jurisdiction over nuclear regulatory and energy resources on the Outer Continental Shelf from Interior to the new Energy Committee. This was an attempt to counter the Bingham substitute, which had attracted strong support among Democrats allied with Dingell and other subcommittee leaders. Another goal of the substitute was to indicate the support of Republicans who wanted an Energy Committee with the broad jurisdiction described above. This desperate attempt by Patterson to salvage some sort of Energy reform was early and compelling evidence of reform's bleak prospects.

The Bingham substitute was adopted on March 25, 1980 by a 300-111 vote, drawing broad support from Democrats, including every committee chairman except Rules Committee Chairman Richard Bolling. The attempt by Patterson, Cleveland and Frenzel to recommit the bill to the Select Committee in order to report it later in expanded form was defeated 125-282, falling victim to essentially the same coalition against any revision of the existing jurisdiction.

In adopting the Bingham substitute, the House designated the new Energy and Commerce Committee as the House's lead committee on energy policy, but did nothing to wrest energy jurisdiction from the other committees and subcommittees. The House had once again voted for its fragmented, but comfortable, system.

Chairman Patterson described the vote as "self-serving and damaging to the nation's energy future" and lamented the failure of the range of his Select Committee's initiatives. He went on to suggest that a Select Committee was not the right vehicle for reform—that the Rules or House Administration Committee or some other established entity was needed to marshal the necessary support for reform. Patterson's parting remark upon the fate of the Select Committee's work revealed the extent of his frustration:

"I'm relieved and pleased that the committee is completing its one year of operations, because I don't think there would be many more successes if we continued."[9]

The demise of the Obey and Patterson attempts at consolidative reform marked the eclipse of reform in the House. Even the term "reform" by the late 1970s had ceased to carry with it the positive image of freshness and innovation; many members had not been in Congress during the earlier encounters over reform, and the institutional history recounted by more experienced colleagues was not always flattering toward reform. But perhaps more significantly, members were immersing themselves in the practice of the newly entrepreneurial politics of the reformed Congress. Members of Congress settled into working and tilling the turf of the existing Congress. Engaging in new battle over this turf—and jeopardizing what had been hard-fought gains for many middle ranking and junior members—just did not hold much attraction for a majority of members.

Notes

1. Final report, U.S. House of Representatives, Commission on Administrative Review, H.Doc. 95-272 (95th Congress, 1st Session, 1977).
2. See "House Adopts Tough Ethics Code," *CQ, Weekly Report,* March 5, 1977, pp. 387–391.
3. This applied to both the House and Senate. In 1982 the Senate lifted the ceiling as it applied to its members so as to allow unlimited honoraria instead of a pay raise; in 1983, after revelation of large honoraria received by senators, the Senate re-imposed a limit, compensated for by a raise in salary.
4. Members who were not in the Congress in 1973–1974 for the Bolling-Hansen rift relied on colleagues for their interpretations. Hence, the lack of first-hand historical knowledge on the part of new members made it such that either they had little perspective on the issue or that their perspective was colored by the views of the particular "reference group" of colleagues.
5. "Study Gives Committee Reform a Push," *CQ,* September 3, 1977, p. 1855.
6. H. Res. 404, H. Rept. 96-426, parts 1 and 2.
7. Indicating that even innocuous proposals could spur strong opposition.
8. "House Committee Changes," *CQ Almanac,* 1979, p. 596.
9. "Committee Reorganization," *CQ Almanac,* 1980, p. 563.

Nine

Campaign Finance Reform and Special Interest Influence

An influential political science book of the early 1960s about interest group politics included the following comment on the politics of Congress:

> Congressmen have a great deal more freedom than is ordinarily attributed to them. The complexities of procedure, the chances of obfuscation, the limited attention constituencies pay to any one issue, and the presence of countervailing forces leave the congressman relatively free on most issues. He may feel unfree because of the great demands on his time, but, consciously or unconsciously, by his own decisions as to what he chooses to make of his job he generates the pressures which impinge on him. He hears from voters about things in which he himself chooses to become involved.[1]

This observation is an appropriate starting point for discussion of the campaign finance reforms of the 1970s. This characterization of Congressional "freedom," however, was by the early 1980s only a quaint reminder of simpler times. Members of Congress found themselves not "free to choose," but bombarded by demands for action on a myriad of issues, praised or vilified for positions taken, and thrust into a system in which large sums of money—campaign contributions for members, or for their opponents—hung in the balance.

The most prominent overall effect of the Party and Committee reforms was the dispersion of power. This created opportunities for broader participation and, putatively, for increased policy innovation and freedom on the part of members. While these opportunities were unlikely to lead to the programmism or policy coherence sought by the consolidative reformers inside Congress, or the party responsibility desired by outside theorists, an argument could be made in favor of a system which ostensibly encouraged individualism and creativity.

The reason that these positive developments failed to occur is not due entirely to the intrinsic tendencies of a fragmented decision-making system. A fragmented structure certainly laid a solid foundation for construction of the special interest edifice, but it was the effects of a series of campaign finance reforms in the middle 1970s which helped create and formalize the external special interest infrastructure. These reforms superimposed on this dispersed structure a new and formalized set of powerful special interest linkages to the subcommittees, committees and members—with significant implications for the Congressional agenda.

The prime engine of this development was the Federal Election Campaign Act and its amendments. The new instruments of special interest influence were the PACs—with continued clout on the part of wealthy individuals constrained only by the $1000 limit per candidate per election (up to a limit of $25,000 per annum). If the Party and Committee reforms formed the reform "roots" of the modern Special Interest Congress, the campaign finance reforms provided the water, fertilizer and sunlight required to make the special interest ecosystem grow and thrive.

The results of the campaign finance reforms compounded the effects of the earlier structural reforms and produced a process in which members of Congress found themselves increasingly confronted by issues packaged and shaped by special interest PACs and Washington-based lobbyists. The consideration of these issues was increasingly influenced by PAC money, actual and implied threats, and by the lack of effective countervailing pressure to PACs generally and the interests represented by large contributions often complementing, rather than challenging, PAC funds.[2] (The PACs in many instances do exert countervailing pressures against each other, but rather than this neutralizing the influence, it can have the effect of immobilizing Congress on the issues which most bitterly divide PACs.) The key point here is not simply that PACs can affect or even determine election outcomes (which they sometimes do); rather that the most effective of the Washington-based PACs influence votes, policy-making, and in some cases the Congress's ability to make effective policy at all. While an original goal of many reformers was to make Congress more capable of passing coherent and comprehensive national policy, the grafting of "PAC power" onto the already diffuse Congressional structure signalled the triumph of particularism over universalism in Congressional policy-making.

9:1 THE REFORM OF FEDERAL CAMPAIGN FINANCE LAW

The evolution of campaign finance law reform gave rise to the explosion of PACs, and PACs in turn came to play a large new role in the Congressional process.[3] A patchwork series of legislative, judicial and regulatory decisions constituted a virtual long march to a heightened and more formal special interest influence. The Congress's own attempt to "clean up" campaign finance law in the form of the Federal Election Campaign Act (FECA) and its amendments, was ironically a critical factor in that development. The combined effect of Congressional, Court, and Administrative decision-making was the proliferation of PACs and the creation of the elaborate—if at least more accountable—apparatus of the Special Interest Congress.

The Federal Election Campaign Act—the most recent and sustained attempt to address the problem of money in national politics—had its direct (and ironic) impetus from the veto by President Nixon in 1970 of a rather modest bill to give candidates lower rates for buying broadcast advertising air time. The Congress's response to the veto was to pass a more sweeping bill, the FECA of 1971, which (with a focus on Congressional, as opposed to Presidential campaigns) included the following provisions:

- Limiting the amounts that candidates for federal office could spend on media during primary, runoff, special and general election campaigns (this provision was later invalidated as unconstitutional in *Buckley v. Valeo* except with respect to publicly financed presidential campaigns);
- Imposing ceilings on contributions by any Federal candidate or his immediate family to his or her own campaign—$50,000 for president or vice president, $35,000 for senator and $25,000 for the House. (This limitation was also ruled unconstitutional in *Buckley v. Valeo,* and was replaced in the 1976 FECA amendments by a limitation of a $50,000 personal contribution for a presidential candidate who accepts public financing. Congress failed to pass public financing for its own elections, and hence no limitations on Congressional candidates' contributions have been imposed);
- Vesting supervisory authority over campaign finance laws in the clerk of the House for candidates for the House of Representatives, the

secretary of the Senate for candidates for the Senate, and the Comptroller General for presidential elections. (This was a half-step toward regulatory control, trying to keep autonomy over the process in each Congressional chamber; this approach was discarded in the 1974 FECA amendments, establishing an independent agency, the Federal Election Commission (FEC));

- Establishing filing requirements, including filing reports as to campaign contributions and expenditures with secretaries of state or equivalent officials;
- Establishing reporting requirements that all political committees and candidates report expenditures and itemize individual contributors along with identifying information concerning the dates, amounts of purchases in excess of $100—as well as personal services, salaries, etc. over $100 (in 1979, raised to $200);
- Setting forth scheduled dates for the reporting of contributions and expenditures. These dates were the tenth day of March, June, and September each year, the fifteenth and fifth days before election and on January 31. Contributions of $5,000 or more after the last pre-election report were to be disclosed within 48 hours of receipt. The 1974 FECA Amendments replaced this process with quarterly disclosure dates along with a report date ten days before, and thirty days after an election. The 1979 FECA Amendments reduced the maximum number of filings over a two-year reporting period from twenty-four to nine in response to criticism of burgeoning paperwork.

Section 205 of FECA departed from the traditional preclusion of direct corporate and labor union political contributions by allowing the following activities to be paid for out of corporate or labor union general funds:

- communications by corporations to their stockholders and their families or by labor organizations to their members and their families on any subject no matter how partisan, including advocacy of candidacy;
- nonpartisan registration and get-out-the vote campaigns by corporations aimed at their stockholders and their families or by labor organizations aimed at their members and their families; [and]
- the establishment, administration, and solicitation of contributions to a "separate segregated fund" to be utilized for political purposes by a corporation or labor organization . . . (18 U.S.C. 610).

This later provision provided the opening for establishment of the modern PAC—with the stipulation seeking to prohibit coercion of rank and file would-be PAC members:

. . . it shall be unlawful for such a fund to make a contribution or expenditure by utilizing money or anything of value secured by physical force, job discrimination, or financial reprisal; or by dues, fees or other monies required as a condition of employment, or by monies obtained in any commercial transaction.[4]

Possible Prohibition on Government Contractors?

One early impediment to broad-based establishment of PACs by major corporations and unions was confusion over the meaning of Section 200 of FECA which prohibited political campaign contributions by whomever held government contracts. The 1971 FECA extended the ban on contributions by government contractors to "indirect" contributors—i.e. those contributions which "indirectly" flowed from corporate and labor treasuries. Hence, major corporations and unions that might otherwise have leapt into the PAC business did not because they were legally prohibited from doing so as long as they were government contractors. This became an item of major concern to unions, some of which held government contracts for employee training. Hence the AFL-CIO lobbyists became proponents of amendment of the law to maintain "separate segregated funds," and to operate as any other PAC. The prospect of opening up the PAC process to the American industry was not widely understood or foreseen, certainly not by the labor lobbyists who viewed the amendments as helpful to labor and unlikely to be utilized by big corporations.

The Revenue Act of 1971

Another significant development was the Revenue Act of 1971 which allotted tax credits or deductions for political contributions (for federal, state and local office). This was amended in 1978 to permit only tax credits. A federal tax credit was allowed against federal income tax for 50 per cent of the contribution, up to $12.50 on a single tax return and $25 on a joint return and was further increased to $25 and $50 in the 1974 Amendments and to $50 and $100 in the 1978 Revenue Act Amendments.

Pipefitters Local 562 v. United States and the "Separate Segregated Fund"

In June 1972, the U.S. Supreme Court handed down a decision which constituted the first interpretation of the amended campaign finance law. The decision involved a pipefitters union local—and its three officers—which had maintained a separate segregated political campaign fund, and had solicited the contributions at work sites. The union and the officers had been convicted for violating the provision of the law which held that funds must be *voluntary* and be financed by *organization members*. The contention was that this fund in contrast was apparently *compulsory* and financed by the *union*. The latter interpretation had been upheld by the U.S. Court of Appeals.

On appeal to the Supreme Court, a 6-2 majority held that the amended FECA law had *not* been violated since the union had solicited the contributions on a voluntary basis—there was no evidence of coercion—that the intended use of the funds was within the purposes of the law, and most crucially, that the campaign fund had been kept in a fund "*separate and segregated*" from the union (dues based) treasury. The effect of the "Pipefitters" decision was to put the imprimatur of the highest court on the use of a separate segregated fund for voluntary contributions. The Court thus drew the distinction between the regular funds and operations of a corporation or union and the specific political purpose of the PAC's separate segregated fund. The voluntariness of the contribution was considered critical. But another important implication was that the Court had legitimized corporate and union control over the management and disposition of the funds, so long as they were kept "separate and segregated" from the regular treasury. This clarified the law so that would-be founders of corporate PACs now knew that it was lawful for them to establish PACs, and to run them as they wished so long as they kept the PACs funds separate and segregated. This position is still accepted today.

The 1974 FECA Amendments

Against the background of the mushrooming Watergate scandal of 1973 and 1974, amendments seeking to tighten FECA were adopted. These amendments, not fully implemented until April 1975, included the following:

- Establishment of the Federal Election Commission (taking full powers away from the clerk of the House and the secretary of the Senate, although they were both included as non-voting members of the FEC and remained as the initial repository for the FECA reports of House and Senate candidates, respectively). The Commission was established in a way that apportioned the appointment power among the President and Congress (also later deemed unconstitutional in *Buckley v. Valeo*); the original 1974 process was to have two appointments made by the President and four by House and Senate leaders—with all six voting members to be confirmed by both the House and Senate. The FEC was authorized to promulgate rules and regulations and to monitor compliance. Civil enforcement powers were also included.
- Establishment of numerous contribution limitations: $1,000 for each individual contributor per primary, run-off or general election, not to exceed a $25,000 total annually to all federal candidates; for political committees, a limit of $5,000 per candidate per election (but no aggregate maximum). Cash contributions over $100 were prohibited; and a limit of $1,000 was placed on independent expenditures (i.e. by a political committee) on behalf of a candidate.

- Spending limits for Presidential campaigns and House and Senate campaigns
- Various disclosure and reporting procedures similar to the original FECA
- Public financing for presidential campaigns was made available in the pre-nomination primaries, convention campaigns and the general elections. In the primaries, individual contributions up to $250 to major party candidates were matched with public funds; in the general election an outright grant of $20 million from the Federal Treasury (with inflation adjustment provisions) was provided for campaigns of major party nominees. The major parties for running their party conventions.

A key 1974 FECA Amendment was the Congress making it clear that Government contractors could establish PACs with separate segregated funds. Section 103 of 18 U.S.C. 611 provided:

> This section does not prohibit or make unlawful the establishment or administration of, or the solicitation of contributions to, any separate segregated fund by any corporation or labor organization for the purpose of influencing the nomination for election or election of any person to Federal office, unless the provisions of Section 610 of this title prohibit or make unlawful the establishment or administration of, or the solicitation of contributions to, such Fund.

This clarified that government contractors were entitled to form PACs just like any other corporation or other entity. This provision, pushed by organized labor which was worried about its own position since it received Federal training contracts, opened the floodgates for major corporations, which also held Federal contracts, to form PACs. Labor had also been concerned that the courts might invalidate labor's right to operate PACs; hence labor wanted a specific recognition of PACs in FECA. Labor, and most other participants, failed to foresee the long term implications.

Another key point was that the 1974 FECA Amendments effectively established a full-scale public financing system for presidential elections (i.e., for all who chose to accept public funds—conditioned on compliance with spending limitations for candidates who accepted such funds), *while not establishing any public financing component for Congressional elections.* The effect of this would become obvious: to make Congress the target, and beneficiary, of the vast sums of special interest money, which had previously been directed toward influencing the race for the White House. Common Cause and other reform groups that backed public financing of Congressional races in 1974 view this as the critical failure of the campaign finance experience. Certainly, the creation of a dual system allowed special interests opportunities for access to Congress; in addition, the move to curtail the influence of wealthy individuals gave rise to PACs and a whole new array of organized entities in American politics.

The Sun-Pac FECA Advisory Opinion

Another development, this time an interpretive advisory opinion by the FEC, further facilitated the establishment of corporate PACs. The Sun Oil Company, which was considering the formation of a PAC, had sought an advisory opinion from the FEC essentially seeking FEC approval of its intended course of action. SUN-PAC's intention was to use corporate funds to solicit contributions not only from stockholders and their families but also from all corporate employees and their families. The company proposed to establish two separate entities, SUN-PAC, a PAC which would funnel the collected contributions to candidates based on decisions made by corporate PAC managers, and SUN-EPA, an automatic check-off pay-roll deduction plan similar to a "Christmas Club" pursuant to which individual donors themselves would designate campaign contributions.

In approving the Sun Oil plan to solicit employees as well as stockholders,[5] a majority of the FEC Commissioners relied on the fact that, although the statute restricted to stockholders and their families the class of persons to whom the corporation could direct political communications and get-out-the-vote and voter registration drives, there was no similar restriction on the class of persons who could be solicited for contributions to a PAC. However, the view taken by both union officials and two minority FEC commissioners was that allowing corporate management to solicit all of a corporation's stockholders and employees (most of whom were not members of unions)—in contrast to unions who could solicit only their members—gave the corporations greater leeway than unions in soliciting contributions to their PACs, thus resulting in unequal treatment and upsetting the delicate political balance between them. At a time of general backsliding as far as membership and national political clout in the American trade union movement, this development was greeted by union officials as a disquieting development. The 1976 Amendments, however, restored the balance somewhat by limiting solicitations by corporate

PACs to stockholders and their families and executive and administrative staff and their families, rather than all employees.

Nevertheless, the SUN-PAC opinion was viewed as a catalyst for the formation of corporate PACs and as a major breakthrough for corporate PACs both intrinsically and in their status vis-a-vis labor unions. The Sun Oil plan served to establish the general *modus operandi* of future corporate PACs. The approved procedures included:

- use of general corporate treasury funds to create and run PACs and to serve as the base for solicitation of contributions;
- establishment of the right of management (Sun Oil) to solicit on behalf of its PAC (Sun Pac) contributions from persons other than stockholders;
- establishment of the right of a corporation to set up more than one PAC; and
- establishment that payroll deduction plans were acceptable methods for corporate PACs (in striking contrast to a prohibition on similar methods for labor unions included in the 1946 Taft-Hartley Act but repeated in the 1976 Amendments).

As Edward Epstein, a leading authority on campaign finance, has noted: "While it was the 1971 and 1974 amendments that provided the legal authority for business PACs, it was *SUN-PAC* that provided the imprimatur in their size and numbers."[6]

The Supreme Court Alters Campaign Finance: Buckley v. Valeo

The combined effect of the 1971 and 1974 FECA set forth a fundamentally new regulatory framework and set of practices and limitations on Federal campaign finance. The act raised both constitutional questions and the ire of individuals and groups poised to litigate such questions. As tough political questions have a tendency to do in American government, FECA became a matter for the Courts. The suit was filed by a group of strange political bedfellows: the liberal activist, Stewart Mott, the former liberal Senator and Presidential candidate, Eugene McCarthy, and Conservative Senator James Buckley of New York. *Buckley v. Valeo* became the occasion for a detailed constitutional review by the Supreme Court of the FECA provisions. Some of the Court's holdings have earlier been alluded to; and some are by now well-known guidelines in American political circles. For brevity's sake, the key points of the January 30, 1976 decision were as follows; the Supreme Court:

- struck down expenditure limitations on candidates for their own campaigns as unconstitutional abridgements to the First Amendment's constitutional protection of free speech; the only limitation which was deemed to pass constitutional muster was the limit on overall campaign expenditures by presidential candidates who accepted public financing—i.e., as a condition of such acceptance. Independent expenditures by political committees and individuals (so long as not coordinated with candidates' campaigns) also were seen to fall within the constitutional protection and thus are without monetary limitation;

• upheld limitations on group and individual campaign contributions, finding that such limitations amounted to less onerous encroachments on constitutionally protected speech. The Court also noted that these limitations serve to blunt the disproportionate influence on the political process that large contributors either did have, or could have, and that limitation of this influence, as well as the avoidance of the appearance of undue influence, was a legitimate public policy goal;

• upheld the disclosure requirements, presidential public financing provisions, and the FEC as an executive branch entity—this required reconstitution of the FEC to make all Commissioners appointees of the president. (424 U.S. 1, 46 L.Ed. 2d 659, 1976.)

The *Buckley v. Valeo* decision inspired (indeed, in several areas *required*) Congress to adopt further amendments of FECA. In 1976 the Congress amended FECA, initially to comport with *Buckley v. Valeo* but finally going far beyond it. In so doing, Congress completed construction of the foundation for the evolving system of PAC-dominated campaign finance.

1976 FECA Amendments

In 1976 Congress reconstituted the FEC, giving either the House or Senate (a "one House" veto) on FEC regulations, and amended FECA in the following ways:

• limited individual contributions to a maximum of $5,000 to a PAC and $20,000 to national party committee;

• sought to restrict the proliferation of PACs by treating as a single committee (for purposes of contribution totals) the contributions of membership, corporate and labor union PACs. This limitation was $5,000 total to any one candidate in any election;

• Circumscribed the fund-raising methods of PACs—so that corporate PACs could solicit contributions only from corporate stockholders and executive and administrative staff and their families (save for solicitations twice a year from all other employees); labor union PACs were restricted to soliciting contributions only from union members and their families (except twice a year, they too could mail appeals to non-union, i.e. executive or administrative corporate personnel);

• Granting specific authority to establish separate segregated funds on behalf of trade associations, membership organizations and other entities;

- Labor was placed on an equal footing with corporate PACs insofar as it gained the right to establish payroll deduction plans which had been permitted to corporate PACs by SUN-PAC but denied unions by Taft-Hartley.

The 1976 Amendments sought to redress both the constitutional problems occasioned by *Buckley v. Valeo* and the political problems (mainly in the eyes of labor, and Democratic members of Congress responsive to their interests) emanating from the SUN-PAC advisory opinion. But in selecting to "cure" problems posed by the *Buckley* decision and perceived encroachments on unions, the campaign finance reformers opened the door for the proliferation of corporate PACs.

The stage seemed to be set for a major new initiative to win passage of public financing of Congressional elections. Bills were introduced in the House and Senate (differing in emphasis) calling for limits on personal expenditures and public funds to match small contributions. But it was not to be. The Senate was unable to block a Republican-led filibuster of Congressional public financing (falling 8 votes short of a move to invoke cloture); the House, despite firm support from the Democratic House leadership, was unable to pass public financing in 1977–1978 and again in 1979. Concern outside Congress that public financing amounted to "incumbent protection" was clearly offset by the view inside that it would provide challengers with a new source of funds. By the late 1970s it became apparent that Congress was unlikely to pass a public financing bill and that the existing system, like it or not, was there to stay.

1979 FECA Amendments

By the late 1970s the basic Federal campaign finance law was in place—and the burgeoning of PACs was proceeding apace. Some fine-tuning of FECA in 1979 included:

- simplifying record-keeping and public reporting, e.g. excusing from filing reports those candidates or party committees which receive or spend $5,000 or less;
- reduced the number of reports candidates must file;
- allowed state and local party organizations to use contributed amounts of "soft money" for "party building activities" such as get-out-the vote drives, buttons, bumper stickers, voter registration etc.

While these were primarily designed to affect presidential politics, there is little question that such party building activities have an effect on congressional races as well.

The Rise of Soft Money

Since the Corrupt Practices Act of 1925, corporations and labor unions have been prohibited from making contributions or expenditures of their treasury funds in connection with federal elections. The substantial revisions made in federal campaign finance laws in 1971 now permit corporations and unions to use their treasury funds to pay the overhead and solicitation costs of separate, segregated funds (PACs). However, these PACs and all other political committees that contribute funds to federal candidates must contain only funds that are donated by individuals. Such funds comprised of individual monies are called, in the political vernacular, "hard money." They are the only funds that may be used in federal elections in ways that fall within the definitions of "contribution" or "expenditure." Corporations and labor unions may make PAC contributions of "hard money" up to $5,000 to state and local political parties' federal election accounts and up to $15,000 (or up to $20,000 if the PAC has no qualified multi-candidate committee) to the national party committees.

In addition to the exemption that permits corporations and unions to use treasury funds to establish and maintain PACs, there are several other exemptions that permit the use of corporate and union treasury funds in ways that indirectly benefit federal candidates. Corporate and union treasury money, when used indirectly in federal elections through the "loopholes" in federal law, is called "soft money." Examples of the use of soft money in federal elections include the use of corporate and union treasury money for internal partisan communication and for voter registration and get-out-the-vote (GOTV) drives aimed at their respective solicitable classes.

The same term, "soft money," applies to the use of such corporate and union treasury money in state and local elections where permitted by state law. In contrast to federal law, twenty-eight states permit the direct use of corporate treasury funds, and forty states permit the use of union treasury funds in state and local elections.

In two early Advisory Opinions, AO 1976–72 and 1976–83,[7] the Federal Election Commission held that the general prohibition against use of corporate and union treasury money in connection with federal elections extended to the full breadth of a party committee's ticket-wide registration or get-out-the-vote effort. This meant that corporate or union treasury money could not be used to defray even that portion of a registration or get-out-the-vote drive fairly allocable to state candidates.

In 1978, however, the FEC reversed itself in AO 1978-10 and held that voter registration and GOTV could be treated as general party expenditures, thus permitting state parties and by logical extension, other party committees, to pay the portion of costs allocable to state and local elections out of funds permissible under state law.

The Commission also approved several different formulae for determining the allocation of costs to federal and state candidates. These formulae were based on the ratio of federal to total candidates on the ballot, the ratio of federal to total funds received, and the ratio of federal to total funds spent. Since there are far more state and local candidates on any given ballot than there are federal candidates, the portion of "soft" state money to "hard" federal funds that may be used in the ticket-wide activity is significantly skewed toward the "soft money," often in the range of 75–90 per cent.

As Commissioner Harris stated in his dissent from AO 1978-10:

> (t)his means that Kansas corporations and unions may now finance a major part of the costs associated with a partisan registration and get-out-the-vote drive out of general treasury funds . . . .

The 1979 Amendments added legitimacy to the use of the "soft" corporate and union treasury funds and provided additional leeway in its use. The 1979 Amendments specifically permitted a state or local party committee to invoke the names of its presidential and vice presidential candidates when conducting a voter registration or get-out-the-vote drives or distributing campaign material which were paid for in part with these "soft" monies. As long as the party threw in the names of a few state and local candidates, it could finance its activities in large part with corporate and union treasury funds. These provisions led to situations in 1980 and 1984 where the staffs of the presidential candidate, and the presidential candidates themselves, solicited soft funds from corporations and unions and coordinated the transfer of the monies down to targeted state and local party committees for use in ticket-wide party activities. And while this new "trick" of soft money does not directly relate to individual House and Senate campaigns, it does provide opportunities for the House and Senate party campaign committees to obtain "soft" funding of various of their activities. It also enables well-financed party efforts on the national and state levels, which clearly can have an impact on the fortunes of individual House and Senate candidates.

9:2 THE PROCESS OF CAMPAIGN FINANCE REFORM

The process of Congressional campaign finance reform differed from the rest of the Congressional reform experience in that it was substantially affected by forces outside the Congress, and was strongly affected by decisions made by the Supreme Court and the FEC. As it evolved campaign finance reform became increasingly a battleground between "good government" reform groups such as Common Cause and affected interest groups. The interest in reform was spurred by the increase in campaign costs triggered by the new technology of politics, especially television advertising, and it was fueled by scandals indicating that wealthy contributors and candidates were increasingly dominant figures in American politics. Hitherto, interest groups generally had only scant involvement in the internal party and institutional reforms in the early 1970s. Reform-minded public interest groups had helped build support for reforms in the early 1970s. And special interest groups such as labor, environmental, and merchant marine groups had weighed in to protect their turf during the Bolling-Hansen and Patterson battles over Committee reform. But campaign finance reform, starting slowly as a reaction to a perceived excessive influence of individual contributors, evolved into a battleground for a relative advantage—or at least protection—by interest groups, the parties, and that other broad category: incumbent members of Congress. By the end of the decade, campaign finance reformers had constructed a complicated body of law and regulations and a special interest edifice which itself became a force against proposed changes in the system.

Unlike other internal Congressional reform matters, the reform of campaign finance triggered opinions from the administrative agency delegated powers under the Act, the FEC, and from the Supreme Court in its landmark *Buckley v. Valeo* decision striking down key aspects of FECA. But perhaps more notable than these inter-branch involvements was the fact that FECA itself created a whole new structure of entities—the PACs—ready to work for their self-perpetuation and self-enhancement. In this capacity, they became potent obstacles to moves to trim back the power of PACs in the form of public financing and limitation of PAC contributions. And PACs became a new counterforce, or potential complement and source of funds, for the parties. Not only did PACs gain the ability to duplicate some of the efforts traditionally pursued by parties, but they also could help the fortunes of preferred parties. Although the rise of the Republican party's financial clout in the late 1970s was largely attributable to small individual contributors through direct mail, PACs have helped the Republicans significantly, not least through independent expenditures by ideologically conservative PACs.

The Dynamics Within Congress

The process of campaign finance reform reveals a distinct institutional bias toward incumbent protection. Those with the responsibility for changing the rules are the incumbent members who have succeeded under the old rules. All proposed reforms are scrutinized for their potential impacts on incumbents. While partisan or ideological advantage is often considered, the most irresistible pressure is against reforms designed to aid challengers. Rep. Wayne Hays, in his capacity as Chairman of the House Administration Committee, was a prime opponent of public financing of elections because he considered it a source of "guaranteed" funding for challengers. This notion was widely accepted despite the counter-argument that public financing of Congressional elections would amount to an "incumbent protection act." This view was that since public financing would carry with it a limit on expenditures which would undermine a challenger's ability to spend the requisite amount—most likely *more* than the incumbent—to compensate for the incumbent's superior recognition. It is unrealistic to expect incumbents to acknowledge their inherent advantages and seek to outfit would-be opponents with compensatory benefits; although a courageous if quixotic Senator James Buckley proposed an amendment during the 1974 debate on FECA—prior to *Buckley v. Valeo*'s invalidation of spending limits unless part of a public financing plan—that challengers be allowed to spend 130 per cent of the limit on incumbents. This amendment was defeated 66–17.

The overall performance of Congress in regard to its own campaign finance calls into question Congress's ability to deal effectively—and dispassionately—with the problem of equal access to office. The instinct to protect incumbents, and additionally, to seek party advantage, seriously undermines the objectivity of the decision-makers. But more than that, the same structure of fragmented power in Congress militates against effective campaign finance reform in ways similar to its more general effects. An obstinate committee or subcommittee chairman (in this case, Wayne Hays when he was Chairman of House Administration) held the power to pigeon-hole reform proposals for years, and to determine the direction of reform. (Hays bottled up a plan for partial public financing through 1977.) The Senate, for its part, was able to stop partial public financing through filibuster when Republicans were in the minority—and since 1981 when the Republicans assumed control of the Senate, by simply denying it sustained consideration.

The opportunities to debate interminably the issues of campaign finance reform are many. First, as the minority party in both Houses until 1981, Republicans could argue against public financing and PAC limitation because it allegedly would help incumbents, a majority of whom were Democrats. This was in addition to other general arguments against "taxpayer subsidies" and the like. But when the Republicans won a majority in the Senate, they still opposed public financing. This was on the theory that public financing would undo their hard-fought gains by undermining the Republicans' superior access to bountiful Business PAC money. While PACs and especially PACs with Washington offices tend to favor incumbents (including Democratic incumbents), the experience of 1980 and 1982 is that many business PACs appear willing to back challengers to incumbents viewed to be too liberal.

There are many reasons for Congress to refrain from action on complicated issues. With respect to campaign finance, it has thought of, and articulated, most of the reasons. But aside from the instinct toward self-preservation, members of Congress (and some interest group allies) can be forgiven if they are wary of new initiatives in the area of campaign finance reform. This is because their past experience has, in several striking ways, not been what was originally expected.

Unintended Consequences of Campaign Finance Reform

A general, though significant, observation about the process of campaign finance reform is that its consequences were largely unintended and to a large extent unforeseen. This was one area of reform in which reformers in many quarters clearly misjudged the likely results of reform. This was certainly the case when organized labor, in seeking to enhance its advantage, actually helped Business PACs construct an imposing counter-force to its own interests.[8] This was also the case more generally: there was little realization—or at least articulation of any realization—of the profound effects which would be wrought by the FECA and its amendments. Certainly the interpretations and changes brought about by the FEC and the Supreme Court were not envisioned by Congressional drafters. And the original goal of reducing the influence of wealthy individuals led to the proliferation of organized interest group influence in the form of PACs—and a whole set of other problems. The campaign finance reform experience stands out as perhaps the best example of reform's unintended consequences—and of the phenomenon of a reform with a momentum and life of its own, which continues to change in different political environments in unpredictable ways.

Campaign Finance and the New Dynamics of Congressional Elections

The cost of campaigning for Congress has increased exponentially during the 1970s and early 1980s. In 1974 the total expenditure of Congressional campaigns was $77 million. In 1982 candidates spent $343 million. Between 1972 and 1982 PAC contributions to Congressional candidates increased from $8.5 million to $83.1 million. During the period from 1974 to June, 1982, the number of PACs skyrocketed from 608 to 3,479. The number of corporate PACs jumped from 89 in 1974 to 1,467 in 1982—as compared to Labor PACs which went from 201 in 1974 to 628 in 1982. (Labor is unlikely to experience much growth in the number of its PACs since most unions already have them. Corporations, large and small, continue to form new PACs.) However, statistics provide only the rough outline of the profound impact that PACs have had on the political process.[9]

The recent literature about Congressional elections has focused on political money and its effects—and particularly on the ability of nonincumbents to mobilize the resources necessary to launch effective challenges. Consequently, the national political and economic outlook early in the election cycle has become an important determinant of strategic decisions by potential candidates and contributors. The work of Gary C. Jacobson and Samuel Kernell, among others, indicates that a critical period influencing elections is the period long before the election when incumbents and would-be challengers survey the political and economic landscape to decide "what kind of year" it is likely to be.[10] Contributors and particularly PAC contributors make the same calculations; indeed, their determination that challengers have dim hopes can be self-fulfilling, drying up funds to the point that challengers decide not to make the race. Jacobson points to the experience of 1980 when PACs and the Republican Party, sensing a possible "good year" for Republicans—especially in the Senate—funneled large sums of money to challengers of incumbent Democrats. This had much to do with the Republican capture of the Senate in 1980. Similar considerations in 1982—only this time causing potential Republican candidates to conclude that their fortunes would not be so bright—have been viewed as influencing who ran, how much was contributed, and of course, who won.[11] It is a generally held view also that the 1982 election showcased the Republicans' ability to use superior financial resources to minimize the Democratic gains—in short, to distort the electoral outcome despite the macro forces favoring the Democrats.

Of course, these macro trends form only a backdrop for the complicated decision-making by individuals and groups over whether to run and whether to contribute. Increasingly in the 1980s the determinative question has become "can the candidate raise the necessary money?" This often has little or nothing to do with macro forces; instead it has to do with personal wealth, strength of opponents, and critically, the issue positions of the would-be candidates which affect the willingness of interest groups to open up their coffers.

These factors shaping strategic decisions by candidates and contributors obviously transcend elections; they are prominent in the new dynamics of special interest interaction with Congress affecting the workings of Congress and its external relationships in several new ways.

"Home Style" Versus "Washington Community"

There has long been a recognition of the conflicting demands on members of Congress of "the district" and "Washington." The importance of the former is expressed well in Speaker O'Neill's maxim: "all politics is local." There is a certain genius of the American system of representation that no matter how grandiose and global the concerns of members of Congress in their dealings with presidents and their work on lofty legislative matters, they still must regularly go back and service their local constituents and voters. In political science terms, it is the clash of the "Washington Community," a concept pioneered by Richard E. Neustadt[12] describing the cosmopolitan political audience based in the nation's capital versus the "home style" of members in their districts. There the constituency pressures and rituals based on local values described by Richard F. Fenno, Jr. in his study of members of Congress in their districts[13] contrast with the heady politics of Washington. Fenno's research into the "world of the shopping bags" (campaign paraphernalia, in this case grocery bags with the candidate's name on them) reveals a complicated set of perceptions as to how members view the constituent composition of their districts. These take the form of concentric circles of supporters within the district characterized by increasing levels of intensity of support: the geographic constituency, the re-election constituency, the primary constituency and then the close band of intimates. The different ways that members feel they must appeal to the different constituencies within the district have much to do with determining their "homestyles." This literature is relevant to the understanding of the continuing—even enhanced—importance of Washington-based special interest opinion leaders despite the continuing importance of grass roots, district-based influence.

The new labyrinth of PACs, lobbyists and Washington-based trade associations—along with a concentration of fund-raising and political opinion-leading in the capital—has had a centralizing effect on politics. This array of PACs constitutes a new concentration of power in Washington, D.C. While Congress itself has become more fragmented, the structure of campaign finance has become more centralized—i.e., nationalized—in Washington. This is true despite the fact that many PACs remain based in other parts of the country, and despite the rise of grassroots lobbying and "coalition building" as a new technique of influencing members of Congress. The reason is that the largest, most active business and labor PACs are based in organizations that wield clout in Washington, and have the access to influence the Congressional agenda. In addition, these grassroots forces often rely on and defer to Washington-wise government relations directors, lobbyists and PAC managers. Hence, rather than the grassroots articulating an indigenous message, often it becomes the grassroots telling Congress what the Washington-based lobbyists told them to say. In addition, large trade association, labor and ideological PACs are most effective when they can become "leaders of the pack." When "coalitions" of like-minded PACs and other organizations agree on causes and candidates, clusters of PACs channel their campaign funds to selected candidates and form a virtual stampede. PAC operatives make important judgments about who should run, who might win, and what "kind of year" it will be. And their judgments are most important with respect to the marginal races and open seats where large sums of money can tip the balance. For challengers it is critical that some influential figures in Washington "decide" that the race is winnable and increasingly this decision is based on candidates' ability to raise money.

Even though the dollars which comprise the PAC funds are generated from the "grassroots" members around the country, the key opinion leaders and decision-makers who shape the conventional wisdom about such electoral matters tend to be in Washington or to take their cues from leaders in Washington. It also does not seem to matter whether this "wisdom" shaped in Washington is based on an accurate appraisal of the facts. Even though conventional wisdom about electoral prospects is often faulty and subject to fast-breaking revisionism, it feeds on itself and is, to a certain extent, self-fulfilling. In other words, if early signs are that it will be a "bad year" for one party or the other, or individual candidates, funds will be hard to raise and many high quality candidates will decide not to make the race. Even the fact that political fortunes often change quickly and that grass-roots concerns often slip by unnoticed by the Washington cognoscenti—which transforms January's certainties into September questions and November surprises—does not change the dynamics of campaign fundraising for most campaigns in ordinary circumstances.

It is worthwhile to step back and assess the assumption underlying, and the context of, the strategic choices made by special interest contributors. The assumption is that campaign contributions to candidates buy at least access and preferably influence with the recipient on legislative matters. Contributions amount to quasi-"investments." In most instances, the safest investment is in solid, blue-chip incumbents. It is a calculated risk to back challengers (the analogy generally applied in Congressional parlance: if you try to shoot the king, you had better kill him). Thus the context of these strategic choices on the part of interest groups is one in which the multitude of special interest groups are seeking to maximize their influence on issues of concern. And the best indication of what a member will do is to examine what incumbents have done. Hence the voting records of incumbents provide a tangible basis for PAC funding decisions. Past loyalty to a favored point of view is typically the best guarantee of future PAC generosity. In the quest for greater access and influence, the overwhelming evidence is that the bulk of the money, and the preponderance of PAC money, goes to incumbents as seen in Table 9:1.[14]

Table 9:1 shows that the advantage incumbents have over challengers in attracting contributions—and especially PAC contributions—is widening at an increasing rate. Consequently, the advantages that incumbents already enjoy[15] are extended further in the arena of fundraising. Moreover, when challengers mount strong challenges, they "bid up" the race and prod incumbents into raising and spending more. This leads to the finding of Gary Jacobson in a series of studies that the most significant factor in the competitiveness of Congressional elections is the amount spent by challengers. Challengers have the hardest time raising early funds, and they are the most substantially helped by infusions of funds early in the campaign. Jacobson's basic point is that the level of funding of a party's challengers has much to do with how those challengers fare. The Republican challengers in 1980, especially in Senate races, were well-funded and did

TABLE 9:1

The Advantages of Incumbency in the Finance of
Campaigns for the U.S. Congress

House of Representatives Campaigns

	Average $ Spent By Challengers	Average $ Spent By Incumbents	Difference
1974	37,000	54,000	(17,000)
1976	50,000	77,000	(27,000)
1978	63,000	111,000	(48,000)
1980	96,000	169,000	(73,000)
1982	128,000	256,000	(128,000)

U.S. Senate Campaigns

	Average $ Spent By Challengers	Average $ Spent By Incumbents	Difference
1974	402,000	556,000	(154,000)
1976	414,000	628,000	(214,000
1978	612,000	1,423,000	(811,000)
1980	897,000	1,377,000	(480,000)
1982	1,213,000	1,748,000	(535,000)

House of Representatives Campaigns

	Average PAC $ By Challengers	Average PAC $ By Incumbents	Difference
1974	5,000	12,000	(7,000)
1976	8,000	25,000	(17,000)
1978	11,000	38,000	(27,000)
1980	20,000	62,000	(42,000)
1982	31,000	101,000	(70,000)

U.S. Senate Campaigns

	Average PAC $ By Challengers	Average PAC $ By Incumbents	Difference
1974	24,000	71,000	(47,000)
1976	53,000	116,000	(63,000)
1978	74,000	194,000	(120,000)
1980	184,000	304,000	(120,000)
1982	167,000	450,000	(283,000)

well; the Democratic challengers in 1982 were underfunded and did relatively poorly. This leads to a conclusion based on recent experience which suggests that three classes of candidates have access to business and trade association PAC money—incumbent Democrats, incumbent Republicans, and Republican challengers. This leaves Democratic challengers in typically dire circumstances, especially since Labor PACs are unable to make up the difference.

There is recent evidence that seeks to rebut the stereotype of PACs as monolithic, Washington-centered and incumbent-oriented influence maximizers. Based on the 1980 PAC experience, Theodore J. Eismeier and Phillip H. Pollock III describe a diverse range of PACs with differing behavior patterns. As Michael Malbin summarizes:

> The typical PAC is a small operation, is based somewhere outside Washington, gives a substantial share of its money to non-incumbents, and follows a 'remarkably unsophisticated' giving strategy if the aim is to maximize legislative influence.[16]

Certainly PACs are an amorphous and varied lot; prominent among the dimensions upon which they vary is effectiveness. While it is probably the case that many PACs are willing to put their ideology or political orientations above practicality by supporting challengers, the point is that the most effective PACs are those that invest heavily in winners—and those winners are disproportionately incumbents. Only if an incumbent has so alienated an interest group is it likely that the PAC will engage in flat-out support of challengers. This, of course, does happen. Sometimes PACs make it a special campaign to defeat an ideological or issue-based opponent. Moreover, PACs are most effective when they serve as financial support bases for skilled Washington lobbyists. The fact that some PACs have non-Washington locations or do not have effective Washington representation does nothing to refute the thesis that many PACs wield considerable clout on Capitol Hill. Instead, like all the rest of the evidence in politics, the lesson seems to be that some interests skillfully see to it that they have an advantage over others.

Hence, while it is useful to understand the diversity of PACs and their varying strategies, this understanding does not, of itself, refute the proposition that PACs have tended to have a nationalizing effect on important aspects of our politics, that they often enhance legislative access and influence, and that they have aided incumbents and Republicans at the expense of challengers, particularly Democratic challengers.

It is also important to note the recent trend toward Washington lawyers and lobbyists finding it useful (or even necessary) to take on the role of fundraisers. Some Washington law firms actually have their own PACs, and many lobbyists with active practices on Capitol Hill serve as advisors to PACs and conduits to members of Congress of PAC and individual contributions. Again, while there are a range of motives and ideologies underlying PAC behavior, the role of lobbyists in channeling money to members is clearly directed toward members' legislative decisions.

The mutually beneficial nature of the lobbyist/legislator relationship often carries with it a darker side; neither likes his or her particular role. The lobbyist hates to have to raise and give money; the legislator hates to have to take it. But it is part of the system as it has evolved; campaigns are tremendously expensive, and special interests are the most logical paymasters.

Campaign Finance and the Congressional Career

Congressional politics is shaped by considerations of campaign finance in many ways. To start at the beginning of the contemporary Congressional career, some new members of Congress seek committee assignments which will provide good fund-raising opportunities. Of course, this is unlikely to be the only, or even primary, motive. But because of the new potency of PACs and the relative vulnerability of freshmen representatives—beginning with the matter of paying off the last campaign's debts—a good fund-raising base in a committee certainly has its allure.[17] The attractions of PAC money—as opposed to individual contributions which are limited to small amounts and harder to raise—continue up the seniority ladder. When members become potent forces on subcommittees and committees—or chairmen—their ability to raise funds from affected interest groups is enhanced further. The factors which might militate against more senior members attracting the biggest PAC contributions are 1) if they are so "safe" they can afford to go without and 2) if they have positioned themselves on issues against a set of interests represented by PACs. However, typically there is at least a potential counter-source of PAC money on the other side of the issue in those cases.[18]

And the preference for PAC money is sustained by several developments in the area of fundraising from individuals. First, only 4 per cent of taxpayers make use of the tax credit for contributions; only a fraction of that number are large contributors. These contributors become well-known in the age of full disclosure. Hence sophisticated direct mail and phone bank techniques make it such that individuals are pretty well picked over—to the point of disgust in many cases! While wealthy individuals might at some point tire of the process, PACs typically have compelling reasons for continuing participation.

The Electoral Disconnection: When Campaign Contributions Have Little To Do With Campaigns

The trend in Congressional elections—especially in the House—has been toward increased advantage to incumbents and a critical importance of the level of the funding of challengers. Incumbents ordinarily have distinct advantages over challengers, and—when significantly challenged—incumbents can respond by raising large amounts to compensate. Moreover, an increasingly elite consensus in Washington among clusters of similarly oriented special interest groups has much to do with shaping the political climate of national elections. To be sure, "home style" is critical in a member's interaction with his or her constituents. But increasingly, the ability to run effective campaigns is heavily influenced by what special interest groups based in Washington decide. But this development grows from another increasingly apparent trend: that special interest contributions are oftentimes only tangentially or superficially related to election campaigns.

This trend is spurred by the fact that well-established members of Congress *perceive*—oftentimes irrationally—that they are vulnerable,[19] and feel it necessary to take all precautions against would-be challengers. It is important to stress that the emphasis here is on *perceptions*. All the evidence supports the position that, especially in the House[20] incumbency remains a huge advantage. And as the aforementioned statistics indicate, it may well be increasingly advantageous. But as members have grown increasingly wary of possible challengers, they have responded in the most tangible way they know: the so-called "deterrence" approach to fund-raising. This involves raising large sums of campaign money to have sitting in certificates of deposit designed to deter a would-be challenger from taking the plunge. It is the ultimate exercise in the law of anticipated reaction; it assumes that a prospective challenger will desist in the face of a big war chest. This type of preparation is justified as necessary because of the new capacity of PACs to "pile on" huge amounts of campaign contributions quickly to a challenger perceived to be making a strong race. (This latter point is often more than perception; it is accurate.

While most practicing politicians do not keep up with the political science literature, incumbent congressmen intuitively grasp the point that the level of challengers' funding is a crucial factor in their likelihood of success. The deterrence approach to fundraising is the incumbents' answer to the prospective challenger.)

A consequence of this new tendency is that members who have no known or likely serious opponent solicit and receive PAC contributions in great abundance. This might otherwise be dismissed as an insignificant "side-effect" of reform, except that it is part of a growing *dis*connection of so-called "campaign" finance from elections. These contributions to "safe" congressmen are only tangentially related to the election process in that they have little or nothing to do with an actual election contest in which one candidate espouses one set of positions on issues and another takes a different set of positions. The timing of the contributions is often far-removed from or unrelated to the election: sometimes *after* the election to pay off past debts, sometimes early in the election cycle to begin the "deterrent" fund. In some cases, contributions are timed to correspond with legislative developments rather than electoral ones.

In short, a system has grown and flourished in which campaign finance is certainly a vital part of the electoral process, but often it has much more than an electoral connection. In new ways campaign finance has become oddly *dis*connected from the electoral process. Increasingly, so-called "campaign contributions" have little or nothing to do with campaigns. Except in those unusual circumstances when ideologically oriented PACs sense the chance for significant gains by challengers—as in 1980—most PACs play both sides of the aisle by contributing to incumbents of both parties, and sometimes hedge their bets by giving to both sides in the same race.

When campaign contributions become disconnected from campaigns, one must ask to what they have become connected. The answer quite clearly is access and influence within the newly decentralized Congressional structure. This unsurprising answer takes the form of several major tendencies, which manifest themselves in the form of various Congressional biases: first, PAC money tends to follow *relevant* power—i.e., the key points of access including committee and subcommittee members, and especially chairmen and other important players; secondly, PAC money tends to follow specific legislative issues; and increasingly PAC money appears to be simply a general "access fee" on a host of issues. The access and influence add up to Congressional biases which, significantly influence politics and policy. The overall reform experience helped to shape these biases.

Notes

1. Raymond A. Bauer, Ithiel de Sola Pool, and Lewis Anthony Dexter, *American Business and Public Policy* (New York: Atherton Press, 1963), p. 478.
2. As Senator Robert Dole (R.-Kansas) told Elizabeth Drew, "there aren't any Poor PACs or Food Stamp PACs or Nutrition PACs or Medicare PACs." See Drew, *Politics and Money, op. cit.,* p. 96. Robert J. Samuelson has questioned the relevance of this remark by observing: "But, of course, there is a food stamp program, a medicare program and a substantial array of welfare programs. They were enacted because they were thought to be good ideas and even if recently trimmed, they survive because people still believe them to be good ideas and because they have substantial constituencies." See Samuelson, "Campaign Reform Failure," *The New Republic,* September 5, 1983, *op. cit.,* pp. 33–34. A specific rejoinder to Samuelson is to question whether proposals for similar broad-based social programs would stand much chance under the present system as opposed to when they were originated. A general point is that there is clearly a disparity between interest groups which are represented and active, especially through PACs, and those which are not. Increasingly, representation of Washington is a prerequisite for effective access. To be sure, this does not extend to many broad areas of policy-making where public opinion, constituency, party and ideological factors hold sway. But many interests never have their ideas heard, or proposals even placed on the agenda, because they are either not organized or not effectively represented.
3. See Herbert E. Alexander, *Financing Politics: Money, Elections and Political Reform* (Washington, D.C.: CQ Press, 1980); Herbert E. Alexander, *Political Finance* (Beverly Hills: Sage Publications, 1979); Edwin M. Epstein, "The Emergence of Political Action Committees," in Alexander, *Political Finance, Ibid,* pp. 159–198; Joseph E. Cantor, "Political Action Committees: Their Evolution and Growth and Their Implications for the Political System," Congressional Research Service, U.S. Congress, Report No. 82–92 Gov, November 6, 1981; Updated May 7, 1982 and Gary C. Jacobson, *Money in Congressional Elections, op. cit.* In addition, an excellent short report by Peter Fenn and the Center for Responsive Politics contains many incisive tables, some of which are provided later in this chapter; see *Money and Politics: Campaign Spending Out of Control* (Washington, D.C.: Center for Responsive Politics, 1983).
4. 18 U.S.C. 610, at _____.
5. Federal Election Commission. Advisory Opinion 1975-23, Federal Register, v. 40, no. 233, Dec. 3, 1975, p. 56584 *et seq.*
6. Edward M. Epstein, "An Irony of Electoral Reform," *Regulation,* Vol. 3, May–June, 1971, p. 36.

7. See RE:AOR, 1976–72 f 6034, October 6, 1976 and RE:AOR, 1976–83 f 6036, October 12, 1976 in *Federal Election Campaign Financing Guide* (Chicago: Commerce Clearing House, 1976). These opinions are letters from the FEC in the unusual circumstance of the FEC having been un-constituted" pending revision of FECA by Congress. The citation for AO-1978-10 below, issued after the FEC's reconstitution, is *Fed. Elec. Camp. Fin. Guide, Ibid.* f 53–30, July 21, 1978.

8. This involved the ability of government contractors to operate PACs. See above and Epstein, "Irony of Electoral Reform," *op. cit.* and Mark Green, "Political PAC-MAN," *op. cit.*

9. See Elizabeth Drew, *Politics and Money, op. cit.* and Mark Green, "Political PAC-MAN," *The New Republic,* December 13, 1982, *op. cit.,* pp. 18–25 for journalistic accounts of the impact which stress the deleterious impact on Congress, and for a more detailed and less critical view of PACs, see Malbin, ed., *Money and Politics in the United States, op. cit.* The Malbin book provides a useful counter-balance to some of the more polemical asser-tions about the untoward influence of PACs. However, its convincing portraits of the diverse roles, strategies and influences of the different kinds of PACs do not, in my view, undermine the general argument here that Congressional reform in general and campaign finance reform fos-tering PACs in particular led to a significant new fractiousness and special interest orientation of the recent Congresses. The Malbin book does valu-ably point out the complexity of the process and the difficulty of prospec-tive reforms.

10. See Gary C. Jacobson, *The Politics of Congressional Elections* (Boston: Little, Brown, 1983) and his *Money in Congressional Elections* (New Haven: Yale University Press, 1980); Gary C. Jacobson and Samuel Kernell, *Strategy and Choice in Congressional Elections* (New Haven: Yale University Press, 1981); for an update covering the 1980 and 1982 Congressional election experience, see Gary C. Jacobson, "Money in the 1980 and 1982 Congres-sional Elections," in Malbin, ed., *Money and Politics in the United States, op. cit.,* pp. 38–69; and for an extended analysis of the effects of economic conditions, see Edward R. Tufte, *Political Control of the Economy* (Prince-ton: Princeton University Press, 1978). Also important in the expanding literature on Congressional elections is Thomas E. Mann, *Unsafe at Any Margin* (Washington, D.C.: American Enterprise Institute, 1978) as well as Fiorina, *Congress: Keystone of the Washington Establishment, op. cit.* and Mayhew, *Congress, The Electoral Connection, op. cit.*

11. Of course, as for the results of the 1982 elections, it is fair to point out that the ability of the Republican Senatorial Campaign Committee to funnel large amounts of money (some of it raised earlier from PACs but substantially from small individual contributors) to its candidates in close races helped stave off worse defeat. In fact, it helped five incumbent Republicans win razor thin victories over Democratic challengers. Simi-larly the House Republicans were able to avert an off-year loss of seats of major proportions (as it was, they lost 26) by supporting incumbents under stiff challenge—not least of whom was the Minority Leader Robert Michel. Thus it is worthwhile to note that the *tail end* of the election cycle is important too. This point is accentuated by Jacobson in his analysis of

the 1982 election, citing the Republicans' ability to distort the electoral trends by using superior financial resources to those of the Democrats; see Malbin, ed., *Money and Politics in the United States, op. cit.,* pp. 65–67.

12. Richard E. Neustadt, *Presidential Power, op. cit.* and also see a trail-blazing study of the early Congress, James Sterling Young, *The Washington Community, 1800–1828* (New York: Harcourt, Brace and World, Inc., Harbinger Books, 1966).

13. Richard F. Fenno, *Home Style* (Boston: Little, Brown, 1978).

14. See Peter Fenn, *Money and Politics: Campaign Spending Out of Control, op. cit.,* p. 13.

15. In staff, office space, the franking privilege, other perquisites and the incalculable advantage of prestige and access to both information and people which goes with being a sitting member of Congress.

16. Michael Malbin, ed., *Money and Politics in the United States, op. cit.,* p. 3 and see pp. 122–141 for elaboration.

17. A point which is not lost on PACs, as indicated by the evidence from the first six months of 1983 which showed freshmen House members to be among the leading recipients of PAC contributions: with median total receipts of $15,497 versus $5,115 for all other House members. See David Shribman, "House Freshmen Take the Money to Run," *New York Times,* October 30, 1983, p. 4E.

18. An example here is John Dingell and Timothy Wirth on telecommunications policy in the 98th Congress. In staking out a position hostile to ATT on the issue of long distance telephone rates, Dingell and Wirth alienated ATT, but in so doing pleased labor and consumer groups. See John D. Dingell and Timothy E. Wirth, "The Great Phone Robbery," *The Washington Post,* October 26, 1983, p. A27 and Jeanne Saddler, "Limit on 1984 Rise in Local Phone Bills Clears House Over Opposition by AT&T," *The Wall Street Journal,* November 11, 1983, p. 4.

19. See Thomas E. Mann, *Unsafe at Any Margin, op. cit.* and Elizabeth Drew, *Politics and Money, op. cit.*

20. The Senate has been a different story in recent years, with senators being much more vulnerable than House members in the late 1970s and in 1980. Very recently, i.e., 1982, incumbents were successful in every case save for Senator Howard Cannon (D.-Nevada) defeated by Republican Chic Hecht and Senator Harrison Schmidt (R.-New Mexico) defeated by Democrat Jeff Bingaman. It should be noted that five Democratic challengers very nearly upset incumbent Republicans, but the superior Republican resources helped avert loss of control of the Senate.

PART IV

Rethinking Reform: Ramifications and Recourses

Ten

The Overall Reform Experience

The United States Congress is characterized by a highly developed committee system. The inequities in apportioning power within this system early on attracted reformist critics. Reformers, particularly liberal Democrats in the House of Representatives, fixed upon the party (most prominently, the House Democratic Caucus) both as a forum for reform debate and as an object of reform. Their efforts were directed to strengthening the Democratic party—its leadership, subcommittee leaders, and its rank and file—at the expense of entrenched (often Southern and conservative) committee leaders. A review of the Party reform developments has revealed that, although there were conflicting currents and goals in the Party reform effort, the predominant original goals of Party reformers were greater party leadership, programmism, and discipline. However, the result was substantially less of each. The movement was sharply toward the entrepreneurial, individually beneficial politics of every member for him or herself.

The experiences of the Bolling-Hansen battle, one portion of the Obey Commission and the Patterson Committee were focused on that other crucial portion of Congressional terrain, the committee system—and were all serious attempts to reform it. If Party reform in large part was seen as a means of taming unresponsive committee leaders, Committee reform was a more direct approach to accomplishing the same goal. An analysis of Committee reform provides the most revealing insight into the effectiveness of direct consolidative reform, and the formidable opposition it engendered. The fact that attempts at consolidative committee reform in the House[1] were still-born—not once but several times in the space of six years—underscores both the tenacious individualistic values of the House and the immediate and tangible dispersive effects of Party reform.

The major effort at Committee reform (the 1974 Bolling plan) came at the most inopportune time. The Democratic Caucus reforms had "spread the action" to subcommittees and a broader base of members, helping to make Committee consolidation all the more unattractive to newly empowered, middle-level members. Despite the Watergate era, political climate in which anything labelled "reform" was likely to meet with at least some approval, the Bolling plan encountered stiff opposition. Party reform had helped build a high, sturdy wall to block consolidative Committee reform. This became evident when the Bolling Committee plan was rejected in favor of the watered-down Hansen plan; and it was even more obvious in 1977 and 1980 when the Obey Commission and Patterson Committee respectively were overruled by the entrenched defenders of existing House turf.

These developments had profound implications for Congress's performance, both intrinsically and in conjunction with the other branches and levels of American government. To the extent that greater fragmentation made Congress less able to speak with one voice or concur on basic policy, the post-reform Congressional structure also made Congress less cohesive as an institutional counterbalance to the President. However, to the extent that the increasingly diffuse and rambling structure of Congress defied *anyone's* attempt at domination or even persuasion, the Congress had made itself (at least in part) all the more impervious to attempts by the President (or others, including programmatic liberals in Congress) to achieve broad policy goals. Beginning with his much ballyhooed National Energy Bill—President Jimmy Carter's unsuccessful experience with his own Congressional party and Congress generally, was a major factor in shaping his image as politically ineffective. These factors certainly contributed to the perception of a deteriorating Carter Presidency, culminating in his defeat in 1980.

10:1 REFORM AND THE MULTIPLICATION OF ACCESS POINTS

The above-mentioned inter-branch concerns are obviously important, and already have been explored elsewhere.[2] However, the focus here, which has received considerably less attention, is the extent to which reform actually played a role in making Congress more responsive to outside special interest groups. From this standpoint it is clear that the proliferation and ascendancy of subcommittees—the implementation of the Subcommittee Bill of Rights shifting power to middle-level and junior Democratic members—created new and more numerous access points for special interests. At the beginning of the 1970s, the House had 118 regular subcommittees; and at the end of a decade of reform, 131. In 1970, 95 Democratic House members chaired 112 regular House subcommittees; and 109 Democrats chaired subcommittees including the 146 subcommittees of the regular, special and select committees at the time. In 1980, 147 House Democrats chaired 147 different subcommittees (including regular, select and special committees).[3]

These chairmen and newly empowered subcommittees constituted new power centers in an increasingly inchoate Congress. While it is difficult to identify a precise date when, or example of how, the essential nature of Congress's overall relationship with special interests changed as a direct result of reform, by the end of the 1970s it was clear that Congress and its essential workings had changed. This was an evolutionary process by which a combination of reforms and evolutionary "events" made the system increasingly diffuse. Different parts of the structure were subject to "critical events" at different times within this period. For example, the expansion of the Ways and Means Committee in late 1974 from 25 to 37 members and the establishment of subcommittees on the Committee for the first time since 1957 exemplifies how reform expanded access points and changed the substantive orientation of one extremely important committee. It is also necessary, however, to understand the special political dynamics of that Committee. In this case, the demise of Wilbur Mills in 1974, a largely self-inflicted fall from grace due to personal problems, had as much or more to do with the change of politics at Ways and Means as did the specific reforms. It is impossible to know how the enlarged Committee would have performed under a Mills in high dudgeon; although it is probable that the effects of further dispersed power would have been felt eventually in any event.[4] Yet, Mills' demise combined with reform to produce more rapid change.

The most glaring effect of the structural reforms was the proliferation of new power centers—which quickly became special interest access (i.e., veto) points. No longer was there an omnipotent committee chairman or a handful of party or committee leaders who, in any given policy area, might speak for the party or committee and instill confidence that a final "deal" had been struck. The expanded number of subcommittees, their newly empowered chairmen and the general democratization of committee procedures as well as floor and party processes saw to that. The growth of both the range and complexity of legislation and larger, more expert and entrepreneurial staffs to deal with it,[5] added to the absolute number of access points and the character of the process by which interest groups related to Capitol Hill. This period of the seventies witnessed a heightened "permeability" and fractiousness of Congress, and especially so of committees, many of which earlier had traditions of considerable cohesiveness and relative insularity from interest group pressures.[6]

There is no better example of this new permeability than the post-1974 Ways and Means Committee, with its infusion of new members (the Democrats, younger and more liberal; and the Republicans, younger and more conservative) and its new difficulty in formulating coherent policy.[7] This is hardly a reflection on the two post-Mills chairmen, Al Ullman (D-Oregon) and Dan Rostenkowski (D-Illinois), both of whom presided over stormy years on the Committee. This turmoil included Ullman's inability to carve out a legislative agenda on tax reform, energy and welfare policy or successfully to spearhead support for President Carter's initiatives in a Democratic-controlled committee and a Democratic Congress. Rostenkowski has shown impressive political skills in working toward consensus in the Committee—showing both the potential and limits of effectiveness of chairmen in the face of circumstances at once more democratic in the Committee and House. Of course, after 1980, Rostenkowski's job was that much more difficult, since he was forced to contend with both a Republican President and Republican-controlled Senate. Despite his considerable political acumen, he has presided over a committee which has been divided, and in some cases paralyzed, over key policies. Three major pieces of legislation illustrate not only a new tumult on the Committee but also a marked proclivity toward accessibility to special interest appeals. One example was the 1981 "bidding war" on the tax bill by which Democrats and Republicans sought to outdo each other in bestowing tax breaks on special interests in the heady atmosphere of freewheeling tax cuts of the early stages of Reaganomics.[8] Another example (in which Democrats on the committee chose inaction rather than action) was the Ways and Means performance on "TEFRA," the Reagan Administration's "reverse of direction"—i.e., significant tax increase—tax reform bill of 1982 which was written in the Senate Finance Committee. Notwithstanding the House's constitutional prerogative to originate tax bills, this legislation was not taken up by Ways and Means. This was so as not to put Democratic "fingerprints" on a major tax increase.[9] A third example is the late 1983 stalemate over a tax bill when the Ways and Means Committee's proposed $8.3 billion tax increase (in the face of $200 billion deficit projections) was stalled due to stiff opposition in the Rules Committee and from other House members because of the bill's inclusion of a provision putting a cap on the use of Industrial Revenue Bonds ("IRBs"). These bonds, popular devices for states and municipalities to provide below-market tax exempt financing for private enterprises as an incentive to locate facilities in their locales, were viewed by Chairman Rostenkowski and a majority of the Ways and Means Committee as prone to abuse and too much of a drain on revenues. But state and local officials as well as the beneficiaries of "IRBs" fought hard to thwart the Ways and Means attempt to limit their use. These major bills indicate not just the newly topsy-turvy quality of the process, but also the arrival on the scene of intense, fully disclosed, PAC-based and money-tinged special interest-dominated policymaking. These were perhaps exaggerated examples played out on the grand scale of macroeconomic politics and Federal tax policy. But the new fragmentation-cum-special interest orientation was perhaps more outsized in *scale* in comparison to many other issues—but not different in *kind*—from the new politics-as-usual in the House.

In sum, each individual member, and particularly the middle-ranking majority members, became newly potent forces in policy-making. A subcommittee chairman in a given field became the most important person in the lives of entire industries and policy areas.[10] A related point is that the importance of subcommittees was not limited even to the political orientation and control of their chairmen. New, more democratic procedures, and ultimate accountability to Democratic Caucuses on Committees inspired lobbyists to lavish attention on most or all the members of subcommittees—visits, campaign contributions, honoraria, and other "massaging." Under the new dispensation, even relatively junior members had become at least potentially important players in the process.

Several other areas of reform activity—including some surprising ones—also held out opportunities for special interest access and influence.

10:2 "SUNSHINE" AND DOLLAR SIGNS: WHEN MIXED, NOT THE BEST DISINFECTANT

Beginning with the Legislative Reorganization Act of 1970 and subsequent reform efforts from inside and out to "open up the system," the drive for open government was one of the most compelling and persistent themes of the 1970s reform movement. It was also, however, an area which had paradoxical implications in the form of new access for, and accountability to, the special interests. (They had obvious reasons to want to monitor the activities of the beneficiaries of their largesse.)

The "record teller" breakthrough in 1970 was only one aspect of the anti-secrecy thrust of the Legislative Reorganization Act. The act also sought to open up committee business meetings and hearings, and mandated roll call votes in committee and recording such votes in committee reports. The reorganization act also required public notice of at least a week of impending hearings and allowed for committees to open up their public hearings (although not mark-ups) to television and radio coverage. Following the Legislative Reorganization Act, the "sunshine" movement brightened even further.

In 1973 the House passed rules requiring that all sessions of committees and subcommittee business meetings, hearings and "mark-up" drafting sessions be open unless a majority of the committee voted in open session to close them. This was later amended to require that each closed meeting be the subject of a separate vote to close, making it all the more difficult for members to choose to operate in secrecy. This development was followed in 1975 by the opening of conference committee sessions (subject to a right of either house's conferees to vote in public to close a session), and the partial opening of party caucus meetings.[11]

Another effect of "sunshine" reform was the expanded access of the electronic media to House proceedings. Building on the 1970 Legislative Reorganization Act's allowance of broadcasting of committee meetings, and after two Congresses of review and reflection, in the 95th Congress the House authorized opening its floor proceedings to closed-circuit television and radio coverage. In the 96th Congress, the members of the House approved live cable television coverage (under the control of the Speaker).

Yet despite the irresistible appeal of increasingly open politics in a democracy, no area of reform activity better demonstrates the subtle perils of even the most putatively beneficial reform proposals than the anti-secrecy drive in Congress.[12] The notion that "sunshine is the best disinfectant" is deeply ingrained in the modern American political consciousness. The idea of maximizing public scrutiny of Congress in its transaction of the public's business seems uncontroversial—even a necessary concomitant of public accountability. The record teller break-through as part of the 1970 Legislative Reorganization effort, and the "sunshine" movement for open committee meetings, television coverage of committee and House proceedings, greater public disclosure of members' personal assets, campaign contributions and honoraria and disclosure of activities by lobbyists all appear to be natural ingredients of a well-functioning contemporary government.

Some of these reforms were neutral in their effect vis-a-vis special interest influence (e.g., television of House proceedings perhaps resulted in more one-minute tub-thumping speeches, a preponderance of blue Oxford shirts and blown-dry hair, and subject matter tailored to "national news" programs). To its credit, television coverage has broadened public awareness of Congress, or at least has provided continuous coverage for those political participants and "Congress addicts" who have reason to follow Congressional actions very closely. But the question must be asked: who are the main beneficiaries of all the information generated by open meetings, hearings, and disclosure? One might argue that the press and the public are important beneficiaries, and to some extent this is accurate. However, it is also true that this access to information often is best utilized by the lobbyists and campaign contributors who monitor meetings to see how members of Congress vote. Public-spirited citizens do not generally frequent committee and subcommittee mark-ups of highly technical bills or inhabit the halls of Congress wielding costly analyses and briefs marshaling evidence for or against particular courses of action.

A series of reactions to the new openness of proceedings in the Ways and Means Committee in 1976 sheds light on both the benefits and disadvantages of the sunshine reforms. During 1975, the first full year of the expanded Ways and Means Committee and its first without Mills as chairman, the Committee evidenced great divisiveness. It had a particularly difficult time reaching agreement on a tax revision bill,[13] and demonstrated both fractiousness and a susceptibility to a committee "conservative coalition" thwarting majority Democratic goals. As Tom Arrandale of *Congressional Quarterly* observed at the time, some of the blame for the committee's difficulties in agreeing stemmed from the new open mark-up sessions. Rep. Joseph Karth expressed the view:

> Had it not been for the open mark-up sessions, we would have come out of committee with a much better bill, . . . The press should be allowed in, but that's a different thing from allowing lobbyists to sit in the audience and corral members in the committee room.[14]

Congressman Waggonner suggested that closed meetings resulted in "more honest effort to find accommodation," and Congressman Rostenkowski added that "I don't necessarily mean that we'd make better legislation in closed meetings but that we'd get to where we're going faster." The theory, then, was that one of openness's side-effects was greater accessibility to lobbyists and press—and concomitant posturing of members.

These opportunities for access—enhanced by contributions—have a distorting effect on the process, and the sunshine reforms, for all their benefits generally, provide, at best, a "check" and opportunity to monitor the process for the special interests.

Disclosure of campaign contributions, of course, was a major step in preventing obvious *quid pro quo* dealings. And in addition to these anti-secrecy reforms, the revelations of Watergate and several waves of scandals touching the Congress itself during the 1970s spurred Congress to adopt a series of ethics reforms designed to disclose information about members' personal finances, their official and unofficial office accounts, foreign "junkets," use of the Congressional mailing frank, and outside earnings and honoraria. These ethics requirements were kept separate from the whole other area of financial disclosure surrounding campaign finance. But the disclosure made as a result of these provisions tend to be "one day stories" except in the most egregious circumstances, more likely than not to fade quickly from the public consciousness. And the requirement of disclosure of personal financial dealings has probably had more of an effect to make members more cautious about their investment decisions and "outside" business activities than they have revealed conflicts of interest in members' voting.

Openness, then, brings along with it an intrinsic tension between healthy scrutiny and greater opportunity for the exertion of influence. The mere presence of a well-known industry lobbyist in a mark-up can have an unspoken but profound effect on the substance—and outcome—of consideration. Indeed, overt participation by such lobbyists in drafting sessions and open mark-ups is not uncommon. This is a trade-off inherent in the process, and one which is simply the risk that reformers run when they adopt reforms which are intrinsically "right" as a matter of process—although with possible negative consequences in practice. And on balance, the sunshine reforms are a prime example of such intrinsically "right" processes. But the side-effects which redound to the advantage of special interests must not be overlooked. This is especially so in light of the explosion of PACs and the increasingly related, sprawling apparatus of Capitol Hill lobbyists. By the late 1970s the structure of PAC relationships to committees and subcommittees created a pattern of campaign contributions with specific legislative purposes. If Justin Dart is right that "politicians always listen, but with money they hear you better," then it is also the case that openness allowed contributors to see better the performances of the objects of their bounty. In short, sunshine reforms brought a new and salutary accessibility and accountability to the public, but did so in spades to the special interests. Sunshine reform has been mixed in its effects. It has enhanced public access to Congress, but has probably aided most those who have the resources to monitor closely the process. Despite the intrinsic benefits, that has been to the overall advantage of the special interests.

10:3 THE RESURGENCE OF CONGRESS—AND THE ASSERTION OF SPECIAL INTERESTS

Another major theme of the reform movement was reassertion of Congress's power against that of the president. As James L. Sundquist details in his masterly study, *The Decline and Resurgence of Congress*,[15] the Presidential accretion of power in the years since FDR had been greeted substantially by Congressional deference and complacency. But the experiences of Vietnam, followed by Nixon's contemptuous treatment of Congressional spending decisions, followed in turn by the web of abuses collectively known as Watergate all served to awaken Congress from its long slumber. Sundquist provides a detailed chronicle of both Congress's decline as an institution and its quest to wrest back power from the president. For our purposes, it is enough to focus on the main elements of the reform of Congressional institutions and processes designed to reassert Congress against the president with an eye toward the implications of these reforms for Congress's relations with special interests.

Budget Reform and Impoundment Control

This was a major area of "consolidative" reform activity aimed at both greater Congressional coherence and capacity in the budget-making process, and more Congressional leverage against the president with respect to the same.[16] The overall impact, or success, is difficult to determine—since the record has by virtually all accounts been mixed. The answer tends to be significantly shaped by how the question is framed. In short, as a reform the major thrust of which was to consolidate power and impose some central control over the Congressional budget process, the Budget Act has been moderately successful in bringing both greater coherence and in equipping Congress (with its Congressional Budget Office, two Budget Committees and professional staffs) to deal more effectively as a counterweight to the president and the Office of Management and Budget.

What is less clear is whether the consolidative intent of the Budget Act has served, to any significant extent, to blunt the multifarious effects of the trend toward dispersed power which developed during the same period. The budget process certainly works better than if there had been no Budget Act. But the overall goal of budget reform to consolidate power has been undermined to some extent by its own terms: i.e., having created two new power centers (in the form of Senate and House Budget Committees—new staff and information bureaucracies, the Committee staffs and CBO), reform created a whole new layer of process, and another important access point for special interests. This led to a whole new setting for conflict in Congress—especially a Congress confronting a weak economy and an era of decremental rather than incremental budgetary policy.[17] The establishment of budget priorities has become a new threshold battleground for interested parties—especially for industries dependent on high levels of Federal expenditures in certain areas such as defense, synfuels and other government-dependent industries, loan guarantee programs, as well as other interest groups dependent on entitlements or social spending. While this may be a more rational, and thus "better" process than the previous one, it does not *replace* the old process; it has been grafted on to the other layers. As another level of process, it has evidenced a remarkable malleability to prevailing political trends. (Perhaps its most brilliant usage was President Reagan's 1981 use of the reconciliation process as the instrument of his budget cuts, but the process is also susceptible to being embraced or circumvented, depending on the political circumstances.) And Congress continues to govern by "continuing resolution"—not yet able to meet deadlines established by the Budget Act.[18] While flexibility and adaptability to changing political winds might be lauded as a hallmark of good pragmatic process, the impact for special interests has been either neutral, or not necessarily bad. In other words, as consolidative reform, the Budget process has achieved partial success, but it has certainly not constituted an impediment to the general workings or functioning of the Special Interest Congress.

Oversight and the Legislative Veto

Probably the two most ballyhooed devices of Congressional resur-gence against the president during the 1970s were the expanded committee oversight of executive agencies and the greatly increased use of the legislative veto over administrative rules and regulations. Congressional oversight had been much talked about ever since the Legislative Reorganization Act of 1946, but—as noted by the Bolling Committee in 1973 and 1974—had been more talked about than acted upon. Members of Congress paid lip service to Congress's oversight function, but there were few political incentives to engage in the humdrum task of exhaustive review of agency actions. The legislative veto was used as early as 1932, but became a major instrument of Congressional sabre-rattling at the executive in the conflict-ridden 1970s. Although this surely was not the overriding intention of the backers, each proposal provided new opportunities for issue en-trepeneurialism on the part of members and, as such, new avenues of access and policy influence for special interests.

As James Sundquist has shown, the use of oversight—never Congress's strong suit—grew substantially during the period from 1974 to the end of the decade.[19] Of course, there remain questions as to the quality of oversight. The point to be stressed, however, transcends both quantity and quality, and looks to interest—i.e., the motives of members using oversight and the outside interests, if any, which have a stake in the use of oversight and the legislative veto.

When examined from this standpoint, several points become clear. First, as Sundquist concludes in his review of oversight in the 1970s:

> . . . in the field of oversight as in every other area of legislative activity, decentralization is the order of the day. Any notion of central control, or discipline, within each house as a means of improving the quality of oversight is wholly foreign to the temper of the new, resurgent Congress.[20]

Attempts to coordinate Congressional oversight or to use it as a means of coherent Congressional action in opposition to the executive have achieved little. Committees develop "oversight plans," required pursuant to the Bolling H. Res. 988, but there is no requirement that oversight be undertaken with vigor, comprehensiveness, or great effect. As a general matter, oversight, as well as the legislative veto, reflects the overall theme of 1980s structural fragmentation. To the extent that oversight has elicited concerted Congressional action, it has usually been in a clumsy rush of subcommittees with overlapping jurisdiction seeking to leapfrog over each other to oversee or investigate the day's clamant issue. Energy policy (generally during the 1973 and 1979 crises), the near-calamity at the Three Mile Island nuclear plant, and the Reagan Administration's scandal at the Environmental Protection Agency in 1983 are all examples of issues which brought out the Congressional overseers *en masse.* The combined effect of several different subcommittee chairmen threatening to bring contempt of Congress proceedings ought not to be minimized. Such several-pronged attacks may bring action more quickly than a more deliberate or focused approach. The point here is simply—and not surprisingly—that a diffuse Congress has taken on its oversight functions in a diffuse fashion. This allows substantial autonomy for subcommittee issue-entrepreneurs, and opportunities for outsiders with patrons in Congress who have issues that need overseeing.

A second point is that oversight provides a forum for the issue priorities and positions of the subcommittee chairman doing the overseeing. As the demands of the job multiply, the day-to-day priorities are shaped by professional staff: in a busy Congress, oversight orientations often reflect the personal concerns of subcommittee or committee staff.

Sundquist has noted that oversight hearings often are shaped by the motives of their sponsor. For example, Congressman Brademas conducted his oversight hearings on aid to the handicapped because of his personal goal of increasing this program's appropriations.[21] Similarly, concern for policy and special interest implications of oversight of an agency can *deter* members from pursuing oversight at all. As Chairman Poage of the Agriculture Committee observed as justification for limited oversight activity:

> About all we would accomplish, as I see it, is to create hard feelings, a loss of confidence on the part of our farmers that the Department of Agriculture could render their service, because we can be so critical of the Department . . . that there won't be any farmer in the nation that will have any confidence.

In some cases, the oversight becomes virtual intervention in agency management; or what some agency personnel view as attempts by members of Congress to run their agencies. Sundquist reports on the typology of three different kinds of oversight hearings in the view of a Congressional staffer: one "being objective and bringing out both sides of an issue"—which the staff viewed as a "small percentage" of the hearings, and the other two being "it stinks" or "it's great."[22] These latter two types represent the part where the policy dispositions of the members and staff hold sway in both the selection of witnesses and the *modus operandi* of the hearing.

The different uses of oversight are so wide-ranging, and often concern such apparently mundane day-to-day activities of agencies, that it is difficult to find "smoking pistols" of special interest involvement as the force behind the hearings or the beneficiaries of the approaches taken at such hearings. These instances are of their nature anecdotal, and in any event, not likely either to be identified willingly or to appear obviously in the public record. But there is little doubt that interest groups view oversight as one weapon in their arsenal.

More direct evidence of special interest use of Congress is found in what was the reform era's biggest Congressional growth industry: the legislative veto—apparently brought to a hasty demise by the Supreme Court in *Immigration and Naturalization Service v. Chada.*[23] The legislative veto—even with its constitutional questions—emerged as the favorite instrument of Congress to tighten its control over the executive. While the Flowers and Levitas bills to attach a legislative veto over *all* administrative rules and regulations (variously estimated to be between 7,000 to 10,000 annually) failed to gain passage in the Congresses of the 1970s and early 1980s, there had been, until *Chada,* an explosion in the attachment of *ad hoc* legislative veto provisions to specific bills across a wide range of legislative subjects. Between 1973 and 1980, more than sixty pieces of legislation contained legislative veto provisions,[24] and the House attempted to attach a veto to many more.[25]

Clearly the most telling example of a nexus between the legislative veto and special interest influence is the experience of the Federal Trade Commission in the late 1970s. The FTC, the federal government's chief regulator of business and protector of consumers, was in a particularly activist phase under the leadership of Chairman Michael Pertschuk. The FTC had initiated regulatory proceedings in such controversial areas as:

- television advertising directed at children, such as sugar-coated breakfast cereal and the like;
- funeral home practices and services—including alleged deceptive practices;

- alleged unfair practices by used car dealers;
- regulation of trade groups which set "voluntary" self-regulatory standards for consumer products and industry-wide codes;
- trademark and patent law—bringing petitions to the patent office arguing that a brand-named item had become so common as to be "generic" and thus should be stripped of patent and trademark protection;[26]
- various practices in the insurance industry;
- a range of anti-trust and restraint of trade issues, including a specific focus on monopolistic practices by agricultural cooperatives;
- regulation of professionals such as doctors, lawyers and others some of whose activities could be construed as anti-competitive;
- a policy particularly irksome to business by which the FTC provided taxpayer funds for public participation by individuals and small business if they could not afford to do so themselves.

Business—especially the lobbyists and PACs for the affected groups—reacted strongly against what they considered encroachment, or threatened encroachment, by the FTC. They resorted to the Congress. Congress resorted to the legislative veto.

The legislative veto may have been born and sustained on the lofty principle of Congressional coequality. But its use in the matter of the FTC, the veto proved a less lofty vehicle for special interests to undo agency policies—in this case virtually threatening the existence of the agency. (Amid bitter Congressional disputes over the controversial policies, the veto, and the funding level of the FTC, in the absence of such funding the agency actually shut down for a day, May 1, 1980.)

The affected groups—broadcasters, advertisers, and cereal manufacturers, lawyers, doctors, funeral parlor operators, used car dealers, insurance industry representatives, along with particularly aggrieved corporations—worked the Commerce Committees of the House and Senate and whipped up enough collective hostility to produce a major Congressional uprising against the FTC. It also resulted in Congress seeking to use the veto to prohibit or severely circumscribe FTC authority on very specific areas of policy.[27]

The Senate and House vied with each other over exactly which areas and in what ways the FTC ought to be allowed to continue proceedings. Matters which had been earlier a matter for formal FTC regulatory proceedings became the occasion for private "hat-in-hand" negotiation between lobbyists and members on Capitol Hill. As it turned out, a compromise conference agreement with a two-chamber legislative veto provision was reached, and the FTC was not emasculated or even trimmed back nearly as far as veto proponents in both the House and Senate had wanted. However, the FTC experience put it and other independent regulatory agencies on notice that any over-zealous pursuits could once again provoke Congressional scrutiny and opposition.

The legislative veto, and also importantly the threat of a veto, were powerful tools. Indeed, the threat of such a veto, like the fact of oversight hearings, could alter agency policy and practice in ways which are difficult to document or quantify, but are nonetheless real.

The legislative veto, while it flourished, was seized upon as a convenient device not just by members of Congress—but by interests with axes to grind against agencies. It is too early to know how the process will change in the post-legislative veto era, but it is possible that stricter Congressional control over policy in the first instance will take its place, and interest groups will be at the forefront of the move to draft the terms of such statutes. The supposed "victory" over the veto for executive power may only spur Congress and special interests to be more careful about delegation at the legislative threshold.[28]

Foreign Policy and Congressional Special Interest Politics

Although not directly a procedural "reform" issue, the area of Congressional resurgence in foreign policy matters bears mention here as one also characterized by increased interest group activity. The more visible incidents of Congressional reassertion in foreign policy—the 1973 War Powers Act and the anti-Vietnam War McGovern-Hatfield and Cooper-Church resolutions of the early 1970s—were reactions by Congress to what many considered to be deceptive (or worse) actions of presidents (namely Johnson and Nixon) in Tonkin Gulf, the Dominican Republic, Vietnam and Cambodia. Congressional assertion on these matters of peace and war were designed to recapture Congress's constitutional war-making power, a power which had been substantially ceded to the presidency.[29]

But beyond the constitutional and foreign policy concerns, it is also worthy to note during this period the rise of a related "Foreign Policy/Special Interest" axis. This is not to say that foreign policy had been previously untouched by domestic public opinion and ethnic political considerations. The point is simply that the growth of the special interest apparatus—and particularly the rise of issue-oriented PACs—did not stop at the water's edge. Batteries of defense contractors and ideological "big defense" groups pursued their ends with money and influence on Capitol Hill. Great questions of defense policy—MX, B-1, Cruise missiles, AWACS, stealth technology, the whole arsenal of the Reagan Administration's high-technology "Star Wars" defense strategy—are not only matters of national security: they also are constituency jobs programs and corporate special interest projects, with all of the attendant political machinations and ramifications (countered gamely by the liberal defense monitoring organizations such as the Union of Concerned Scientists and the press).

Similarly, the politics of Presidential and Congressional policy with respect to various of the world's trouble spots are the subject of intense special interest activity—most notably the pro-Israel groups and PACs on matters involving the Middle East and particularly the security of the State of Israel, the "Greek Lobby" on matters of Cyprus and aid to Turkey and Greece, and the web of groups on various sides of the American policy toward Central America—as well as other, less well-known groups. This kind of participation is certainly not new; nor in any way untoward. What is new and perhaps an unfortunate departure is the fact that the politics of the 1970s and 1980s have demanded that many of these groups become full-fledged participants in the PAC-money/lobbying process, with all that comes with it.[30]

10:4 MEMBERS OF CONGRESS FOR THEMSELVES: THE RESISTANCE TO "STREAMLINING" REFORM AND THE SIDE-BENEFITS FOR SPECIAL INTERESTS

During the 1970s and 1980s there has been more than occasional carping at the House leadership for their alleged shortcomings. Yet the record of the reform experience clearly shows that when given the chance to enact reforms designed to strengthen the leadership, or to implement convincingly those reforms which might imbue the leaders with greater power, a consistent majority of House Democrats were opposed. While centralization is not inherently positive, the fragmentation of Congress has had decidedly dysfunctional consequences.

There were diverse reasons that the Bolling, Obey, and Patterson reforms were derailed, not least of which was that the urge toward decentralization and individualism simply proved irresistible to many members. Rather than Congress being arrayed "against itself," it simply was a collection of individual members acting and voting *for themselves.* In an age of individualism, the need for quick accomplishments for the electorate back home, and the limited attention-spans of the television generation, the traditional norms of apprenticeship and deference—"waiting one's turn"—were bound to be swept away. However, a different and more surprising point to be made is that *even some of the reforms designed to strengthen the leadership* ended up further fragmenting the Congress and aiding special interests.

Multiple Referrals and Multiplied Opportunities for Access

A prime example of the irony of reform designed to enhance the leadership actually resulting in fragmentation is the multiple referral process. This was the technique recommended by the Bolling Committee to allow the Speaker (usually on advice by the parliamentarian) to refer bills to committees jointly, sequentially or to split the bills and send different parts to different committees. The original goal was to coordinate and rationalize the process by which the various committees with concurrent or overlapping jurisdiction consider a bill. One clear objective was to build consensus and thus to smooth floor passage. Another was to assert leadership priorities and in selected legislative areas to *expedite* the process. The result has been the opposite.

It should be remembered that the Bolling Committee multiple referral recommendation was part of their larger package to overhaul Committee jurisdictions. In a more streamlined system with fewer jurisdictional overlaps, multiple referral would presumably be of limited applicability, a mechanism for fine-tuning and coordination in the limited cases where overlap remained. Of course, the jurisdictional shifts envisioned by the Bolling panel never passed. Hence, the inclusion of the Bolling multiple referral piece in the different Hansen puzzle (i.e., virtually no change of jurisdictions) changed substantially the dynamics of multiple referral. The consequence was that the use of multiple referral escalated, since the number of committees with a claim on a "piece" of a bill remained large, the multiple referral mechanism proved a convenient device to "spread the action" on individual House bills.[31] Moreover, the multiple referral option (rather than a clear-cut assignment to one committee or a declaration of the primacy of one committee) actually exacerbated pre-existing rivalries between committees. If there was any reasonable justification for assertion of an interest in a bill, a committee could now be expected to assert that interest. Multiple referrals also increased the jockeying among committees and "forum shopping" by special interests. If a special interest group has good access to one committee and more tenuous ties to another, the group will encourage assertion of a legislative interest by the friendly committee. The consequence is that if there is any colorable jurisdictional claim, it is likely that a committee will assert it. The effect of this process is to multiply not just the number of committees and subcommittees involved on a given bill but also to ensure in many circumstances that special interests will be asserting their maximum clout—i.e., be able to present their views to the most sympathetic panel.

The success rate of bills subject to multiple referral (as compared with bills referred to only one committee, and as compared with all bills) suggests that multiple referral resulted in both a lower rate of bills reported out of committee and a lower overall rate of House passage. These aggregate statistics in the 95th and 96th Congress reveal that a bill reported only to one committee has twice (8.7% versus 4.35%) the chance to be *reported* than a multiple referral, and better than three times (9.6% versus 3.0%) the chance than a multiple referral to be passed by the full House.[32] While these aggregate statistics do not provide great insight into the specific legislative pattern and implication of the diminished rate of passage of multiple referrals, they do show that multiple referrals did precisely the opposite of their intention. Instead of expediting the process, they expanded the number of possible access points to influence the course of a particular piece of legislation. And while these statistics do not control for the complexity and controversiality of legislation, it is fair to say that multiple referrals often were used on the more important and complex bills. The overall impact of multiple referrals is to slow down the process, enhance the opportunities for exerting influence, and generally to blur substantive consideration of the legislation in a maze of often duplicative hearings, reports, mark-ups, and other committee deliberations. As indicated by the statistics above, the race here usually goes to the *slowest*, i.e., those who seek delay and are most effective in prolonging the process.

In the case of multiple referral, a procedural mechanism with the goal of greater consolidative effect,[33] ended up having the opposite, i.e., further decentralizing, result—and one which dovetailed nicely with increased opportunities for special interest influence.

10:5 THE SENATE REFORM EXPERIENCE

The Senate during this period had an experience with reform different from that of the House. This owed to several factors, including the "upper" chamber's already firmly established decentralization rooted in the 1950s changes in rules and ambiance, its tradition of individualism and informality, and its smaller size and larger forum. Senate "action" had already been "spread" by the beginning of the 1970s. The so-called Johnson rule of 1953 was Majority Leader Lyndon Johnson's dictum that every Democratic senator would have at least one "major" committee assignment. This created opportunities for meaningful participation by even the lowliest freshman Democratic senator, and as the system grew and developed, members rapidly moved up to positions of power and authority on subcommittees and committees. Hence the structural roots of special interest access were already in place in the Senate at the time that they were only being planted in the House.

There were several efforts in the Senate—partially successful—to tidy up the committee system—the Stevenson-Brock Committee on Committees in 1976–1977[34] and the Culver Commission on Senate Administration support services (Commission on the Operation of the Senate).[35] The Stevenson-Brock Committee accomplished the feat of actually eliminating three committees, bringing the number of standing committees from eighteen to fifteen and also reduced the number of subcommittees (in one swoop from 135 to 100 in 1976; they have since grown to 112 in 1984).[36]

The Stevenson-Brock Committee operated under tight time constraints. Appointed in April 1976, the Committee resolved to bring a package to a floor vote by the October adjournment in order to achieve whatever it might prior to the new assignment of committee places the following January, 1977. While this goal was not achieved, it did motivate the committee to concentrate its efforts and establish both an efficient work schedule and realistic set of objectives. The committee adopted a consciously consensus-oriented approach, and it sought to achieve what it could by securing prior agreements whenever possible. This 1976 effort—staffed by people familiar with the Bolling-Hansen experience—was designed to avoid a similarly bruising reform battle. The hallmarks of the Senate Committee reform effort were speed, cooperation by the respective party leaders, accommodation, and above all else a quest for consensus.

When the measure was taken up it was dubbed a "reorganization," fully supported by the leadership at the beginning of the new session. It was also, it is important to note, the occasion for the unprecedented agreement not to make assignments to committees until the reorganization package was dealt with. Moreover, all efforts were directed to assuage and accommodate the committee chairman.[37] This concerted effort at minimization of conflict resulted in a consensus plan which produced a small-scale rationalization of the Senate committee system.

But, while the Committee's accomplishments are not to be minimized,[38] the effects of this consolidation on the Senate's overall *modus operandi* were limited. The main point is that the Senate, with its smaller membership and larger per capita workload still provided more than enough choice assignments to go around.

To the extent that the Stevenson-Brock reorganization sought to move toward a more equitable apportionment of workload and power, there was an incentive for a majority of members to support the plan. The success of the accommodations reached with virtually all the key committee leaders revealed both the genius of the strategy and the limitations of the accomplishment: there was some modest reshuffling and rationalization, but no fundamental revision of the Senate power structure. Fundamental change was soon to come to the Senate but not in the form of rules changes: the 1980 election catapulted Republicans into control of the Senate and augured new dynamics in the workings of the Senate power structure.[39]

The diffuse structure of the Senate remained largely intact after reorganization. That structure was still essentially decentralized; it too was significantly affected by the FECA campaign finance reforms, especially after 1976. Data on Senate elections reveal that senators—particularly those from larger states who needed huge campaign war chests for media time—became increasingly dependent on PAC contributions. And a new wrinkle was the growth of ideological PACs like NCPAC (the National Conservative Political Action Committee, leader of the Moral Majority) and their negative targeting of liberal Democrats in 1978, 1980, and 1982,[40] making large "independent expenditures" against incumbent senators. This was followed by a growth after 1980 of a spate of liberal PACs seeking to counter the conservative attack.

The campaign finance nexus to the special interests was all the more pronounced in the Senate, particularly during the rise of corporate PACs from 1976–1980; and the new impact of hefty PAC funding of Republican Senate candidates had a considerable effect on both the 1980 Republican Senate victory during the Reagan presidential landslide and the Republicans' retention of that Senate majority in 1982.

The impact of some of the reform efforts, of course, was significant, and their results, when complemented by the right other political circumstances (e.g., an activist Democratic president and Democratic majorities in both Senate and House), could produce more programmatic and effective performance. The House reform experience—along with concomitant change in composition—did achieve a remarkable new participatory democracy and openness in the way the House allocates power and performs its work. Considering the many antediluvian and cloistered practices characterizing the public's business as recently as the late 1960s, the changes wrought by reform are no small achievement. The system is now more open, accountable and participatory—and to the extent that this may be viewed as intrinsically beneficial—the results can clearly be seen as positive. And it should be further acknowledged that the many instruments that are now in place, especially those party power levers such as the Democratic Steering and Policy Committee, the Speaker's power over the Rules Committee, and the rejuvenated Democratic Caucus and its task forces, all offer the prospect of greater party responsibility and leadership in future political circumstances more congenial to liberals and Democrats.[41]

But in recognizing the possible future consequences of reform— even assuming some developments closer to what the original reformers intended—it remains necessary to focus rigorously on the reform results and consequences thus far. These results—in their entirety—must be presented in darker colors.

10:6 GOALS, TENDENCIES AND TRENDS OF THE CONGRESSIONAL REFORM EXPERIENCE

Congressional reform is a complex, dynamic and often contradictory process, and while there may be some relatively simple conclusions to be drawn from it, these conclusions were not simply arrived at. The description and analysis which constituted the bulk of this book detail the various strands, motives, and directions of the reform efforts. Several major themes have emerged.

- *Mixed motives underlay the various reform efforts.*

There was not one monolithic "reform bloc." There were several reform movements, operating simultaneously, sometimes in opposition to one another. At times individual reform blocs sponsored proposals which worked at cross purposes with their own stated goals.

The several main goals (not always pointing in the same direction) can be summarized as follows:

1. Congressional Reassertion Against the President, especially the Republican President, Richard M. Nixon—To improve Congress's effectiveness against the executive branch on a host of issues.
2. Congressional "Leadership" and "Streamlining"—To strengthen the power of the leaders of Congress in order to improve Congress's performance, and to rationalize Congressional structures and procedures in order to make Congressional operations more efficient.

3. Party Responsibility and Policy Efficacy—To enhance the role of the parties, particularly the House Democratic Party as an instrument of policy-making, and in so doing to pass more coherent, comprehensive, i.e. universalistic—programs.
4. Congressional Democracy—To broaden participation by members of Congress in Congressional decisions.
5. "Sunshine"—To open up Congressional processes to public view, as both an intrinsically worthwhile "process" goal *and* because it was widely believed that public scrutiny would make Congress produce "better" legislation and policy.

One major motivating factor behind reform was to assert Congress against the President in budget-making, war powers and in a host of other legislative arenas. Another important goal of several leading Democratic reformers was greater capacity for strong leadership of Congress—for more "party responsibility" at least in theory. In practice, of course, there were strong pressures for reforms which "spread the action"—i.e., which diffused power more evenly throughout the House. Still other reforms were designed to accomplish specific "process" goals—to be sure, with implications for power relationships and policy—but mainly based on notions of the intrinsic worthiness of certain ways of conducting business. These included "sunshine" reforms to open up the Congressional process and some of the "streamlining" reforms to make Congress more "efficient."

To put the point simply, the reform process was complicated and often inconsistent, and there was no monolithic reform effort or one discernible "legislative intent" which tells the whole story about the diverse motives behind reform. What finally emerged as "the reforms" were the product of the clash and then compromise of these goals arising from the mixed motives. Of course, they also were affected by the equally complex post-passage process by which some reforms were seized on and others circumvented, some embraced and others ignored—in sum, the process of implementing reform and reconciling it with the emerging values of the changing Congress.

- *While the overall reform process had mixed results, some results were positive. . . .*

Reform during the 1970s accomplished much that was positive. There were reforms which must be judged simply on their intrinsic merits to have been beneficial to Congressional operations. A system that had been largely closed to public view and access was substantially opened. A power structure which had ceded much of Congress's authority to a cloistered elite of preponderantly conservative and

Southern committee chairmen was made more democratic. Congressional procedures were updated, staffing increased and professionalized, and Congress's informational and analytical capacities vastly modernized. Congress took steps to exercise its oversight powers more fully, and in several ways to reassert itself against the Executive branch. Congress also reacted to Watergate and a succession of smaller scandals closer to Capitol Hill by adopting self-regulating ethics codes and generally, more effectively monitoring the conduct of its own members.

In short, reform must be accorded its due in thoroughly recasting a tradition-minded and inertia-bound institution. And to the extent that reform *was* a success, it did combine with changes in the internal composition of Congress and in the outside environment to transform essential aspects of the workings of Congress. However, the recognition of a series of reform accomplishments, certainly does not imply that all—or even most—of the reform experience was positive.

- . . . *Disjointed, contradictory, and fragmented reform efforts produced reforms which further fragmented Congress.*

The overall reform process had at least one major deleterious effect: by diffusing power within Congress and then establishing the basis for PAC-based formal links to special interests, reform served to expand, enhance, and systematize the responsiveness of Congress to the most well-organized, well-heeled, and politically active special interests. While reformers of various stripes at least implicitly believed that a reformed Congress would make "better" policy—i.e. more comprehensive, less parochial and less narrowly based—the result has been the reverse. Reform has heightened the Congress's tendencies toward fractiousness, incoherence and in some cases indecision. The profoundly negative implications for both the Congressional and American political process have only begun to be understood.

Scattered, confused and often contradictory reform efforts led to overall reform results which often were mirror images of their contradictory origins. Specific reform efforts begun with the intention of strengthening the party leadership led to aggregate effects making it weaker. "Sunshine" reforms designed to open the system to public and press dove-tailed with campaign finance reforms to provide PAC-based lobbyists with ring-side seats from which to participate in key Congressional decision-making (and from which to monitor their "investments"). Major efforts to consolidate and streamline the House committee system substantially failed, running headlong into the effects of party reforms which had succeeded, conferring new power on middle-level Democrats on subcommittees. Party reform's success, then, preordained committee reform's failure—since newly ensconced middle-level subcommittee chairmen had no wish to alter a system which had just been reoriented in their favor. Procedural reforms designed to expedite the process under one plan for reform found themselves grafted onto another plan, with results directly counter to the original intention.

- *A further fragmented Congress became more responsive to new and more numerous special interests.*

The aggregate effect of reform was to reallocate power within the committee system and particularly to the subcommittees and more broadly to rank and file members. An inherent accompanying effect was to multiply access points, which in Congressional practice means potential veto points. In short, reform served to open up new avenues of influence for special interests. To the extent that *new members,* of differing regions, ideologies, ages and orientations, acceded to positions of power, *different special interests* were provided new opportunities to exercise influence. The overall effect of reform, then, even aside from and prior to the campaign finance reforms, was to attract a new wave of special interests into the process. Reform made influencing Congress a more highly regulated activity, but in doing so it spurred interest groups to feel the necessity of forming PACs in order to influence Congress. A new activism on the part of American corporations and the new domestic and international competitiveness of business heightened this tendency. And of course, campaign finance reform provided the crucial nexus between the Congressional structure and the special interests. But the "Special Interest Congress" was well on its way to creation even before the campaign finance reforms. The structures and procedures of Congress *intrinsically* encourage the fragmentation of legislative performance and product.

- *The new politics of campaign finance formed a strong link between special interests and Congress. Increasingly campaign contributions had less to do with campaigns. For incumbents, they became "deterrents" to scare off possible challengers and hence make less likely that there would be a campaign. For PACs and other groups, contributions became "dues" for entry into the world of Washington influence. As Congress itself became more decentralized, the special interest appendages of Congress became more centralized—based in Washington and both leader and follower of strategic "national" conventional wisdom about political trends. And while "grass-roots" and region, party, ideology and other factors spurring allegiance to certain interests remained significant determinants of voting behavior, PAC contributions became increasingly important in nudging members toward actions—or inaction—favoring special interests. PACs came to have a distorting effect that is incremental, i.e., their effect is in shaping and changing members' behavior from what it would otherwise be, absent the PAC contribution.*

Campaign finance reforms designed to diminish the role of wealthy individuals in the political process created a new, more anonymous and burgeoning layer of corporate and ideological PACs which came to exert a degree of pressure on Congress which had been unforeseen by the original reformers. A general result of the entire reform experience—despite a new official sensitivity to ethical concerns and sharper scrutiny of Congressional deportment and the dangers of money influencing politics—was a Congress all the more susceptible, indeed *inevitably* and *systematically* susceptible, to money-based influence.

The "incrementally distortive" effects of PAC contributions—in prodding members to act more favorably toward special interests than they might otherwise—are subtle and difficult to measure. But they are pervasive and increasingly evident.

• *Reforms designed to accomplish legitimate institutional objectives—e.g., asserting Congress against the executive in the Nixon era—were seized upon and used by special interests to accomplish their own goals. To a certain extent, the resurgence of Congress offered new opportunities for the assertion of special interests.*

The Vietnam War, Watergate, and Executive impoundment of Congressionally approved funds served as a triple-threat provocation of Congress to assert itself against the Presidency. With strong public support, and based on legitimate and substantively defensible motives, Congress pushed forward on a wide range of reform issues such as budget reform, oversight of the executive branch and independent agencies, foreign policy, and on a number of legislative subjects by extensive use of the legislative veto. Many of these moves toward Congressional coequality achieved a measure of "success"—i.e., enabled the House and Senate to reassert themselves against the Presidency in ways that can be adjudged as constructive. The accomplishment of the Budget Reform and Impoundment Control Act of 1974—giving Congress better information, new budget-making capabilities and an unprecedented overall "picture" of its spending programs—was probably the most positive outgrowth of the reassertive Congress. There were some other bright spots manifested by Congressional checks on executive abuses and by a greater willingness to challenge the president on policy or criticize agency performance. This was especially the case in contrast to the era of Congressional timidity and deference to the Presidency of the 1950s and 1960s.[42]

However, that is only part of the story of the reassertive Congress of the 1970s. Another part is the way that special interests built on Congress's accessibility and responsiveness, seized on Congress's new activism, and used the resurgence of Congress as a tool of special interest assertiveness. Oversight became a mechanism for prodding an executive agency into action favorable to a commercial, industrial or other interest. The budget process provided an early forum for ensuring that an advantageous spending priority was established. Congress's new assertiveness on defense and foreign policy issues opened up opportunities for ethnic and ideological groups to mobilize sectors of the Congress in directions they preferred. Most significantly, until the June 23, 1983 U.S. Supreme Court *Chadha* decision[43] struck down virtually all uses of the legislative veto, this device afforded great opportunities on domestic policy issues for special interests to use their friends and allies on subcommittees in Congress as instruments to de-fang, intimidate or otherwise influence independent agencies, notably the Federal Trade Commission. If there remained any timidity on the part of Congress, it was a timidity not toward the president, regardless of party, rather a susceptibility to the blandishments of the newly potent special interest groups.

- *The legislative process has always been subject to biases. But the reformed process has created new biases which, while subject to greater public disclosure, are more directly based on campaign contributions than in the past. Special Interest Groups and particularly PACs, now exert substantial influence in both mobilizing Congress to action on certain issues and immobilizing it on others. Further, PAC money is selective and mobile. It clusters around the new, decentralized power centers and it follows the issues that affect interest. The issues that committees and subcommittees take up help determine where PACs will "invest" their contributions.*

The legislative process is inherently a series of trade-offs based on a variety of clashing assumptions and values—which, by definition, reflect certain biases. But the skew of politics in a liberal democracy must be approached and understood with sensitivity. Conflicting interest groups must be delicately balanced—and the countervailing interests of the broad public and those sectors of society which are, for practical purposes in the nation's capital, "unrepresented" must be considered as against the well-represented special interests.

An era of reform has strengthened the organized at the expense of those "un-organized." It is not new that money works its will in Washington. But money in the form of campaign contributions *does* work in new ways in Washington, even when fully disclosed and within the law.[44] Money combined with dispersed power within Congress now shapes the parameters of politics in a variety of ways which add up to systematic bias. As E. E. Schattschneider has observed, some political issues are organized in and some out of the process as a matter of course: but *money* now strongly shoves Congress toward some issues and away from others. Such a phenomenon is difficult to measure, especially in the instances where bias leads to inaction rather than action. But just because biases are subtle, and oftentimes leave faint tracks, does not mean that biases do not exist. What can be quantified is where in the committee system the money is contributed and how these contributions correlate with the legislative matters before the committees. The unsurprising conclusion is that PAC money follows structural power, and even more selectively it follows specific issues: i.e., the pending bill as opposed to jurisdiction over *potential* bills.

- *A major effect of a reform effort initiated to strengthen party discipline and to advance liberal Democratic policy was ironically to weaken party discipline even further and make it harder to pass liberal Democratic legislation. On balance, reformers (and their careers) fared better than reform; and liberal Democrats enhanced their individual power bases more successfully than they were able to use them to advance liberal Democratic goals.*

The earliest and most active leaders of the Congressional reform movement were activist liberal Democrats. While the reformers' motives were diverse, and the reform process generally was complicated, one strong discernible current underlying reform was the desire to enable Congress to pass strong Democratic programs. Ironically, what happened was exactly the opposite; reform made it more difficult for liberal Democrats to further their policy goals.

To be sure, American politics changed markedly during this period—in ways not hospitable to the progress of Democrats, especially liberals. Liberal self-confidence, its intellectual initiative, and even basic elements of its agenda seemed to disintegrate or disappear. An aggressive conservative-cum-pragmatic philosophy led by President Richard Nixon, and then by hard-line "neo-conservatives" culminating in the Reagan Presidency, emerged in its stead. Intellectual and ideological currents well beyond the doors of Congress helped to explain the electoral, political and policy changes of the 1970s and early 1980s.

Yet it should not be overlooked that a reform movement whose early leaders sought to renovate Congressional mores and structures in order to make strong Democratic policy ironically led to the construction of formidable obstacles to just these policies. It was not conservatives—or to any significant extent, Republicans—who reformed Congress; hence the process by which Democratic reformers engaged in at least partially self-destructive behavior necessitates close examination.

- *Special interests' stake in the process, and influence over it, now extends not only to policies that concern them—but over policies well beyond their direct special interest concern.*

The expansion of special interests has not been limited to the growth in their numbers, their size, or even their influence over policy areas of direct concern to them. A simple but important point is that their increased power has prompted special interest groups to concern themselves with an ever-expanding range of issues.

Some of this owes to the growing ideological cast of American politics of the early 1980s; this accompanied the rise of single issue groups and ideological PACs. But in addition, issues began to "overlap." It was not hard for anti-gun control groups to notice that pro-gun control candidates also often happened to be "liberal" on defense and foreign policy issues, or vice versa. Bankers, insurers, and realtors focused on issues beyond those directly relating to banking, insurance, and interest rates. There is nothing inherently wrong with this—in fact, to the extent that it represents a growing gravitation of interests to one party or the other, or a set of programs and values, this development might even be salutary. However, the new ideological tendencies have *not* been a positive development. For the most part, they have been a development specifically in the context of the PAC-based politics of *quid pro quo* campaign contributions, skewed rating scores, campaign "hit lists," veiled threats—and other such excesses which have come to characterize Washington politics in the era of PACs.

- *Special interests' stakes in the process also now extend to the process itself. It is difficult enough to reform an institution whose processes serve the needs and preferences of incumbents, but the difficulties of reform are further complicated when special interests themselves have become an additional player on process reforms. Here is the rub: how to pass anti-special interest reforms in an age when reformers essentially need special interest "permission"?*

PACs, trade associations, law firms, and lobbies—as well as the puta-tively "white hat" groups of public interest advocates—have become key players in the legislative process. While Congressional reform issues have historically been in-house affairs—even in our participa-tory times—special interests now have the clout to weigh in on *process* issues that concern them. The most obvious internal reform area involved attempts at Committee reform and the reshuffling of com-mittee and subcommittee jurisdictions. And the most critical "exter-nal" reform area involved campaign finance—e.g., legislation to cur-tail PAC contributions or to replace the existing system with public financing of Congressional elections.

The problem is that these issues are not "free votes" by disinter-ested parties; they are votes by sitting members of Congress, many of whose political lifeblood is the PACs. Even anti-PAC, pro-public financing members find themselves having to accept large PAC con-tributions in order to raise amounts necessary to deter a real or poten-tial opponent. And more than one incumbent has been subjected to subtle intimidation to the effect that PAC contributions will be harder to come by—or withheld—if the member sponsors public financing or PAC limitation legislation. So far has the systemic politics of money and influence come that members are now lobbied hard to sustain that system itself. It is not surprising that a regime and the powerful within it will seek to hold their ground—but the profound dangers—and the alarming implications for the entire political system ought not to be overlooked.[45]

- *A reformed Congress is a "weakened" Congress in the sense that Congress is often hamstrung by the multiplicity of interest groups and its own internal access points. It becomes incapable of achieving consensus on policy or acting in an expeditious, effective fashion. Of course, the other side of this point is that a Congress with an abundance of power centers led by independently entrepreneurial members makes it hard for any leader—including the President—to lead in the direction of universalistic (as opposed to particularistic) policies. However, a "weakened" Congress does not necessarily mean a strengthened President; in fact, the opposite appears often to be the case: i.e., a diffuse Congress weakens the entire American political system.*

A "resurgent" Congress composed of bright, dynamic, and activist members obviously has its merits. Informed and articulate members no doubt have much to contribute to Congressional decision-making. But, excessive individualism accompanied by rampant accessibility to outside interests is bound to have negative consequences for both the Congress as an institution and the American political system generally.

An assertive Congress is not necessarily a Congress positive in its contribution to policy-making. Nor is a "strong" Congress *ipso facto* a contributor to the "strength" of the political system. The "reformed" Congress has become a source of diffusion of policy and power. Certainly an important function of Congress on occasion is to stymie unwise executive initiatives and to improve on presidential proposals. But such a role is most effective when used sparingly. When Congress itself becomes an habitual impediment to consensus, and the court of last resort for the mobilization of *dis*sent, then a rethinking of Congress's proper role is in order.

- *There has to be a better system. While it may not be realistic to try to "dig up" the roots of the present system, it is possible to identify "piecemeal" and "wholesale" reform proposals designed to fashion a system by which the Congressional process is rendered more efficacious and the financial link between special interests and individual candidates is at least loosened and preferably severed. In addition, while the increasing importance of money is certainly a major problem, it is not the only problem. New ways must be found to make Congress more capable of rationally dealing with national problems. This involves the creation of new political incentives and structures within Congress.*

There are "piecemeal" and "wholesale" approaches to reform. After exploring some of the implications of the present system in Chapter Eleven, Chapter Twelve considers both, and reasons its way to a proposed "package" for comprehensive reform. The package constitutes an attempt to address both the external and internal structural problems of special interest influence.

Notes

1. The modest success of the Stevenson-Brock Select Committee on Committees in the Senate—how it avoided the typical pitfalls of consolidative reform but also how it did little to alter the Senate's decentralized tendencies—is discussed below.
2. See for example Sundquist, *Decline and Resurgence of Congress, op. cit.* and also Nelson Polsby, *Consequences of Party Reform, op. cit.*, pp. 89–130 with an emphasis on the dysfunctional consequences of reform of the presidential party nomination process on the presidency's ability to govern. Of course, in contrast, the present study views consequences of reform of Congress *on Congress* and the broader political system.
3. A key point here is that the absolute number of subcommittees in the House did not rise during this period; the number of members chairing them rose from 109 to 147. Numbers here were compiled from the *CQ Almanac*, 1970, *op. cit.* and the *Almanac of American Politics*, 1980, *op. cit.*
4. For example, there had been growing opposition to the use of closed rules on tax bills on the House floor prior to the onset of Mills' personal problems. This opposition came from some liberals and other non-Ways and Means members who wanted to be able to amend tax bills on the floor or at least do more than vote "up or down" on large tax measures.
5. See Michael Malbin, *Unelected Representatives* (New York: Basic Books, 1979); Harrison W. Fox, Jr. and Susan Webb Hammond, *Congressional Staffs: The Invisible Force in American Lawmaking* (New York: Free Press, 1977).
6. Fenno, *Congressmen in Committees, op. cit.* and for an up-to-date account, see Steven S. Smith and Christopher J. Deering, *Committees in Congress* (Washington, D.C.: CQ Press, 1984). Smith and Deering stress that reform had different effects on different committees and subcommittees. Following Fenno, they have found that the nuances of reform are applied unequally across the committee system—since member goals and orientations affect the extent to which the goals of reform are embraced and implemented.
7. For a good analysis of the post-reform difficulties of the Ways and Means Committee, see Catherine Rudder, "Tax Policy: Structure and Choice," in Schick, *Making Economic Policy in Congress, op. cit.*, pp. 196–220. Ms. Rudder details how reform helped weaken the Ways and Means Committee as a "control" committee, with adverse consequences for tax policy.
8. Drew, *Politics and Money, op. cit.*, pp. 38, 43, 46, and 113.
9. This can be construed to mean both or either that the Democrats on House Ways and Means preferred not to risk alienating the electorate by raising taxes or the lobbyists whose clients had won major benefits in the 1981 tax bill—and suffered major losses in 1982. The Democrats' reasoning probably included both considerations.

10. E.g., a John Brademas on education policy, a Phil Burton or John Dingell on Interior Committee and public lands environmental matters, a Lionel Van Deerlin and then Timothy Wirth on telecommunications and securities industry policy, Paul Rogers followed by Henry Waxman on health issues, Jonathan Bingham and then Don Bonker on foreign trade—and this list could go on and on.

11. The Democratic Caucus in 1972 with respect only to legislative proposals as opposed to internal matters such as leadership elections or party rules remained closed; the Republication Party Conference had held open sessions since the 1960s.

12. As indicated earlier in the discussion of the Record Teller Amendment in 1970, the implications of "sunshine" reform were never clear-cut. While it was most likely accurate for liberals to think that openness would do away with "closet conservatives" and secret votes where special interests could more easily work their will, there also were situations in which closed doors allowed liberals and others to vote *against* particular special interests and not risk their wrath. This is one of those ironical aspects of reform in which reform process and "progressive policy results" sometimes were at odds with each other.

13. See "Ways and Means in 1975: No Longer Pre-eminent," *CQ Weekly Report,* January 10, 1976, pp. 40–44.

14. *Ibid.*, p. 43.

15. *Ibid.*

16. Alan Schick, Joel Havemann, Sundquist and others have provided analysis of the background and history of the 1974 Budget Reform and Impoundment Control Act and there have been numerous accounts of the tribulations of the Congressional budget process. Alan Schick, *Congress and Money* (Washington, D.C.: The Urban Institute, 1980); Joel Haveman, *Congress and the Budget* (Bloomington, Indiana: Indiana University Press, 1978).

17. See Allen Schick, ed., *Making Economic Policy in Congress* (Washington, D.C.: American Enterprise Institute, 1983) especially the introduction and Chapter 3, John W. Ellwood, "Budget Control in a Redistributive Environment," Chapter 4, Naomi Caiden, "The Politics of Subtraction" and Chapter 9, Allen Schick, "The Distributive Congress," pp. 1–5, 69–99, 100–131 and 257–274 respectively.

18. This is especially the case in an age when Congress prefers not to face up to the political dilemma caused by huge deficits, i.e., either raising taxes or cutting spending. See Helen Dewar, "Frustrated Congress Misses 2nd Deadline for Cutting Deficits," *Washington Post,* September 24, 1983, p. A2.

19. See Sundquist, *Decline and Resurgence of Congress, op. cit.,* pp. 315–343.

20. *Ibid,* p. 343.

21. *Ibid,* p. 329.

22. *Ibid,* p. 339.

23. *Immigration and Naturalization Service v. Chadha,* __ U.S. __, 103 S. Ct. 2764 (1983). This decision jolted the whole area of Presidential/Congressional relations into great uncertainty. The consequences are still unknown, although it is by no means clear that special interests will emerge the losers. The subject is treated in greater detail in Chapter Eleven.

24. Sundquist, *Decline and Resurgence of Congress, op. cit.,* p. 350.
25. The list illustrates the breadth of areas and affected constituencies involved in legislation containing legislative veto provisions. See Sundquist, *Decline and Resurgence of Congress, op. cit.,* p. 351 and *CQ Almanac, 1971,* p. 508.
26. This last mentioned issue was of particular concern to the Formica Corporation, which was the target of just such a proceeding.
27. Of course, use of the veto by anti-consumer forces also spurred the pro-consumer groups to fight the legislative veto in the courts. "Public interest" groups were key backers of the *Chada* constitutional challenge to the legislative veto, although liberals were more supportive of the legislative veto on foreign policy issues.
28. See Kevin Phillips' comments in *Business & Public Affairs Fortnightly,* July 15, 1983, *op. cit.,* p. 5.
29. For a good review of the role of Congress in these areas, see Thomas Franck and Edward Weisband, *Foreign Policy By Congress* (New York: Oxford University Press, 1979) and Cecil V. Crabb, Jr. and Pat M. Holt, *Invitation to Struggle: Congress, The President and Foreign Policy* (Washington, D.C.: CQ Press, 1980).
30. See John J. Fialka, "Jewish Groups Increase Campaign Donations, Target Them Precisely," *Wall Street Journal,* August 3, 1983, *op. cit.,* pp. 1 and 13.
31. See House Report No. 96-866, 96th Congress, 2nd Session, April 1, 1980.
32. "House Multiple Referral Procedure," Suggested Revision Staff Report, House Select Committee on Committees, January 23, 1980, p. 8.
33. Although the Patterson Committee failed in its attempt in 1980 to provide the Speaker with more clear-cut authority to set time limits and control the multiple referral process.
34. For a detailed review of the Stevenson-Brock Committee and its accomplishments, see Judith H. Parris, "The Senate Reorganizes Its Committees, 1977," *Political Science Quarterly,* Vol. 94, Number 2, Summer 1979, pp. 319–337. James Sundquist also makes useful observations about the experience in broader perspectives, taking account of the House Committee reform experience and generally, in *Decline and Resurgence of Congress, op. cit.,* pp. 430–439.
35. See, Norman J. Ornstein, "The House and the Senate in a New Congress," in Thomas E. Mann and Norman J. Ornstein, *The New Congress* (Washington, D.C.: American Enterprise Institute, 1981), pp. 363–383.
36. Sources are the Almanacs of American Politics and for 1983 Alan Ehrenhalt, ed., *Politics in America, Members of Congress in Washington and At Home* (Washington, D.C.: CQ Press, 1983); count includes select committees.
37. Successfully as to all except Quentin Burdick of North Dakota, who stood to lose the chairmanship of Post Office and Civil Service due to its abolition and who became the "1" of the 89-1 vote on the final resolution.
38. For example, in contrast to the Bolling-Hansen reforms, Stevenson-Brock did actually achieve something close to a single comprehensive Energy and Natural Resources Committee (minus tax aspects still in Senate Finance).
39. With all sorts of intriguing questions for political scientists. For example, it is generally assumed that a Congress "divided" along partisan lines

would lead to conflict and stalemate. But the experience of the 1981–1983 period, and especially the "post Reagan honeymoon" 1982–1983 session, presents a possible model in which a "divided Congress" has actually served to encourage Congressional consensus. The "moderate" leadership in each body can rein in its own party's extreme wings by saying "we'll never be able to pass that in the other chamber." In such a political setting, Conference Committees become the real "little legislatures," and leaders can exert considerable influence not by use of carrots or sticks but simply by pointing out political realities. Here the law of anticipated reactions fosters consensus.

40. In 1980 NCPAC claimed responsibility for the defeat of well-known liberal Democratic incumbents Frank Church, George McGovern and John Culver among others. In 1982, NCPAC launched a particularly ferocious attack on Senator Paul Sarbanes in Maryland; this attack failed (Sarbanes was re-elected handily) and NCPAC was increasingly seen as a negative factor, being repudiated by some candidates it supported.

41. I have benefited greatly from a running dialogue with Philip M. Williams on this point. In brief, he takes the position that the instruments of Congressional Democratic party control as a result of reform are essentially in place and can be used effectively in the right political circumstances. We both hope he is right. I have darker suspicions that the dispersive tendencies are so ingrained and so politically attractive and utilitarian that strong party leadership—even with the reforms—remains more popular and desirable in principle than in practice.

42. See Sundquist, *Decline and Resurgence of Congress, op. cit.*

43. Also see Joseph L. Bower, *The Two Faces of Management* (Boston: Houghton Mifflin Company, 1983), pp. 153–159, on how the legislative veto "politiciz(es) the Government's technocratic systems," and breaks down traditional insulation of bureaucracy from influences to which Congress is responsive. Bower's book, finished before *Chada*, views the legislative veto as a challenge and threat to technocratic tendencies.

44. See Elizabeth Drew, *Politics and Money, op. cit.*

45. See Mancur Olson, *The Logic of Collective Action* (Cambridge, Mass.: Harvard University Press, 1971) and Mancur Olson, *The Rise and Decline of Nations* (New Haven, Conn.: Yale University Press, 1982).

Eleven

Congressional Biases: Reform and Patterns of Special Interest Influence

11:1 SPECIAL INTEREST INFLUENCE AS INCREMENTAL DISTORTION AND THE SHAPING OF CONGRESSIONAL BIASES

It is difficult to gauge with precision the effects of special interest influence. Unlike the overt *quid pro quo* bribery situation, the typical world of Congressional decision-making finds special interest largesse as merely one of many competing factors.

Several basic points are in order to underscore the complexity of the process. First, the structure of Congress as it has evolved is *intrinsically* oriented toward fragmented, narrow interest-oriented policy-making. An elaborate web of outside special interests has formed around this structure, and an infrastructure of PAC and individual campaign contributions has given sustenance to the inhabitants of the structure; but it is the structure itself which biases the Congress toward individual entrepreneurialism, subcommittee autonomy and disjointed decision-making. Secondly, special interest groups—working with sympathetic members of Congress—exert significant influence by affecting Congress's agenda. The life of an issue is complicated—and the birth and gestation stages are critical. Special interest groups influence Congress's agenda in many ways, often invisibly, or at least in ways not readily detectable. One example of this subtlety is influence exerted before members and issues ever get to Congress. This is the case when interest groups play an active role in the electoral process. To be sure, they do so by means of campaign contributions, but they also increasingly do so by insinuating themselves into campaigns with endorsement conventions, debates, and questionnaires with ratings based on responses. Well-orchestrated efforts by these small groups can swallow up candidates' time and also, to a large extent, shape both the format of debate and the issues that are debated. While entrepreneurial and well-intentioned groups ought not to be faulted for seeking to maximize their influence on issues about which they are concerned, it is still fair to note the often negative effect on the larger electoral and governing processes. The tendency toward candidates' position-taking and government-by-questionnaire is not a positive one: it often distracts from the large arena of non-elite concerns, typically including major economic issues. Elite issue politics often perpetuates misperceptions about the nature of the legislative process, oversimplifying complex issues into a series of questions susceptible to "yes" or "no" answers. Ratings by interest groups similarly seek to reduce broad-ranging Congressional voting patterns into "good" and "bad" votes.

Beyond the electoral sphere special interests have a myriad of ways—many very subtle—to shape the Congressional agenda and to frame issues. Some of the more common include the strategically placed amendment, getting the "right" language in a Committee report, or having a member of Congress ask a question designed to elicit a useful answer (and legislative history) at a hearing. But this special interest assertion of influence rarely surfaces to public view. Even the most overt evidence of influence—campaign contributions—are often just expressions of appreciation for positions previously taken and affinities already displayed (although they are also increasingly *de facto* "entry fees" to access).

Overt special interest influence often distorts only incrementally, i.e. marginally reinforces or discourages already formed predispositions. Because of the difficulty—or impossibility—of precisely measuring influence based on specific instances, an extensive select bibliography on the subject is included, which establishes some connections which are sometimes statistical and sometimes circumstantial.[1] The goal here is instead to set forth a speculative theory of how reform's and Congress's recent evolution generally has helped increase the special interest *orientation* of Congress and has shaped Congressional biases. The objective of this undertaking is to try to provide insight into the patterns and workings of special interests' distortive effects on the process.

Special Interest Influence as Incremental Distortion

The true workings of special interest influence are not the stuff of which headlines are made. While some journalists may delight at the prospect of headlines trumpeting PAC contributions as tantamount to bribery, the reality is somewhat less clear. Special interest influence works in many ways, but at its most effective, it is a matter of shared values and longstanding relationships between Congress members and outside groups. It is exerted in indirect or even subliminal, rather than obvious, ways. Political influence is best accomplished with a grace and deftness that displays no heavyhandedness and which is often invisible to those affected.

Special interest influence often relies on unspoken assumptions and the law of anticipated reactions. A member's party, ideological orientation, personal background (including factors such as region, education, religion, friendship, etc.) all have significant predictive value as to voting tendencies.[2] Members come to their jobs with attitudes, biases, political allegiances, commitments and assumptions which predispose them toward, and against, certain interests. The job of PACs and lobbyists is to try to reinforce or weaken those predispositions through campaign contributions. It is in this sphere of activity that PACs and influential lobbyists can be accused of "distorting" the process. But the distortive effect of PACs and lobbyists should be seen as an incremental effect—i.e., a distortion to the extent that it changes members' votes or dispositions from what they would otherwise be, absent the special interest influence. When seen in this context, it becomes clearer how difficult it is to measure special interest influence or gauge the impact of reform on the Special Interest Congress. For example, it is not enough to conclude that Congressman X's $5,000 contribution from a dairy PAC spurred him to vote for dairy price supports. It is necessary to examine how Congressman X was otherwise disposed to vote—based on his party, region, other group influences and allegiances—absent the dairy PAC contribution. For the dairy district congressman there is likely to be no distortive effect, because he or she would have voted for price supports anyway. For the non-dairy district representative, the contribution may well be distortive. Dairy price supports are an example of an issue on which members have clearly discernible "district interests"—i.e., they are either from dairy districts or are not. It is not surprising then that members from non-dairy states who vote for dairy price supports are often accused of "caving in" to dairy contributors.[3] But this situation bears closer analysis. The probability appears high that the contributions had something to do with the favorable vote—because, except in the event of concerted consumer awareness and criticism of the costs of dairy price supports, this is a relatively "free" vote for the non-dairy district member. Hence it is possible to conclude that the special interests' likelihood of success is greatest when it has one group already favorably disposed (the dairy representatives) and another bloc without strong reasons to oppose them. The dairy lobbyists can "reward" members who vote "right" anyway, based on constituent preference; and go to the other group and say "your constituents don't care; so vote with us."

But even this apparently simple scenario is actually more complicated, because the "incremental distortion" of the non-dairy district representative may vary. For a member with a strong pro-consumer record, the incremental distortion from what he or she would otherwise do is great; the non-dairy representative less responsive generally to consumer groups has less to distort. Of course, other factors must be taken into account, prominently including "logrolling," i.e. trade-offs by which members otherwise disinclined to vote for dairy (or tobacco, etc.) subsidies may do so in exchange for support on their favored legislation. These "deals" are often unrelated to PAC contributions, which is to say that a member's vote might be "distorted" from what it would otherwise have been by a "deal" on another bill rather than a PAC contribution. But the member might still get the contribution. And a journalist or other observer might come along and draw specious conclusions. The situation then is complicated, and certainly more complicated than a simple correlation between campaign contributions and votes.

The subtlety of these distortive effects, and the existence of a vast array of other independent and often conflicting factors, makes a comprehensive, conclusive explanation of precisely how reform promoted special interest influence difficult to establish. In addition, it is important to note that there is a relative absence of *overt* special interest influence or even involvement in many areas of Congressional activity. A review of large issues of foreign and domestic policies might lead an observer to conclude that special interest involvement is limited to a small group of Congressional issues. The analysis which follows will address this matter in some detail. However, several conceptual points are in order. Contemporary political scientists disagree as to the accuracy of two different models of American government. The one which has achieved a significant degree of support in the literature is the so-called pluralist or "partisan mutual adjustment" model—that interest groups articulate their interests and bargain for partisan advantage; the outcome of this process is government policy which has aggregated, reconciled and adjusted these interests. Major criticisms of this model have been described earlier in this book, mainly in literature relating to the structure of urban policy-making (Schattschneider, Bachrach and Baratz, Crenson, et al.).

A recent book on Congress presents an intriguing alternative model (both normative and empirical) which focuses on the political community. Arthur Maass in *Congress and the Common Good* argues that a more desirable and realistic model of the workings of Congress involves groups and individuals articulating their various conceptions of the "common good," i.e. their preferences for the political community as a whole, as opposed to their narrow economic preferences.[4] The debate is an important one, and as noted earlier, a concern of this work is the extent to which Congress fails to address the needs of the broader political community. For the purposes here it is enough to make the following points about reform and interest groups (which embrace aspects of the competing models).

Reform helped to make Congress more responsive to interest groups by 1) organizing itself to cater to them, and by 2) revising the law and regulations to enable interest groups to organize themselves more effectively to influence Congress (mainly through PACs). But further, these effects of reform have put special interest groups in a position where they not only are well-situated to articulate their interests and needs on their own partisan and parochial matters, they are now in a position to influence (electorally, through influence over the agenda, etc.) larger issues affecting the political community as a whole. It is even arguably the case that interest groups are in a better position than Congressional sub-units to articulate and express a coherent set of preferences for the political community. For example, a conservative-minded business, trade association or ideological PAC can seek to influence a broad range of issues extending across Congressional committee and subcommittee lines which amounts to a coherent political agenda. Most Congressional entities—with the exception of parties—simply do not have the jurisdictional or conceptual ability to do that. In short, reform has enhanced fragmentation as well as special interest access and influence—not just on issues of direct concern to the groups. And of course to the extent that PACs involve themselves in elections and Congressional agenda setting, special interest group activity clearly extends to the broad realm of the "common good." The analysis which follows seeks to identify some of the patterns of special interest influence and to clear the path for both speculation on the future and recommendations for alternative directions. The approach is to assess the different ways in which Congressional organization and special interest influences (and values they manifest) help shape the biases of Congress. These biases, in turn, have an impact on what Congress does. What emerges is a system of individually and group-oriented clusters of bias favoring and opposing certain issues, positions and issues.

11:2 VALUES: THE BIAS TOWARD INDIVIDUALISM

The reform of Congress was essentially a clash between two conflicting value orientations. The first involved all those previously mentioned values which cluster around two, essentially individualistic concerns on the part of members of Congress: the desire for *Constituency and Special Interest Support* (most obviously re-election, but other district-based concerns as well), and the quest for Washington-centered political clout, or what might be dubbed *Empire-building*. The second focused on collective institutional goals, as seen in the most ambitious reformers' designs for *External Institutional Efficacy* and *Internal Institutional Rationality*. The first two concerns served as an impetus to dispersion of power. The second two aimed at greater consolidation of Congressional resources and power.

The debate over reform became an extended playing-out—on many sub-institutional fronts—of this contest between dispersion and consolidation, more specifically, between procedures favoring individualistic concerns and those seeking to advance greater collective functional capabilities.

The reform proposals that most threatened individualistic values were either pre-empted from serious consideration, sidetracked, or— if they ever got to the realm of decision—rejected. Those reforms that might possibly have aided greater aggregate institutional efficacy were re-shaped and molded in design and enactment to comport with individualistic values. Those proposals which aimed to serve the functional goals and power interests of independence-minded and entrepreneurial individual members were carefully nurtured upon consideration, and wholeheartedly embraced in implementation.

The result of this tension was that a reform movement which had as its early, dominant philosophical impetus the goal of greater institutional clarity of function was seized upon—albeit subtly and incrementally—as an opportunity to serve desires leading precisely in the opposite direction. Rather than a careful re-examination of institutionally dysfunctional individualistic values and their systemic implications—much less a concerted shift in another direction—the reforms became an occasion for the expansion, refinement, enhancement, even celebration, of those very values.

Congressional reform in the 1970s helped make an already decentralized, incohesive institution even more so. And this bias toward these behavioral values has manifested itself in Congress's individualistic and entrepreneurial performance on policy. These values merit further exploration. The classic typology of Congressional norms is Donald K. Matthews' 1960 study[5] of the Senate, in which he identified apprenticeship, legislative work, specialization, courtesy, reciprocity, and institutional patriotism as the major institutional "folkways." Although there have been obvious disparities between the Senate and House owing to size, structure, and different historical development, this typology can be applied to overall contemporary Congressional behavior.

There is no doubt that in varying degrees these values continue to exist. But it is important to note that they are by no means static; they are affected by changes in members' attitudes and goals, and most fundamentally by turnover in members themselves. These values are the key to institutional change. While there is certainly a chicken and egg problem here—with no simple resolution—it seems probable that changes in institutional orientation and performance generally follow changes in individual members' preferences and values. Reforms and new institutional forms certainly alter old norms and spawn new ones. Individual member values have great impact not only on how an institution functions but in what way it seeks to restructure itself. Hence reform of Congress was most likely heavily influenced by the values a majority of its members sought to enhance.

What were these values? In part, they were variants of those identified by Matthews. But more specifically, they were ones which heightened individual autonomy, and allowed freer opportunity to accomplish those individual goals of constituency support and Washington-based efficacy.

Apprenticeship has probably been the value most seriously eroded. Members are clearly not willing to serve a lengthy apprenticeship before taking part in the gamut of activities. Members elected in times of political tumult, often from marginal seats, want to be able to show constituents quick results. They are not prepared to wait. Stress on performing legislative work and specializing have probably not changed so much in their existence as in their new meanings for most members. In the "pre-reform" Congress legislating and specializing meant taking a seat on a committee or committees—deferring to the committee chairman and elders, performing minor legislative tasks such as participating in hearings, voting, and generally doing what one was told, and waiting for more power and responsibilities by accruing seniority. The forty or fifty House members and twenty or so Senators who sat atop their institution's power structure wielded great power, while the rest made do with less influence, biding their time and in some cases growing frustrated.

These values broke down first in the Senate. Greased by the Johnson Rule of 1953 the Senate structure began to provide a substantial majority of its members with worthwhile duties and powers (if they were clever enough to use them effectively).

The values proved more tenacious in the House, but eventually gave way. They were overcome by reforms that catered to the political needs of the disadvantaged in the old system along with the new generation of members who were simply not willing to wait to experience being disadvantaged in the new. In the latter instance there was at least the perception that constituents were not willing to wait for results from their representatives.

Consequently, assertive new members wanted to participate in all phases of Congressional activity, resulting in increased activity but also a newly sporadic and uneven quality to much of the legislative activity. The implications for specialization illustrate this point in that the specialization norm has been both weakened and strengthened in the new system. To the extent that members are pulled in many directions it is weakened. But in other ways specialization is now actually greater in that members take on important roles on subcommittees, committees in the party and informally much earlier in their careers. They are motivated to specialize in those areas of prime responsibility. However, they also feel it necessary to take stands—"position-taking"—on a wide range of issues, and especially on whatever happen to be the most clamant issues. (During and after the 1973 and 1979 energy crises many members suddenly became "energy specialists" of one sort or another; during recessions, members became "experts" in jobs programs; the nuclear freeze and domestic environmental issues have also attracted Congressional single issue crusaders.) The new norm is to try to specialize in several issues which are the subject of particular committee or other sub-institutional based concerns (empire-building), but also to be flexible and adaptive enough to specialize in popular national issues (more empire-building) and targeted local concerns (constituency support).

Courtesy, reciprocity, and institutional loyalty are still in evidence—to the extent that they are expedient for individual members. But to the extent they are not expedient, they are typically eschewed. In some cases members refuse to engage in (and indeed, blow the whistle on) vote-trading or deal-making. In the most generalized recent trend: members "run for Congress by running against it," no doubt in recognition of Congress's low public standing.

The overall trend during the period is that virtually all of the individual member roles which involved individual autonomy and a degree of flexibility in their assertion, and had evolved to some extent in the circa 1968 Congress (particularly in the House) had been noticeably strengthened by the late 1970s. Members found themselves better able to represent those constituencies they chose, in many different roles. Indeed, the only individual roles which seem *less* highly developed in the post-reform period are ones which inhere some sort of concerted action: party representation, comprehensive policy-making, and "gatekeeping"—screening out certain fractious issues. Also less in evidence are supportive roles involving acceptance of, or allegiance to, authority figures such as the President, or the Congressional leadership, although a persuasive president (Reagan as opposed to Carter) can still marshal Congressional support for certain macropolitical national policies. Despite Reagan's success, a general tendency has been for both Presidential and Congressional leaders to encounter resistance from independent-minded members of Congress.

Table 11:1 draws the connection between Congressional functions and the proliferating roles of individual members in the post-reform Congress. It itemizes the many specific—and highly individualistic—roles which members take on in performing those Congressional functions. First, it indicates the large number of such roles, providing many opportunities for individual activity, and secondly, it lays the basis for analysis of how the many different roles lend themselves to use by members—with varying degrees of effectiveness—to serve special interest needs.

The goal is not to find special interest utility lurking behind every Congressional function; instead, it is to assess the extent to which members' different roles allow special interests to achieve their objectives. This analysis should provide the basis for further insights into the particular workings of Congressional biases toward certain kinds of policies and interests.

Table 11:1 shows the multiplicity of roles members of Congress can derive from the essential Congressional functions. These roles compete for their attention in the face of limited time and resources. Members of Congress must not only choose which roles to play but how to play them—and for whose benefit. The hallmark of the choices, and the roles, is individualism—the individual member's ability to use his or her time, office and resources to enhance his or her standing—electorally, in the Congress and in selected spheres of the outside political community.

TABLE 11:1

Congressional Functions and the Proliferation of Individual Members' Roles

Congressional Functions	*"Practical" Individual Member Roles*

Representation	*Representative:*
	—of individuals
	—special interest groups/affinity groups
	—District/State/Region
	—Ideological or other philosophical bent in Fenno's constituency terms:
	—Personal constituency
	  —Primary constituency
	  —Re-election constituency
	  —Geographic constituency

Legislation	*Legislator:*
	—distributor of discrete benefits:
	  —pork-barrel politician/bearer of good tidings in the form of projects, grants, and jobs
	—authorizer/appropriator
	—redistributor:
	  —architect of social change/advocate for sectoral interests
	  —tax reformer/raiser, cutter, loophole-opener or closer
	—regulator:
	  —policy-maker/co-participant with bureaucracy (or bane of its existence), friend or foe of private industry
	—delegator:
	  —general policy-maker/*overseer* of implementation

TABLE 11:1—*continued*

Congressional Functions	"Practical" Individual Member Roles

	—friend or foe of industry
	—buck passer?
	—comprehensive policy-maker:
	  —thinker, visionary, architect of grand policy bargainer in subcommittee, committee, floor, conference, other public forums, etc.: deal-maker, pragmatist, underminers of comprehensiveness?
	—budget overseer/position-taker:
	  —priority setter
	  —spending controller
	  —budget cutter
	
	Constitutional Co-participant in Executive Appointments (Senate Advice and Consent):
	—critic or defender of Administration Appointees
	—voter
	  —in subcommittee, committee, floor, caucus, conference
	  —position-taker (on issues that come before the Congress)
	  —coalition-builder
	
	Position-taker:
	—issue-raiser and framer
	—gate-keeper
	—coalition—leader or member
	—advocate
	—publicist
	—interest group or constituency crowd-pleaser
	—moral crusader—leader
	—public opinion—follower
	—symbolist at the expense of substance

Information	*Information Publicist:* —press-releaser —newsletter/franked mail—correspondent —spokesperson —Federal program "contact person," explainer
Investigation	*Investigator:* —muckraker —"white-washer" —crusader —interest group and constituency crowd-pleaser —media-figure

TABLE 11:1—*continued*

Congressional Functions	"Practical" Individual Member Roles
	Ombudsman/Case Worker: —errand person —social security check getter —red-tape cutter —string-puller —job-finder/supporter —government contract-locater/expediter —discrete-benefit provider/trader
Education	*Educator/Leader:* —thinker —opinion-leader —advocate —writer/press releaser —media figure —moral spokesperson
	Mobilizer of Consent: —supporter of government policy —issue and policy—explainer —program "contact person" —aide in bureaucratic implementation
	Mobilizer of Dissent: —opponent of government policy, or proposed policy —special interest advocate 　—single-issue spokesperson —ideologue/programmic policy advocate 　—ideologue —critic —legislative obstructionist/bargainer

11:3 THE BIAS TOWARD DISTRIBUTIVE POLICY

One major focus of political science analysis has been a typology of different "arenas of power." Theodore Lowi's early formulation[6] that the substance of policy influences the role of organizations led to his three categories of policy-making: "distributive" (providing benefits to specific groups without regard to limited resources), "redistributive" (providing benefits and assessing costs to broad categories of citizens) and "regulatory" (a choice as to whether to confer benefits or impose costs to different groups on the basis of ostensibly general rules). This typology, despite some problems of overlap and imprecision, has been helpful in understanding how government relates to society. Its application to Congressional decision-making is best seen in a detailed review of Congress's role in making various kinds of policy. Allen Schick has observed that the Congress of the late 1960s and 1970s essentially organized itself to make distributive policy (i.e., confer benefits and reap the political rewards) but that the economic malaise of the late 1970s and early 1980s required Congress to make *re*distributive policy.[7] A fragmented Congress set up to dole out benefits is not necessarily well-suited to impose restraints—cut spending, close tax loopholes, etc. Hence Schick sees the "paralysis of Congress" as attributable to the distributive orientation of Congress in a political environment which demands a different kind of organization. This squares with the analysis here in that the reform experience diffused power to smaller units and individuals and thus equipped Congress to cater more effectively to special interests. As long as there was economic growth, members of Congress could concentrate on distributing benefits and ingratiating themselves with special interests. Schick makes an important point that a Congress oriented toward distributive legislation faces difficulties when called upon to make effective redistributive policy. This goes some way toward explaining the erratic and ineffective performance of Congress in the late 1970s and early 1980s.[8]

The reformed Congress is biased in favor of distributing discrete benefits; when it is thrust into the role of withdrawing benefits and making comprehensive but reductionist policy, Congress has hardly warmed to the task. The three-fold typology put forth originally by Lowi is useful in helping to make this general observation. It should be noted, however, that the typology tends to oversimplify the realities of Congress.

James Q. Wilson, has noted that there are problems with Lowi's three categories.[9] There is often difficulty in distinguishing between the three policy spheres; there is also a key distinction which should be made between initiating policy and amending an existing policy. As Wilson also observes, while Lowi has made a major contribution by noting that "the substance of a policy influences the role of organization in its adoption, the incidence of costs and benefits of a policy should not be obscured by the use of categories ('distributive' and so on) that are hard to define and to purge of misleading implications."[10] Following Wilson, the focus of the analysis here is on the spheres of Congressional decision-making in terms of how they assess costs and confer benefits on the society—and how Congress biases itself toward certain types of behavior and outcomes.

Costs and Benefits, Special Interests and Congressional Biases

It is most sensible to proceed from the "big" issues to the more narrow in order to identify certain Congressional biases on the basis of the costs and benefits to society. By focusing on these costs and benefits we also see the political costs and benefits to members of Congress, and why these combine to shape biases of Congress in terms of its agenda, decisions and outcomes. And we are also in a position to assess the changes which have occurred recently—some as a result of reforms, some otherwise—in Congress's biases and proclivities.

Distributed Benefits and Distributed Costs

Wilson has noted that the issues least likely to be the subject of organized lobbying are ones which broadly confer benefits and impose similarly broadly the costs. This category includes Social Security and other entitlement programs which had from the New Deal until Reaganomics been viewed as uncontroversial "motherhood" issues. The Wilson dictum that these types of issues attract support from politicians because of their broad appeal—without the necessity of organizational intervention—still is largely accurate. However, recent developments in Congress and in the country make it such that some revision of the traditional view here is in order. The Congressional bias toward virtually unquestioned support of these programs has been eroded.

In normal circumstances it is still fair to say that broad entitlement and social policy issues do not engender the organizational activity that "narrow cost, narrow benefit" issues attract. As Senator Dole and others have observed, there is no "poor people PAC" or "Food Stamp recipient PAC." However, there has been a change in bias in this area which is tangentially related to reform and heavily influenced by the new ideological approach of the Reagan Administration. The new Congressional budget process afforded the mechanism—reconciliation—for the Reagan budget cuts. But the Reagan Administration's proposals forced Congress to ask basic questions about the proper role of government (arguably the first such rethinking in a generation) and changed the political dynamics of broad costs/broad benefits legislation. Existing groups used to virtually automatic benefits (social security beneficiaries and other recipients of government aid) have been stirred to action in defense of existing benefits or to stave off imposition of new costs (Federal employees not wanting to be included in the Social Security system, industries resisting new users' fees and/or the new competition of deregulation).

Some of Congress's difficulty in dealing with these problems is inherent in the problem of the 1980s politics of subtraction versus addition and the point made by Schick about Congress's preference for distributive politics rather than redistributive politics. But it is probably fair also to note that the fragmented structure of Congress and the relative absence of organizational activity on entitlement issues has resulted in several developments. These issues have sparked partisan differences—the Democrats have become the defenders of broad benefit/broad cost programs in defense against conservative Republican moves to trim them. In addition to and perhaps a partial product of this heightened partisanship, solutions have become harder to come by. Some of this may be due to the fragmented Congressional process—which allows the Democratic-controlled House and particularly the House Ways and Means Committee to obstruct GOP Presidential and Senate initiatives. Much of the policy stalemate is due to continuing philosophical differences over the role and scope of government.

One significant reaction to both increased partisanship on these issues *and* Congressional structural fragmentation has been to seek unusual mechanisms to fashion bipartisan compromise solutions. The best example is the Greenspan Commission on Social Security which combined Administration and Congressional principals in the Social Security debate to hammer out a compromise plan to rescue the Social Security System. Two earlier (less successful) attempts at building consensus on issues of broad cost and benefit significance in a fragmented Congress were the efforts by Speaker O'Neill in favor of President Carter's Energy Policy and Welfare Reform in 1977–1978. In the former case, regional and special interest group activity (oil and automobile industry) along with other psychic aspects of American transportation diverted attention from the broad cost/broad benefit nature of the issue. In the latter case, inherent philosophical and moralistic concerns over work and income maintenance clouded debate and also arguably raised questions about whether the cost of welfare—even if broadly distributed—was excessive. In each case, a special committee approach was used to overlay the ordinary Congressional committee structure. In neither case was the legislation enacted, although the Carter Energy package did pass the House.

To conclude, issues involving broad benefits and broadly distributed costs still are notable for the relative absence of interest group activity and the high degree of political acceptance of the basic existence and attributes of these programs. However, recent changes have occurred. Along with a new focus on basic questions about the proper role of government and a new politics of redistribution and retrenchment has come a new, mainly defensive involvement by representatives of threatened groups. The main development has been to activate partisanship, but a likely future development is to provoke increased special interest group formation and participation. Hence Congress's bias toward the status quo on these issues has been affected by the new politics of subtraction. The future most likely will see continued movement in this direction.

Concentrated Benefits and Distributed Costs

These are legislative issues which give rise to programs benefiting clearly identifiable special interests but which broadly distribute costs so that they are typically not visible or politically contentious. Wilson cites as examples in 1973 such issues as veterans' benefits, agricultural subsidies, oil import quotas and tariffs on many commodities. Here too there has been change—some attributable to the new politics of redistribution and reduction and some of it related to institutional change and changed political dynamics stimulating different actions by interest groups. A basic change has been a new visibility of the beneficiaries and awareness on the part of those paying the costs. This has spurred heightened interest group activity on both sides.

Perhaps the most significant general development in this area has been the taxpayers' revolt which spread from state taxpayers' initiatives (e.g. Proposition 13 in California) to the Federal policy arena after 1980. The drive by conservatives to cut spending has been complemented by liberals seeking to cut Federal subsidies. The decline of the American economy and the rise of the deficit have increased the public outcry for more cutting in these areas.

In response to the "popular" move for spending reductions, the affected interest groups have been spurred to defend their benefits. Farmers and other traditional beneficiaries have been activated. In addition, groups which have only recently come under threat—e.g. automobile workers lobbying for domestic content legislation in the face of competition from Japanese manufacturers—have lined up to push for this sort of help from the Congress. As international trade becomes more competitive and American producer groups come under greater pressure the calls for protection will increase. As Robert Pastor has pointed out, there may still be strong reasons to continue to act as free traders even as we rattle the protectionist sabres.[11] Moreover, while the Congressional bias toward helping friendly client groups may continue to be strong, the deficit and the pressure of public opinion against preferential treatment of well-organized economic groups will continue to generate strong counter pressures.

Distributed Benefits and Concentrated Costs

Legislative programs with distributed benefits and concentrated costs present difficult political problems. First, they are difficult to achieve *because* the benefits are diffuse and the targets of the costs are likely to mobilize in opposition. Moreover, if the target group has political clout, it most likely will develop relationships with the relevant Congressional actors and units. Traditional accounts of "iron triangles" and agencies "captured" by regulated industries lead one to conclude that Congress would appear to have a bias against programs which assess costs so narrowly. To a significant degree this has been the case: Congressional chairmen and committee powerhouses are typically hesitant to impose heavy costs on patrons, especially when those patron industries are well-organized and active on Capitol Hill—for example, the American Medical Association, the National Association of Broadcasters, the National Association of Realtors, etc.

This presumed bias against broad benefit/concentrated cost programs, while certainly still present, is also undergoing change. Increasingly in an era of limits it is programs that require sacrifice from these groups which are seen as necessary to reduce excessive costs in vital areas of the economy. To the extent that deregulation of major sectors of transportation and communications involve increased competition and less preferred status for commercial entities, there are new concentrated costs on a small group of (previously advantaged) corporations. To the extent that *new* regulation is proposed—for example, government-set fees for doctors under the medicare system or FTC regulation for a host of professional groups—relatively narrow groups are being asked to bear costs in the interest of larger societal benefits.

As the politics of subtraction continues, the Congressional bias against this sort of program is likely to continue to weaken. The best reason for this is that it is likely to become not only good policy but good politics—as entrepreneurial members of Congress or public interest advocates can mobilize public support behind policies and against less-than-popular groups like doctors and lawyers.

Concentrated Benefits and Concentrated Costs

The major sphere of special interest conflict is where both benefits and costs are concentrated. It is here that it is most likely that competing interest groups will be locked in head-to-head battle over who gets benefits and upon whom costs are imposed. This includes much of the debate over tax legislation and federal budget-making, especially recently when the defense budget has been virtually sacrosanct and social programs have been the constant target of cutbacks.

The traditional view has been that where both costs and benefits are concentrated, and special interests are in an adversary relationship— such as tax treatment of mutual versus stock life insurance companies or independents versus big oil companies—that policy changes will be affected only by negotiation and bargaining among the interests or after shifts in the political complexion of the decision-making body. This remains true to a large extent; increased PAC and lobbyist activity is concentrated on maximizing advantage in this bargaining process. And both internal reform and electoral shifts provide examples of policy change following change in political coloration: the reduction of the oil depletion allowance followed the "opening up" of the Ways and Means Committee in 1974 and the range of cutbacks and conservative policy shifts which followed the Republican assumption of control of the Senate in 1981.

It is this last area of concentrated costs and benefits where the lion's share of special interest activity occurs. And the committees concerned with industries most heavily regulated (e.g. broadcasting or transportation as to regulatory policy) or affected (e.g. corporations, partnerships and wealthy individuals as to tax policy) are the ones most likely to attract special interest clusters around their relevant subcommittees and individual members. For members, their legislative efficacy is often directly related to the degree of potency of their committee assignment. Traditionally favored in the House have been the most powerful: House Ways and Means, Energy and Commerce, Budget and Appropriations. Other committees have less in-house power but in some cases take on virtual "life support" responsibility for the interests of certain groups, e.g., Agriculture, Merchant Marine and Fisheries, Education and Labor, Post Office and Civil Service, Interior, and Science & Technology. The dependency of these groups on their committee-based benefactors was highlighted by the desultory experience of House Committee reform in the seventies.

Elizabeth Drew and others have cited a number of examples of the workings of PAC and lobbyist-based special interest influence. In *Politics and Money,* she provided new insights into the workings and implications of the new "Special Interest Congress." In her journalistic exploration of the role that money plays in both contemporary Presidential and Congressional politics, Drew delved into how special interests, rooted in PAC money, have taken on a new and powerful influence. She describes the 1981 "bidding war" over the tax bill in which Democrats and Republicans vied with each other to bestow greater special interest benefits, to the glee of the interests and to the intended benefit of members' and the parties' campaign coffers. She also describes the behind-the-scenes struggle between "independent oil" and "big oil" over tax policy that affect them—with profound campaign finance overtones. This tax policy-making in the 1982 Reagan tax increase (TEFRA) which found the House Ways and Means Committee taking a seat on the sidelines, i.e. not taking up or reporting out a bill to avoid putting its "fingerprints" on a major tax increase whose passage was considered to be macroeconomically essential. The point made well by Drew is that the substance of policy became a bargaining chip in the later battle for campaign funds. This tendency was strikingly illustrated by exchanges over oil policy, and their not coincidental relationship to party fundraising activities. The evidence here is necessarily anecdotal. It is not the purpose of this section, or the larger study, to engage in investigative reporting of behind-the-scenes "deals" or to allege untoward Congressional behavior. Rather the goal here is simply to identify tendencies and contours of the new process that reform was instrumental in creating.

In addition to Drew and other journalists, the "public interest" organizations Common Cause and Congress Watch have collected a good deal of material documenting the various effects that special interests have on Congress's specific policy performance. In a 1979 study entitled "How Money Talks in Congress," Common Cause identified a number of areas where special interest campaign contributions appeared to exert substantial influence on matters of policy. These areas included the maritime-related unions on cargo preference and other legislation before the Merchant Marine and Fisheries Committee; dairy and sugar interests on issues before the Agriculture

Committee; the American Medical Association on health issues before the Ways and Means and Commerce Committees;[12] and the National Education Association on education issues before the Education and Labor Committee. Other examples abound: the American Trial Lawyers Association and industry on national no-fault automobile insurance and capping product and toxic liability damages; realtors on a range of tax issues affecting investment, depreciation and ownership of real property; oil companies on tax and general regulatory and environmental matters; other resource companies on environmental matters; banks on regulatory and tax matters; manufacturers on occupational safety and health issues; agribusiness on agricultural issues; defense contractors on defense spending and procurement issues; big business representatives on tax and corporate matters; and the list could go on and on. Perhaps the ultimate proof of the perception that it is necessary to gear up a Washington presence is the explosion of the number of business and trade association PACs. A more specific example is the new activism of small business associations and high technology companies and associations—sectors not hitherto active in Washington which now understand that decisions made in Washington have great impact on their futures.

The general point made in the Common Cause report, articulated by then-Republican Congressman John B. Anderson of Illinois, is that "Special Interest contributions are often targeted at incumbents and all too frequently are used as a form of investment."[13] This supports the proposition that PAC contributions are more than a healthy manifestation of corporate participation in democracy; put bluntly, they are designed to buy access and influence votes.

Common Cause has also identified a broad range of government subsidies which it alleges are natural concomitants of special interest influence on Congress. And, Common Cause further argues that it was these economically inefficient policies which served to fuel the inflation of the late 1970s and early 1980s. In a 1980 study entitled "The Government Subsidy Squeeze," Common Cause provides an authoritative analysis of Congressional catering to special interest demands. These include:

Direct subsidies

—agricultural subsidies; using breakfast cereal as an example of the influence of a web of government subsidies including price support and set aside programs on grain production, Interstate Commerce Commission regulation of transportation, not to mention similar factors influencing the sugar and milk which accompany the cereal to the breakfast table;

—the range of agricultural subsidies including price supports, commodity loan programs, deficiency payments between target prices and what farmers actually receive, etc.

Indirect subsidies

—The whole area of tax expenditures (also covered in another Common Cause study "Gimme Shelters"), i.e. those indirect benefits conferred as part of the tax code which allow exemptions, deferrals, deductions or exclusions from tax and which represent lost revenue for the government and constitute an "expenditure" as if the government had actually authorized and appropriated funds for a program. Examples cited here include:

—DISC, the Domestic International Sales Corporation, an opportunity for corporations which export to set up "shell" subsidiary corporations which can defer indefinitely taxes on half of the profits off the subsidiary. Enacted in 1971 as an incentive for U.S. corporations to export, Common Cause and other critics contend that this constitutes a tax benefit for corporations to do something that they would be doing anyway—and a drain on revenues.

Income Tax Deferral for U.S. Owned Subsidiaries

This allows U.S. owned foreign corporations to escape (indefinitely) U.S. corporate tax. In its indefiniteness, it amounts to a virtual permanent tax exemption.

Deduction of Interest on Consumer Credit

This allows consumers to deduct the interest paid on all loans for consumer purchases—serving as an actual inducement to borrow.

Deferral of Tax on Shipping Companies

This allows shipping companies to deduct from taxable income all deposits into capital construction funds. Income tax on earnings on assets held in these funds can be deferred indefinitely; and when ship owners can further escape tax when they withdraw assets by "rolling over" the money into the purchase of new ships.

Timber Tax Exemptions

These allow earnings from the sale of timber to be taxed at capital gains rates (in 1980, 28%), as opposed to higher rates for products in

other industries. Also certain costs of managing and preserving forests are allowed to be "exposed"—i.e. deducted as current expenses.
Another tax break in the timber industry allows shifting earnings to
tree cultivation, which is taxed at a lower rate.

Common Cause goes on to identify regulatory "subsidies" in the
airline industry, trucking, maritime, rail, Federal work laws (the
David-Bacon Act requiring "prevailing wage rates" on Federal or
Federally-financed construction projects, dairy, loan guarantee programs, irrigation subsidies, Small Business disaster loan programs,
and other.

The Common Cause analysis does not in all cases draw direct links
to specific activities of affected interests. The important point is that
there are infinite possible ways that the government can hurt, or if it
chooses, help different economic groups, and this importance of the
government role elicits—some would say, commands—active interest
group involvement. The conclusion drawn by Common Cause and
others is simply that these special interest activities add up to a number of special interest biases which steer Congress away from what it
might otherwise do—and away from the public interest.

Special Interests Inside the Gates: The Proliferation of Internal Caucuses

The mushrooming growth of special interests outside the Congress
during this period and the steady march of structural fragmentation
inside the Congress led to the perhaps inevitable marriage of the two
in internal, informal ad hoc "issue caucuses."[14]

These groups have developed and proliferated, from the beginning in the early 1960s when DSG for liberal Democrats, the Wednesday Group for liberal Republicans, and Members of Congress for
Peace through Law for peace-oriented foreign policy activists in both
House and Senate had the field to themselves. Beginning in the early
1970s and becoming especially pronounced after 1975, it was the rare
"cause" around Capitol Hill which had not set up housekeeping as an
issue-oriented caucus.

It is difficult to gauge in general terms the policy impact of these
groups or the extent to which they serve simply as the means of
information-gathering and disseminating "think tanks" on Capitol
Hill, supplementing the jurisdictions of the formal committees and as
in-House lobbying operations.

It is difficult to find evidence that the caucuses have themselves become important policy tools; but there is evidence that they provide additional research and a means of mobilizing support or opposition to specific policies. What they also illustrate is the mushrooming special interest consciousness and orientation on Capitol Hill, i.e. the mind-set that virtually every public policy issue has a web of special interests which should be addressed in a "we" versus "they" manner. The caucuses also serve as public relations and, to some extent, policy and "position-taking" vehicles for members—especially for those whose committee assignments do not provide a forum for taking strong positions on these particular issues. The caucuses thus become further instruments of individualistic "crowd-pleasing," and to the extent that they are at all important simply add to the rambling character of the Congressional structure.

11:4 SPECIAL INTERESTS VERSUS THE COMMON GOOD: THE BIAS AGAINST UNIVERSALISM

Congress is characterized by an inability—and unwillingness—to subordinate its individual members' roles to the larger interest of collective institutional efficacy. There are few incentives to do so. And there are plenty of outsiders whose activities indirectly serve to capitalize on, and perpetuate, this individualism.

The reform experience highlights the tenacity of the very values which underlie this institutional incohesiveness. Individual member autonomy and responsiveness to constituents is connected to increased malleability in the face of multiple and competing special interests. These special interests urge members of Congress to deliver particularistic benefits—including everything from various forms of political plums to massive sums of Federal largesse, "tax expenditures" and other favors to individuals and groups. All these are at the expense of the formulation of universalistic, coherent national policy. It is important to realize that this occurs not so much because members consciously or conspiratorially[15] want this to be the case. Indeed, most members can wax eloquent about their lofty *positions* on issues, and grand schemes or "visions" of comprehensive policy—even if exigencies of legislative politics rarely provide the opportunity to act upon the same. Instead, the contemporary American political system can rarely achieve consensus on important public policies (or sometimes even relatively minor ones). In a polity characterized by pronounced sectoral cleavages, the legislative product (due to legislative compromise, inaction or ill-considered forays into new areas) is often innocuous or in other ways deficient. Often lost in the legislative shuffle are creative new ideas for large-scale policy changes or carefully crafted legislative initiatives. This is not to say that innovative ideas and proposals are lacking; to the contrary, the newly entrepreneurial tendencies of diffuse power and strong staffs encourage innovation, and many a Congressional career has been made by championing a new cause or legislative initiative. Yet the same diffuse and entrepreneurial system which spawns new ideas also often swallows them up—i.e., makes it very difficult for those ideas to reach fruition.

The legislative product is uneven—shaped by a bias toward incrementalism and a limited institutional attention span. In the area of comprehensive policy-making, Congress does not formulate coherent plans to reduce inflation or stimulate the economy, provide for national health care, manage energy, tax or employ or re-train, or provide for welfare—or make other broad national policies even in an age when government is at least a potential participant in most spheres of American life. True, we are a diverse society. But this diversity is manifested in a disjointed Congressional process (as part of a complex and multi-layered Federal structure of government) which has trouble producing consensus on the proposed solutions.

There are presently strong incentives for members of Congress to concentrate on satisfying constituents' and special interests' immediate needs, and not coincidentally, their own political careers. Hence members of Congress (and their abundant staff) immerse themselves in the work of helping out constituents and special interest clienteles with their narrow energy, health, welfare and other legislative problems. This is at the expense of time and resources spent on broad-based policies on these and other general problems. Moreover, considerable effort does go into committee, subcommittee and other case-based individual work. However, too often that work is unrelated to anything approaching broad-based legislative policy-making. The service of narrow interest groups, and of other near-term political demands, has contributed to the growth of a structure mired in its own disarray.

But this disarray is not neutral, it favors certain interests. This is the value to this subject of the political science approaches taken by Messrs. Schattschneider, Bachrach and Baratz, Friedrich, et al.: i.e., the structure and process of the decentralized Congress constitutes a collection of many "mobilizations of bias." Each subcommittee, committee, special interest caucus—even individual Senate or House offices—can be seen as a manifestation of certain values and incentives which influence what and who gets screened in, and out, of the process. And members, PACs, lobbyists and special interest groups seek to manipulate the structure and process to mobilize that bias in favored directions. There is nothing new about structure and process amounting to the mobilization of bias—or of interests shaping that bias. What is new in Congress is that there are now so many narrow and active interests working to achieve their goals within a political structure which has become as diffuse as the outside interests themselves. Also new is the systemic implication: a political process whose biases and overall agenda are heavily influenced by campaign contributions and lobbying—and whose institutional resources are fractionated and to a considerable extent, dissipated. It is a system in which substance can easily be overwhelmed by process. And the process often serves the interests of the most astute, effective, usually narrow—and well-heeled—special interests. An irony of reform is that Congress actually helped special interest groups dominate it by making them organize themselves in a way which is most effective for the special interests. The literature of social science—notably Mancur Olson in *The Logic of Collective Action*[16]—has pointed out that often the most efficacious interest groups are those narrowly based and small. These groups have the singularity of purpose and incentives paralleling those of individuals and thus have the advantage over larger, more multi-interest (and thus diffuse) interest groups. In dispersing power within Congress[17] and then empowering interest groups to establish narrowly based PACs and lobbying arms, Congress created the conditions for the optimum impact of special interests—and its own reliance on them. And all this has been at least partially an outgrowth of reform.

The Myth of PAC-Based "Freedom of Choice"

There is one large myth about the Special Interest Congress which needs to be debunked. This is the idea that with all the competing PACs and lobbies a member of Congress is "free to choose" the PAC or special interest group with which to ally.[18] This ostensibly justifies or legitimizes the system, presumably since it enables members of Congress to act as they would have absent the special interest influence. This is fallacious on several counts.

First, PACs and questionnaire-wielding advocacy groups have an impact at the very outset of each Congressional career—candidates must "choose" sides early on. Hence there is little opportunity to "reserve judgment" or wait to decide on the merits later; the politics of position-taking is so well-established that the freedom to refrain from choice among special interests is no longer an option.

Secondly, once having staked out positions roughly corresponding to certain group preferences, candidates and members of Congress are hardly "free" in terms of future voting patterns except in the most formal sense. In a more cynical formulation: "once bought you must stay bought." Rival groups will consider the member an adversary. And the supportive group will often hold their own Congressional allies to the most exacting standards of loyalty. This is especially so of the single-issue and ideological organizations, both left and right. It is only slightly less the case with industrial and commercial interests, although they are more accustomed to members of Congress having to be against them on occasion. The key for commercial interests is to keep the lines of communication open—and to obtain the best results possible in the political circumstances.

And of course the most glaring fallacy of the "freedom of choice" theory is that members are truly able to choose on the merits on a case-by-case basis. For many members this was never an option based on the political makeup of their districts, their partisan or ideological support, or the composition of their electoral base. But increasingly through ratings and organized efforts by interest groups to inform and mobilize their "grass roots"—Congress is depicted as being composed of a collection of "friends" or "foes" of particular interests. Once labeled a friend or foe it is difficult to become otherwise. And once so designated it is inaccurate to describe members as truly "free to choose." That is perhaps the most basic—and pernicious—bias of the Special Interest Congress, an increasingly evident bias against an important freedom—the freedom of individual members to decide each vote on its merits.

Notes

1. See Select Bibliography on Special Interests and Congress. For political science background see James Q. Wilson, *Political Organizations* (New York: Basic Books, 1973) and Jeffrey M. Berry, *Lobbying for the People, op. cit.* Also see Robert Salisbury, "An Exchange Theory of Interest Groups," *Midwest Journal of Political Science*, Vol. 13 (February 1969), pp. 1–32 and David B. Truman, *The Governmental Process, op. cit.* for differing theories as to the "events" and forces which bring together people around interests.
2. For evidence of ideological influences being stronger than traditionally thought, see Jerrold E. Schneider, *Ideological Coalitions in Congress* (Westport, Conn.: Greenwood Press, 1979). Other comprehensive analyses of Congressional voting behavior, both published in 1973 and hence based on evidence which does not include the period after the major reforms, are John W. Kingdon, *Congressmen's Voting Decisions* (New York: Harper & Row, 1973) and Aage R. Clausen, *How Congressmen Decide: A Policy Focus* (New York: St. Martin's Press, Inc., 1973).
3. See Brooks Jackson and Jeffrey H. Birnbaum, "Dairy Lobby Obtains U.S. Subsidies with Help from Urban Legislators," *Wall Street Journal*, November 18, 1983, pp. 33–34.
4. Arthur Maass, *Congress and the Common Good, op. cit.*
5. Donald K. Matthews, *U.S. Senators and Their World* (Chapel Hill: University of North Carolina Press, 1960).
6. Theodore Lowi, "American Business, Public Policy, Case Studies and Political Theory," *World Politics*, XVI (July 1964), reprinted in Randall B. Ripley, *Public Policies and Their Politics* (New York: W. W. Norton, 1966), pp. 27–40 and James Q. Wilson, *Political Organizations, op. cit.*, pp. 327–346.
7. Schick, ed., *Making Economic Policy in Congress, op. cit.*, is particularly helpful in focusing on Congressional policymaking in distributive, redistributive, regulatory, and international trade issues. See pp. 257–279.
8. This performance is analyzed in depth in Schick, ed., *Making Economic Policy, op. cit.*
9. James Q. Wilson, *Political Organizations, op. cit.*, p. 332.
10. *Ibid*, p. 332.
11. See Robert Pastor, "The Cry-and-Sigh Syndrome: Congress and Trade Policy," in Schick, *Making Economic Policy in Congress, op. cit.*, pp. 158–195.
12. A 1983 update on AMA contributions in Common Cause's study: *Take $2,000 and Call Me in the Morning* (Washington, D.C.: Common Cause, 1983) which tracks AMA PAC contributions and voting records of recip-

ients on issues of interest to doctors, including the exemption of doctors from FTC antitrust regulatory jurisdiction. See Select Bibliography for citations of these and other relevant Common Cause studies.

13. "How Money Talks in Congress," *Common Cause* Report, p. 14.

14. See Susan Webb Hammond, Arthur G. Stevens, Jr. and Daniel P. Mulhollan, "Congressional Caucuses: Legislators as Lobbyists," in Cigler and Loomis, *Interest Group Politics, op. cit.,* pp. 275–297 and their *Informal Congressional Groups in National Policy Making* (Washington, D.C.: American Enterprise Institute, 1984). For a case study of the functioning of one active House caucus, the Northeast-Midwest Congressional Advancement Coalition, see Robert Jay Dilger, *The Sunbelt/Snowbelt Controversy: The War Over Federal Funds* (New York: New York University Press, 1982).

15. See David Mayhew, *Congress: The Electoral Connection, op. cit.* for an analysis of how the dynamics of re-election shape Congressional behavior.

16. See Mancur Olson, *The Logic of Collective Action, op. cit.,* chs. 1–2.

17. See James Q. Wilson, *Political Organizations, op. cit.,* pp. 337–338 on the general tendencies: "special-interest associations are more powerful where formal political authority is weak or diffuse. . ." and "if the party is lacking in cohesion, lobbying will be directed at key individual legislators, especially committee and subcommittee chairmen."

18. This is a by now hackneyed argument of defenders of PACs. A perceptive early articulation of the point in political science terms was James Q. Wilson's observation in 1973, in *Political Organizations, op. cit.,* pp. 337–338, that: "If one organization enjoys greater access in a noncohesive party system, then all organizations will enjoy greater access, and the chances of any one prevailing over the others is accordingly reduced except in those issue areas where the benefits it seeks impose small, highly distributed, or low-visibility costs on others. Furthermore, in a political system which is fragmented, individual officeholders are freer to choose which organization, if any, to heed."

Twelve

Conclusion: The Congressional Future, Lessons for Future Reform Efforts and Recommendations

12:1 THE EXERCISE OF POLITICAL INFLUENCE AND THE PROBLEM OF MOBILIZING CONSENT

The quest for a system which simultaneously values both democracy and consent—requiring both active citizen participation in government and deference to, and support for, government decisions—poses the most perplexing problems for the future of Congress and the American political system. The problem of how to democratize political influence, during and especially *between* elections, is intrinsically a thorny one. But it becomes especially difficult when viewed in the context of the problem identified by Professor Samuel Beer, that of "mobilizing consent."[1] The quest for democracy calls for fashioning a political process which maximizes access to the system and opens up participation within it. The quest for consent calls for building the legitimacy of government and sustaining support for its programs. Each is a delicate process. Reconciling the two is especially problematic.

The process of reform described in the preceding chapters has made things worse in both areas, and the negative consequences are related to each other. The proliferation of access points has afforded new opportunities for special interest influence. The multiplication of corporate and other PACs has expanded the number of groups clustered around those access points. But this increase of access points and participation has failed to enhance or expand democracy. It has only made access more expensive, and accessibility more likely to be conditioned on campaign contributions, honoraria, or other behind-the-scenes "plums." Clear-eyed conceptions of the "public interest"—difficult in the best of circumstances—are all the more frequently lost in a welter of money-blurred, special interest machinations.

Even if this new system of special interest-oriented political influence has putatively "increased" the volume of quantitative "access," it has more importantly decreased the quality of political responsiveness and responsibility. "Checkbook" participation, characterized by only fleeting and tangential contact between Washington-based PAC staffs and their members, reveals a dubious case for any of the claims of an uplifting, mass-based democracy in the new politics of PACs.[2] On the contrary, even though the most recent two victors in presidential campaigns, Reagan and Carter, have both run "against Washington"—the insulated power center of information and political access still lies securely in Washington. In fact, despite the rhetoric of devolution of power in the Federal system,[3] and the reality of decentralization among the Washington power centers, Washington itself retains significant power, arguably even more insulated and distant than in the past.

Since Washington is where the special interest infrastructure plies its trade, it is there that the interests contribute to a growing "consensus gap" between Washington and the rest of the country. This gap is between the government, which seeks to devise and implement policies, and the people who must first understand, then—one hopes—support and comply with these policies or proposals. This is what Samuel Beer refers to as "the problem of mobilizing consent."

In 1966 Beer wrote an article on the British Parliament and what he perceived to be both an increasingly important governmental function and a possible new role for Parliament, a "legislative" institution more in name than in fact, subject to the domination of strong governments drawn from its majority party's ranks, and presumably looking for a new *raison d'être*. This function, which Beer noted was inspired by a speech by Representative John Brademas (D.-Indiana), was to "mobilize consent" for government policies. After a review of the difficult British economic problems of the 1960s, Beer observed:

> The economic problems of which I have spoken are essentially political problems. I do not deny that there is a good deal more that economists would like to know about the causes of inflation and the condi-

tions of economic growth. At the same time, modern economic analysis does give Governments far greater understanding of these matters than was possessed by Governments and their advisers in the 1920s and 1930s. The problem is, therefore, not so much to devise economic programs which, if they were carried out, would meet the problems. It is, rather, to win such understanding and acceptance of Government programs among the public, as individuals and as members of producers' and consumers' groups, that they will adjust their own behavior to the requirements of these programs. The central problem, in short, is to win consent—and winning consent is a political problem and a political process.[4]

What Beer identifies is the growing complexity of both modern problems and their governmental solutions and argues that the job of *building acceptance for government policy*, i.e., mobilizing consent for government programs, is a vital job that needs to be performed. "A Government today is strong for any purpose—economic, social, or military—only so far as it can mobilize consent among its citizens."[5]

This is perhaps the critical problem faced by the contemporary Congress.[6] As prime intermediaries between the government and the governed, members of Congress have immense potential as explainers, facilitators and interpreters of government. They do, and ought to, take on the role of cajolers of the executive branch when necessary, but they ought also to be the ones who defend and articulate government policies. In short, they ought to be prime movers, in normal circumstances, to mobilize consent. Yet, if there has been one role which has seldom been taken on by members of Congress since Beer identified it in 1966, it has been this one. On taxes, welfare reform, energy policy, immigration law reform, criminal code revision, defense and major foreign policy issues—to name but a few—Congress members have often assumed the role of critics of the administration or at least purveyors of alternative policies. If there is an ultimate built-in bias of the new entrepreneurial and decentralized system, it is that of the cult of Congress member as "mobilizer of *dis*sent."

The United States and particularly its Congress have never been noted for an ability to adopt and win consensus for comprehensive national policy. Something ingrained in our Constitution and society seems to inveigh against it. Hence, we are the only major industrial country without a national energy policy, national health insurance, a coherent federal welfare system, and other policies in broad issue areas. We have been chronically incapable of revising our Federal Criminal Code, rewriting the Communications Act, modernizing immigration law and facing up to the constraints of our entitlement burdens. In other spheres, such as pension reform, airline deregulation and some well-intentioned regulatory schemes, we move too hastily: Congress has passed sweeping legislation which emerges in a form quickly criticized as flawed—and targeted for early revision.[7] Our collective inability to marshal consent—especially recently—owes in large part to our fractious and fragmented institutional structures. And during the period under study the forces of the mobilization of *dis*sent have been greatly strengthened, at the expense of the system's capacity to mobilize *con*sent, which has never been great in the best of circumstances.

The subcommittee chairman, the individual member, the concerned Congressional staffer, when moved to do so by a constituency or other interest, can become a spearhead of campaigns against government policies.[8] In many instances, these efforts involve limited institutional "guerrilla" activities designed to pressure bureaucrats or at least to show members of Congress to be sympathetic with some group or constituency adversely affected by a government action. But this tendency becomes a more serious problem when it concerns broad national policy initiatives. This is an instance where the mobilization of dissent can become instrumental in the *immobilization* of policymaking.

The Carter Administration was unable to mobilize consent for a number of its initiatives: the Carter National Energy policy, the gas tax, welfare reform, hospital cost containment, and a host of smaller issues. This is not to say that all of these proposals were well-advised or that the political management of these matters was adept. Congress has sharpened its skills in defeating executive initiatives; and while sometimes this is to the good, it is unhealthy for the system when the politics of dissent and guerrilla-warfare becomes *the norm*. The Reagan Administration won early success on its major tax and budget bills in 1981, but much of that early success owed to the fact that the Reagan tax and budget packages catered *both* to the many corporate special interests and a broad-based public desire for a tax cut. This broad support managed, for awhile, to outweigh the labor and "public interest" advocates who objected to cuts for social services. But even as President Reagan was able to "communicate" his way to public and Congressional consent on some early major policies, by 1982 the forces of dissent began to nibble away quickly thereafter. On tax policy, barely a year after his stirring victory on tax cuts, President Reagan was forced to make a U-turn, acknowledge the huge federal deficit, and reluctantly support TEFRA, a tax bill notable for its large tax increases.[9] The Reagan Presidency proved susceptible to the piecemeal attacks of dissenters in Congress—including defectors in his own party (e.g., the "Gypsy Moths" in the House and the few remaining liberal Republicans in the Senate who defected on budget and some defense and foreign policy issues). And perhaps the ultimate example of a special interest-tinged process of mobilizing *dissent* is the successful effort of the American Bankers' Association and allies to persuade the Congress to reverse its previously adopted policy and repeal the plan for withholding of taxes on dividends and interest during the first session of the 98th Congress.[10]

In what was perhaps the most sustained "grassroots" national special interest lobbying campaign in history, the national bankers' PAC leaders mobilized bank customers, consumer groups and the citizenry into thinking that the government was making a new "raid" on their bank accounts—rather than simply trying to prevent cheating on tax returns. In the face of the blizzard of mail from both consumers and bankers, a large majority of members of both Houses relented. Life was made particularly unpleasant for members who stood firm against repeal.

These problems of democracy, consent and legitimacy loom large in questions about the future of Congressional reform, and of Congress. The remainder of the book considers the portents for reform of Congress and the American political system; in the context of these two critical political values: democracy and consent. It further considers the difficulty of institutional and systemic leadership when democracy becomes democracy for certain organized interests and consent becomes a rare event reserved only for uncontroversial and typically inconsequential matters.

12:2 REFORM AND
THE FUTURE OF CONGRESS

Congress has never lacked for critics, and it is in the nature of American democratic politics that it is unlikely to do so. At the time of writing, there are critics of Congress residing everywhere from the White House to the local street corner, from foreign capitals to the Capitol lobby and from editorial rooms to the corporate board rooms. Most of these criticisms can be traced to something Congress either did or did not do which affects the interests—economic or otherwise—of the particular critic. These criticisms themselves should not be particularly worrisome because they are inherent in politics. The pronouncement made in a best selling book about the American future that Congress has become "irrelevant" in the face of a new localism in American politics[11] should also not be too troubling to Congress. In short, while innovations on the state and local level are notable developments in recent American politics, the continuing relevance of Congress and the Federal government can be demonstrated easily—usually as quickly as one can say the word "preemption,"—Federal takeover of an entire sphere of authority and policy.

Yet, the criticism that Congress has grown hopelessly fragmented and that special interest groups' influence has increased out of control should be more worrisome—although it too has its precedents in the cyclical pattern of American politics:[12] scandal followed by disclosure, followed by indignation—followed by reform, boredom and politics-as-usual.

It is clear that Congress has indeed grown too dependent on, and inextricably linked to, special interest groups. But it is important to note that Congress got to this state of affairs *by reforming itself,* with ostensibly good intentions. And yet there is a paucity of clear-eyed proposals for changing direction.

If Congress continues on its present path, what will it look like and what are the implications for American government?

Some Possible Scenarios

The Future of Congressional Structure

The recent trend has been toward fragmentation of power; there is little political interest in reining in the new subcommittee-based power centers. While there has been realization of some of the negative consequences for coherent policy and overall Congressional performance there has been little—other than the typical lamentations about the lack of leadership—to indicate any serious new push to consolidate power in Congress or to reclaim from subcommittee chairmen and individual members their recently won rights and perquisites. Nor is there any suggestion from the chairmen and rank and file members that they would be willing to give up any of these rights and perquisites.

The future, then, left to natural evolution would appear to be an increasingly stable regime of fragmented Congressional decision-making—along with both its positive attributes of great autonomy and flexibility for middle-level and rank and file members and its negative implications of institutional inefficacy and policy incoherence.

The Future of Campaign Finance

The future of campaign finance appears less certain than that of Congressional structure. While stability (albeit incoherent and fragmented stability) would appear to be in store for Congressional structure, campaign finance is rapidly changing, uncertain, perhaps even out of control. The costs of campaigns increase at geometric rates; the already huge advantage of the Republican party over the Democratic party in fundraising ability seems likely to widen; and the growing link between special interest group preferences and Congressional votes raises the spectre of either a major scandal or pent-up public disapproval at the cumulative effects of the process. In short, there is a strong possibility of a critical event triggering change. But as often occurs in American politics there is greater likelihood that the system will muddle along with disjointed, incremental adjustments. This sort of change is typically evolutionary, often not very thoughtfully formulated, and not necessarily positive. A few possible trends are discernible. One clear goal of one set of proposals for reform is to place a limit on PAC contributions—to allow candidates to accept only a certain amount (e.g. $90,000) of PAC contributions. Another variant is to restrict contributions to groups and individuals from the district or state of the candidate (or to provide a tax credit only for such home-base contributions). Another direction of possible campaign finance reform—also indirectly aiming to reduce the power of PACs—is to increase the limit on individual contributions from $1000 per election to as much as $5000 per election. This would place individual contributors on the same level as PACs. It would be a retreat from the original rationale behind FECA's creation of business, trade association and ideological PACs, i.e. to decrease the influence of wealthy individuals. By placing individuals on the same plane as PACs it would simultaneously decrease the importance of PACs and increase the relative power of wealthy individuals. There is also the move for full-scale public financing of Congressional elections, an idea which has never won the full-hearted support of Congressional incumbents and which continues to face rocky prospects.

The best guess as to likely scenarios in the area of campaign finance would appear to be continuing primacy of incumbents (especially in the House), increasingly good prospects for well-financed Republican candidates for Congress and especially challengers to Democratic senators and for open seats, and the rapidly escalating cost of campaigns.

Toward PACless Politics?

There are strong rumblings but only scant tangible movements toward abolishing PACs. PAC money became an embarrassment in 1984 and the Democratic presidential candidates foreswore it. Limitation of PACs found its way into the Democratic platform, and similar sentiments have been expressed by several Congressional and Senate candidates. Hints and moves in that direction bear scrutiny because they raise intriguing issues both as to the functioning of the existing system and the best direction for reform.

One verity of the present system is that only certain kinds of candidates have access to any significant amounts of PAC money. Incumbents and Republican challengers are generally the best situated, but generally only the most likely winners, and usually only after the primaries, have the potential to collect substantial PAC backing. This tendency has spurred a logical reaction on the part of candidates lacking any real potential for PAC funds—i.e. to try to make a virtue out of their disadvantage. Without disparaging the sincerity of anti-PAC candidates, it makes perfect sense for candidates running against candidates with significant PAC backing to try to make an issue of the "special interest influence" in the race. There is little public opinion data to suggest that this is a cutting issue.[13] There is evidence to suggest that opinion leaders (such as editorial writers and Common Cause members and the like) care about the issue, but the public remains either uninformed, confused or not terribly interested. Moreover, to the extent that PACs have been seeking to convince their grassroots members that PAC giving is the best way to influence public affairs in a positive manner, attempts by anti-PAC candidates to characterize PAC contributions as "sleazy" have had a negative and confusing effect. One thing is certain: such anti-PAC campaigns cause resentment on the part of the PACs themselves. The candidate renouncing PACs experiences misunderstanding at best, even among groups that remain sympathetic to his or her candidacy. In addition, there is an ironic tendency of the nascent anti-PAC movement: despite the fact that many opponents of PACs are progressive, the repudiation of PACs by candidates is most likely to work to the disadvantage of progressive candidates. This is so because the PACs most likely to be deprived of influence in races where PAC contributions are absent are labor PACs. Labor union members are typically small contributors who are long used to giving to campaigns through their PACs. They are also very unlikely, in contrast to business, trade association and ideological PAC members, to have their money find its way into campaigns through individual contributions.

The impact of PACless politics, then, is difficult to gauge based on only the few, very isolated experiences thus far.[14] However, some basic lessons are already obvious. One is that it is intrinsically unhealthy to have a system in which one perfectly legal aspect of the system can be used as a stick to beat on the candidate who accepts that part of the system—PAC contributions. Another is that condoning selective observation of the law holds out the spectre of each contest becoming one in which the candidates at the outset, based on perceptions of their own advantage, jockey for position as to what the rules will be for that particular race. If this tendency spreads, along with the message that PACs are all inherently corrupt, the medium and long-term implications for the system will become increasingly cloudy. If nothing else, it is unfair to candidates, and probably unfair to PACs, to place each candidate and PAC in perpetual uncertainty as to what the rules of the game will be for each contest. Over the longer term, if there is to be reform, change or even abolition of PACs, so be it—but it makes little sense to have a system which allows selective adherence and which itself becomes a target of attack.

The outbreak of anti-PAC sentiment may be an experiment that fails, or a passing fad. To be sure, it creates *ipso facto* a cash crunch for candidates seeking to finance PACless campaigns. The trend is certainly discounted by incumbent-oriented national political observers and experts. But it may be more than a blip on the political seismograph. And of course much will depend on how skillfully Common Cause, other anti-PAC groups and opinion leaders orchestrate the issue—along with exogenous factors—in determining whether the public will countenance the continuation of the PAC-based system.

The Future of Lobbying

Lobbying of Congress, PAC-based and otherwise, will continue to be a desirable or even necessary, sideline activity of many American businesses, interest groups, ideological, religious and other organizations. With the great technological breakthroughs in information dissemination, lobbyists will be more dependent on demonstrating their ability to mobilize grassroots support and large amounts of campaign contributions than traditional abilities to control the flow of information and access to Congressional decision-makers. Moreover, while traditional skills of framing and presenting issues, agenda-setting and control and other Washington-based activities will continue to be important, increasingly grassroots-based "coalition building" and media-oriented public relations "issues management" will be essential adjuncts to effective Washington representation. The connection between PAC contributions and effective lobbying will, absent path-breaking reform, continue to be close.

The Future of Congressional Performance

The future of Congress's performance is likely to continue to be characteristically spotty—and its public approval low. The Congress tends to be unpopular as an institution except when a popular, activist President is successfully passing legislation through it. The Congress of the foreseeable future would appear to promise more of the same—and more of the tendency Richard Fenno has pointed out: people admiring their own representative in Congress but mistrusting Congress. There will most likely also continue to be demands for stronger leadership—as against what James MacGregor Burns calls the "King of the Rock" syndrome by which each politician pursuing self-aggrandizement militates against the exercise of effective institutional or systemic leadership.[15]

Some may find this characterization overly pessimistic. To be sure, the Congress and the American political system certainly have significant strengths. For all their faults they serve as cornerstones of a government and society which continues to conduct a remarkable and grand national experiment in political democracy and freedom. There are some defenders of the system who contend that the decentralized structure and maze of special interests accurately—and admirably—capture a peculiar American imperviousness to centralized power. Another optimistic view of the present system is to see the devolution of power in Congress as part of the larger move toward participatory democracy in the United States and the Western democracies generally. But even conceding that a degree of decentralization is a good thing, the view here is that the present system is *too much* of a good thing.

The effectiveness of American democracy and the efficacy of the national legislature are intertwined. While it is true that special interests have historically wielded power in American politics, the present situation poses unprecedented problems. An elaborate system of PAC-dominated campaign finance has been grafted onto the newly, and excessively, diffuse structure. There is a new level of sophistication on the part of participants both in Congress and representing the special interests which makes the process at once more and less accessible. It is more accessible in that increasing numbers of interests have formed PACs, hired consultants and lawyers, and learned to "play." It is less accessible in the sense that there are new barriers to entry to all either unwilling or unable to play the above-mentioned game.

The prognosis (and warning) is this: the present system is structurally, procedurally, and ethically coming apart. If American government refuses to face up to its problems of process, our problems of policy will become more and more pronounced. If the structure and process are allowed to drift—further fragmentation of process and geometric rise of PACs and their contributions—the system will continue to move in either of two directions: special interest mastery or special interest-spurred stalemate and drift. The link between special interest campaign contributions and Congressional decisions will become tighter. The integrity of representative government will be further compromised.

The number of people participating with any sense of commitment and conviction will continue to decline. The quality of candidates who come forward may remain quite high in terms of education, ability and certainly their impressiveness as individual political entrepreneurs. But their room for maneuver will grow ever more circumscribed. The politics of special interest position-taking and the need to cater to the narrow needs of increasingly demanding groups will further fractionate the process. The "big picture" of American and world policies will continue to be lost in the competition of small-minded interests. This all creates the ultimate irony: that in the face of increasing sophistication in technology, information, education and insight susceptible to problem-solving, the American political system will grow decreasingly capable of using all this in any coherent way. And the gap between the potential and the performance of American government will widen.

What is needed is an expanded, vigorous debate and a new push for reform. But this reform movement should not be just whatever happens to be labeled "reform" as a matter of political convenience, but a set of thoughtfully formulated proposals which take into account the lessons of the previous reform experience. Some mistakes no doubt will be made; and not all the consequences can be foreseen. Nonetheless, the only corrective to the Special Interest Congress lies in rethinking and redirecting Congress in ways which enable it to deal more coherently and effectively with the job of making national policy.

Lessons for Future Reform Efforts

There is little doubt that the "reformed" system itself is in need of reform. The question is how to profit from the past experience in ways which are at once realistic and bold—politically practical yet designed to address the most serious defects. This chapter seeks to analyze past reform efforts in terms of their original goals, to learn their lessons both procedurally and substantively, and to propose correctives. This consideration leads to a review of possible reform proposals and is followed by a package of suggested proposals. The proposals considered are divided into "piecemeal" reform approaches, which attempt to take into account the constraints of contemporary politics and to make small-scale adjustments and improvements, and "wholesale" reform, which aims at more fundamental change.

Five different goals of recent Congressional reform have been previously identified. All were admirable, although not necessarily consistent. An assessment of each original goal in the context of the experience will inform the formulation of appropriate goals of a new reform effort.

• Congressional Reassertion Against the President

This phase of reform has engendered some constructive new Congressional procedures and institutions allowing Congress to compete more effectively with the presidency. But there has also been a tendency for special interests to convince their allies in Congress to use certain of the instruments of legislative scrutiny of the executive for the special interests' purposes. It is not yet clear what will be the long-term political fallout of the *Chada* opinion striking down for all intents the legislative veto. An ostensible "victory" for presidential power (and defeat of Congressional "meddling"), the ramifications could turn out to be much less clear. Vigilant and savvy special interests, and wily and effective members of Congress, may simply choose not to delegate as much power to the executive, and when they do, they may do so with much greater specificity. From the standpoint of special interests, the loss of the legislative veto simply constitutes a loss of one device and creates a vacuum out of which may emerge some new opportunities.[16] This vacuum simply calls for new creativity and adaptability, traits special interest groups have evidenced in abundance in the past.

In the area of Congressional-Presidential relations, the future of reform remains uncertain. Congress's reassertion has had positive and negative consequences. While Congress has been more active and arguably "effective" against the Presidency—especially so on budget policy and sometimes through use of the oversight function—this has not always had positive consequences for the overall functioning of the political system. What needs to be assessed is exactly which functions Congress performs in a way which is constructive for the overall system and which functions bring out Congress's more meddlesome and less constructive tendencies. With some obvious exceptions, Congress's new participation in the budget process, and much of its exercise of oversight, is a positive development which ought to be further developed—in quest of greater Congressional budgetary discipline and better conformity of executive action to Congressional intent. Congress's entrepreneurial members and staff have also contributed to policy innovation and "issue development" in their subcommittees and caucuses. But at the risk of some oversimplification, the involvement of Congress in the details of bureaucratic rule-making and administrative policy decisions as contemplated by the more zealous proponents of the legislative veto was not a shining example of Congress at its most constructive. And much of Congress's assertiveness on the details of foreign policy has not been generally positive—although obviously important on broad foreign policies such as Central America and Middle East policy, the Congress's constitutionally prescribed war powers and other required roles such as the Senate's treaty-approval, advice and consent on nominees and the difficult area of intelligence operations.[17]

• *Congressional "Leadership" and "Streamline" versus "Democracy"*

There are few goals more talked about and less practiced in American government than strengthening the Congressional leadership. Even passage of reforms ostensibly designed to enhance leadership control do not necessarily lead to the desired result. The proper balance between individual members' autonomy and the leadership's authority must be re-examined. The history of the Congress's internal allocation of power has been cyclical, and is presently at a point where individual members are often impervious to leadership requests for support. We live not in an age of "King Caucus" but of "King Congressman." This longstanding dilemma in its contemporary context should be resolved in favor of the leadership. But this most likely will not be accomplished by yet another attempt at consolidative internal reform. An effective solution must take into account internal power dynamics and incentives in today's complex, special interest-dominated politics; it must include external political factors and forces as well. Any solution must deal with the growing problem of money influencing politics, but it must do more than just deal with money: it must also involve some rationalization of structure. Comprehensive correctives to Congress's contemporary deficiencies necessarily involve changes in the role and function of special interests. And some of the most constructive changes involve the portion of the political system which was the original focus of the reform effort, i.e., the parties.

• Party Responsibility and Policy Efficacy

The goal of greater coherence of party remains substantially unfulfilled; it continues to elude yet another generation of Party reformers. While new mechanisms for party influence are in place—the Democratic Caucus, the Democratic Steering and Policy Committee and their Republican counterparts (newly sophisticated party campaign committees which, at least in the case of the Republicans, have built up huge coffers)—the goal of party responsibility remains a political science pipe dream. Many would argue that it should remain so in a society as disparate as that of the United States. However, the fact remains that Congressional parties have established the structural *potential* for party-based potency, but have accomplished little in practice. American parties remain noticeably lacking in self-discipline and are not taken seriously as instruments of policy-making. Thus the one segment of the political system which has the potential to concern itself with formulation of national, "universalistic" policies remains hobbled on the side-lines of American government. This seems increasingly the case as PACs, lobbies, television and direct mail fund-raising grow increasingly important while the traditional techniques of campaigning are replaced by the new technology and its expert practitioners.[18] To the extent that one of the parties, the Republicans, have mastered these new techniques they have improved their electoral fortunes and ability to shape policy. But better mechanisms are needed for both Congressional parties to formulate overall, nationally-oriented party policies, especially better ways to enable parties to translate policy positions into legislative reality and to mobilize electoral coalitions. This is not an argument in favor of a new party hegemony (of which we are in no jeopardy); rather it is a plea for more programmatic and efficacious Congressional parties to serve as effective intermediaries between special interests and individual members of Congress.

• *"Sunshine"*

The Sunshine reforms have opened up the process, with some benefits and some negative consequences. The intrinsic and aesthetic desirability of public disclosure and access clearly outweigh the side-effect that Sunshine also affords new accessibility to special interests. Sunshine goals, then, were largely accomplished and ought not to be undone. It would, however, be desirable to broaden the *use* of the Sunshine reforms to make the Congressional process more accessible and understandable to the general public. This can be accomplished by added exposure through televising of Floor, committee and sub-committee proceedings and computer-based dissemination of detailed information on legislative developments. There is also a need for better methods of tracking and disclosing the ways that public access is used—and abused— by special interest groups and lobbyists.

The Dubious Prognosis for "Digging up the Roots"

The prognosis for "digging up" the entrenched roots of the Special Interest Congress is not encouraging. The results of reform, the values reflected by them and the effects of Congress's instinctual individualism are deeply imbedded. The Congressional incentive system is strongly tipped toward individual autonomy. Members thrive in such a system. It effectively serves electoral and constituency service needs. The decentralized internal structure is well-suited to the demands and requirements of the outside interests.

In such circumstances it might seem appropriate to recommend new reform initiatives targeted on the committee system: e.g., a new Bolling-style effort, mandatory rotation of committee chairmanships, a limitation on the number of terms a member could serve, a bold rationalization of committee jurisdictions along lines of executive departments, consolidation of the authorizing and appropriating functions in subject matter committees, strict limits on the number of subcommittees, bicameral joint committees[19] or other devices aimed at reversing the individualistic and dispersive tendencies of the structure. One or more of these *may well* be appropriate. But as the reform experience described here has indicated, it is precisely these sorts of reforms directly challenging the individualistic values which have provoked the most tenacious institutional resistance. These reform proposals tend to be altered, "reshaped," defeated, or, if passed— blithely ignored. In short, it is difficult to conclude, in light of the previous experience, that a broad new push for consolidative structural reform holds promise. What seems a more promising prospect for reform is a "package" of targeted reforms which recognizes the considerable existing structural and behavioral constraints, and is sensitive to prevailing values and incentives. The goal is to shift institutional values and practices by means of a series of complementary reforms of both internal structures and external processes and relationships. This can be done effectively only if the challenge to the ingrained values of the committee and subcommittee-dominated structure is done in a politically sensitive way. And this must recognize the political incentives inherent in the proposed reforms. The package must build on the lessons of previous reform efforts. A basic lesson is that, like any good political campaign, a reform effort needs a coherent set of assumptions, methods, and goals—and a workable strategy. The specific components include the following:

- Clearly define the problems and identify the objectives—structural, procedural, political, and understand the values and assumptions underlying the objectives.
- Calculate the trade-off in any reform effort between the "intrinsic process" and substantive policy implications.
- Consider the political dynamics of internal and external support and opposition.
- Decide on a clear-cut "destination" of the reform efforts (i.e., the power structure of the reformed institution); also consider possible unintended consequences, but do not let the fear of these consequences serve as an excuse for inaction.
- Consider whether a "piecemeal" or "wholesale" reform effort will lead to the destination.
- Adopt an overall "package" and strategy, and stick to it.
- Be prepared to compromise, but not on points that lead to the wrong destination. (It might be better to have no reform than to have counter-productive reform.)

Some Contemporary Proposals and the Problem With "Piecemeal" Reform

In recent years, there has been scant interest in, and slim prospects for, internal structural reform.[20] To the extent that there has been interest in any reform, most of the attention has been focused on the area of most glaring abuse, campaign finance reform. Recent proposals suffer from many of the inherent pitfalls of piecemeal reform, but they present some hope, and more significantly, they provide a reference point from which to develop ideas for more comprehensive reform. The overall goal is to formulate a package which will have a positive impact on the overall structure and performance of Congress—not just a part of it. By beginning with campaign finance reform we can work backward to the requisites of structural reform and the ingredients of comprehensive reform.

Recent Proposals for Campaign Finance Reform

The leading campaign finance reform proposal in recent years has been the Obey-Leach (in earlier form, Obey-Railsback) public financing bill. In a recent version in the 98th Congress it provided for limitation of the amount of contributions House candidates could accept from PACs, established partial public financing of general elections based on matching grants and required that free radio and television time be provided to candidates who have been "targeted" by independent expenditure PACs.[21] The bill's sponsors in the Autumn of 1983 concluded that the public financing component remained an obstacle to House passage.[22] (Even though the bill would not apply to Senate races, the prospects of passage in a Republican Senate notably hostile to any form of public financing remained bleak.) Based on this perception of the unpopularity of public financing, the originators of the bill proposed a revision which removes the provision for direct public financing and replaces it with an indirect public expenditure in the form of a 100 per cent tax credit up to $100 for contributors who are residents of the same state as the recipient candidate. The bill establishes a strict limit of $90,000 for PAC contributions (to a single candidate) and would impose an overall spending limit on candidates who accept the 100 per cent tax credit-subsidized funds: candidates would have to agree not to spend more than $240,000 in the campaign and not to contribute personally more than $20,000 to their own campaigns.[23]

This is an intriguing (and laudable) attempt at "piecemeal" campaign finance reform. In recognizing the opposition of powerful outside groups and many members to "raiding the treasury" for public financing, this bill employs the tax credit approach, as opposed to direct public financing. Like the Conable-McHugh "Political Tax Credit Reform Act" bill,[24] the proposal would use the device of a tax expenditure as a "back door" public subsidy of campaigns. The Conable-McHugh bill would provide a 100 per cent tax credit for contributions to candidates and PACs of up to $50 for an individual and $100 on a joint return for contributions to House and Senate candidates from the contributor's own state. A 50 per cent credit would be allowed for contributions to political parties. It would abolish the 50 per cent tax credit on contributions up to $100 and $200 on a joint return for non-Congressional races—and otherwise seek to ensure that the political tax credit will not result in a loss of revenue to the Federal treasury (by abolishing the credit for non-Federal election contributions).

Current battles in Congress have pitted defenders of the present system (and the ever-increasing power of PACs) against reformers who endorse some combination of public financing of Congressional elections and a limitation on the percentage of campaign funds candidates can accept from PACs. Passage of the original Obey-Leach bill for partial public financing or something like it (including the increased tax credit approach) would be an immense improvement over the *status quo*. This would place a cap on PAC contributions and provide a component of public financing (based on public funds matching private contributions); it would also guarantee media response time for candidates attacked by "independent expenditure" PACs. Such a plan would certainly improve on the present system.

However, it must be recognized that these approaches and their variations also have serious flaws. They deal *only* with campaign finance, seeking to trim back PAC power through limits on acceptance of PAC contributions and partial public financing. And, it also must be said that passage appears unlikely in the circumstances of the Congress as presently constituted. There remains substantial opposition to this type of reform in both parties (although more so from Republicans). On campaign finance reform the most significant dividing line is not so much between the parties but between incumbents and challengers. And while any imposition of limits on overall expenditures or amount of contributions would probably aid incumbents (and thus they might be expected to support them) many incumbents who typically have strong fundraising capabilities mistrust any limits which might constrain their ability to withstand serious challenge. Moreover, incumbents tend to be extremely wary of public financing since it would "automatically" bankroll challengers, who in the present system are chronically poorly funded. While the revised Obey-Leach bill *might* muster a majority in a contemporary Democratic House, a continuingly Republican-controlled Senate would probably remain inalterably opposed to any public financing scheme and any limitation on PAC contributions. And while the prospects of passage would be better in a Democratic-controlled Senate, incumbents of both parties have evidenced qualms about a major break from the status quo. Moreover, while Democrats, especially those in key committee positions in the House and others in "need" such as funds-starved freshmen, receive their share of PAC contributions, the explosion of corporate PACs has been a particular boon to the fortunes of the Republican party. Barring some major scandal involving PACs and campaign finance or some other inspiration for a public outcry for change, the outlook for this sort of campaign finance reform is dim. In any event, as long as Republicans have a "veto" on PAC limitations and public financing in the Senate, the Obey-Leach approach faces virtually certain defeat. The Republicans are not and ought not to be expected to vote against their party self-interest in a system which has helped facilitate their recent rejuvenation—and in the case of the Senate, their accession to power. Moreover, in fairness to the Republicans, the amendment omitting direct public financing by the backers of the original Obey-Leach bill can be seen as a play for Democratic party advantage—i.e. to force a vote which would have revealed reform supporters to be mainly Democrats and cast Republicans as the defenders of PACs prior to the 1984 election.

The Need for Comprehensive Reform

Yet even the original Obey-Leach public financing approach suffers from its limited focus: it seeks to redress *symptoms* of the present, essentially inequitable system, rather than addressing the dysfunctional aspects of the Congressional structure and campaign finance law which spawned the PACs in the first place. Even if Democrats were to win back the Senate and a Democratic Congress were to pass PAC limitation and public financing, this would do little to alter the sources (internal and external) of continuing Congressional incohesion and disarray. These sources include the excessively fragmented power structure, and the lack of workable instruments of party leadership and discipline. The manifestations of this system are the absence and/or incoherence of program, a pronounced susceptibility of Congress's various power centers to outside influence and a notable disinclination toward mobilizing consent. In short, a "piecemeal" approach centered on campaign finance reform would only be a small step to arrest the growth of special interest influence and Congressional ineffectiveness. In practice, the matching grant aspect of public finance in the original version and the $90,000 limit of PAC contributions would encourage PACs to "buy in" early—i.e., contribute early enough in the campaign to help a candidate qualify for public financing. The $90,000 limit on PAC contributions would similarly spur PACs to "sign on" early enough in the election cycle to ensure that their contribution became part of the $90,000. The provision of an opportunity for candidates to respond to independent expenditure PACs or candidates who exceed the spending limit is positive, but it essentially reacts to, and tinkers with, the present process rather than create a better one.

The Frenzel-Laxalt bill,[25] another proposed "reform," does not even seek to correct a defect in the process; it seeks instead, to enhance the role of parties by among other provisions, removing the limit on coordinated expenditures by party committees. The sponsors, both prominent Republican party leaders, articulate the need for stronger parties; their intention appears to be to achieve greater Republican party advantage in the name of enhanced party responsibility. In removing the cap on coordinated expenditures, this bill would remove all limits on the amount that the party campaign committees could contribute to their candidates. This bill offered by Frenzel, a Minnesota Republican and defender of PACs, grows from the fact that the Republicans have had no trouble building huge campaign chests on PAC contributions, but they have been frustrated by limits placed on the amount parties can give in each state and district.[26] The Democratic campaign committees, on the other hand, have had trouble mustering enough money to provide the maximum amounts to their candidates. The Frenzel-Laxalt bill would complete the evisceration of limits on expenditures by party committees; it would do so by opening up television and radio advertising using the candidates' names to party funding. As it stands, there are already so many loopholes through which party committees can spend money on behalf of candidates (that is non-allocable to the limit to a particular candidate), the one limit with any teeth is on media expenditure. Consequently, removing all limits really has the effect of removing only the media expenditure limit. The Frenzel-Laxalt bill would enhance the substantial advantage the Republicans already enjoy in attracting small donor and corporate PAC money. A goal of reform more worthy than partisan advantage would be to advance the cause of systemic fairness. While it will not be possible to remove money as a major factor in politics, inequities based on campaign money should not be allowed to result in further systematic distortion of the currents of public opinion.

These proposals for "piecemeal" campaign finance reform, then, emerge as either somewhat flawed but sensible proposals which have little chance of passage or seriously flawed proposals which could pass but might only exacerbate existing inequities. When viewed in this light, it seems less fanciful—and more important—to consider ambitious proposals which seek to deal more comprehensively with this growing national problem. It is appropriate, then, to consider fundamental, "wholesale" reform.

12:3 ASSUMPTIONS, GOALS AND A PACKAGE OF "WHOLESALE" REFORM

A comprehensive "package" can be strategically planned, adopted and implemented, although the impediments are by now well understood. The prime objectives, based on the conclusions set forth in this study and particularly what the last reform movement did *not* accomplish, are as follows:

1. To establish a more rational process of evaluating and planning reform.
2. To reduce Congress's direct linkages to special interests in the form of PACs and individuals; i.e., strengthen Congress's ability to make decisions on the basis of the merits of issues.
3. To strengthen the Congressional leadership, enhance Congress's ability to pass legislation which deals comprehensively with large national issues, and endow Congress with the capacity to adopt more coherent and effective policies; this requires a more rational, yet politically sensitive structure.
4. To provide Congress with new political incentives to seek to mobilize consent for, rather than dissent from, governmental proposals and policies.

Not everyone will agree that these are realistic—or even desirable—goals. While conceding that the chances of imminent success are slim, this is an attempt to outline what *ought to be* the goals of reform and to provide the means to achieve them. That is, if we were to fashion an "ideal" or model comprehensive package of reform, what would it look like?

Selected Approaches to "Wholesale Reform"

1. REFORM IMPACT STATEMENTS

The first suggestion is procedural. The Congressional reform experience has evidenced a pronounced tendency toward unintended consequences. Some individual reforms wrought changes which were not foreseen or desired; and the collective impact of reform had consequences different from what many reformers intended. To be sure, such uncertainty is inevitable. But it would be useful to integrate into the reform process a more rigorous consideration of what the consequences of reform will be. At the very least there should be a record of the "legislative intent" of the Congress when it undertakes reform.

Admittedly, clarity of intentions is often elusive. But it would be helpful to impose some sort of requirement of hard-nosed consideration of the matter of intentions. One way to accomplish this would be to require a report similar to environmental impact and inflation impact studies: any reform of party, committee or institutional rules should include a report on the *intended* and *expected* effects. There should also be provision for periodic reports monitoring and analyzing the effects. While this approach will not foreclose the possibility of unintended consequences, it would at least create a record and a basis upon which to draw conclusions. It would also make it easier to adjust the reforms or undertake moves in a different direction after assessing the effects. Such a procedure might also require "benchmark reports" requiring reports on the results at predetermined intervals.

2. REDUCING SPECIAL INTEREST INFLUENCE

The goal is an ambitious, comprehensive and efficacious proposal—one which deals with both campaign finance and structural reform: *party*-based public financing of Congressional Elections.[27] PACs would be banned from contributing directly to the campaigns of individual candidates. PACs would be permitted to contribute, subject to limits,[28] to the party campaign committees. In addition, the major party campaign committees, and qualifying minor party and individual independent candidates, would receive public financing on the basis of a formula which counted the number of candidates fielded multiplied by the eligible voters in those districts, then multiplied by a set number of cents per vote.[29] The formula would be established by Congress and administered by the FEC.

The party campaign committees would then be in a position to provide campaign funds in the general election to their candidates on the basis of party priority, candidate need, and the particular circumstances of each local election. It is assumed and intended that the party committees would become instruments of the respective party leaders. Party leaders could pick and choose, perhaps subject to some upper limits, which candidates got significant, as opposed to token or zero, party campaign fund support. The leaders could take into account candidates who have little or no need for party contributions—because of adequate financing from private sources—and which candidates who, by virtue of their voting records, are not deserving of significant party assistance. Similarly, the leaders could channel large resources to candidates deemed especially deserving of party backing. The system could work either of two ways: publicly financed party contributions only in the general elections, or party contributions allowed in primaries as well, perhaps subject to limits (for example, under the present system, party committees are limited to $5000 per candidate in the primary; i.e. they are treated like any other PAC). The preference here would be for the former. By limiting party contributions to the general election, the system would afford maximum access to attractive political "unknowns" who can emerge from the grassroots in a primary. Toward the same end, banning PAC contributions directly to candidates would mean that organized, usually Washington, D.C.-based special interest money would cease to flow into primary campaigns. This would put a premium on candidates' ability to raise individual contributions in the primary. But the assumption is that it is more likely that candidates will attract individual contributions from their local areas than from national organizations. The further hope is that the exposure provided by free air time—suggested below—would reduce campaign costs and enable to run a new crop of candidates who are not personally wealthy or likely to have pre-existing relationships with interest group benefactors.

The two values advanced by such a system would be 1) in primaries, local responsiveness—i.e., the likelihood that candidates with strong local roots and support will emerge in party primary campaigns (absent national PAC money) and 2) in general elections, a stronger assertion of party positions on national issues and greater focus on policies rather than personalities. A key goal of this system, if administered equitably by the party leaders, would be to provide a new base of campaign funding for challengers of both parties and the incumbents who need it most. Incumbents would still have significant advantages; however, party leaders could channel campaign funds to challengers, instead of having funds sit in the bank accounts of "safe" incumbents. The ultimate winners would be an electorate presented with at least two candidates in each district who have the resources to wage credible campaigns. Of course, some would fear giving the party leaders such political clout, suggesting that an unenlightened Speaker might misuse or abuse this power. This, of course, is always a possibility. But a process must achieve and then sustain its legitimacy and in supporting a strong leadership one must be prepared to accept a strong leader with whom one disagrees. This idea of strong party leadership is propounded here because it is felt that it would be systemically beneficial, regardless of the strong leader's political disposition.

Some might argue that a system of public financing through the parties would move too far toward parliamentary-style "party government." The view here is that there is no such jeopardy. Rather, the centripetal forces of individualism and electoral entrepreneurialism are so firmly entrenched in the Congress of the present and foreseeable future that it would be desirable to endow party leaders with a significant counterweight to that tendency. More traditional suggestions for structural or even constitutional reform[30] to strengthen the parties hold out little hope. The most effective counterweight to the forces of diffused power is a new role for parties in the campaign finance process; and further, it would be intended and expected that such a reform would assert party influence on structure and policy-making as well.

This proposal for a party-based system of public financing would be preferable to the proposed direct public funding of Congressional candidates along with a cap on PAC contributions in that it would simultaneously advance several of the most important goals of reform. First, it would break the direct link between special interest PACs and candidates (and in doing so, the direct link between special interests and sitting members). It would set up the parties in several constructive new roles that have chronically eluded them in recent American politics: as power centers in their own right over candidate recruitment and support, and critically, as wielders of both carrot and stick to party members in Congress. In addition, in an age when special interests are unlikely to wither away, the proposal would establish party leaders, through the campaign committees, as intermediaries between special interests on the one hand and candidates for and members of Congress on the other. PACs would still be free to give to party committees, and thus indirectly to party candidates. And of course, special interest group advocates could continue to contribute as individuals directly to candidates of their choice (subject to the present or perhaps inflation-adjusted limits). And the PACs and/or their lobbyists would continue to be able to marshal all their information, resources, and grassroots support behind particular positions on issues. Gone, however, would be the conflict-ridden situation in which contributors to Congressional committee and subcommittee members sit in judgment on issues of vital interest to the contributing PACs. The fact and appearance of such direct *quid pro quo* politics would be banned.

Would special interest influence and "deals" be abolished at a stroke? Of course not. As long as there are interests there will be special interest influence and perhaps even the spectre of *quid pro quo* politics. However, eliminating direct campaign contributions would insulate to some extent individual members from overt financial pressure, and would establish parties and particularly party leaders as brokers on policy. They would then be in a position to say "yes," "no," "maybe," and "let's discuss this further" to supplicant interests. In other words, such a system would provide leaders with greater leverage over their rank and file members and increased legitimacy as buffers and intermediaries between Congress and external interests. By presiding over party fundraising and distribution, party leaders would have new tools to exercise leadership. And the ability of special interests successfully to circumvent the leadership, while not eliminated, would be lessened.

Hence, unlike the direct public financing of candidates, party-based public financing unabashedly aims to change the balance of power in the system. Instead of merely seeking to limit the opportunity for money-based, direct influence over individual members, party-based public financing aims to ban it. Instead of creating an incentive for PACs to "buy in" early in support of certain candidates and strategically positioned incumbents, this system would urge PACs to cast their lot with a party. Undoubtedly, there would be the time-honored hedging of bets—i.e., contributions to both sides. However, to the extent that PACs throw in with one party or the other, this may also lead to a healthy development of greater party programmism in America. While it is unlikely that American parties will under any circumstances become significantly more ideological on the European model, it is reasonable to expect that different PACs representing diverse interests would gravitate toward the party most responsive to their concerns. This probably would mean that generally the large corporate PACs would gravitate toward the Republicans and labor PACs to the Democrats, with different geographical, professional, ethnic, ideological, and other sectoral factors leading PACs toward one party or the other. To the extent that American parties become less hollow "catch-all" parties, this would be salutary. And since the public financing component would provide money on a matching basis with established limits—on a formula set by the FEC, the two major parties would receive a set amount for the election cycle, and minor parties and independents would receive money according to a formula; the FEC would see to it that the overall effect of public financing would be to equalize the competition between the major parties. The goal would be to allow each party and its candidates to get its message to the people—and to prevent one party from distorting the results of the elections or the functioning of the legislative process on the sole basis of its financial advantage.

Such a system would seek to correct several of the more glaring inconsistencies left in the wake of *Buckley v. Valeo*.[31] In passing a system of Congressional public financing, the plan would put Congressional elections on a par with presidential elections. Insofar as this would be a system of public financing, this proposal would appear to pass the *Buckley* test on the issue of limits, i.e., the ban on PAC contributions and limits on contributions would arguably pass constitutional muster because the limits are all incidental to the system of Congressional public financing. Finally, such a process would seek to alter institutional mores and practices in a significant way *without* either resorting to constitutional change or a head-on challenge to the existing Congressional structure. It is intended that, over time, this process would strengthen the leadership's hand vis-a-vis committee and subcommittee chairmen and members generally. But this would take place via reform of campaign finance rather than another bruising attempt at committee or other structural reform. While such reform would not likely be easy, there is gathering momentum for campaign finance reform.

"Backdoor" Public Financing

Many will see a move toward party-based public financing as improbable at best. In seeking to imbue parties and particularly leaders with new, money-based clout, it may plausibly be argued that individuals and special interest groups would never agree to such a system. This is, of course, the problem with reform: if it is to mean anything it involves the redistribution of power. A more subtle but intriguing alternative approach is what we shall call "backdoor" public financing. This is to provide public financing through the back door, i.e. by a series of indirect rather than direct mechanisms for government-encouraged public subsidy of political campaigns. One major ingredient, discussed below under the reduction of campaign costs, is to require free television air time for candidates as a condition of FCC licenses. This would address the problem of huge media costs—presently the most expensive portion of most campaign budgets. Another aspect of this is use of a "campaign frank" for a certain number of free mailings during the course of Federal campaigns (similar to incumbents' Congressional mailings). One of the more effective, and increasingly expensive, means of communication is direct mail for both persuasion and fundraising. By allowing candidates a mechanism for free campaign mailings (subject to regulations and limits based on the number of voters and the allowable format), each qualifying candidate would have reasonable access to the voters' attentions. While it is impossible to guarantee that each candidate "gets his message out," this would certainly increase the likelihood. And a third significant approach to "backdoor" public financing would be to use the tax code to encourage the broadest possible base of small political contributions. The tax code is already used in various ways to provide incentives and disincentives for certain kinds of social and economic behavior. At present approximately four per cent of taxpayers take the 50 per cent tax credit on political contributions up to $100 or $200 on a joint return. Broader political giving by taxpayers at all levels could be encouraged by providing a 100 per cent tax credit up to $500 per annum. This credit would be provided on the short form and there would be an educational campaign to apprise all taxpayers that this is their opportunity to have a major voice in political campaigns beyond the act of voting.

To Reduce Campaign Costs: Free Television and Radio Time as a Condition of FCC License Renewal

In addition to, and consistent with, the above proposal there must be an effort to reduce the cost of campaigns. With the rise of PACs and the increase of overt special interest politics has come an explosion of campaign costs. Million dollar campaigns for the House are not unusual and have become standard for Senate races. Senate races in populous states are necessarily multi-million dollar contests.[32]

To a large extent, spiraling campaign costs are attributable to the increasing costs of media exposure. Newspaper and radio ads are big ticket items in candidates' budgets, and of course, television time, consulting, and production costs are extremely expensive.[33] The Television Bureau of Advertising reports that $117 million was spent on political advertising in 1983, 29 per cent greater than the $90.6 million in 1980, for a presidential election year, and 103 per cent above the $57.6 million spent in 1978.[34]

Especially if public funds are to be expended and, in any event, in the name of attracting candidates who are not necessarily wealthy, it is essential that any reform of campaign finance seeks to limit and preferably reduce the costs of campaigns. A proposal to that effect would be that as a condition of receiving a license from the Federal Communications Commission, each radio and television station would be required to provide free air time to Congressional candidates on the basis of a formula to be devised and administered by the FCC in conjunction with, and on the advice of, the FEC.

The formula would include some combination of candidate debates, question and answer sessions and other formats, as well as free time to run campaign advertisements produced and furnished by the candidates.[35] This provision of free air time would replace all paid television and radio advertising: as another condition of FCC license, no stations would be permitted to sell advertising time to Congressional candidates.

This proposal, unlikely to warm the hearts of television and radio station owners, seems a small condition in return for their lucrative licenses in the greater interest of contributing to the health of the political system.

The Campaign Frank and
Tax Credits for Newspapers to Provide Free Space in Print Media

Candidates for the House and Senate should be allowed free postage (a "campaign frank") similar to incumbents' Congressional frank. This would be regulated to allow equal access to the electorate by all candidates. True equality would probably require a limitation on privately financed mailings by candidates using the "campaign frank."

In addition, while the following could not be mandatory since it would violate First Amendment free speech requirements, newspaper publishers should be encouraged to contribute similarly to the health of the political system by donating free advertising space to Congressional candidates or at the least, to provide space for the airing of candidates' views. The high costs of campaigning forces candidates to go out and raise the oftentimes objectionable special interest money. While public financing through parties would have a positive link-breaking effect on the process, it is also necessary to ensure that candidates have adequate opportunity to get their messages across to the electorate. Free television and radio time is critical. But in addition, newspapers of all sizes and orientation should provide free space to candidates to respond to questions, print columns expressing their views on issues, and in certain circumstances, be given a small amount of free space to run ads of their choosing. The combined effect of reduced media costs would be a significant decrease in the cost of the most crucial and expensive aspects of contemporary campaigns. Of course, this would not be *guaranteed* to reduce, in absolute terms, campaign costs because campaigns have a way of inexplicably eating up however much money is available. In short, less money spent on media might "free up" amounts for direct mail, door-to-door campaigning, staff, etc. But public financing and free media exposure would create significant new opportunities for access to the electorate, attracting candidates who previously have not felt it financially realistic or practicable to run. And well-run campaigns could make the most of these opportunities and obviate the need for huge private sources of campaign funds. While incumbents would continue to have distinct advantages, the free time would help to create a greater degree of fairness, and a more informed electorate.

It is probably the case that a truly fair system of public financing of individual candidates would be one in which challengers receive *more* funding than incumbents. However, as long as incumbents in Congress decide the process, the likelihood of this ever happening is slim to nil. But in the proposed process of public funding through the parties, the door is left open for parties, within the context of their national priorities and strategy, to channel amounts to challengers against "targeted" opponents, which might accomplish something like this equalizing effect.

To Make All PACs "Non-Connected"

. If much of the above seems complicated and perhaps impracticable, there is a simple, targeted approach which could go a long way toward reducing the effective operation of corporate, trade association and labor PACs. This would be to abolish separate segregated funds by which "connected" PACs are presently bankrolled by corporation, trade association and union treasury funds. These funds provide for overhead and other administrative costs, and they absorb the substantial direct mail solicitation costs that are the big-ticket items of PAC operations.

Such abolition would place corporate, trade association and labor PACs on the same financial footing as ideological PACs; i.e. they would be banned from using their sponsoring entities' treasury funds. Instead, they would have to use internally-generated funds for administrative and solicitation costs.

Assuming that such a reform could pass—it is extremely unlikely because it cuts right to the heart of PAC power—there is the other problem that these PACs are already in existence, and hence less likely to be dealt a death-blow by the cut-off of treasury funds. While this might certainly be the case as opposed to a system which banned use of treasury funds from the outset, it might be expected that *over time* such a system would render business and labor PACs more like to-day's ideological PACs. That is, significant amounts of their resources would be expended on solicitation, overhead and self-preservation; less would be available for contributions to candidates. If one quick blow to business and labor PACs is desired, this is not a knock-out punch. But if a gradual diminution of PAC influence is the aim, the abolition of treasury-funded PACs would be a big step in that direction (although the reemergence of contributions to candidates by individual executives in place of PACs would likely result).

Tightened Disclosure and Limitations on Lobbyist-Financiers

Another approach to reducing special interest influence would be to tighten disclosure and contribution-limitation requirements. To some this carries with it the alleged futility of most regulatory schemes—and the response that it will only be a matter of time before people figure out means of circumvention. Perhaps. But several ideas hold promise if there were a concerted desire to identify fundraisers and key contributors with precision, and to limit the more pernicious aspects of the recent trend toward convergence of lobbying and fundraising.

First, if the FEC disclosure forms were to be truly revealing, they should require disclosure of individual fundraisers, the listing of events at which specific funds were raised and the identification of solicitors of funds when there is no event (e.g. direct solicitation or direct mail). What is presently lacking in disclosure is any real insight into who *raised* the money. While this may not seem significant to the uninitiated, who raises money is deeply significant to politicians.

Secondly, if there were to be a serious attempt to circumscribe the permissible roles of lobbyists, this might include a ban on registered lobbyists soliciting or contributing money for the benefit of legislators whom they lobby. Of course, lobbyists derive their power and influence from many sources other than campaign contributions. But increasingly, lobbyists are the first ones in the door of Washington fundraising events—even if preferably they are delivering other people's or PACs' money. This reform would not necessarily reduce the influence of lobbyists (it would save them some money!). But such a ban would attack a rather obvious conflict of interest in the existing system by which lobbyists are a ready source of support and solicitations for members of Congress with whom they transact business.

3. TO STRENGTHEN CONGRESS'S ABILITY TO MAKE COMPREHENSIVE POLICY: BACK TO THE NECESSITY OF CONSOLIDATIVE REFORM

Congress has proven itself effective in a number of areas: responsiveness to, and representation of, diverse constituencies and interests, articulation and "gestation" of ideas for innovative policy initiatives, and as a forum for the discussion and arbitration—if not always the resolution—of conflicting political and economic ends and interests. Perhaps the flip-side of these strengths is one glaring weakness. Congress has historically been extremely poor at making broad-based, comprehensive policies—and of mobilizing consent for national policies.

Some of this is part and parcel of American society's diversity—and even its ideological disposition against concentration of power, "quick fixes," and national—as opposed to local or regional—policy solutions. We also live in an era, at least temporarily, of reaction to the New Deal legacy of grandiose national initiatives. And this ethos of targeted, decentralized policies has been picked up not only by Republicans of various stripes but by "neo-liberal" Democrats as well. Ideological configurations aside, the point to be made here is that as a result of the reforms and parallel developments, the contemporary Congress is so decentralized in its structure that it is often incapable of making effective comprehensive policy even when it wants. In short, in key areas of national policy—energy, defense, health care, welfare, tax reform, immigration law and industrial policy—we perpetuate *fragmented, piecemeal* policies, or the lack of clear-cut policy, simply because we are organizationally incapable of fashioning *national* ones. The vast and competing assemblage of interest groups help guarantee this tendency.

There is no simple solution to this problem, certainly not as simple as such proven "non-starters" as the time-worn suggestion of a parliamentary system,[36] the single six-year term for presidents, the balance-the-budget amendment, or the line-item veto. Perhaps the best course of action in the direction of a greater capacity for comprehensive policy-making is encompassed in the earlier stated proposal for party-based public financing. Giving party leaders greater power in electoral politics and in the role of intermediary with special interests would greatly strengthen the leaders' hands in the formulation of policy. Of course, the prospects of this occurring in the near-term are unlikely. And in any event, the existing committee system with all its built-in overlap and inertia militates against leaders asserting a wide-angle view over their narrow spheres of policy formulation. Hence, it is necessary to consider what else might be done to enhance the Congress's capacity for comprehensive policy-making.

A Radical, One-Shot Approach to Subcommittee Reform

It is by now apparent that one of the major effects of reform was the enhancement of subcommittees—particularly the power of sub-committee chairmen and the rights of rank and file members of sub-committees. It would be difficult, perhaps impossible and certainly undesirable to turn back the clock to the days of unbridled power exercised by aging, seniority-entrenched full committee chairmen. And it is arguably the case that subcommittee chairmen and members are so content with their bailiwicks and perquisites that little or nothing in the way of consolidative reform is worth attempting.[37]

One bold, admittedly controversial step would go a long way toward redressing the problem of dispersed subcommittee power. This would be to assert the party leaders and party steering committees in the areas of deciding the number of subcommittees, their titles and jurisdictions and most importantly, the chairmen. This proposal would run headlong into opposition from the beneficiaries of past reforms. It would directly challenge the cornerstones of the present decentralized regime. However, a system which accords great authority and power over substantive policy-making to its subcommittees ought to think long and hard about the process by which it chooses who runs the subcommittees—and what the subcommittees do. If future reformers really want stronger leadership and more accountable and programmatic parties, the most direct, albeit radical approach would be to give the Speaker power over the subject matter, agendas and leadership of the subcommittees. Stability among the members of subcommittees is probably desirable in light of the modern demands for legislators with expertise on their committee's policy areas. But leaders of subcommittees (also full committee preferably) should be responsive to a higher authority in determining issues, agendas, time tables, even substantive orientations. There is enough independent-mindedness built into the system among committee and subcommittee members that mavericks would continue to have opportunities to have their say. But a coherent overall game plan for each Congress in the new workplaces of the Congress, the subcommittees, is the proper concern of leaders of both parties, but particularly for the majority party leadership.

4. LEGISLATIVE "PACKAGING": POTENTIAL USES AND ABUSES

Another area of activity which bears scrutiny is the recent attempts at the commission approach to controversial issues. There has been increasing use recently of such "packaging" of policies by use of outside special commissions on such national policy areas as Social Security, the MX missile system, Educational reform and Central America. There has been discussion of a commission on the deficit, on entitlements and a host of other problem areas. In Congress itself in 1977 and 1978, Speaker O'Neill used a variant of the form in the House on the Carter Energy bill (successfully, but only so in the House) and welfare reform (with less success). In the latter two instances the mechanism used was an *ad hoc* committee composed of key members of the several committees with overlapping jurisdiction on the issue. One approach, and by far the best one, to deal systematically with the problem, would be by means of strong party leadership through the party apparatus—e.g., the House Democratic Steering and Policy Group and ad hoc Task Forces—to take on such "big" issues and fashion proposals which command overwhelming majority party support.

However, others favor an approach which recognizes institutional leadership and responsibility in certain defined areas on a bipartisan basis. This approach recognizes that there are some issues which defy piecemeal and scattershot solutions and arguably transcend party politics. At least it is fair to note that decades of fragmented consideration of the issues—and either absence of party leadership or partisan bickering—have yielded little in the way of legislative output. There is a tradition of trying to produce at least nominally bipartisan solutions to key foreign policy and national security issues. There are some who contend that broad areas of domestic policy might lend themselves to similar approaches. The leaders would have to acknowledge first that Congress can only concentrate on so much at a time, secondly that Congress is ill-equipped generally to make comprehensive policy due to its party and committee structure and thirdly, that a bipartisan, focused attention on a selected subject—with active participation by both Congressional party and committee representatives—

might succeed wearing bipartisan commission "hats" in areas where they might otherwise fail.

The view here is that such commissions have a strong proclivity to being window-dressing, dilatory tactics or deliberately stacked decks in favor of a predetermined solution. They are not cure-alls for most broad issue areas. In any event, bipartisan "packaging" should be viewed as a distant second-best to stronger party leadership and action on these issues.

The desultory reputation of Presidential Commissions as producers of ineffectual dust-gathering tomes owes at least in part to the lack of coordination between the executive branch and the Congress. Some of the poor track records of commissions are products of the actual political intent: commissions often are used as diversions from, and alternatives to, concerted—or any—action. The Congressional approach to commission work, including enlisting the help of outside experts and citizens, should be directed toward problem-solving and action. And while this is certainly not a panacea, it might constitute one experiment to fill a vacuum in the present Congressional process, but it is best done by and within parties—with only a handful of issues lending themselves to bipartisan approaches.

A Balanced Package of "Wholesale" Reform

What is needed is an overall strategy for achieving efficacious Congressional reform. This strategy should have as its centerpiece, a balanced package which, although composed of different "pieces," constitutes a reasoned approach to comprehensive reform.

A worthwhile package should include the following:

- Keep the limit for individual contributions to candidates per election at $1000 but provide a 100% annual tax credit up to $500 for every taxpayer. This would encourage taxpayers at every level to participate in the funding of campaigns through "backdoor" public financing.
- If a total ban on direct PAC contributions to candidates is considered impracticable, then an alternative would be a severe limit on PAC contributions directly to candidates. (The preference here is to ban them in primaries, and/or limit them to a 6-month period preceding elections.)
- Party-based Public Financing through the Congressional party campaign committees, on a formula that would provide each party committee with an equal amount of federal funding—and a proportionate amount to minor party and independents. (An alternative would be to reward parties on the basis of registration, although Republicans would strenuously object and independents would immediately become national power-wielders.)

- Mandatory Free Air Time as a condition of FCC license.
- The Campaign Frank for all qualifying candidates; to qualify candidates would need a certain number of certified signatures.
- Strict limits on subcommittee growth and increased powers of the Speaker of the House and Majority Leader in the Senate to set the agenda not just of floor business but of committees and subcommittees as well.

Getting From Here to There

Of course, before even getting to the problem of possible unanticipated consequences of reform, there is the substantial problem of the process of consideration and adoption of reform. Just as there is no guarantee that the best-laid reform proposals will work as intended or expected, it is improbable that a reform proposal will emerge from the reform process in its original form. Hence the ambiguous and multi-directional results of many "piecemeal" reforms observed in the previous chapters.

It is necessary to consider not only where to go, but also how to get there. The basic problem of self-interested decision-makers must be recognized. Members of Congress make the rules which decide not only how Congress operates but also, to a large extent, who will participate—i.e., to a significant extent, who will be members of Congress. In addition, as noted at the outset, increasingly the special interest groups have become "players" who have a say in any changes in the overall "game." Hence on basic issues of process, the temptation to seek partisan and other forms of advantage is typically irresistible. Short of a dream-world "veil of ignorance"[38] (in which the founders of the system do not know where they will end up as participants in that system) it is likely always to be the case that incumbents will seek to protect incumbents, parties will seek to advance their own party interests and at the very least, the present inhabitants of the system will have disproportionate say over reform of that system.

The difficulty of winning passage of reform makes it easier to prescribe what "there" looks like than to suggest ways to get there. No such suggestions are foolproof of course, but here is an approach. There should be a bold attempt to take issues of process and structural reform outside the routine of Congressional business. The beginning of a Congressional session is probably the best time for an initiative for structural and process change, especially at a time when there has been significant turnover of membership. The best time for such reform is when there has been a change in party control (as in 1947 and 1981).

The obvious characteristic of these periods is temporary dislocation of established power configurations. Congressional norms of seniority and ongoing political coalitions provide continuity and serve to inhibit sweeping change. Efforts should be made to create a climate in which the status quo orientations of the members are minimized and the diversions of routine business and subtantive policy matters are not present. The beginning of a session would provide such a time—especially if the leadership stipulated that no other business would be taken up until the proposed reform package was acted upon. Holding everything else temporarily hostage would concentrate wonderfully the minds of members of Congress. To be sure, matters of turf would remain important—but they might be somewhat less so if committee assignments were not made until the reform package was acted upon.

The following might be a possible scenario. In December caucuses, the majority party hammers out a reform package which deals with the need for stronger leadership within Congress and a less money-tinged system of campaign finance. Discussions and negotiations with party leaders in both Houses seek consensus on the ingredients. The crucial agreement is for both Houses not to appoint committee members or take up regular business until the reforms are acted upon. Early January until the State of the Union becomes virtually a "special session" of the Congress to work out the details of reform. Unprecedented, certainly. But also increasingly necessary. The alternative is to let reform proposals become turf battles and bargaining chips interchangeable with other legislative battles. And the upshot of that has been drift and increasing Congressional inefficacy. It would take leaders of daring and persistence to attempt such a task. But the goal of greater systemic coherence and efficacy demands it.

There is probably a case to be made for participation by citizens other than members of Congnress in at least an advisory capacity, with final authority over rules and procedures remaining in the members of the particular parties and chambers. There is clearly a need for greater public awareness of the importance of Congressional rules, structure and procedures, and the exigencies of the reform process. There is, of course, no single, sweeping answer. But we must strive for a better system and attempt to produce reforms that are designed to lead in a direction beneficial to the overall workings of the system.

Conclusion

It is early 1985. The 99th Congress has convened and there are winds of restlessness, rebellion and maybe even new reform in both the House and Senate.

In the House, for the first time in ten years, the Democratic Caucus has used its reformed procedures to depose a seniority-ensconced, sitting committee chairman. Eighty-year-old Melvin Price, Chairman of the House Armed Services Committee, was dethroned by a bloc of younger, more liberal Democrats who replaced him with forty-six-year-old, liberal Les Aspin. Much has been made of the generational shift and the policy implications of an anti-Pentagon chairman (albeit one who was a leader in the move to save the MX). Aspin's victory was not just a rejection of the infirm Price and Speaker O'Neill's plea to re-elect him, it was also a rejection of the top six Democratic members of the Armed Services Committee. Aspin was the seventh-ranking member.

Aspin's victory sent shock waves throughout Capitol Hill and inspired speculation that more such rebelliousness might be forthcoming.

- A black minister from Philadelphia, Rep. William Gray, a moderate Democrat, has been elected to chair the Budget Committee, an extremely visible and important post in a deficit-conscious time.
- 117 Democrats in the House have served four terms or fewer.[39]
- The Democratic Caucus has voted to elect the party whip the next time the post is vacant.
- A "radical" new budget process seeking to consolidate budget, taxes and appropriations into one mammoth bill has been proposed by Rep. David Obey, a veteran of past reform efforts.[40]
- In the Senate, Senator Dan Quayle (R.-Indiana) and others reflect a disillusionment with existing Senate procedures which elevate individualism over efficiency and provide myriad opportunities for obstruction. Former Majority Leader Howard Baker (R.-Tennessee) has retired, in part out of frustration at the Senate as an institution. Senator Quayle hopes to win passage of a reform plan that would streamline Senate procedures. There is new talk of consolidating committees, perhaps reducing the number of subcommittees.[41]

The recent restlessness seems familiar. Yet, what is striking about the Aspin victory over the seniority system is not that it happened but *that it is the first time in ten years that the seniority system was violated.* What is striking about "radical" reform proposals is *that there are so few of them.* And what is notable about the moves for Senate reform is *the absence of significant progress toward any significant reform in an institution which has been drifting toward chaos for more than a few years.*

The most striking characteristics of the contemporary Congress in the "post-reform" era are its stability and resistance to organized efforts at change. Reliance on a complicated infrastructure of outside groups for direction, influence and political sustenance (i.e. money) is another by now obvious characteristic.

There is no good reason why the American people ought to continue to be ill-served by Congress. The present Congress has a structure and process better suited to serving the special interests of associations and groups, and the political interests of incumbent members of Congress, than the larger interests of the American people. It is too easy to lament the recent reform experience and use that as an excuse to eschew new attempts at reform. There must be ongoing and rigorous rethinking. And that rethinking must lead to readiness. The time for serious consideration of reform will come again. Next time reform must help equip Congress for the job of coherent policy-making. Next time reform must be tailored to the needs of the "Public Interest Congress."

Notes

1. Samuel Beer, "The British Legislature and the Problem of Mobilizing Consent," in Bernard Crick (ed.), *Essays on Reform* (London: Oxford University Press, 1967), p. 91, and reprinted from Elke Frank (ed.), *Lawmakers in a Changing World* (Englewood Cliffs, N.J.: Prentice-Hall, 1966). Citations herein are from the Crick book.
2. See Michael T. Hayes, "Interest Groups: Pluralism or Mass Society," in Cigler and Loomis, *Interest Group Policies, op. cit.,* pp. 110–125.
3. And the reality of it to the extent that the Reagan Administration has sought to shift the financial burden of many social programs to the states.
4. Beer, ". . . Problem of Mobilizing Consent," *op cit.,* p. 91.
5. *Ibid,* p. 100.
6. A series of incisive observations using different terms but focusing on the important role of legislators as educators—i.e., as leaders and shapers of public opinion—is found in an article by a former legislator/educator, Senator J. William Fulbright (D.–Arkansas). See J. William Fulbright, "The Legislator as Educator," *Foreign Affairs,* v. 57, Spring 1979, pp. 719–732.
7. See, for example, the Occupational Safety and Health Act (OSHA), Clean Air Act, the Federal Insecticide, Fungicide and Rodenticide Act (FIFRA), Employee Retirement and Income Security Act (ERISA), Airline Deregulation, the Foreign Corrupt Practices Act and Superfund environmental legislation. This is not to disparage the goals or terms of these broad-based legislative initiatives. One point is that most of these bills became law *before* Congress's decision-making process became so fragmented and the rise and influence of PACs so pronounced. They also came at a time when Federal intervention in the economy and society was much more in vogue than later in the 1970s and early 1980s. A contention of my argument herein is that much of this legislation would not have passed in the present structure and dynamics, or would have emerged in forms much less comprehensive. As it is, various special interest groups see as part of their contemporary mission the vitiation or amendment of what they consider to be the more onerous aspects of these laws. The Reagan Administration has in many areas perceived its role similarly, as summarized by the early Reagan Administration's motto posted on a Reagan official's wall: "Don't Just Stand There, *Un*-do Something!"
8. A view of Congress and its members' roles as parts of triangles of power among Congress, bureaucracy and affected interest groups is found, most recently, in Morris Fiorina, *Congress: Keystones of the Washington Establishment* (New Haven, Conn.: Yale University Press, 1977). Fiorina does not make the point made here about the role of Congress in mobilizing dissent from government policy, but he does criticize the consequences of

these triangles and the negative impact of Congress as "Keystone of the Washington Establishment." The concept of "iron triangles" has a longer history, going back at least to Douglas Cater, *Power in Washington* (New York: Random House, 1964). For another recent view of the problems and prospects for so-called "cozy triangles," see Roger H. Davidson, "Breaking Up Those 'Cozy Triangles': An Impossible Dream?" in Susan Welch and John G. Peters, eds., *Legislative Reform and Public Policy* (New York: Praeger Publishers, 1977), pp. 30–51.

9. Tax Equity and Fiscal Responsibility Act of 1982.

10. See Thomas B. Edsall, "Bankers Flex Muscles Again," *Washington Post*, May 5, 1983, p. A10, Thomas W. Lippman, "Effort to Repeal Interest Dividend Witholding Law Advancing," *Washington Post*, July 21, 1983, p. A11 and Paul Taylor, "The Death of Witholding, Or How The Bankers Won a Big One," *Washington Post*, July 31, 1983, p. A12.

11. James Naisbitt, *Megatrends* (New York: Warner Books, 1982), pp. 97 and 103.

12. See Grant McConnell, *Private Power and American Democracy, op. cit.*

13. See MRK Research Data contained in *Insight Massachusetts,* a private polling service in Boston, Mass. which has focused on this in their ongoing polling service. I am grateful to James Kerasiotes for providing me with their findings.

14. One example is Elizabeth Mitchell's 1984 challenge of Senator William Cohen in Maine in which Ms. Mitchell repudiated PAC contributions at the outset of the campaign. Another example is the 1984 Massachusetts Senate race for the open seat of the retiring Senator Paul Tsongas. In this context, all candidates, Republican and Democrat, agreed not to accept PAC contributions. The author should disclose a particularly direct experience of the effects of this decision; he was Finance Director of the campaign of one of the candidates.

15. James MacGregor Burns, *The Power to Lead* (New York: Simon and Schuster, 1984), see pp. 147–166.

16. At this writing, special interest groups were weighing the implications of *Chada*—along with Congress and the Executive—to see what is left when one takes out the severable legislative veto section of the 200 or so pieces of legislation with such provisions. The problems, and opportunities for new special interest initiatives, are many. See Kevin Phillips' observation that *Chada* might not be such a disappointment to special interest lobbyists after all, since it will force Congress to be more detailed in its drafting in the first place. *Business & Public Affairs Fortnightly,* Vol. V, Number 10, July 15, 1983, p. 5.

17. Globe-trotting congressmen and senators sometimes make for dubious diplomats. Of course, Congress is most effective in this arena as a check on Administration policy: on such broad policy fronts as Vietnam, Angola, Central America and the Middle East. To be sure, it would hardly be beneficial to remove Congress and its responsiveness to public opinion from a role in this sphere. Yet it should be noted that Congress is not particularly well-suited to taking a leading role in formulating foreign policy. See, Franck and Weisband, *Foreign Policy By Congress, op. cit.*

18. See Larry Sabato, *The Rise of Political Consultants* (New York: Basic Books, 1981).

19. All of which are intriguing but impracticable ideas.

20. Former Senators James Pearson and Abraham Ribicoff have suggested proposals for reform in the Senate which are recent suggestions for overhaul; despite recent dissatisfaction with the Senate by many of its members, including a move by Senator Dan Quayle of Indiana, there appears to be little broad-based interest in Senate reform.

21. H.R. 2490, 93rd Congress, 1st Session.

22. Dennis Farney and Albert R. Hunt, "Backers of Public Funding of House Races Drop Idea, Will Seek New Curbs on PACs," *Wall Street Journal*, September 16, 1983, p. 5.

23. An additional proposal considered to put teeth in the limit was that if an opponent went above the $240,000 limit the candidate would have access to free air time.

24. "The Political Tax Credit Reform Act of 1983," *Congressional Record*, August 2, 1983, pp. H. 6330–6331.

25. H.R. 3081, 98th Congress, 1st Session, May 23, 1983 sponsored by Rep. Bill Frenzel of Minnesota.

26. See 441(a–d) of the FECA.

27. Variations of party-based public financing have been floated by Herbert E. Alexander and others, and most recently by Rep. Tony Coelho (D. California) and Chairman of the DCCC. The Alexander proposal would funnel public money through state and local party committees. The Coelho idea is to provide matching grants to the part campaign committees, along with the existing PAC contributions to individuals and the committees. The Coelho proposal has not yet surfaced as a bill or full-blown legislative initiative, probably due to a lack of party backing. It should also be noted that the so-called Long Act of 1966—made inoperative in 1967 before it took effect—would have provided for a taxpayer checkoff for public finance of presidential elections. In Long's scheme, the two major national party committees would have received the money. Indeed, it was mistrust over the power imbued in the two national party chairmen which inspired the move for suspension of the act. See Gary C. Jacobson, *Money in Congressional Elections, op. cit.*, pp. 177–178 and Herbert E. Alexander, *Financing Politics, op. cit.*, p. 28.

28. These would be based on formulas established by Congress and administered by the FEC. They would be based on the number of candidates fielded and adjusted for inflation on a periodic basis. There would be provisions for minor parties and independents based on this formula.

29. This could be done in a fashion similar to provisions for minor party and independent public financing of the presidential elections.

30. For recent examples, see Charles Hardin, *Presidential Power & Accountability: Toward a New Constitution* (Chicago: University of Chicago Press, 1974) and Lloyd Cutler, "To Form a Government," *Foreign Affairs*, Vol. 59, No. 1 (Fall 1980), pp. 126–143, advocating adoption of a parliamentary system. Of course, the goal of stronger parties has a long history in American political science. Some older sources are William Yandell El-

liott, *The Pragmatic Revolt in Politics* (New York: MacMillan, 1928) and *The Need for Constitutional Reform* (New York: McGraw-Hill, 1935); E. E. Schattschneider, *Party Government* (New York: Farrar Rhinehart, 1942) and *The Semi-Sovereign People, op. cit.* And of course, the classic statement "Toward a More Responsible Two Party System," *American Political Science Review,* Vol. 44, No. 3, Part 2 (1950).

31. See *Buckley v. Valeo,* 424 U.S. 1, 96 S. Ct. 612, 46 L. Ed. 2nd 659 (1976).

33. See Fenn, *Money and Politics, Campaign Costs Out of Control, op. cit.*

33. The costs of time vary among media markets. But even at the lowest-unit-rates, television and radio time absorb a major chunk of campaign budgets. Charges for air time in major media markets can run in excess of $10,000 a minute. While the fragmentation of the communications industry may augur lower costs, for example for cable television ads, the overall cost of reaching a wide audience will likely continue to spiral.

34. And although no hard numbers are available, it is estimated that between 30% and 70% of campaign budgets are spent on media—with somewhere in the range of 50% being typical. See materials of "Non-voter Study," '80–81, Release, January 14, 1981.

35. There might be a requirement of a certain amount of time for straightforward appearances of candidates looking directly at the camera (i.e., the so-called "talking heads" proposal). While I do not support this proposal because I think freedom of expression as well as maximum creativity in political persuasion is important in the realm of campaign advertising, there might be an argument for a certain amount of required percentage of "talking heads" time to be provided as part of the free media requirement by the FCC.

36. See Charles Hardin, *Presidential Accountability, op. cit.* and Lloyd Cutler, "To Form a Government," *Foreign Affairs, op. cit.*

37. The proliferation of subcommittees has leveled off in recent years. The House Democratic Caucus approved a cap on subcommittees in 1981 which provided that, except for the Appropriations Committee, standing committees are limited to eight subcommittees. Committees having more than thirty-five members and fewer than six subcommittees may increase the number to six or, with approval of the Steering and Policy Committee, seven. One tangible result of the cap was that no House committee added subcommittees at the outset of the 97th or 98th Congresses.

38. John Rawls, *A Theory of Justice* (Cambridge: Harvard University Press, 1971).

39. *The Busby Papers,* Vol. IV-20, January 9, 1985, p. 2.

40. Julia Malone, "Getting the House in Order: Changes in Rules Proposed," *Christian Science Monitor,* November 21, 1984, p. 4.

41. Helen Dewar, "Senate Faces Institutional Identity Crisis," *Washington Post,* November 29, 1984, pp. 1, 6, 7, 8.

Select Bibliography
On Special Interests and Congress

Adamany, David W. and George E. Agree, *Political Money: A Strategy for Campaign Financing in America.* Baltimore, Johns Hopkins University Press, 1975.

Alexander, Herbert E., *Financing Politics: Money, Elections and Political Reform.* Washington, D. C.: CQ Press, 1980.

Anderson, Jack, "The Power Behind the Dairy Industry," *The Washington Post.* March 6, 1981. p. C15.

"Banker's Political Action Committee: One Honest and Effective Way to Participate," *ABA Banking Journal,* v. 72, Apr. 1980: 76–79.

Broder, David, "Studies Intensify Vote-Buying Debate," *The Washington Post,* September 4, 1983. pp. A22–23.

Chappell, Henry W., Jr., "Campaign Contributions and Voting on the Cargo Preference Bill: A Comparison of Simultaneous Models," *Public Choice,* v. 36, 1981: 301–312.

Common Cause, *Guide to Money, Power and Politics in the 97th Congress.* Washington, D.C., 1981.

Common Cause, *Campaign Finance Monitoring Project. 1972 Federal Campaign Finances, Interest Groups, and Political Parties.* Washington, D.C., 1974. 3v.

Common Cause, *Campaign Finance Monitoring Project. 1974 Congressional Campaign Finances. Volume 5: Interest Groups and Political Parties.* Washington, D.C., 1974.

Common Cause, *Campaign Finance Monitoring Project. 1976 Federal Campaign Finances.* Washington, D.C., 1977. 3v.

Common Cause, *AMA Campaign Contributions Helped Kill Hospital Costs Containment Bill.* Washington, D.C., 1979.

Common Cause, "Take $2,000 and Call Me in the Morning," *A Common Cause Study.* Washington, D.C., 1983.

Congressional Quarterly, Inc. *Dollar Politics.* Washington, D.C., 1971–74. 2v.

Cottin, Jonathan. "Washington Pressures: BIPAC Seeks to Elect Pro-business Members to Congress," *National Journal,* v.2, July 18, 1970: 1525–1531.

Demkovich, Linda E., "The AMA-Reports of Its Death Have Been Greatly Exaggerated," *National Journal,* v. 11, Dec. 1, 1979: 2017–2022.

Drew, Elizabeth, *Money and Politics.* New York: MacMillan, 1983.

Edsall, Thomas Byrne, *The New Politics of Inequality.* New York: W. W. Norton, 1984.

Epstein, Edwin M., "Corporations and Labor Unions in Electoral Politics," *Political Finance: Reform and Realty.* Philadelphia, American Academy of Political and Social Science, 1976. *Annals,* v. 425, May 1976, p. 33–58.

Etzioni, Amitai, *Capital Corruption,* San Diego: Harcourt Brace Jovanovich, 1984.

Green, Mark, "Political PACman," *The New Republic,* December 13, 1982. pp. 18–25.

Green, Mark, and Jack Newfield, "Who Owns Congress," *Washington Post* magazine, June 8, 1980: 10–19, 21.

Gordon, Michael, "The FTC Exemption Vote: Did the AMA and ADA Gift Givers Carry the Day?" *The National Journal,* December 11, 1982. p. 2127.

Graves, Florence, "The Power Brokers," *Common Cause,* v. 7, Feb. 1981: 13–20.

How Money Talks In Congress: a Common Cause Study of The Impact of Money on Congressional Decision-making. Washington, D.C., 1978.

Isaacson, Walter, "Running with the PACs," *Time* Magazine. October 25, 1982. pp. 20–26.

Jackson, Brooks, "Doctors and Dentists Prescribe Donations for Some in House," *The Wall Street Journal.* September 17, 1982. p. 20.

Jacobson, Gary C., *Money In Congressional Elections.* New Haven, Yale University Press, 1980.

Keller, Bill, "In a Bull Market for Arms, Weapons Industry Lobbyists Push Products, Not Policy," *Congressional Quarterly Weekly Report,* v. 38, Oct. 25, 1980: 3201–3206.

Keller, Bill, and Irwin B. Arieff, "As Campaign Costs Skyrocket, Lobbyists Take Growing Role in Washington Fund-raisers." *Congressional Quarterly Weekly Report,* v. 38, May 17, 1980: 1333–1346.

Maass, Arthur, *Congress and the Common Good.* New York: Basic Books, 1983.

Malbin, Michael J. ed., *Money and Politics in the United States.* Chatham, N.J.: Chatham House, 1984.

Malbin, Michael J., "Campaign Financing and the "Special Interests," *Public Interest,* no. 56, summer 1979: 21–42.

Maraniss, David, "PAC Heaven," *The Washington Post.* August 21, 1983. pp. A1, A16.

Mayer, Caroline, "Study Links Funds, Legislation" *The Washington Post.* November 25, 1981. p. D9.

Mintz, Morton, "House Tax-Cutters Got Large Donations from Business PACs," *The Washington Post.* July 2, 1981. p. A9.

Mintz, Morton. "Savings and Loans Associations Deposited Half A Million on the Hill," *The Washington Post.* July 9, 1981. p. A10.

Muller, Nathan J., "Political Action: What's It All About?" *Practical Politics,* v. 1, Sept.–Oct. 1978: 6–10.

" 'Must Not' Legislation (Cont'd.)" Editorial. *The Washington Post.* December 6, 1982. p. A10.

PACs: What They Are, How They Are Changing Political Campaign Financing Patterns. Washington, Center for Information on America, 1979 (Grass roots guides on democracy and practical politics; booklet no. 62).

Public Citizen, Inc. Congress Watch, *Nader Study Links Oil Contributions to Pro-oil House Vote,* Washington, D.C., 1979.

Reeves, Richard, "When Reform Backfires," *Esquire,* v. 93, Mar. 1980: 7, 11. v. 93.

Roeder, Edward, "18 Finance Panel Members got $300,000 from Chemical Industry" *The Washington Post.* July 2, 1981. p. A9.

Rothenberg, Randall, "The PACs Go to Market on The Hill," *Nation,* v. 227, Nov. 18, 1978: 536–539.

Sabato, Larry, *PAC Power.* New York: W.W. Norton, 1984.

Samuelson, Robert J. "The Campaign Reform Failure," *The New Republic,* September 5, 1983. pp. 28–36.

Schellhardt, Timothy, "Builders Try to Wield Political Cash to Get Housing Aid from Congress," *The Wall Street Journal.* March 25, 1982.–. 31.

Sedacca, Sandra, *Dirty Money . . . Dirty Air? A Common Cause Study of Political Action Committee Contributions to House and Senate Committees Reviewing the Clean Air Act.* Washington, D.C., 1981.

Shields, Mark, "The Coming Campaign Scandal," *Washington Post,* February 25, 1983.

Taylor, Paul, "Auto Dealers" Money Adds Octane to Drive Against FTC Regulation," *The Washington Post,* February 18, 1982. p. A2.

The Wall Street Journal, Series on "Cash Politics:" Hunt, Albert, "Special Interest Money Increasingly Influences What Congress Enacts," *The Wall Street Journal.* July 26, 1982.

Farney, Dennis, "A Liberal Congressman Turns Conservative: Did PAC Gifts Do It?" *The Wall Street Journal.* July 29, 1982.

Perry, James. "How Realtors PAC Rewards Office Seekers Helpful to Industry," *The Wall Street Journal.* August 2, 1982.

Index

411

About the Author

Burton D. Sheppard, a lawyer and political scientist, practices law in Boston and Washington, D.C. Sheppard was a Rhodes Scholar from 1973–1976 at New College, Oxford University where he tutored in comparative government. He was Assistant Professor of Political Science at Wellesley College from 1977–1982. He is active in Democratic party politics, has worked in the U.S. Congress and state government, and has served as Vice-Chairman and Chairman of the Issues Committee of Massachusetts Common Cause. Sheppard holds a B.A. with General and Departmental Honors from The Johns Hopkins University, a doctorate from Oxford University and a law degree from Boston College Law School. A native of Newton, Massachusetts, Sheppard grew up in Natick, Massachusetts and now divides his time between Massachusetts and Washington, D.C.